IN THE SHADOW OF THE SIGN

My Life in Pictures

by Renée Patin Farrington

Produced by Gretchen Van Tassel

Book design, cover and map art by
Lorne C. Dokie, Razorwire Design

ReneeFarrington.com

In the Shadow of the Sign
My Life in Pictures

By Renée Patin Farrington

©2021 Renée Patin Farrington

All Rights Reserved.

No part of this book may be reproduced in any form or by any means, electronic, mechanical, digital, photocopying, or recording, except for the inclusion of a review, without permission in writing from the publisher.

Published in the USA by:
BearManor Media
4700 Millenia Blvd.
Suite 175 PMB 90497
Orlando, FL 32839
www.BearManorMedia.com

ISBN: 978-1-62933-637-4   In the Shadow of the Sign (paper/bw)
ISBN: 978-1-62933-638-1   In the Shadow of the Sign (hardback/bw)
ISBN: 978-1-62933-743-2   In the Shadow of the Sign (paper/color)
ISBN: 978-1-62933-744-9   In the Shadow of the Sign (hardback/color)

Book design and layout by Lorne C. Dokie

In Praise of *In the Shadow of the Sign*

Renée Patin Farrington has given us a highly personal, evocative picture of growing up in Los Angeles as the daughter of a Disney animator. She parallels her own story with that of her dad, who went on to launch his own commercial studio in the 1950s. This candid reminiscence manages to capture the dreams and realities of two generations.

Leonard Maltin
Renowned film critic/historian/author

This richly illustrated memoir is not only an extraordinary journey through a family's history as reflected through the eyes of its daughter in her golden years, but it shows the breadth and depth of the creative force of Hollywood's animation community, the central role played by The Walt Disney Studios, as well as how everyday people lived almost like bit players in Southern California's real life world that was as beautiful as a movie set. There real people went to a high school attended by Debbie Reynolds and had a best friend who married a movie star. Our author was a baby at the Disney strike, taught in a boarding school in Switzerland, built a boat with her husband and sailed from coast to coast. By drawing on a rich set of home movies, photo albums, and illustrations from Ray Patin's work, Farrington allows readers to discover an enchanted time and place in the American past while taking them on a magical personal journey through it.

Vanessa Schwartz
Professor of Art History and Director of the Visual Studies Research Institute, USC
Author of *Jet Age Aesthetic: The Glamour of Media in Motion* (Yale UP, 2020)

What a trip! What a tour guide! Renée Patin Farrington's observant, insightful, whimsical memoir transported me back to the time and place where we both grew up. Seen through the eyes of a child and written in the voice of a marvelously mature woman, the details in this life-journey are drawn with literary strokes equal to her talented father's legendary cartooning. Ray Patin was a brilliant animator who executed the genius of one of America's greatest artists in classic films like *Fantasia* and *Snow White and the Seven Dwarfs*, the film that gave birth to an empire. Revisiting the studio where he did his memorable work and I did voices for The Lost Boys in *Peter Pan* was a favorite stop for me on a route that vividly and accurately illustrates a golden time in the history of California and American culture.

John Wilder
Award-winning writer, producer and director. Author of *Nobody Dies in Hollywood*

Renée Farrington is the daughter of Disney artist Ray Patin. Her heavily illustrated and beautifully written memoir takes us from the Golden Age of animation all the way to her most recent adventures in the shadow of the Hollywood sign. This is truly a delightful read.

Didier Ghez
Author of the *They Drew as They Pleased - The Hidden Art of Disney* book series

Ray Patin is a name many outside the animation business haven't heard of, but his career in the field is filled with many accomplishments during the medium's golden age. From Krazy Kat to the Disney Studios, and then onto Warner Bros. cartoons, Patin later became a pioneer in the burgeoning field of animated TV commercials in the 1950s. He quietly made his mark, but left a legacy of indelible memories. His daughter tells his unique tale from her front row seat.

Jerry Beck
Author and animation historian, www.cartoonresearch.com

Los Angeles and Burbank can be wacky places, but Renée Patin Farrington makes sense of it in this engaging, fondly nostalgic book which will make you wish you, too, had grown up in the "Shadow of the Sign."

Wes Clark and Mike McDaniel
Authors of *Lost Burbank, Growing Up in Burbank* and *True Tales from Burbank*

I've just read a thoroughly entertaining book, and if you want to read something charmingly out of the ordinary, try it. Most have seen pictures of the famous HOLLYWOOD Sign on the hill overlooking that glittering town, but did you know that on the other side of that hill—in the shadow of the Sign—lay a magic kingdom? Farrington's father was one of the pioneering animators who brought life to those enchanting Walt Disney classics so many of us grew up with, and her mother was a noted artist. The book tells of her life growing up in sight of the Disney Studios with those talented parents and the famous people with whom they came into contact. Then, as icing on the cake, she tells the story of the amazing sea voyage she and her husband made on a 50-foot cement yacht—which they built themselves.

Patrick Shannon
Author of four award-winning books

The golden age of Hollywood animation was driven by an army of immensely talented artists, all of them human beings with lives and loves of their own. Ray Patin was part of that legion of talent, and in this lively, playful biography his daughter brings him to life on the printed page, along with the world he lived in. This is an engaging read, filled with warmth, affection, and a wealth of delightful visual surprises.

J.B. Kaufman
Film historian and author, www.jbkaufman.com

For my parents, Maxine and Ray,
and for Gretchen
who lit the spark that brought them and me back to life.

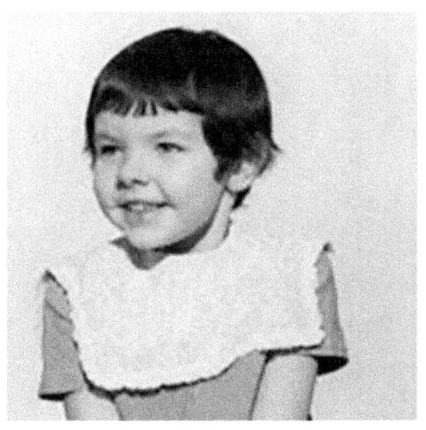

Renata at rest

*We shall not cease from exploration,
and the end of all our exploring will be to arrive where we started
and know the place for the first time.*

T. S. Eliot

Before Beginning

A view of Burbank, 1924

Before we begin, I thought it apt to say a few words about the picture storybook you are about to read. It is a chronicle of my voyage of discovery. As I meandered along my eighty-year journey, I gathered memories that form the lens through which I now look at what was and what is.

My exploration is documented in photo-memorabilia that help tell the story when words aren't enough. Let's start with a 1924 photo of my hometown taken almost a century ago. I'm not talking about the advertising sign that shouts along the hillside, touting a brand-new housing development. My childhood homestead is on the other side of that hill in those bare fields that became Burbank. I grew up behind the bright white letters of the beacon that shines down on the would-be stars of Hollywood. Our house was in the metaphoric shadow of the glamour and glitz of a town that is mostly in our imaginings.

When the picture was taken, my father Ray was eighteen. He was living with his family in another part of Los Angeles, drawing cartoons for his high school yearbook. My mother Maxine was ten, reading fairy tales to the younger kids at a little schoolhouse in Culver City. Eight years later, Ray was drawing cartoons on love letters to Maxine. Soon they were married and settled into a love nest near the Hollywoodland sign that advertised their neighborhood. In 1937 Ray got his dream job animating cartoons for Walt Disney. And in 1938 Maxine also acquired a new job—raising me, their first and only child. When Mickey Mouse and company moved to Burbank in 1940, so did we.

I thought you might appreciate this little chronology because my time travel navigation tends to jump back and forth. But isn't this how we remember our lives, in glimpses, all tumbled together, viewed backward through our magic memory lens?

I tried to recount my journey as truthfully as I can. But the story is narrated as viewed from the perch where I now rest looking back from a bird's eye view. It all happened, and the people are all real though some names are not. My truth-telling is supported by almost a thousand photographs dating from the 1920s. Many of these are taken from home movies my father made. These will be available from time to time on my website ReneeFarrington.com. You can also see photos in color where available on the site and in the e-book.

I have had help in telling my story. You'll note throughout the book the name Gretchen popping up. Gretchen Van Tassel is a lifelong dear friend who has been like a daughter to me since I was her mentor early in her career. She has since proved the old adage of the student surpassing the master by initiating and guiding every step of the production of this book. You'll see us posing in many guises in many different venues on our world travels.

Perhaps it is from growing up Disney that my tale tends toward the lighter side. There are times I skip-a-dee-doo-dah through the scary forests and other moments when I savor a frolic with bluebirds on the grassy hilltops. We will travel light. After all, you can't have shadows without light. And it just may be true that the reason angels can fly is that they take themselves lightly.

Renée Patin Farrington
Monterey County, California

Contents

The contents of 75 years as depicted
in 75 miniatures on a 75th birthday collage

Part I Beginning
  1 Announcing Potsy 1
  2 Maxine Once Upon a Time 9
  3 Ray Dreams of Disney 14
  4 A Cartoon Courtship. 27
  5 Burbank, Thanks to the Seven Dwarfs. 44
  6 A Visitor's Guide to La La Land 50
  7 The Girl with Two Faces 68
  8 School Days ABCs. 74
  9 War on the Home Front 86
  10 Old Kids on the Block 103
  11 Grown-Ups, Relatively Speaking. .116
  12 Sex Lessons and How I Learned Them 133
  13 Dear Diary 143
  14 Fast Times at Burroughs High 155

Part II Becoming

15 A is for Academia 171
16 B is for Beach 174
17 C is for Campus 177
18 D is for ΔΓ 184
19 E is for Entertainment 189
20 F is for Fashion 195
21 G is for Gaucho 202
22 H is for Hollywood Calling 207
23 I is for Imagineering® 216
24 J is for Joint 220
25 K is for Knowledge 224
26 L is for Light Fantastic 229
27 M is for Music 237
28 N is for Nautical Interludes 244
29 O is for Old Santa Barbara 254
30 P is for Picture-Making Patins 263
31 Q is for Queens 271
32 R is for Renée Reanimated 277
33 S is for Smokes, Spirits and Suds .285
34 T is for Teacher 293
35 U is for Under the Sign 299
36 V is for Virtue and Vice 310
37 W is for Writer 319
38 X is for XOXO 334
39 Y is for Youth Begone 342
40 Z is for Zip-A-Dee-Doo-Dah 349

Part III Being

41 I Gotta Have Art 353
42 Potsy in Grown-Up Land 365
43 Marriage Afloat and on the Rocks 374
44 Adventures Far from the Sign 397
45 The Cast of Characters 413
46 Ray Redux 427
47 I Remember Mama 436
48 Lessons from Beyond the Shadow 451
Afterword 460
Acknowledgements 462
Credits 464

Part I Beginning

1
Announcing Potsy

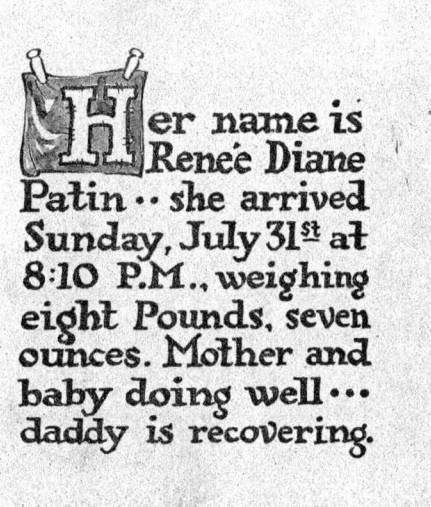

How a cartoonist and his wife announced their firstborn

They called me "Potsy." I didn't understand it was because of an overabundance of baby fat until I looked back at my infant photos with a more critical eye. By this time, they were calling me "Stinky Pee Tail." But I get ahead of myself.

Separated at birth

I feel sorry for the first visitors who came to admire me. What could you say about a bouncing baby girl who looked like she was separated at birth from Winston Churchill?[1]

---

[1] Prime Minister of Great Britain during World War II who is rumored to have said that all babies look like him, but then…he looks like all babies.

 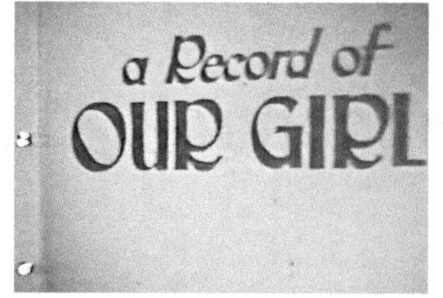

Debut film performance: *My Life in Pictures*

Not only did I bear a striking resemblance to a corpulent cigar-smoking star on the 1938 world scene, but I was born to be a star. My father documented my first years in 8-millimeter[2] movies entitled *Renée, A Record of Our Girl.* The series alternates between black and white and color stories, all creatively produced and introduced with hand-lettered signs in the place of sound. Now 80 years old, the film clips and I can be a bit blurry, but here is my story.

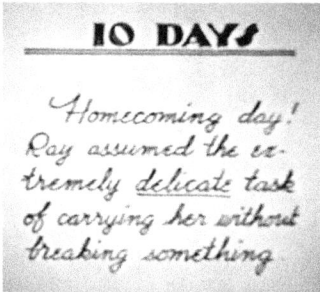  

Cinematic debut: *The Homecoming*

My debut performance was in 1938 at 10 days of age. I wonder how many times my father directed, posed and shot my mother to get the 22-second segment celebrating my homecoming from Physicians and Surgeons Hospital in Glendale, California. A title card announces the plot: "Homecoming Day! Ray assumes the extremely delicate task of carrying her without breaking something."

The location is a suburban street in Glendale's Atwater district near the now-trendy Silverlake/Los Feliz enclave of Los Angeles. It is August and probably very hot. A raven-haired beauty, my mother, is smiling and waving from the passenger seat of a 1936 Dodge sedan—one of those round body cartoony cars. She looks as if she has been driven there by the now missing chauffeur and is waving at hosts who await her on their porch. Suddenly a handsome balding young man in a sports coat (my father who has left the camera rolling on its tripod), rushes into the frame. My parents greet each other fondly whereupon he opens the car door with a flourish to reveal a blanket lying across her lap. He merrily swoops it up, and we catch a tiny glimpse of me. A star is born! My mother looks worried—probably not that my father will drop me, but that the scene will have to be shot again and she's dying to get out of that stifling car.

---

[2] Very narrow film used by early movie-makers

Daddy worked for Mr. Disney

Opening episodes of the Potsy movies feature cozy, domestic infant care scenarios filmed in my first home on Revere Street, around the corner from the Tam O'Shanter, still touted as the oldest restaurant in Los Angeles. If you've seen Laurel & Hardy comedies, 1940s films noirs or HBO's *Mildred Pierce,* you know the neighborhood with its tar-patched streets, pseudo Spanish bungalows and palm-lined courts. Our apartment was a few minutes from the studio that the Disney brothers, Walt and Roy, had established on Hyperion Avenue—as close as possible to Hollywood. This is where Daddy went to work to draw the "sound cartoons" called *Silly Symphonies*.

Ray, photographer/director/father, and me (not ready for my close-up)

My father's camera recorded each phase of my development. Everything was fodder for his little Bell & Howell that could pop out of its leather case at any minute.

Nana in her cameo

My father's mother whom I would call Nana once my vocalizing was intelligible, is featured in the dramatic bottle warmer segment with the opening title: "Mother Patin was our baby's roommate and tended to her majesty's night and early morning needs during these important early months." Nana is directed to test the warmed milk on her wrist, then, in an Orson Welles-worthy close-up, tap her fingers to indicate impatience while the milk cools to a temperature suitable to my awaiting maw. I am shown in my bassinette ravenously guzzling the large-nippled glass bottle—mandated after I over enthusiastically and painfully gummed my first and last meal at my mother's small-nippled breast.

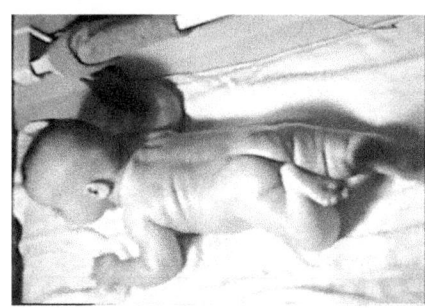 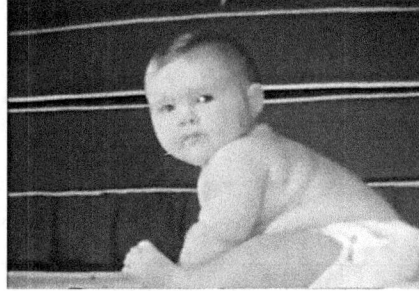

Intimate moments

Then there is the bathinette episode where, oiled like a squirming miniature Michelin man, I am examined from my top to tush to toes. Close-ups reveal baby booty and booby cleavage. Titles remark on my heft calling me "Fatty Pants," and record my weight: "Ten months–21.5 lbs.!"

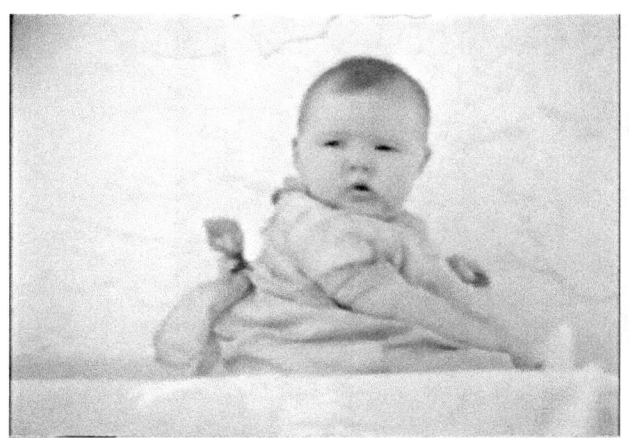 

Pretty baby

Mother told me, when I was old enough to wonder, that my plumpness was a sign of a healthy baby. She didn't seem to resent having to cut the sleeves of my hand sewn baby dresses, so my cherubic arms could fit. Far from hiding the fact that his daughter was blessed with an overabundance of baby chubbiness, Daddy seemed to relish photographing his darling, dimpled daughter. He filled reels with scenes of his first—and only—born performing obliviously for his camera.

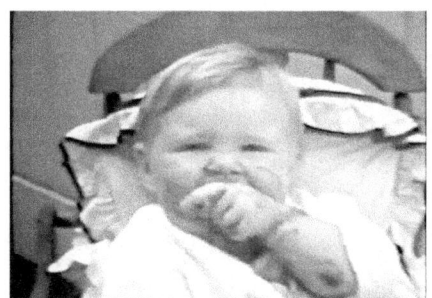  

Milestones….and more milestones

After cocktails and dinner *chez nous,* my parents' guests were invited to the living room unrolling of the silver screen. Hidden in the room next door, my father would beam double and triple features through a special cubbyhole he had designed for the purpose. To the accompaniment of the loud whir of the projector, and occasional narration shouted from the next room, the audience was treated to each of my milestones: the first tooth, prunes smeared on the face, and rolling everywhere before crawling–usually accompanied by Pluto. Mother, always beautiful, is shown with a perpetual smile entertaining and nurturing me, rocking me in her lap where she would sing the not-very-lulling lullaby called "Rock-a-Bye Baby"—wherein the bough breaks and the baby and cradle plummet to the earth. I, an early rhymer, renamed the song "Apple Pie" for the apple blossom print chintz covering the rocking chair.

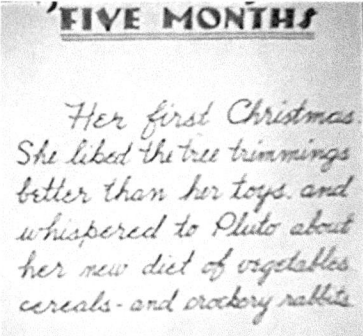 

Babe in toy land

My first Christmas was captured on film in great detail. Daddy's introduction to the festivities reads: "Her first Christmas. She liked the tree trimmings better than her toys and whispered to Pluto about her new diet of vegetables, cereals—and crockery rabbits."

Daddy's description of my reaction to the display he and my Mama provided for me might reflect a little tiredness after a night of preparation. His expectations were dashed at my five-month-old preference for the tree trimmings over Disney-themed toys like ceramic reproductions of the Three Little Pigs, and the rabbits Snow White gamboled with in the forest. He was wrong. Although I love the sparkle of a well-trimmed tree, my joy of toys like those I gummed at my first Christmas has lasted a lifetime.

Mother and child

Daddy's movies record my progress from head-bobbing infant oblivion to non-stop rushing, hands outstretched to embrace each new adventure. As my infant needs decreased and my mobility increased, we started filming at remote locations. My mother and I would stop whatever we were doing, wait for the camera to be wound, stand still for the exposure meter, and, often reluctantly and repeatedly, pantomime our delight with whatever had been amusing us before my father called "Action!" The documentaries of our outings often end with the two of us posed against the sun for dramatic sundown silhouettes.

My outfits are a fashion parade of hand knits from soakers[3] to sweaters, puff sleeves and pinafores. Mother's ensembles often matched mine. She is always at the height of thirties/forties fashion. My reddish hair goes from the curl in the middle of the forehead, to braids that start on top of my head and inevitably fall down. Mama, too, sports braids as well as a pompadour and

---

[3] A sort of knit diaper cover

the occasional snood.[4] There is a famous scene in Proust's *Remembrance of Things Past* where the taste of a Madeleine cookie floods the narrator with memories. For me it's not pastry but pictures, these eighty-year-old movies that recreate my first years.

 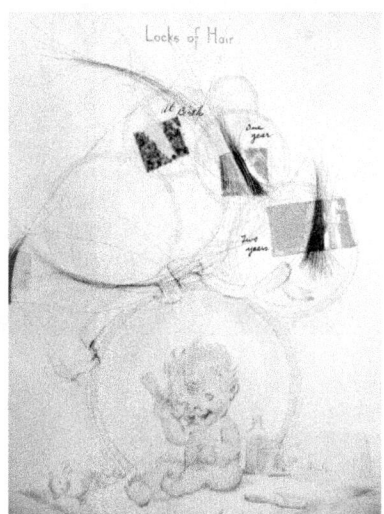

Precious moments   Locks of love

A chronicle of youth

While Daddy was recording my every twitch on film, Mama documented my progress in my *Precious Moments* baby book. She celebrated each accomplishment with as much joyful pride as if I were a cherished gift she was surprised and delighted to have received. She noted: "Renée surprised us both by being such a fat, chubby baby." My petite mother's appreciation of my comeliness was reflected in my first words: "pretty baby." My father made a rare entry after the query about "Difficulties in Pronunciation: orange juice." There's even a page where my strawberry blond locks of hair are lovingly taped for posterity.

---

[4] A sort of knit hair cover

The voyage begins

On the first page of the album, my Aunt Vinnie, Daddy's sister, wrote a propitious preface under the title "Stepping Stones:"

> *Dear little girl, may you dance over them throughout life with a minimum of tumbles and a maximum of happiness is the sincere wish of your aunt who loves you dearly.*
>
> *Vinnie*

My path has indeed been filled with not only lesson-learning tumbles, but also a maximum dose of happiness. I have raced headlong, hungry to devour all the wonders on life's menu. I invite you to join me on a nostalgic trip through the early stepping-stones along my way out of La La Land to Grown-Up Land. Fasten your seat belt. It may be a bumpy ride. But isn't that true of the best of Hollywood movies?

2
Maxine Once Upon a Time

Maxine at one and two

When my 23-year-old mother gave birth to her one and only me, she had been married six years. She weighed 105 pounds. My father, boasting eight more years of experience and wisdom, told her when they were married that she wasn't mature enough to have a child. This was made clear three months later on their first Christmas when he gave her one of her beloved Oz books. She was furious, thinking—not without foundation—that he thought she was childlike.

Maxine Jane Riley was born in 1914, the year World War I began. She was premature, weighing, I was told, two pounds and placed in a cotton-lined shoebox. They called her a "miracle baby." As a child, she remained tiny, barely bigger than the dolls with whom she could pretend the kind of life she could only fantasize.

When little Maxie was seven, she climbed up on a ladder leaning against the house on the Sunset Strip where the Rileys lived before their move to Culver City. The occasion that prompted her ascent was to show off the doll that she obtained, despite a severe stutter, by going door to door selling magazine subscriptions. She celebrated her triumph posing between her brother Bob and sister Fran. They were the oldest three of what would be a set of six siblings.

Many years later when she was a grown-up, still shyly signing her work just "Max," my mother painted a picture of her family in front of their

Bob, Maxine and Fran,
the older three Riley kids

Culver City homestead. In her early Grandma Moses-esque style, she pictured the clapboard house built by my carpenter grandfather. It still stands, graced by a few upgrades. Most plumbing was indoors, with a washing machine out back. Also, in the back was a little house occupied at various times by several family members, including us Patins.

Gerry, Dick, Mother Ida with baby Jack, Father Clint, Maxine, Fran, Bob

The farmlike spread was close to the hills of Palos Verdes, and, although they weren't actually visible from the house, Mama included them in her painting to enhance the somewhat stark setting among the lima bean fields that stretched all the way to Beverly Hills. The rising smoke from a nearby house, laundry drying on the line, a bucolic menagerie and hovering angels add a Thomas Kinkade[1] idealized tranquility to the scene.

Lined up like a welcoming committee, are the matriarch, Ida, with baby Jack in her arms, prematurely white-haired Clint, the patriarch, and the other children in their Sunday best. At the end of the retinue is the dog, one of many named Jimmy, and the legendary turkey couple, Mr. and Mrs. Wurtle—distinguished by Mrs. Wurtle's wooden leg. According to Riley family lore, she had lost her leg in a tragic mowing incident, and my grandfather fashioned a series of wooden legs that she found serviceable and the family found fascinating, particularly when they stuck out stiffly from her perch on the clothesline.

The idyllic rendering of the Riley homescape covered the reality of my mother's painful childhood. Her father, who worked at the nearby MGM Studio making movie props and sets, abused both her and the oldest boy Bob. For Bob, it was explosively physical and loud. She remembers her father as a strikingly handsome man with a violent streak who would pick up four-year-old Bob and throw him across the room. Mother's abuse was psychological, secret and shameful.

---

[1] American painter (1958-2012) known for the mass popularity of his idyllic domestic scenes and marketing savvy.

In a newspaper article written when she was in her nineties, my mother told the interviewer, "He was such a mean man that none of us felt sad when he died. And I grew up thinking all handsome men were mean."

Little Maxie on left dances in fairyland

My mother was left alone with her fears and with her responsibilities for a growing family. My grandmother, a plump picture of domesticity, was too busy with pregnancies (some of which she terminated) and working in the grocery store around the corner to pay attention to anything that ailed her brood—or, if she did pay attention, she chose not to protest. Maxine's only escape was to fairy tales and art. She created lands she read about and saw in her own imagination.

Back: Frances, Maxine, Ida, Clint, and Bob; Front: Jack, Dick and Gerry

A photo of an older Riley clan pictures them lined up on Venice Beach. Was their uniformly glum demeanor because they were squinting into the sun, or does the photograph reflect the harsh truth that my mother's family painting hid?

Maxine's bathing costume has sleeves because she was always very self-conscious about her upper arm and back covered with angry scars from third degree burns suffered when she was three and stuck a celluloid comb into a heater. She still had the childhood stutter she claimed was from being forced to switch from left- to right-handedness. It disappeared after she left home, but the humiliation experienced from teachers and classmates endured as did the stings from her father's mistreatment.

An artist graduates

Her father never let teenaged Maxine participate in any school activities. Her Venice High School senior picture stuck in the lower right corner of a page shows a shy, lovely girl with no activities listed. Her world was a quiet, hidden one. She loved art, and spent hours drawing ensembles for twenties fashion plates. Gerry remembers paper doll clothing designed by her big sister Max whose dreams were filled with making real outfits for the movie stars. Their glamorous lives had become the fairy tales of my mother's teen years.

Maxine and Vivien as Scarlett

My mother was totally unaware of her beauty that was often compared to Vivien Leigh's.[2] But she was never allowed to go out with boys until my father came along and my grandfather let her date the nice young cartoonist the family had known for years. She must have been enchanted by the fantasies my father drew in his cartoons.

---

[2] British transplant, Vivien Leigh was best known for portraying Scarlett O'Hara in *Gone with the Wind*.

Congratulations from the Sailor Man

He even had his friend E. C. Segar, the creator of *Popeye,* make a cartoon to congratulate Maxine on her graduation. Below a scene of the sailor man in his usual feisty mode, the inscription reads,

> *To me fren Maxine Riley*
>
> *Congratcherlations on account of yer gradyeration*
>
> *Popeye*

The tumultuous Riley homestead was at times as raucous as Popeye's. It must not have been an easy place for mother to bring her first and only beau, Ray. She was ashamed of their deep Depression poverty and always remembered when five-year-old Jack jumped up and down with glee after a county charity food package was dropped from a truck in front of her and her older, more sophisticated gentleman caller.

And so it was that, once upon a time in 1931, along came, if not a charming prince, something even better—another artist, kind and handsome, but not threateningly so. My mother recalled in her interview, "I didn't date him for very long before we got engaged. He was a wonderful person to me."

Just like in one of her pretend scenarios, Ray whisked Maxine away into adulthood and Hollywood. She began a life lived—if not always happily ever after—with fulfillment and often the joy she had been denied as a child.

3
Ray Dreams of Disney

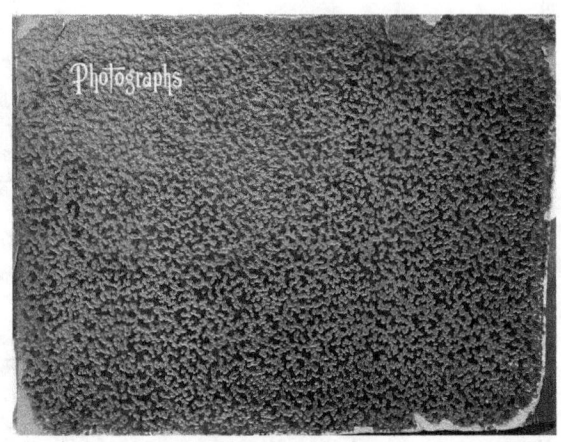

A story begins

The antique album is stamped in gold with the word "Photographs." Some of these are over a hundred years old. They were pasted on the black pages with care by my father who wanted to tell a picture story of his family from his boyhood in Louisiana through his early thirties in California. He meticulously labeled the pages in white ink with informative and often humorous commentary and illustrations. On the photo of the house where he was born, he wrote: "Vin and Ray's birthplace." It was located in Breaux Bridge, Louisiana, the "Crawfish Capital of the World." In the picture his mother, who was visiting the site long after they had moved away, poses perkily in front of the shotgun house, so named because those who were so inclined could shoot a shotgun in the front door and the bullet would go out the back door. A more practical use for the lined-up room layout was its ability to catch the rare breeze on a muggy day near the Bayou Teche in what is called "Cajun Country."

Therese, Ray and Maurice

My father was named Ray (not Raymond) Patin (French for "skate"). His middle name was Maurice like his father. His earliest appearance in 1906 shows newborn Ray in a white lacy dress sliding off the lap of his adoring mother. Behind them his father follows instructions to look into the camera.

Vinnie and Ray

In another formal portrait, Baby Ray is again precariously perched in the same dress, this time next to his sister, Vinnie (which also is not short for anything). She had been born in the same house a year before and looks not at all happy to be sharing it with the new arrival. Is she clenching her jaw as well as a fist, ready to pinch the wide-eyed little pest? In any case, a lifelong sibling rivalry was underway.

In a more mature photograph, again posed with Vinnie, Ray's dress is replaced by floppy shirt and trousers. Mother Therese dominates the tableau in all her Edwardian Era finery. My grandmother's proud smiling face is capped by an elaborate hair/hat concoction, outdoing her daughter's jaunty foliage fascinator. A sense of pride and exaggeration were but two of my grandmother's traits as we will see later. Now neither child looks at all happy. It's a good thing my grandmother was one of thirteen Durand children scattered nearby in St. Martinville so that Vinnie and Ray could have playmates other than each other.

Ray, Therese and Vinnie

The old Louisiana home in flood   In the land of Evangeline

Daddy's documentation of the people and places of his home on the pages of the album include a scene of his cousin navigating a flood, showing inundated Evangeline Oak "as it never has been seen before." The massive live oak was named after the heroine of Longfellow's love poem, "Evangeline, a Tale of Acadie," about the French Canadians called Acadians who migrated to Louisiana. The word Cajun is a corruption of the French "Acadien." I grew up thinking Evangeline was some sort of saint the way my Louisiana relatives talked about her and all the things named for her.

I learned a lot about my Louisiana heritage from Daddy's album and from the stories passed down from my grandmother who was very proud of her Durand heritage.

A wedding in the family

Most vivid of her accounts was the story of the plantation called Pine Alley and its Tara-esque double marriage of the Durand sisters. With her honed talent for storytelling, Nana told and retold me about my great-great-grandfather Charles Durand's 1850 Hollywood-worthy epic. Her recounting of the story grew more dramatic with each telling. I heard of how he brought millions of spiders from China (or some say from nearby swampland). The industrious arachnids were set loose among the trees that lined the three-mile alley (allée) leading to the plantation mansion where the altar was located. They wove yards and yards of delicate webs into the branches and mosses of the trees. They were followed by waves of slaves who stuffed bellows with hundreds of pounds of gold and silver dust from California and pumped it onto the gossamer canopies. They say the grand entrance of the brides riding in their gold embellished carriages through the magnificent arboreal display was like something out of a fairy tale. And it may very well have been. But, it is true, if not in all the details. There is documentation. Daddy pasted a postcard of the famed avenue in the family album and labeled it "In the Land of Evangeline." I'm sure that Longfellow, who wrote "Evangeline," could have written a smashing poem about Pine Alley. Later my father visited the historic venue and filmed "Pine & Oak Alley, Scene of Louisiana's Most Fabulous Wedding." As further proof, the Louisiana Tourist Commission found the site of the over-the-top extravaganza worthy of a plaque.

Unlike Evangeline, our relatives came directly from France, not Canada. Therefore, we are not officially Cajuns. One of our ancestors, Louis Jucereau de St. Denis, sailed to Louisiana in the navy of none other than Louis XIV.[1] He was a key figure in colonizing the land of our Patin progenitors for the French.

---

[1] That's Big #14, the Sun King, the one who built Versailles.

Family skeleton

But the man I knew as Daddy showed no hint of his Louisiana childhood, no accent,[2] no zydeco rhythms, no cravings for jambalaya or gumbo. He never spoke French like his forebearers for fear of being laughed at. He didn't mind being laughed at when he made fun of himself, though. Even as a kid he joked about his skinny figure, labeling one shot of himself in Louisiana in a track ensemble, "Family Skeleton."

My grandfather Maurice's biography was greatly overshadowed by the Louisiana legends my grandmother dramatized about her own family history. I know little about my father's father and never met him. He died at fifty-five the day after Christmas two and a half years before I was born. Those who knew him spoke reverently of him as a kind, sensitive man with great intellectual curiosity. In rare photographs, he always hid a mangled hand resulting from an early encounter with a cotton gin—or a printing press—depending on who was recounting the catastrophe.

Some say that Maurice Patin always carried a certain sense of sadness. Perhaps the melancholy came from the bottle he hit a little too hard, or from a chronic case of wanderlust. Perhaps he lost his spark after giving in to my domineering grandmother when she prevented him from taking the job he was offered as an editor of a Parisian newspaper. I was told that my grandmother broke into hysterical tears sitting atop a trunk at the Louisiana station where they would board a train for New York and their ship to Europe. She bemoaned leaving her large family for the perils of the Old Country.

---

[2] The Louisiana (loo - ziana) accent, depending on who exhibits it. It's not really typically southern, it's almost like Brooklynese and at times French.

California, here we come

But Maurice's wanderlust wasn't quenched. When Ray was ten, the family of four packed up and headed west to follow Nana's brother Oscar. They traveled in an old Oldsmobile called Horace. In the family album, Daddy pictured the car from the inside and out with meticulously cut out photos. He added the title, "The reason we got there." The "there" was Albuquerque, but when Uncle Oscar moved to California, the Patins did too, arriving just as the Roaring Twenties began. In Los Angeles my grandfather, former newspaper publisher and intellectual, found work checking the manifests of foreign ships at the port of San Pedro.

Pacific playtime in 1920s Santa Monica

Album snapshots show that the Pacific Coast agreed with the Patins. Father and son fished off the pier in Santa Monica and young Ray showed off his more mature, but still skeletal, physique.

 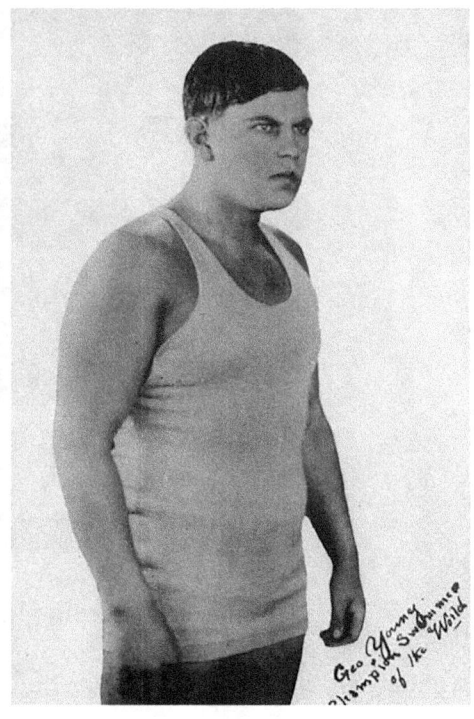

Artist and athlete

Many photos of early Catalina Island appear throughout the album. In one we see my father, again kidding about his not-so-buff body, comparing himself to mighty George Young, the first man to swim the channel between the mainland and Catalina. One incident that is not pictured is when he and his best friend Leslie were arrested there for not wearing a tie at the Casino. I imagine the lack of neckwear may have been secondary to their hooch-inspired revelries on the beach.

My father found his treasured isle romantic as we shall see in his courtship of my mother. His sentiments were matched by The Four Preps who in the mid-fifties rhapsodized the romance of the isle:

"26 Miles (Santa Catalina)"

Twenty-six miles across the sea
Santa Catalina is a-waitin' for me
Santa Catalina, the island of romance, romance, romance, romance

Introducing Master Ray Patin

But life in California was not all a day at the beach. Young Ray needed to find gainful employment during his school off hours. If Maurice didn't find newspaper work, his son Ray Maurice did. A profile of the industrious lad appeared in a copy of the *Los Angeles Evening Express* along with a photo of him suitably clad in knickerbockers and "newsboy" hat selling the paper on an LA street corner. His shiny change-maker at his belt and best salesman's smile in place, he poses in front of a rapt customer in front a Los Angeles department store window. The piece is written in the kind of purple prose that was acceptable in 1921 when sentences were stretched to their lengthiest conclusions rather than clipped into digestible bytes. It is prophetic that the writer used the word "animated" to describe my father's artistic impulses.

He is a sturdy lad of fourteen, as full of joie de vivre as other chaps of that age…But given a pencil and scrap of paper, or even a pen or brush, and he becomes animated by different impulses, for Ray Patin is … a prodigy, and his drawing, impromptu sketches and clever cartoons are the delight of his school friends, and decidedly of interest to more mature critics.

Beneath his thatch of auburn hair his fertile brain is busily planning new worlds to conquer, and when he is not cleverly constructing mechanical toys – his airplane won a prize at the Bullocks contest last month – he is doing sly cartoons which have a feeling and flair one does not expect of a youngster of his age and experience. Since he was eight or nine, Ray has been drawing; he has executed portraits of friends and relatives that are actually startling in their characterization of the subjects and his cartoons promise a keen and appreciative sense of humor as well as unusual ability in the actual drawing.

           Published!   Budding cartoonist collects kudos

Not only did he sell newspapers, but Ray contributed to them, especially the *Junior Times* supplement for the *Los Angeles Sunday Times.* He won several prizes, including one for his cover featuring a mounted crusader touting "Truth, Love and Courage." It reflected a strong moral sense that would be a lifelong trait.

Cartoon by resident artist Ray whose photo in newspaper is bottom right

Ray's newspaper efforts continued when he entered Polytechnic High School in Los Angeles. He became that clever fellow found in many high schools who did all the illustrations for the school paper and yearbook. He amused his friends by flipping animated cartoons that he created in the margins of his textbooks.

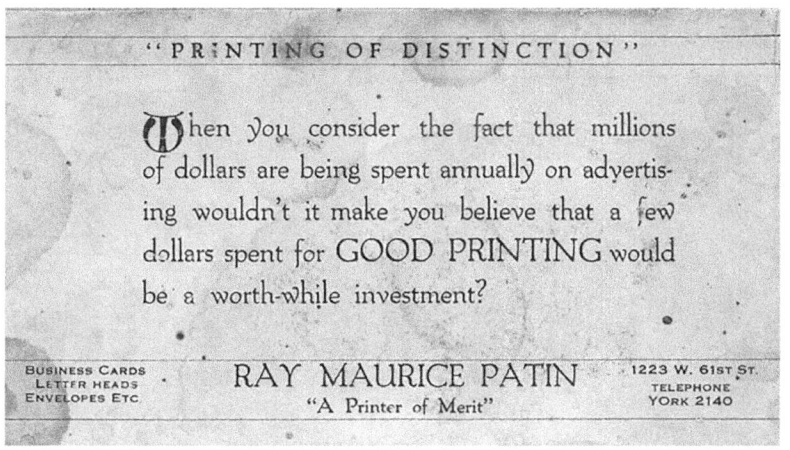

A printer of merit, age 18

But, the Depression hit, and, in a move he would always regret, Ray dropped out of school to support the family. At the Patin house on 61st Street, he set up various artistic endeavors. Following in his father's footsteps, he set up a printing business. He used a small hand-operated black iron press upon which, also echoing his father, he lost the tip of his finger. His "Printing of Distinction" business card was a harbinger of advertising in his future.

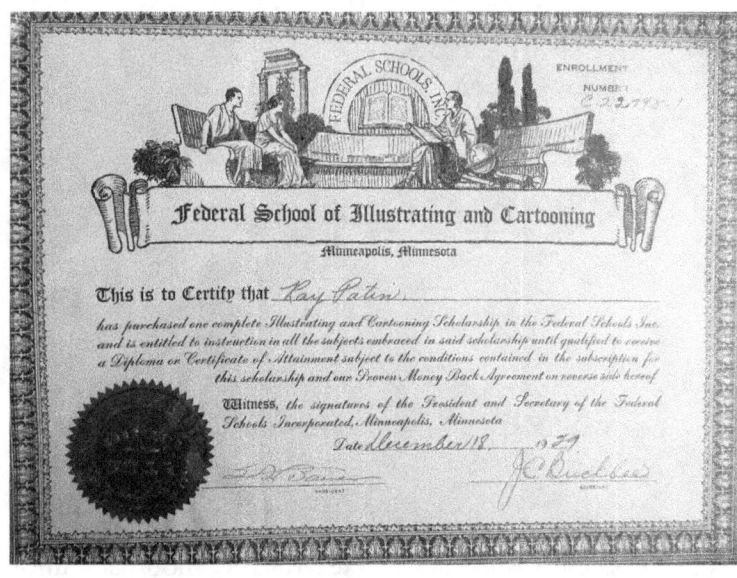

Portrait of the artist as a young hopeful   Certificate of authentic artistry

Young Ray echoed the educational path of his future boss, Walt Disney, who having been the school newspaper cartoonist, dropped out of high school. My father also enrolled in art school, though not the Chicago Academy of Fine Arts, which Walt attended. In 1929, Ray enrolled in a correspondence course with the Federal School of Illustrating and Cartooning. One of his assignments for the course was a pen and ink cartoon, dated 1931. He called it "The Starving Artist Gets a Break Thanks to Walt Disney." In a pastoral landscape, the old-style, skinny-faced Mickey Mouse from *Steamboat Willie* gestures at a red-haired artist speeding out of the frame. (As in many of my father's cartoon self-portraits, the hair was the only element in color.)

The starving artist gets a break...almost

Mickey's speech balloon says, "Hey Red! C'mon back an' finish your picture!" The artist answers, "Can't do it! Your boss is advertisin' for artists an' I've just gotta eat!"

The year before, Walt Disney's secretary informed my twenty-four-year-old not yet father that they were returning the sample drawings he had sent. She informed him that "should Mr. Disney decide to interview you at some further date, we will call you for an appointment."

Draw me a Mickey Mouse!

It would be several years before Mickey's "boss" would become my father's boss. For the time being he landed a job with Charles Mintz who ran a studio producing Academy Award-nominated work. My father animated the hugely-popular Krazy Kat cartoons at $27.50 a week.

One of the many cartoons from the period shows my father's frustration at not being a Disney artist. A crowd of clamoring children surrounds a frantic red-haired Ray. One little girl is holding a pencil and implores, "Won't You Draw Us a Mickey Mouse?" The caption explains, "How Krazy Kat Kartoonists Get That Way."

So, Ray's cartooning was actually earning a salary and, along with teaching cartooning and freelance work, kept the artist and his family from starving. A 1935 letter addressed to my father working at Harman-Ising[3] declares that his salary for 1934 as reported to the Internal Revenue Department was $1,267.50.

---

[3] Yes, the surnames of the animator partners are propitiously real. They were a very successful animation team who went on to found animation studios at Warner Bros. and MGM.

My father was twenty-five when he drew a rabbit painting a modernistic egg. The cartoon reflects his never-dying desire to be become a successful working artist at a time when Picasso and Cubism were all the rage. The caption reads, "The world is getting so tired of conventional things– I'm sure it'll welcome my design for a modernistic egg."

The unconventional egg

Photo and copy of Maurice Patin drawn by his son. Which is which?

And so it was that in 1931, Ray Patin was living at home with his parents, Therese and Maurice, on 61st Street in Los Angeles. He practiced his art copying a photograph of his father at his age of 25, and he continued his cartooning. But most importantly to our story, one auspicious day, Ray suddenly realized that the shy little girl who often visited her grandmother next door had grown into a charming, beautiful sixteen-year-old.

The rest is my parents' history.

4
A Cartoon Courtship

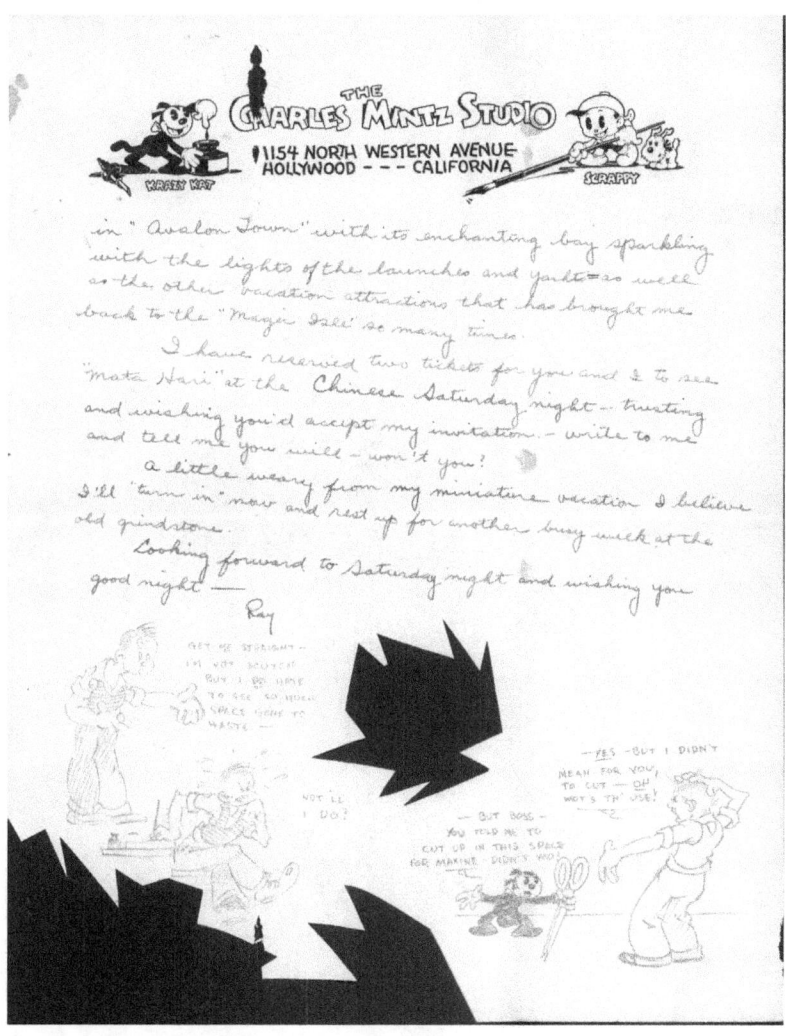

A written invitation with Krazy Kat cutting up–literally

My father wooed my mother with a lover's serenade of cartoon-covered letters. Ray wrote of his admiration for Maxine, at first tentatively, lest she think he's too mushy or the letter should land in the wrong hands. He created the billets-doux[1] while he was animating Krazy Kat at the Charles Mintz studio in Hollywood, sometimes using his boss's stationery to create the letters he would send across the county. He often used numbers to key his drawings to the text, and characterized himself falling asleep at his drawing board after one of their dates. He sometimes added cutouts for embellishment– or perhaps to cut out passages he felt weren't worthy of his dream girl.

---

[1] Note to younger generations: a billet-doux was a popular term for a love letter. It's from the French, literally "sweet note." Lest you think it is out of favor, it was the Word of the Day on the Merriam-Webster website on Valentine's Day 2017. Now go look up Merriam-Webster on Google!

The suitor with his drawing pencil

Heart to heart with Krazy

One of his offerings pictures the smitten suitor with pencil and drawing board on the top of which sits the star of the film he had been drawing. The speech balloon reads:

> *Krazy, is there any other language I can use to better convince Max that I'm really plum nerts* (nuts in 1930s slang) *about her?*

His communications are chatty, filled with news of his day, with questions about her high school life and musings on their budding relationship. Many have invitations to a date. On the final page of one letter, Ray describes the location of their future honeymoon, his old favorite haunt as:

> *"Avalon Town" with its enchanting bay sparkling with the lights of the launches and yachts as well as the other vacation attractions that have brought me back to the "Magic Isle" so many times.*

Just like my father's rumble seat

He goes on to invite her to see the movie *Mata Hari* at the Chinese (Grauman's) Theater that Saturday. He would no doubt escort her in his spiffy little convertible with a rumble seat in the back.

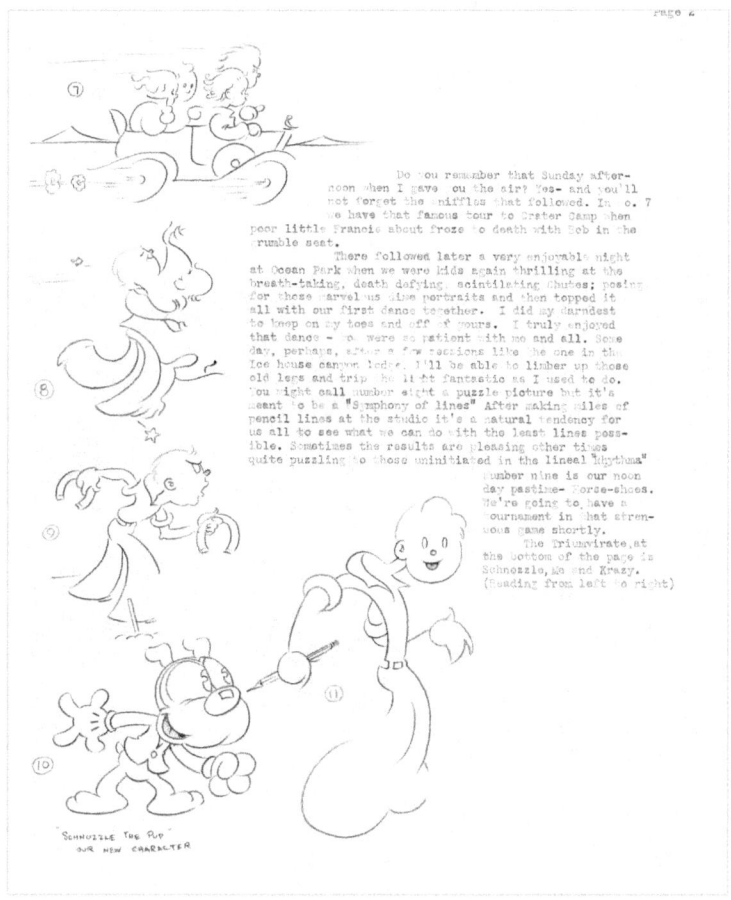

Rumbling…

The rumble seat of my father's courting car was the subject of another letter where my father described an outing that might have been less than ideal. This time the rumble seat was filled by my mother's brother Bob and her sister Frances whose name my father misspelled. However, I'm pretty sure the faint little "g" at the beginning of the word rumble was not a mistake.

...and grumbling

*Do you remember that Sunday afternoon when I gave you the air?
Yes – and you'll not forget the sniffles that followed. In No. 7 we have
that famous tour to Crater Camp when poor little Francis about froze
to death with Bob in the (g)rumble seat.*

The letter continues with a description of far more romantic activities, but we'll save that for the "L is for Light Fantastic" chapter.

The object of his affection

In one correspondence, he drew a picture of a Betty Boop-ish preschooler and commented on having met an equally beguiling Maxine Riley in her grandmother's house next to his.

*Picture number one is the coy Miss Riley at the tender age of (?) in a pose
in which I last remember her. My how she has changed! By what queer pranks
of fate had she been kept from my sight until that memorable night that I again
"Found You."*

The prenuptial love letter

I can imagine my father as a sort of good-humored, doting protector, treating my young delicate mother with great tenderness. In a prenuptial letter written right before their wedding, Ray offered future domestic help and declared his love. The letter is alive with cartoons showing household chores that red-haired Ray is at the ready to perform. He shares thoughts on their upcoming I Do's and Catalina honeymoon—complete with a map of the island on which the newlyweds are pictured cuddling. He wrote:

> *I hope that your washing wasn't too heavy. Speaking of domestic duties– mebbe you have realized since last night that I may be able to give you quite a few tips on housekeeping such as cooking pies and trimming them like this* (with giant scissors) *or causing a stir among things by wielding the old spoon to the "Rhythm of a one-man band."*

The letter ends with a hug and kisses:

> *Honey, it's almost one o'clock so I have to close this hurriedly and get back to the galleys–it's a job to keep my noodle on my work let me tell you! With thots running thru my brain about the day when I say "I do" and sail to Catalina to start our life together. I could fill up the rest of the space with love and kisses like this* (a line of X's). *But you told me not to make this a mushy love letter so I'll just close with a big bear hug for you.*
>
> *Ray*

Wedding in Grandma's garden and honeymoon on the magic isle

And so, it came to pass that on September 17, 1932, Maxine and Ray were married in a very small family affair in the garden of her grandmother's house where they met. In their wedding portrait, my mother is modestly attired in a sleek turtleneck gown that hugs her slender frame almost hidden behind a giant bouquet.

My parents' honeymoon began on the *SS Catalina* steaming to the island where my father could share his favorite stomping and splashing grounds with his bride (and hopefully avoid the hoosegow[2] in which he had been confined during his roaring youth). In a snapshot in front of the ship's gangway and life ring, Ray at twenty-five looked quite respectable in white flannel pants and dark blazer. Maxine, seventeen, sported a fashion-forward suit she tailored herself with a cloche hat and leather gloves, adding an air of maturity she didn't yet feel.

Once on land they photographed their love of each other and of the island at every opportunity. On the back of one shot she took of her new husband, my mother wrote:

> *Casino Way is beautifully lighted at night–leading to the two-million-dollar casino which holds the gorgeous ballroom on the entire upper floor and a beautiful theater below.*

Ray's photos of his bride shine with the romance of a besotted new husband.

---

[2] It has come to the attention of the author that there may be readers to whom this colorful word for a place of incarceration may be unfamiliar. She apologizes.

Santa Catalina, the island of romance

A declaration of love

During the honeymoon phase, Ray, no longer constrained by pre-wedding propriety, declared his love with a self-portrait, jumping for joy, shouting, *"Hello Honey I Loves Ya!"*

A view of Hollywoodland and the "dangerous" dam

The newlyweds nestled into the guest quarters of a large Spanish style estate on Holly Drive in the hillside district called Hollywoodland. They lived near the actress Peggy Entwistle who, the day after my parents were married, had tragically leapt to her death from atop the letter H of the Sign nearby. The Sign, erected in 1923, had been the beacon of hope that lured her to Hollywood from Broadway. But she became despondent over not being offered any roles and took her life from atop the symbol of all she thought she lost.

The Mulholland Dam and Lake Hollywood Reservoir

But my parents' story living in the Hollywood Hills was a far happier one. In one dramatic, oft-told tale, my father practically carried my mother to safety behind the Hollywoodland Sign as they fled the house during the 1933 Long Beach magnitude 6.4 earthquake. They feared the Mulholland Dam would break and that the reservoir would flood their neighborhood. I've always found the story ever so romantic, like the mighty ape's rescue of Fay Wray in *King Kong,* the movie that came out that year.

Hollywoodland home

On my recent visit to the location to photograph the gateway to my parents' first love nest, a couple of passing hill walkers recited a list of show biz types who've stayed in the neighborhood, including The Rolling Stones and Marilyn Manson. From their photos in the early thirties, I'd say Mr. and Mrs. Patin brought a bit of their own glamour to the spot.

Artist at work

Still feeling the effects of the Great Depression, Ray undertook freelance projects in addition to hopping between animation studios. He drew ads for the Earle C. Anthony[3] car dealership. One piece called "Rich diggings" aimed to convince the salesmen to boost their profits by selling accessories for Packard Motor Cars.

Coaching cartooning

---

[3] Much more than a car dealer, Mr. Anthony was one of the most prominent movers and shakers in Los Angeles. He owned TV and radio stations, was a songwriter, journalist, playwright and a philanthropist who saved the Hollywood Bowl from going under. He even helped bring the Dodgers from New York to Los Angeles and gas stations to early motorists.

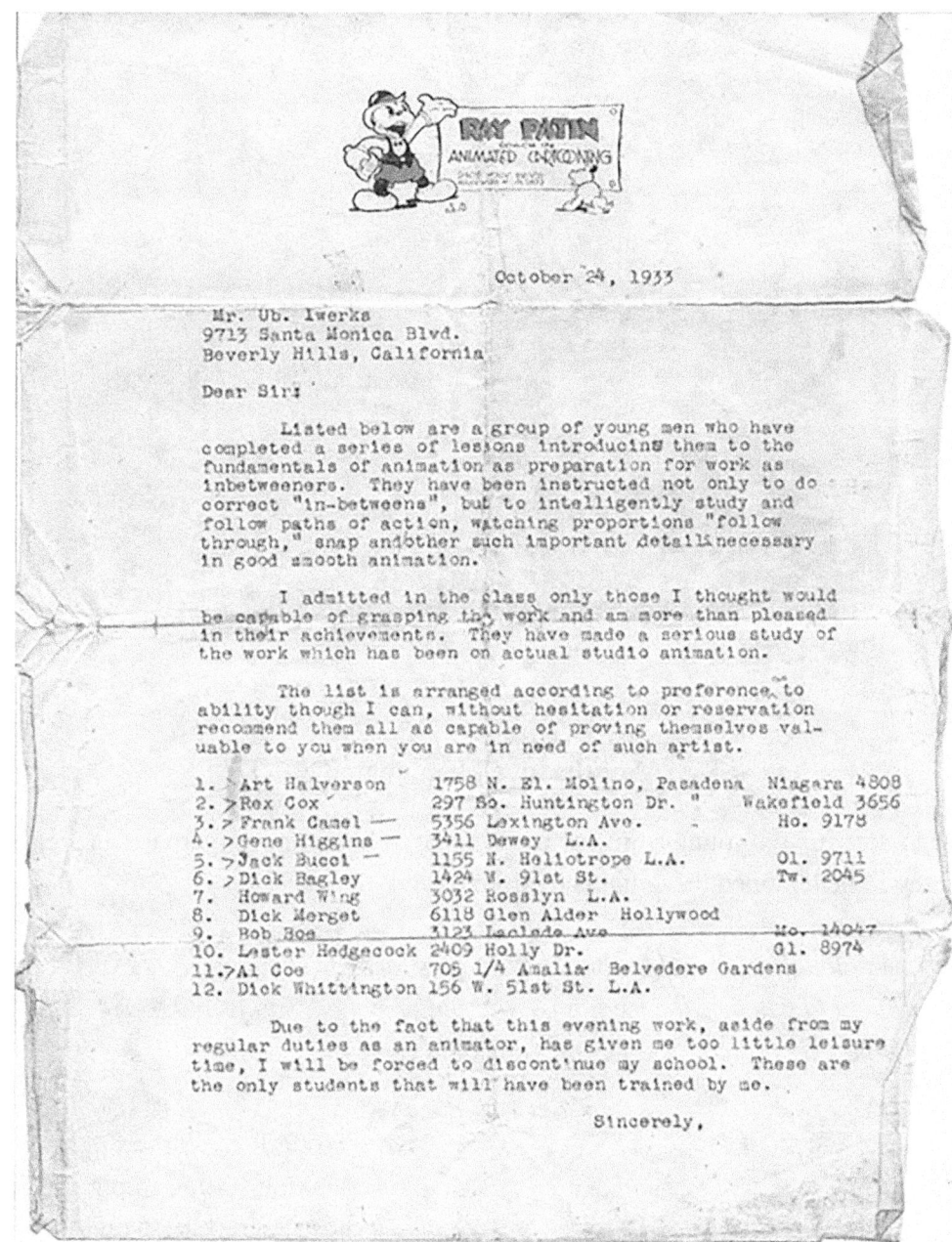

Accolades for animators

He taught "animated cartooning," at the Holly Drive house. In a letter written in 1933 to Ub Iwerks,[4] he recommended a list of students he trained as animators. In closing, Ray wrote,

> *Due to the fact that this evening work, aside from my regular duties as an animator, has given me too little leisure time, I will be forced to discontinue my school.*

---

[4] Another animation star who opened his own studio after leaving a distinguished career working side by side with Walt Disney, most notably as co-creator of Mickey Mouse. Iwerks has received many awards, including Oscars, for his achievements in visual techniques.

For the love of animation

So, things were looking up for young animator Ray. In one of his cartoons, perhaps an idea for an advertisement, my father extolled the delights of animation:

> *Living laughable lovable comic characters taken from life itself and*
> *brought to you thru the medium of our magic pencil wands and thrust*
> *upon the living screen–that's the animated cartoon!*

What else could she wish for?

While Ray worked at his various jobs, Maxine settled into her role as a housewife. She would see her role in the same way her mother had and the way my father saw it. She was his "little wife." She would be his helpmate. He would make all her dreams of domesticity come true. He pictured her married bliss in a drawing created for drawing school before they were married. Perhaps Ray's offer of domestic expertise in his prenuptial letter was indeed called for, as my mother performed her chores with childlike naiveté. Though the work was a challenge, she delighted in her independence after years of poverty and taking care of five younger siblings in a household where she couldn't indulge her cravings. Once she bought a large jar of mayonnaise and devoured it all in one sitting, leaving none for the artichoke it was to complement–which is just as well because she served the vegetable cold not knowing it needed to be cooked first. I can imagine my father kidding her about her culinary faux pas. She wouldn't have liked the jabs at her culinary skills. They added to her sense of being young and female and therefore inferior.

Getting used to married life

In post-wedding cartoons on the subject of his new bride, my father used his nickname for her, "Ikkus." The unlikely moniker was from a verb describing their name for her favorite playful back scratch/tickling. (Or at least that is what they told me.) In one imaginative drawing dated two weeks after they were married, Ray portrayed Ikkus with a rolling pin demanding his paycheck to buy new clothes. But along with his signature the new husband added:

It might have been this way, but was it Honey? No you're a good kid.

I doubt she would have liked the "kid" allusion either.

Maxine and "Constance" of Hollywood

To relieve the pressure of performing her wifely duties in order to satisfy her more mature husband, my mother indulged in fantasy like she did as a child coping with her father. Aunt Gerry remembers visiting her older sister's seemingly glamorous new home. She says the house was filled with artsy-craftsy furniture and objects d'art created by the newlyweds who seemed to her a most romantic couple.

Mama must have felt as if she was in one of her fairy tales when she posed in a ruffled gown at her equally well-draped dressing table topped with a similarly-dressed doll she had brought with her from Culver City. Indulging in her passion for art she drew a portrait of a beauty called "Constance." The woman, who was probably imaginary, not only reflected the look of the era, but bore a striking resemblance to the artist—even down to trendy penciled eyebrows and ruffled neckline. I doubt my mother had any idea she possessed the same beauty as the woman she portrayed. The fantasy of movies also became an escape to replace her storybooks. Almost every day she would descend the hill to catch a movie at Grauman's Chinese Theater or his Egyptian Theater—elaborately themed movie houses two blocks from each other on Hollywood Boulevard. Perhaps Greta Garbo and John Gilbert or Clark Gable and Jean Harlow offered the teenage Maxine the romance she sometimes found missing in Ray's cartoons. Her humor had been dulled by years of teasing by the Riley clan.

Yuletide romance

The artwork for their first Christmas card picturing a handsome snuggling couple in a snowy wonderland does show a romantic side. Perhaps even more evidence that the honeymoon was still going on three months after their marriage is found in the corner of the drawing. Here my father wrote MAX + RAY. It's not the initials you would find carved on a tree. It is the announcement that the two artists collaborated on the final product, with Daddy doing the drawing and Mama adding the color after it was printed.

Finally, in 1937, Ray realized his dream. He was hired as an animator at The Walt Disney Studios. The couple left their Hollywood home and moved to an apartment near the studio on Hyperion Avenue.

Now able to apply his talents to his dream job, my father worked on bringing Donald Duck to life. He even got to direct the other animators on scenes with an animated Shirley Temple[5] in *The Autograph Hound* where Donald, a big movie buff, pursues the stars for their signatures.

Walt's thank-you party

---

[5] A highly popular, dimpled, curly-topped child star

Having a field day

I liked watching Daddy's movies of the extracurricular antics of the Disney employees and their families. Particularly amusing was the *Field Day,* Walt's thank-you celebration for the tremendous success of *Snow White and the Seven Dwarfs.* He held the extravaganza at the sprawling, sumptuous, now abandoned and deteriorating, 1920s Norconian Resort Supreme, east of Los Angeles and north of Corona (hence the name). The workers were treated to the resort's facilities, dinner and dancing—even a marching band. Daddy's film coverage shows overhead views of the resort shot from a plane that took off from the airfield. I laughed at the photography of his cavorting co-workers as they one-upped each other in the pool and on Lake Norconian. There are no shots of my mother. I'm pretty sure my imminent birth in a month was the reason for her absence.

Ray at play

From a "gag" shot taken of him at the time, I'd say my father had a mighty fine time acting out his dream as a Disney animator. He is shown between two colleagues making comic use of the little hair he had left as well as added facial embellishments. His cohorts were no doubt coached to seem oblivious to his antics.

Ray shoots his leading lady in Santa Barbara and Bryce Canyon

In their six child-free years before I was born, my mother and father seem to have enjoyed their leisure hours romping hither and yon. Wherever they roamed, Ray would proudly showcase his lovely Maxine for his silver screen. She posed perched on the fountain at the Santa Barbara Mission and is seen silhouetted at the end of the day with Bryce Canyon in the background. Mushy? Maybe. Romantic? Definitely!

Rare photo of the newlyweds together

5
Burbank, Thanks to the Seven Dwarfs

The Seven Dwarfs get their due, 11th Academy Awards ceremony, 1939

Walt Disney was presented a special Oscar by Shirley Temple. The award is decorated with one big shiny man and seven tiny ones. The big guy was for the film *Snow White and the Seven Dwarfs,* and the mini Oscars were for the true stars of the movie, the Seven Dwarfs. The proceeds from his first animated feature were so great that Disney could afford to buy fifty-one acres in Burbank and move his studio to the San Fernando Valley.

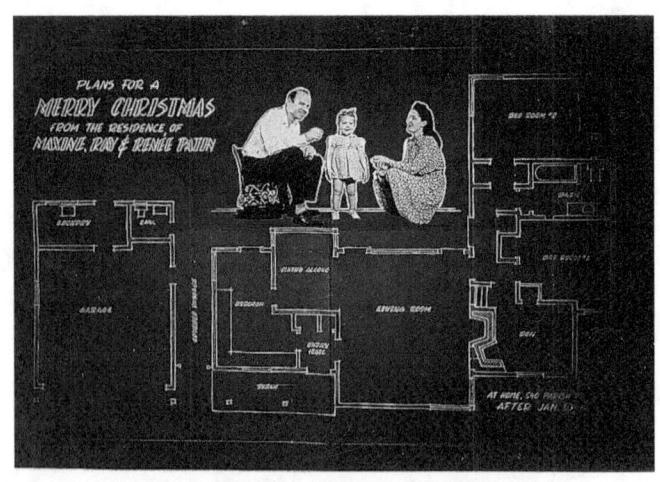

1941 Christmas card from the new Patin "residence"

Since my father was one of Disney's happy merry workers, we moved there too. Daddy had the plans drawn up by Leslie Arthur, his old friend and Catalina partner in crime who was now an architect. Our 1941 Christmas card shows the three of us posed on the plans for our new house, my father perched on my rocking chair. Our new home was in the Burbank subdivision called the Riverside Ranchos, because it is a block from Riverside Drive (named for the trickle of water called the Los Angeles River) and because the neighborhood is zoned for horses in the backyards.

Parish and Parkside, the Patin place

The ranch style house curves gracefully around a corner. From the south side on Parkside Avenue we could see Griffith Park that gives the street its name and looking west from the front porch on Parish Place, we could see the water tower on the Disney lot.

Now Daddy said he would be able walk to work, which we always called "the Studio," but he never did walk, saying it would spoil his work clothes. In the morning, he would get all dressed up in his Maxine-laundered white shirt, tie and pleated trousers. He tried biking a few times, but even with trouser clips to guard against sartorial bicycle chain accidents, he gave it up and drove our moss green Plymouth the three blocks to work.

The Animation building and signpost showing where Daddy worked

The original front gate to The Walt Disney Studios complex my father entered is still on Buena Vista Street. So is the original Animation building where he worked at the corner of Dopey Drive and Mickey Avenue. He worked with other men (and a rare woman) at desks with rotating back-lighted glass plates and metal pegs along the bottom. The animators would attach a pile of thin hole-punched papers to the pegs. The light helped them see through the papers and they would shuffle their drawings back and forth like a flipbook. That way they could change the characters just a tiny bit, watching them come alive the way they would on film—24 drawings per second.

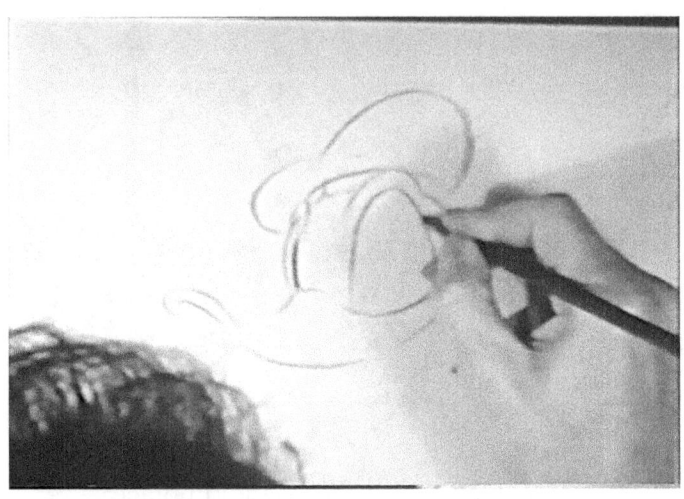

Daddy draws Donald

The art of animation was no mystery to me, no more than Mama's art of vacuuming. Daddy had an animation board on a big desk at home and I loved to stand next to him watching him work. His left hand rapidly rustled his papers using his digits long before animation was digital. He drew with his right hand, the one with the tip missing on the pointing finger because he caught it in his little printing press. In his pencil hand, he kept a gray kneaded eraser, like the ones I tried unsuccessfully to use as modeling clay. To his right was a little cosmetic mirror on a stand for making faces to help him give expression to his characters. He made funny faces even when he wrote his signature too–that distinctive script so many of the animators copied from Walt, now the Disney logo.

Sometimes we went to the Studio for special treats when we kids were shown Disney films at the theater on the lot. But I was always afraid they might have scary parts. That yellow-eyed, warty-faced witch in *Snow White and the Seven Dwarfs* menaced me in my dreams. And I cried for days when Bambi's mother died. Although my father worked on the harmless, though slightly phallic, mushrooms in *Fantasia,* some of that movie's dark dramatic scenes were pretty creepy for a kid.

One day my father took me to the commissary for lunch where I had hoped for a Walt sighting. Although this would never come true, I did get to sit on the lap of Clarence "Ducky" Nash, the voice of Donald Duck, who entertained me with that almost unintelligible angry quack-speak. The sprawling grounds on the other side of the guarded gatehouse bustled with animated workers walking or biking along tree-lined streets fronted by lawns and buildings named for different phases of the production. "In-betweeners" were the artists who did the drawings that linked the key ones the animators did, and the all-female Ink & Paint Department was where the transparent "cels" were painted before they were shot on the great big multiplane camera.

Visiting Daddy at the red and beige streamlined studio was what I imagined a college campus must be like. And from Daddy's movies it looked as if he and his co-workers were having as much fun as a bunch of college kids. I always laughed when I watched the scene where Kae Sumner, the very tall ink and paint lady, jitterbugged with the very short man on the roof of her building.

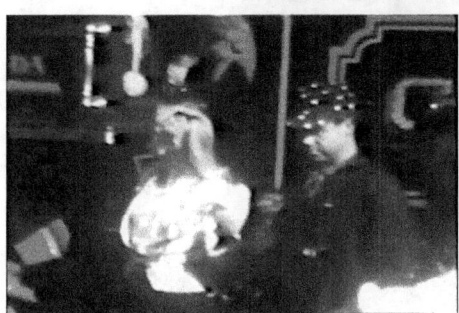
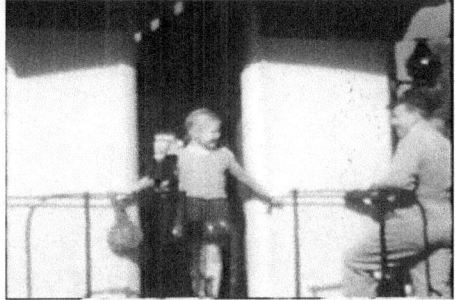

Movie at Grizzly Flats: *Potsy Rides the Rails*

My parents' friends were as much fun as kids. A favorite was Ward Kimball, one of Walt's "Nine Old Men," the elite group of top Disney animators who weren't old at all. Ward was like a big kid. He and his friends had a Dixieland band called the Firehouse Five Plus Two. Once we went to visit the Kimballs. I remember what fun the whole family seemed to have together. They even had a life-sized steam locomotive in their backyard. Ward dressed up like a railroad man in a polka dot engineer's hat. Daddy filmed me taking a trip all by myself on the Grizzly Flats Railroad.

My parents' parties with other artists were filled with the latest in creative cocktails, goofy games and impractical jokes. I would try unsuccessfully to join the fun, then spy on the adult activities through the secret movie-showing opening my father put in the wall from the den to the living room. He had grown tired of the setup and now placed his projector among the guests, so he could treat them to his narration.

Strike!

One home movie that our guests would have sat through was my father's documentation of the five-week strike when the Disney animators no longer whistled while they worked. They wanted more money and more credit, and they wanted to join the Screen Cartoonist's Guild. Daddy's film began with a letter to Walt telling him why they were going on strike.

The film that I also watched over and over shines a spotlight on all the action of the strike beginning in May of 1941. The artists are shown outside the entry guardhouse with pickets bearing sayings like Pluto protesting, "I've got a bone to pick with Walt," and Pinocchio lamenting, "No Strings on Me."

Maxine marches

Ray rolls Renée rocks

While his co-strikers defiantly hoisted their signs in the air, Daddy proudly pushed his on the ground on a disk that made it look as if Donald Duck's webbed feet were waddling along in front of him. It said, "Pin Money Can't Keep Me in Pin Feathers."

Mama is shown carrying a picket for Lab Technicians. Next to her is a lady whose sign pictures a mad Mickey saying, "It's up to Walt to call a Halt."

My father captured in vivid black and white the determined esprit de corps of the strikers as they marched or taunted the "scabs" who drove through the gate to work. He panned over tired marchers giving serious attention to speeches in their eucalyptus grove headquarters across the street from the Studio. There are shots of the workers taking rest and refreshment, and I even have a topless scene at the temporary nursery school where I played with other animators' kids.

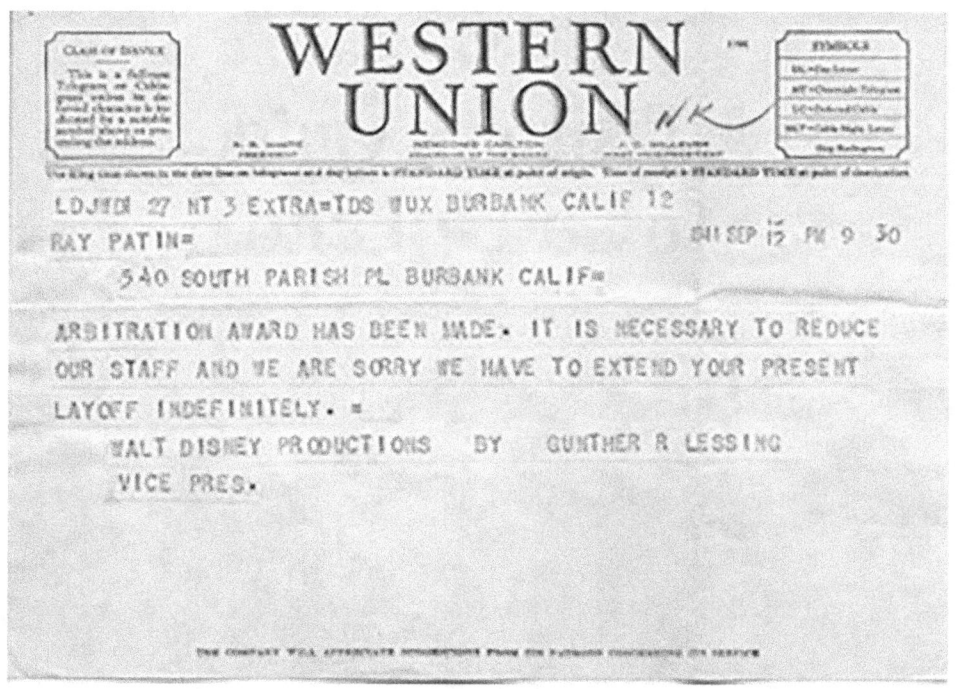

End of a dream

The animators won and joined the Screen Cartoonist's Guild. They went back to work but were soon "laid off"—temporarily fired. In September of 1941 my father got a Western Union telegram[1] from the Studio saying his layoff was extended indefinitely.

He did animation for Warner Bros. and other studios and was president of the Screen Cartoonist's Guild in 1945. He even went back to work for Disney a short time in 1946. He created comic strips and worked at home. Now I watched him in the den using his animation desk with the light behind the glass turned off as he wrote letters to get work.

Whether Daddy was going to the Studio or working at home made little difference to my busy Burbank life. It was just the way things were in the grown-up world. I knew that all was not well, and that Mama had to purée Daddy's vegetables because he had an ulcer. But for this kid, Burbank was the happiest place on earth to grow up. Even if I didn't have Bashful, Happy, Sneezy, Doc, Grumpy, Sleepy and Dopey as playmates.

---

[1] These were hand-delivered messages where continuous strips of type were cut and glued onto a sheet of yellowish paper. If you got one, it meant very important news.

6
A Visitor's Guide to La La Land

In Los Angeles, all the loose objects in the country were collected, as if America had been tilted and everything that wasn't tightly screwed down had slid into Southern California.

Saul Bellow

La La Land. Now remembered as the title of a movie that almost won the Best Picture Oscar in an Academy Awards fiasco, the moniker stands for the initials of Los Angeles, the City of Angels, and for a certain otherworldly bliss displayed by its earthbound inhabitants. With a population around thirteen million, it is hard to imagine that all the inhabitants of the Los Angeles area occupy any common mindset. But the moniker endures, and impressions of Southern California are as varied in their veracity as those who perpetuate them:

- It's a sun-splashed Garden of Eden dotted with palms and orchards as pictured on juicily-colored fruit crate labels and tantalizing postcards.

- It's the sparkling blue Pacific featured on *Baywatch* and the Beach Blanket movies. It's a Lotus Land for A-listers who saunter on the sands romantically and emerge from the surf muscularly in the pages of *People* magazine.

Mountain dwelling, Santa Monica Mountains

- Traffic is bumper to bumper, but you can just get out and dance on the freeway. That is, if you can believe the opening scene of *La La Land.*

- If you want to see what the residents are like, just watch *Saturday Night Live's* mock soap opera, "The Californians," where bleached blond, oddly colored cast members obsess over freeway routes in an almost incomprehensible slack-jawed Valley Girl speak.

- Southern California is covered with hills where split-level houses cling tenuously by the grace of slender stilts.

Tail O' the Pup, West Hollywood, 2005   Randy's Donuts, near LAX

- And you can eat in restaurants shaped like what's sold inside.

The siren Sign

- Movie stars can be spotted almost anywhere. You too can be hounded by paparazzi if you follow the siren's call of the Hollywood Sign. Its 44-foot tall letters dance along the hillside like an undisciplined chorus line.

Southern California is perhaps a crazy quilt stitched together of all of these fictional and not-so-fictional patches. But for me, it is HOME. I understand that the eccentricities of my homeland precede me. It was perhaps inevitable that I would tend to view the world through lenses tinted with the glaring colors of the Land of La. My reality was shaped by this many-storied place and by the imaginations of a fantasy-loving mother and a cartoon-drawing father.

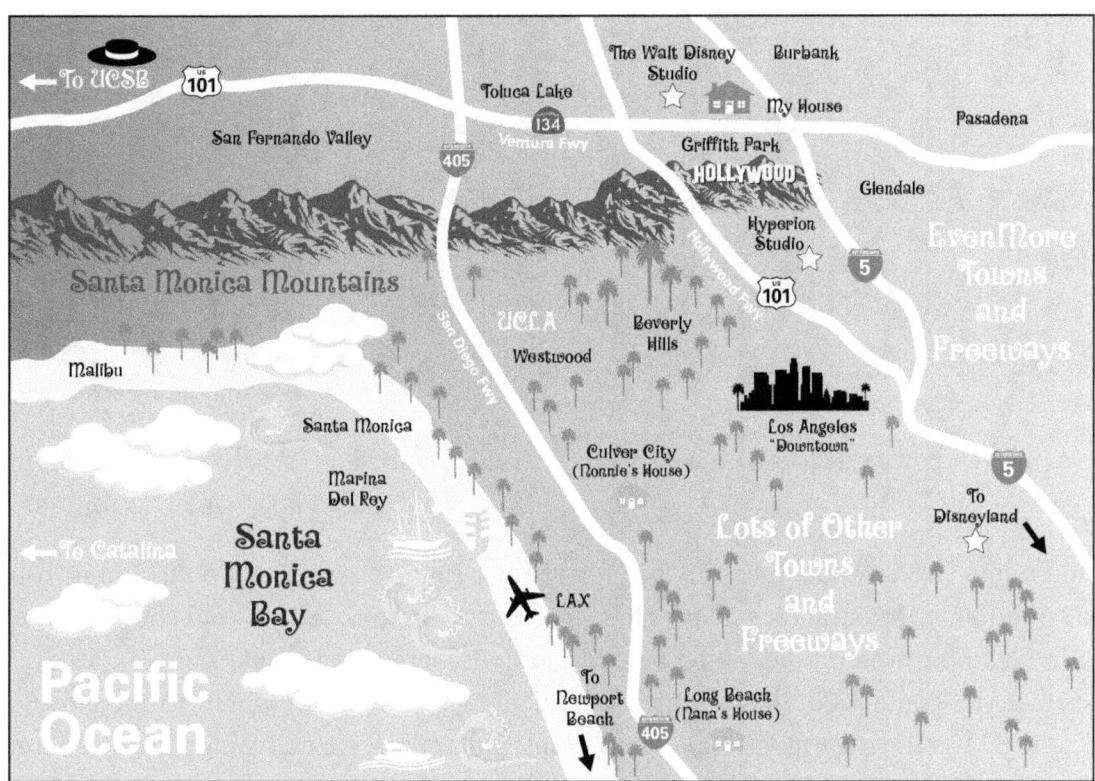

La La Land

It seems fitting that my story include a guide to these stomping grounds as they were and are. Let me take you on a tour of my childhood homeland. There is a map for your touring pleasure. In order to better blend in with the Southland's car centric culture, let's imagine we are crossing into LA County, one of several that form the Southland, by car. Let's imagine it's a convertible—a fire engine crimson convertible. We'll wend our windswept way east on the 101 Ventura Freeway, one of the oft-clogged arteries that hold the county together.

If it's a clear day as we descend the grade, we'll get our first glimpse of my old stomping grounds known for its oranges and a song where Bing Crosby croons that he's going to make the San Fernando Valley his home. Squinting and using our imaginations, we can perhaps picture how what is now a usually hazy urban sprawl might have been viewed by Bing or by the eighteenth-century missionaries who "recruited" the native population to help them stake a claim here for God and Spain.

Those are the Santa Monica Mountains to your right. If you cross them on one of the zigzaggy canyon roads, you could dip your toes in the Pacific. But we'll keep on course to the western part of the Valley, passing homogenized bedroom communities like Tarzana, home of the ape-raised hero's creator, Edgar Rice Burroughs.

You know you're in movie-making country when we reach Studio City. Here the Ventura Freeway becomes the 134 and the 101 goes south to Hollywood and north to North Hollywood (no resemblance to the "real" Hollywood which is barely real anyway). Don't worry–your guide is a native freeway navigator. We'll keep heading east on the 134.

Bing's place, a postcard from Toluca Lake

Bob Hope's Toluca Lake estate, for sale in 2014 at $27.5 million

If my grandmother were conducting this tour for visiting Louisianans, she would stop in Toluca Lake, the community that straddles North Hollywood and Burbank. She would show us where we could see the lake if it weren't hidden by homes and golf course. She would point out celebrity residences that you could see if they weren't behind gates, the locale of which seemed to change from trip to trip. The itinerary always included Frank Sinatra's place and Bing Crosby's family home though the house had burned down, and the crooner and his family had moved to Beverly Hills long before we admired the replacement. Then we would ogle the shrubbery around the home of Bob Hope, Toluca Lake's most influential citizen who, like a twentieth century feudal lord, owned much of the surrounding countryside.

The next off-ramp past Toluca Lake is Bob Hope Drive. We'll leave the freeway here and drive east on Riverside Drive. It parallels the Los Angeles River, a waterway that is most often a damp streak in the middle of a concrete pathway, great for skateboarding, graffiti-tagging and action movie chase scenes.

Forest Lawn: the mansion across the river

Gene Autry's headstone lists his many roles topped by "America's Favorite Cowboy"

Bette Davis's classically styled monument is etched: "She did it the hard way"

We are now in my hometown Burbank, founded by Dr. David Burbank, who was not the famous botanist. He was a dentist who purchased Spanish rancho land here after leaving the northern California gold rush. That Tara-esque mansion across the river is not another movie star's home (nor mine as I would joshingly tell my dates). It's a branch of Forest Lawn Memorial Park. The complex is the current home to a panoply of stars who have taken their final bows such as Gene Autry, whose museum is nearby, and Bette Davis whose home was too.

Before it was developed as a cemetery, that field was the location for the climactic battle scenes in D.W. Griffith's 1915 *The Birth of a Nation,* a three-hour silent film about the Civil War where African-Americans were portrayed by whites in blackface and the white-hooded Ku Klux Klan comes off as almost heroic. The controversial epic has been the subject of much discussion about its racism. Growing up in Burbank, I did not see black faces. I don't know if this was because of real estate covenants or perhaps, as some say, that Burbank was a "Sundown Town" where African-Americans had to leave before the sun set. It was only through the years that I began to learn of the subtle segregation that surrounded my youth.

The dusty hills that form the cemetery's backdrop are part of Griffith Park, another setting for countless big and small screen shows like the bat cave from the sixties Batman series. The park ranges over 4,000 rugged, chaparral- and oak-covered acres in the Hollywood Hills that are part of the Santa Monica Mountains. It is the largest urban park in the U.S., five times bigger than Central Park. Although I grew up thinking it was named for D.W. Griffith, it was actually named for Colonel Griffith J. Griffith who endowed it.[1]

For me, those hills were the touchstone of my home turf. As a child, I would lie in bed at night listening to the plaintive howl of the coyote packs that inhabit the park. And I could see some of their kin in the Griffith Park Zoo. From time to time we would hear of marauding wild coyotes attacking the caged animals in the zoo.

Transmitter on top of Mount Lee and the "right" side of the Sign

From our front yard, I could see the highest peak in the hills, Mount Lee, topped by LA's first television transmitter. What I couldn't see near that tower was the iconic Hollywood Sign. It stretches for 352 feet along the other side of the hill like one of the Seven Wonders of La La Land. Now, the Sign ubiquitously graces any TV broadcast that mentions Tinseltown. It shines its grace on that magic magnet attracting all who seek showy glory. And in my youthful mind, it turns its back on those of us who dwell behind it.

---

[1] In a less magnanimous deed, Griffith shot and severely wounded his wife and went to prison.

The "wrong" side of the Sign and the lights beyond

Yes, I grew up on the "wrong" side of the Sign—in its metaphoric shadow. I have used that fact as one of many excuses for a failure to bring stardom to the family name. Those lights I could see beaming from over the hill in Hollywood shown on premieres of films in which I was never to star.

Sunset Ranch, established 1929

Nestled right under the Sign, in what looks like another movie location sits the Sunset Ranch. Here you can rent a horse and ride western saddle over the hill to Burbank, hitching your mount to a post at a trailside café near where we lived. If you were making this trek in the fifties, you might have spotted a teenaged girl all dolled up in rolled up Levi's, plaid shirt, strawberry blond ponytail and a rather shocking dash of red lipstick. That would have been me, out on a male equestrian-attracting foray. We're on our way there. But first let's look at the house the Mouse built. It's on our way.

As we head into Burbank on Riverside Drive, you may wonder if this typical bedroom community can really claim to be a part of La La Land. About this time, you may notice Mickey ear-topped wrought iron fences and the super-sized wizard's hat Mickey wore in his role as the Sorcerer's Apprentice in *Fantasia*. The fences mark the boundaries of the Walt Disney megalopolis and the hat is the entrance to the Roy E. Disney Animation Building, brother of Walt.

You have arrived at the land of Disney

Where the magic happens

If you look to the left, you'll see the water tank on stilts that, like many of the Hollywood studios, stands as signage for the productions generated there. I could see the tower from our house. It was my other touchstone to knowing I was home, along with the radio tower in the Hollywood Hills. If we turn left on Buena Vista ("good view" in Spanish and a brand of The Walt Disney Company), we will see the old gatehouse my father entered and the location of the strike where the hospital now stands across the street.

The house that Walt built

Around the corner on Alameda we will find the new entrance and one of my cherished landmarks. Peek through the cartoony metal palm tree gateway and through the real eucalyptus trees to glimpse the semi-classical façade held up by the Seven Dwarfs. My favorite dwarf, Dopey, is topping them all—a tribute to the film that financed Disney's move to Burbank.

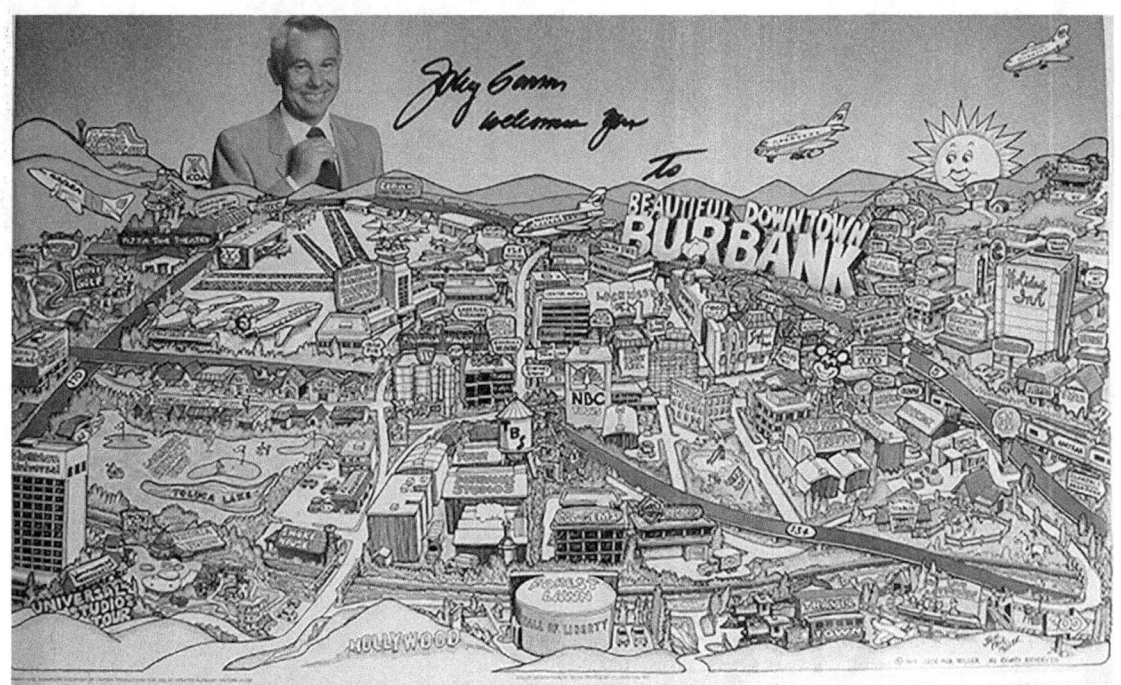

Johnny's Burbank

Nearby is NBC, the birthplace of Johnny Carson's popular name for my hometown, "Beautiful Downtown Burbank." Oh, there really is a Downtown Burbank (there was never an Uptown), but it is two and a half miles from the Media District where it was lauded by *The Tonight Show* when it was based here. And it was never beautiful, even between 1967 to 1989 when it was converted to the "Golden Mall," a never-popular, pedestrian-only shopping area—a sort of beautiful downtown Tomorrowland.

Downtown Burbank on San Fernando Road is where Mama and I would do our errands. We would shop at J. C. Penney where I watched transfixed as our money traveled back and forth in vacuum tubes from our clerk to an unseen cashier on the mezzanine. I felt more mature than my grade school self as I wandered on my own through Woolworth's on a mission to decide how to spend my allowance. Standing on tiptoe at the wooden display bin, I longingly admired the blue bottles of Evening in Paris cologne, and then ambled to the back with the bolts of smelly oilcloth and chirping canaries in cages. But I always ended up with a selection from the stationery counter, perhaps a jumbo-sized Red Chief tablet or an official receipt book complete with carbons. Our lunch was in the same store perched on revolving leatherette stools at the lunch counter. My selection was always a melted cheese sandwich and thick chocolate malt poured from the frosted metal container where it was freshly frothed by a uniformed waitress.

Horse-high crossing button and rent-a-ride barn

We will now return home from my nostalgia trip in downtown Burbank to the Patin residence in the Riverside Ranchos. We will see signs warning that equestrians might cross the street after pressing one of the rider-high street-crossing buttons, and there may be a mobile blacksmith working in a driveway. I often heard the clomp of horse hoofs as I lay in my bed for an afternoon nap. We didn't have a horse. But when we were kids, Mary Jane and I saved up a dollar a week to hire one at the nearby stables to ride for an hour. Our mounts led us across a rickety swinging bridge over the river and into Griffith Park on trails the horses knew so well we didn't have to guide them. Our mounts were usually well behaved until they sensed home when, ignoring our rein signals, they galloped back to the comfort of their rent-a-steed stable as we hung on for dear life. A jaunt down the bridle path to the nearby café for the aforementioned male adolescent sighting was always last on our Saturday's itinerary.

The Wonder Years house

If you experience a sort of déjà vu feeling as we enter my old neighborhood, it may be because you have seen it in a movie or commercial filmed by one of the local studios. The tree-lined streets easily pass as Any-where Any-era USA as they did in *The Wonder Years* TV series. The University Avenue house where Kevin Arnold and his family played out their episodes is a typical Burbank ranch house. Our house was of the same style on a similar tree-lined street. Parish Place was often jammed with stars' trailers, camera equipment and craft (food) trucks catering to cast and crew of various productions. Our house was never chosen for the honor. Or maybe it was, and Mama kept the offer from me because she knew it would be a hassle despite the remuneration, and she didn't want to encourage my thespian ambitions. The house across the street on Parkside had a particularly photogenic Cape Coddish-look surrounded by a white picket fence. It was used for the *Our Miss Brooks* TV show and lots of commercials. I would always try for a star sighting, but Henry Winkler was the only one I can claim.

Our own neighborhood movie location

I *can* claim that I grew up in the same town with other screen stars—though in full disclosure, our wonder years there were on different time lines. Ron Howard spent his happy days in my hometown too. We went to the same high school though by the time he graduated in the seventies, I was *teaching* high school kids. Another show biz notable of a slightly different ilk was Tim Burton who lived on the other side of town near Lockheed and a cemetery that inspired his *Frankenweenie* movie with Disney. And then there was Mary Frances, a local Girl Scout, whose movie stardom we'll talk about later.

Our house doesn't look a lot different today than it did when my father's Catalina carousing buddy-turned-architect friend designed it for us. The current owners may from time to time find relics from the Patin past like a scrap of one of the many layers of wallpaper or paint that fit the decorating trends of the times. They may be puzzled by a few custom-designed relics found around the property.

Would they understand that the rusted pole in the backyard was part of a clothesline where my mother hung our laundry to dry and my father rigged a stepladder into a jungle gym? They may be equally intrigued by the hole for the garbage can next to the two-part kitchen Dutch door or the compartment inside the kitchen where the milkman deposited his wares from the outside.

Big Boy with Mary Kate, granddaughter of my childhood neighbor Mary Jane

Before saying goodbye to Burbank, let's stop at Bob's Big Boy Restaurant on Riverside at the border of Toluca Lake. Bob's was our "Mel's Drive-In" where we starred in our own *American Graffiti* dramas. It was the teen temple where we had to be seen in the right car driven by the right boy. There was no better feeling than meeting both prerequisites as you took your place in the line of "cherry chopped and channeled"[2] cars that filed down the alley and found a parking place in an imaginary spotlight. As my driver date and I waited for a comely carhop to hop onto our running board (hence the name), I tried to look blasé, primping in the angora fuzzy dice-embellished rearview mirror. In a uniform topped with a hat befitting a hurdy gurdy monkey, our waitress attached the metal tray to our window and returned to fill it with our Big Boy Combination Plates: double-decker burgers dripping with Bob's secret sauce, wedges of iceberg lettuce slathered with Thousand Island dressing and hot, salty fries (all for 65 cents).

---

[2] "Cherry" is an adjective meaning the cars have been well fixed up by their young owners. "Chopped and channeled" connotes technical tinkering I never did learn to understand except that it was a good thing.

Warner Bros.

We'll leave the chubby boy's illustrious presence and drive west on Riverside, taking Pass Avenue to Olive Avenue where we are met with a gigantic sound stage at Warner Bros. Studios, whose animated productions were once drawn by my father after he left Disney. Today Bugs Bunny and other real-life stars are heralded in mega posters lining the walls on our left. Like Disney's water tank, the logo-bearing tower no longer stores water to douse fires. And gone are the rows of huge painted background landscapes I could see stacked in the back lot. I was fourteen when ashes from these burning sets fell on our house two miles away. If there was water in the tower, it wasn't enough to douse the huge blaze.

As we cross the river, Olive becomes Barham and we enter the pass into Hollywood. In the hills on our left are homes to the stars and lesser beings like my newlywed parents. On the right is yet another studio/entertainment complex, Universal Studios Hollywood, spread across a vast expanse much of which was owned by Bob Hope.

We're following the route to Hollywood my father took to work in his animation studio in the fifties. We turn left on Cahuenga (Ka-Wang-Ga) and know we have made it to Hollywood when we pass the Hollywood Bowl outdoor amphitheater. After Cahuenga becomes Highland Avenue, we pass the United Methodist Church where I strutted down the aisle as a four-year-old flower girl. Soon we pass the corner of Hollywood Boulevard with the looming Dolby Theater and amusement area where stars strut the red carpet in hopes of receiving their Academy Awards.

Which one is real? Hint: Look for the Mouse on top of the world

The next big intersection is Sunset Boulevard where we turn left to number 6650, the much-renovated building that housed Ray Patin Productions. We'll get to that part of his story later, but for now, let's look at Crossroads of the World across the street from what was his studio. It is a little street of internationally-flavored cottage offices. Today's owner has big plans to modernize the site with many new buildings–apartments, retail, underground parking...even a hotel.

Imagine my delight when I visited Disney's Hollywood Studios in the Walt Disney World Resort, Florida, for the first time and came upon a perfect reproduction of the Crossroads standing as the entrance to a 5/8 scale clone of the city as it was in the forties! I reveled in nostalgia as I wandered through the streets of an untarnished Hollywood of yore, smugly recognizing storefronts that few would know to be anything other than more Disneyesque buildings. I mean, really, how many La La Land outsiders would know that the shack selling turkey to go, called Toluca Legs[3] "The Best Legs in Tinseltown!" is a nod to Toluca Lake?

Also at Hollywood Studios, you can see the 1989 dedication plaque at the end of "Hollywood Boulevard." It bears the words of then Disney CEO Michael Eisner:

> *The World you have entered was created by The Walt Disney Company and is dedicated to Hollywood–not a place on a map, but a state of mind that exists wherever people dream and wonder and imagine, a place where illusion and reality are fused by technological magic. We welcome you to a Hollywood that never was–and always will be.*

It may have been Los Angeles that gave Southern California its nickname, but it is the dream factory of Hollywood that is the spirit of La La. Today it is easier to revisit my old favorite Hollywood haunts in Florida than in California. Hollywood Boulevard is a mecca for tourists in vehicles and on foot seeking glimpses of the movie capital of the world as they imagined it to be. The main activity appears to be shooting selfies with costumed celebrity sorta look-alikes.

---

[3] Update for all SoCal nostalgia and turkey leg lovers: Toluca Turkey Legs Co. closed in 2016 and was renamed "Sunshine Day Café."

Star sightings

Now as I revisit the sites of Hollywood, I need to hunt through decades of development to get to familiar sights. But the hunt is worth it, as each brings back a memory. Let's visit some of these touchstones from the past. We'll begin at a place where you can get a great view of Los Angeles and feast your eyes on the Hollywood Sign not far away. The maps to the stars that are sold within the Griffith Park Observatory are far more factual than the maps to the stars' homes that are offered on the streets below. We will aim at the same veracity in our guided tour.

Young star

As you look over at the Sign, note the memorial bust of James Dean. It immortalizes the young star's role in the movie *Rebel Without a Cause* where he had his famous fight in the Observatory parking lot. The fight was over Natalie Wood, who was the hero's lover on and off screen. My childhood schoolmate was, like me, sixteen when she made the movie where Dean's red jacket served as a rebel call to teenagers. Both Natalie and James died young; he, in a crash of his speeding Porsche at twenty-four before *Rebel* was released, and she at forty-three, drowning off her yacht anchored in Catalina. In more recent times, the Observatory was the sight for a much happier scene when Emma Stone and Ryan Gosling danced their way into romance in *La La Land*.

More memorials line Hollywood Boulevard and parts of Vine Street. In 2018, there were more than 2,600 five-pointed terrazzo and brass stars embedded in the sidewalks. You are free to walk the Hollywood Walk of Fame to do some star gazing. Be sure to look for Walt Disney. He has two, one for motion pictures at 7021 Hollywood Boulevard and another one for television at 6747 Hollywood Boulevard. Donald Duck is nearby. Mickey Mouse and Tinker Bell and Winnie the Pooh are all star-worthy, too.

Idol worship

Footprints of fame

The movie houses my mother walked to in the thirties still stand on Hollywood Boulevard. At what was Grauman's—now TCL—Chinese Theater, look for more star signs. These are the celebrities' hand and foot prints that, like the sidewalk stars, are added in great ceremony and listed online.
In 1963, I went to watch Paul Newman make his impression. I missed the ceremony but watched his movie *Hud*. Driving away, I stopped for a light next to none other than the man with the magic eyes himself. Nervously, I called over that I liked his movie. His retort was to ask me what I was doing inside watching a movie on such a lovely day.

Though not everyone has had such an in-depth conversation with Paul Newman after his cement ceremony, most have heard of the venue. But if we go over a few blocks, in a quieter part of town, there is a monument that many miss.

Home to a little tramp and a little frog

That little-known monument is the jolly frog tipping his bowler hat from atop the gatehouse of an English-looking building near the corner of La Brea at Sunset. This is where a nattily dressed Kermit pays homage to the fact that his creator Jim Henson's studio is in the former Charlie Chaplin studios where my father at one time had his offices.

Tower of legend

That cylindrical building is the home of Capitol Records. Some students of Hollywood lore say that the building was designed to look like vinyl records stacked on a spindle and that the blinking light atop the tower spells out the word "Hollywood" in Morse Code. Fact or legend? In a land where truth and tale often blur, does it matter? It's fun to imagine how tomorrow's archeologists will interpret the memorials to the stars and their works that make up today's Hollywood.

It is now time to conclude the narrated portion of our tour and let you explore La La Land at leisure. It still surpasses anything our imaginations can conjure up. Its myths survive in as many guises as those who may or may not believe them. Maybe the San Fernando Valley exists to some only in song, "Beautiful Downtown Burbank" only as a joke, and Hollywood is just a dream. To me, they exist both as I remember them and as they are–with a delicious dollop of La La thrown in to sweeten the mix. As a native of the fabled county, I am grateful to my forebearers who were not screwed down, but instead tumbled blissfully into Southern California. My geographical roots may have led to a skewed worldview, but I love this corner of the country.

7
The Girl with Two Faces

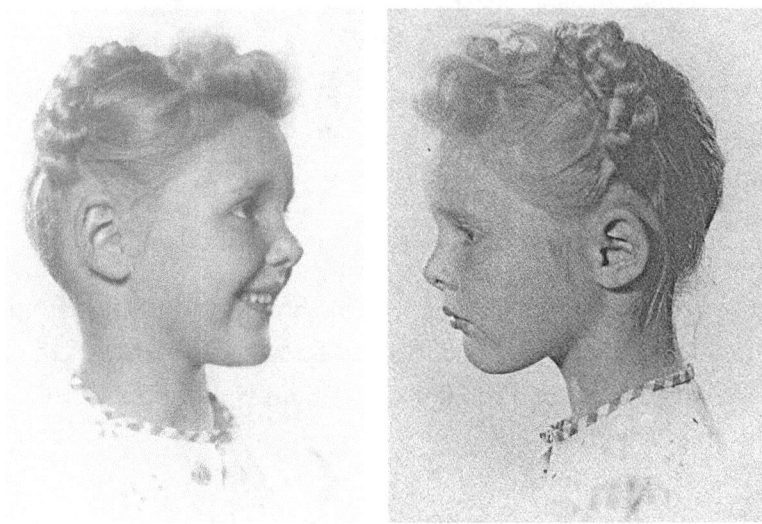

The two faces of Renée

I was a kid of many moods and inclinations. My Riverside Rancho playmates had as many Renées to play with as Snow White had dwarfs. In one of my yearly professional portraits by Jose Reyes of Hollywood, Mr. Reyes either tired of my seven-year-old insistence on frowning or was coached by my parents to capture it.

I was the "The Little Girl with A Curl" in Longfellow's poem:

> *There was a little girl who had a little curl*
> *Right in the middle of her forehead;*
> *When she was good, she was very, very good,*
> *And when she was bad, she was horrid.*

I don't really understand what the curl had to do with the girl, except that the words rhyme. But like that nameless child, I did nothing either naughty or nice without excess. As I grew older, my hair became less red. And my curly bangs—so lovingly crafted in a torturous metal curler by my mother—drooped unattractively on my brooding forehead. The deeper I got into mischief, the more the curl unfurled.

Tomboy

My mother did her best to boost my adorability factor. She knitted and sewed lovely ensembles, many of which matched hers, and she decorated me with them daily. As thanks, I didn't hide my displeasure at being dragged reluctantly to the smelly fabric stores downtown and suffering through the pinpricking fittings. When she wasn't sewing my garments, Mama was washing them in the big round metal machine, wringing them out on those dangerous finger-grabbing rollers, drying them on the backyard line, sprinkling them and ironing them. I protested the injustice of the non-Renée time resulting from my mother's continual efforts on behalf of my presentability.

I was careless of my couture. Those sweet little sashes were gone as fast as the curl in the middle of my forehead. The sweaters unraveled along with my braids, and my moods. As proof that kids should be kept in overalls until they reach puberty, I always ended the day tattered, torn, stained and often bloodied from a full schedule of activities, many involving tree climbing, puddle hopping and (literal) mudslinging. My manners were usually impeccable when away from home. The exception was at Mary Jane's next door where I had the mysterious habit of throwing my glass to crash into the sink after thanking her mother for a glass of water. I'm not sure of the psychological motivation for this bizarre behavior, perhaps it was to see the sparkly shards spread out on the porcelain. It wasn't long before Emma began to offer my beverages in paper cups.

A Hollywood wedding

At four, I put on my angelic face serving as flower girl in the posh wedding of an oft-removed cousin. The wedding took place at the massive Hollywood United Methodist church at Franklin and Highland in Hollywood, in the shadow of the "right" side of the Sign. The church now displays huge AIDS awareness ribbons on the sides of its bell tower. It was featured in films starring such notables as Michael J. Fox, Tom Hanks and Whoopi Goldberg, all of whom may have trod the same aisle where I dumped all my flower petals in one fell swoop feeling, perhaps, that it was more dramatic than a gradual strewing. Besides, I was upset because I thought my blue taffeta dress wasn't as feminine as the other girls attired in apricot.

Dick Winslow at 9, brother of the bride

The bride was from the Johnson family of seven kids, all child actors. There was a saying around Hollywood that when they needed a kid for a part, someone would call for one of the Johnson children because there was one the right size for any role. The family lived in a house of many floors filled with tons of toys. The bride's brother, whose stage name was Dick Winslow, had been "The Boy Reporter of KHJ," an LA radio station. He later played many roles in movies and television. He played the pipe organ, piano, marimba, bag pipes, accordion, drums, saxophone and other wind instruments. And when he got older, Walt Disney asked him to be the one-man band at the opening of *Mary Poppins*, and Dick even went on to entertain at Disneyland Park. In another of his many roles, he played the piano aboard champagne flights to Las Vegas.

Ready for my close-up

Perhaps Mama was trying to show my own child star potential when she had Mr. Reyes photograph her little darling as a plantation owner's child—or perhaps Little Bo Peep. Or maybe she was noticing that baby Potsy wasn't so baby plump any more. By the time I turned five at one of my elaborate birthday parties (always documented on film), my resemblance to Winston Churchill and the baby fat had gradually disappeared. But the Potsy moniker endured as a family endearment. I didn't mind. It was recognition. Hearing the name Renée called usually meant I was in trouble—which I often was, as seen in full-on Renée rampages where I would perform an aria of high-decibel bawling or hold my breath till I turned blue. As I grew older and began to socialize, my little play pals gave me the not-so-precious pet name "Stinky Pee Tail" due to my unfortunate incontinence-while-laughing incidents.

It was lucky I had friends at all as I also developed a coping mechanism to demonstrate my displeasure with them. I would bite them into compliance. That is until my mother cured the habit with a serious bite of her own, a punishment that far surpassed her usual *Snow White* "mean Evil Queen" look where she would open her eyes into a not very scary attempt at a menacing silent warning. I called her an ogress and used my budding acting ability to affect deep disdain at my mistreatment. This was often followed by her favorite "damn it to hell" oath and a threat to tell Daddy. Even though the biting demonstration hurt a lot, I usually escaped the wrath of Ray who administered justice with painful spankings that were not uncommon among my misbehaving peer group. I learned to anticipate my punishments by watching Daddy's lips tighten and the throbbing of a vein in his neck.

My detractors might have labeled my demeanor "wanton willfulness," or the acts of a spoiled child. Those more generous might have described me as a bright, outgoing kid who knew what she wanted. My Aunt Gerry says that it didn't take me very long to wrap my doting parents around my chubby finger and have them dancing to my toy drum.

One happy family   Daddy-designed Christmas card

On our 1942 Christmas card, I am portrayed as an over-indulged child glaring my disapproval at my fun-loving parents as they frolic on my hobby horse. Daddy had created the spring-activated mount for my fourth Christmas along with a teeter-totter that went up and down and around. These were but two selections among the avalanche of gifts from Santa. I judged their worth against my long list of desires recited to the scary Santa at the Bullocks Department Store in downtown Los Angeles.

My father's cartoon renderings of me were a key to the bafflement my parents must have experienced as their little Potsy grew up. My determination to have my own way was usually contrary to their better judgment and led to many contretemps, none ending well for me.

Movie moment: *The Girl with a Curl*

In his movies, Daddy often captured my rapid smile-to-frown mood swings. One of these revealing scenes has me starring in a role that required no acting. It is the story of the girl with two faces. The plot involves a little five-year-old deep in the act of buckling her Mary Janes.[1] Her concentration broken by the whirring of the ever-present camera, she frowns her disdain, her curl falling onto her forehead in its "naughty girl" position.

---

[1] The irony was not lost on my best friend Mary Jane and me that the popular strapped shoe was made of what we thought was "Patin" leather.

At the end of my segment I am coached to turn my other face and assume the lovely profile pose my mother often performed as a sentimental end to my father's home movies. As a true daughter of La La Land, I was learning to put on a happily-ever-after face just like the movie stars on the other side of the Sign.

The Patins' perennial profile pose

I was about six when I ran away from home. I gathered all my freshly ironed dresses, stuffed them into a brown paper bag and trotted off down Parish Place, never again to be subjected to the cruelties of my worse-than-Cinderella's home life. But, because I wasn't allowed to cross Alameda Avenue at the end of the street, I headed home and hung out in the cold, dark backyard with my teeter-totter and hobby horse, waiting to hear a wail of despair over my untimely disappearance. When there was none, I began to sing at the top of my whiskey voice. Finally, I was let back in to little fanfare—the worst kind of punishment.

Tough day on the set

As I matured into young girlhood, my volatility did not abate. Even in the span of one home photo session where I am posed in front of a wrinkled sheet, I transform from suit-and-purse-wearing propriety to disheveled imp to pouting Potsy. My moods unraveled as quickly as my couture and coiffure. I imagine that it was with a sigh of relief that my parents enrolled me in school with high hopes that a little learning might polish off some of my less endearing qualities.

8
School Days ABCs

A model forties classroom just like mine

School. It was at the top of my bucket list, and at four this was already a mighty long list, right up there with being a movie star. My desire to start school was so strong that I would walk around Parish and Parkside with a rolled-up copy of the Sunday paper under my arm, practicing how I would smartly walk to school with a stack of books just like I'd seen the big kids do.

I saved my allowance for pencil boxes with a tiny pencil sharpener and tinier eraser (never used in any classroom I attended). I played school even when I had no one to play with. When I was alone, I got to be both the teacher and pupil. For some reason, I had three copies of *Little Women* and would set up a classroom in anticipation of someone coming over, so I could "teach" them.

My interpretation of my first school—ivy green, if not ivy league

Since flashes of my first academic years are jumbled in no particular order, an **alphabetical listing** seemed appropriate to list my school days' memories.

A is for Assassinated Presidents
My first two grammar schools, as we called them, were William McKinley and Abraham Lincoln. It was undoubtedly a coincidence that these fine institutions of learning had been named for presidents who left office suddenly and tragically. And it was certainly a coincidence that the McKinley principal was named Mrs. Slaughter. The schools held no evil menace—except maybe from the big kids—and from adults who knew how to make me toe the line.

I was transferred from the former to the latter in the fourth grade when my mother was told Lincoln was "better." There may have been reasons undisclosed to me, but I was dubious, having heard my new school called "Stinkin' Lincoln." Sadly, my first real experience with a presidential—or any— passing was the day I heard on the radio of the death of our much-loved President Roosevelt of natural causes. I was eight and still at McKinley.

B is for Balls
Recess was fine for jump rope and jacks and tagging boys to be my boyfriend, but I hated games with balls. The worst was tetherball. Some of those kids put a hell of a wallop on that leather-covered ball, and it would get me right in the teeth, often smashing my nose, making it get all tingly, and sometimes, with luck so I could tattletale to a teacher, even a little bloody. Dodgeball was scary too. Those "safe" big red rubber balls stung legs left bare by short skirts because sensible pants on female students were a no-no.

C is for Cloakroom
None of us Southern California kids knew what cloaks were let alone wore them, but we piled our sweaters, occasional jackets, galoshes and brown-bag lunches in a heap in the dark little room lined with menacing metal hooks. It smelled of rotting apples, feet and wet wool. It was also a room for miscreants who were subjected to the isolation, darkness and odors. I knew from first-hand experience.

D is for *Dick and Jane*
Mrs. Pokinghorn in first grade introduced me to the joys of reading, not through phonics, but through the idyllic, though repetitive, exploits of Dick and Jane. I was envious of their model life, lived the way families should, far removed from the spirited artsy exploits at 540 South Parish Place.

Kindergartener, fifth from right, front row. All proper, hair upswept, hands clasped, no tears

E is for Enrollment
I cried uncontrollably when my mother brought me to enroll in kindergarten at McKinley. My anguish wasn't over separation anxiety, but because I had taken the word "enrollment" literally and had excitedly anticipated the moment when Mama would energetically *roll* me down the broad cement walk to my first ever school. She didn't, and I was angry at missing such a magnificent feat.

The Duchess as a stand-in for Amber

F is for *Forever Amber*

Miss Croft, my beautiful second-grade teacher whose name changed mid-year to Mrs. Froelich, reported back to Mama that I told her that my mother was reading *Forever Amber* and "couldn't put it down." Mother was highly embarrassed. The best-selling novel of the forties was banned as pornography in fourteen states for its sexually blatant content, no doubt leading to its popularity and to my desire to read big books. I must apologize for an unsuccessful and extensive quest for permission to print a photograph of one of the many covers in its seventy-five-year history.
The *Portrait of Louise de Keroualle, Duchess of Portsmouth* and her dazzling décolletage (a common theme) graced *one* of the many covers. Today Kathleen Winsor's historical romance novel is no longer the provocative novel it was in the forties. A Google search will provide you with many more cover examples. You may also be interested in the 1947 movie available on YouTube.

G is for Grocery Store

My first starring dramatic role hooked me on a dream of show business greatness. On the stage of McKinley's auditorium our whole second grade class performed a "play" that demonstrated for a patient audience of families our knowledge of the workings of the grocery store, our current social studies topic. We molded wet gray clay, and when it was dusty dry, we painted it into produce, meat and bakery goods. We brought still-smelly empty milk cartons to line up in the dairy case. We arranged all the goods in colorful displays manned by eager second graders ready to act out their roles in the simulated Ralphs market like the one downtown.

I immortalize my first stage triumph

I, as manager of the grocery store, employed a cone-shaped former orange juice carton as a megaphone to tell all the other workers what they should be doing and alert the shoppers to the best buys. Between my tendency toward overacting and the magnification of my booming voice, no other lines in the play could be heard. My mother was mortified.

H is for Hand Grenade
I didn't really mind being called "Hand Grenade." I suppose I was flattered to have a nickname to describe something other than my figure or weak bladder. After all it was wartime, and the kids called me that just because Renée, a name I shared with no other kids, rhymed with grenade—to a six-year-old.

I is for Imagination
When I started school, I was already an overachiever when it came to one requirement, using my imagination. My mother had filled my built-in bookshelves with her beloved fairy tales. Pretend scenarios danced continuously in my head. My father drew silly imaginary creatures for a living. As an only child, my constant companion was imaginary. Unsuspecting guests were often treated to spontaneous role-playing, and I would create shows and invite the neighbor kids over to watch for a minimum charge.

Kindergarten was a perfect imagination playground. There was a kitchen corner equipped with kid-sized wooden appliances and people-sized rag dolls. We were allowed to play house here and take on different roles from firefighter to cowboy in sets created from giant hollow wooden blocks. Our pretending was supposed to help us understand how we would act as grown-ups.

Later at Lincoln we role-played our social studies lessons. We wore serapes and sombreros to understand Mexico and collected simulated cow plops on the grass to understand how the pioneers found fuel for cooking.

J is for Janie
I gave Mary Jane the nickname Janie because she didn't like it. She was my next-door neighbor and my very best friend, and we fought every day. Janie was in the class ahead of mine at McKinley, and we would walk to and from school together ("a mile and two tenths," I would tell those who asked and who never questioned why I didn't say "a mile and one fifth"). On the way, we always took the alley, so we could feed sugar to Sweetheart, the white horse, who would stick his big head out from his paddock. On the way back, our regular stop was Scoggins or "the little store" on Alameda. Here we bought edible red wax lips and white chalky "cigarettes" with licorice tobacco and red sprinkles for the glowing ash. As we continued on home, "smoking" with sophisticated élan, we agreed that we were far worldlier as the result of our purchases.

K is for Kindergarten
Although it was fun and games, I was impatient to get to the real learning that happened in the other classrooms. My mother wrote in my baby book under kindergarten: "Wished they would get down to work instead of skipping, hopping, dancing and building boats. And she wishes they would teach her to read."

Look what I spelled!

L is for Letters

I always knew I was in the top reading group no matter how the teacher might disguise it with a color or bird name. I would tutor those of lesser talent and was sent to an advanced reading class. But I didn't like the windowless little room and the non-fiction books we had to read and was relieved to go back to my class and find out if Dick and Jane were getting into any new adventures with baby Sally and their dog Spot.

Eventually I learned the joy of arranging letters to make words and then to create sentences. We used picture-story paper that had a blank space for our illustrations and alternating dotted and solid lines to help us form our letters properly. I was proud when I no longer needed the dotted lines, and I could replace block printing with cursive. I began to fancy myself a person of letters.

M is for Microphone

It happened at Lincoln when I was in the sixth grade, my only grade with a man for a teacher, the much-worshipped Mr. Cooke, who taught us how to make model airplanes from balsa wood. But it wasn't the crafts that were my nemesis. It was the microphone. Mr. Cooke had chosen me to be the narrator of an all-school spectacular. After all, I had often demonstrated a gift for gab. (Perhaps my reputation from the *Grocery Store* production at McKinley had preceded me.)

All was ready for the performance, and I was in place and set to begin the festivities. But when I stood in front of a real microphone, not a phony orange juice carton version, I froze. No sound came forth—not until the sound of my sobbing as I was gently led from the dais. The trauma went right to the top of my most humiliating moments along with the time I came to school on a holiday and the day I forgot to wear underpants.

N is for Numbers
Numbers held far less fascination for me than letters. We called it arithmetic, and it meant memorizing rules. It wasn't taught to impart the magic of numbers or the beauty of the logic behind the operations we performed. I found it boring. The number story problems never made much sense and were far less fascinating than make-believe picture books the teacher read to us.

O is for Office
As dreaded a destination as the gulag to ill-behaved Russians or the brig to a mutinous seaman was the principal's office to an unruly grade-schooler. She sat alone behind a giant desk and meted out punishment befitting whatever might have been your infraction or unsatisfactory cooperation. It was a punishment worse than the cloakroom, and I went often, usually for refusing to stop talking when it was the teacher's turn. My visits to the seat of power were seldom for commendation and often for condemnation.

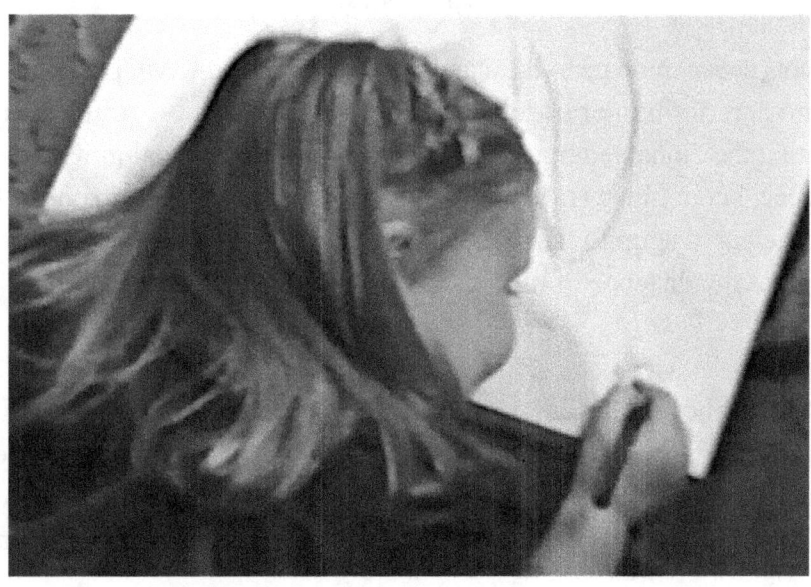

Emerging artist signing her work with a star

P is for Pictures
I showed no tendencies to follow my father into cartooning or my mother into painting. I have found it useful to blame my lack of talent on over-control by my parents who insisted I not put my eyes so close to the paper or outline my coloring book images in black. Sometimes I just stated my own made-up theory that artistic ability often skips a generation. In school my excuse was that I didn't like the awkward, giant "child-sized" brushes and messy, drippy paint the teacher made by mixing colored powder with water into a lumpy goo that invariably dribbled down the rough newsprint paper clipped onto the tippy upright easel. Crayons were easier, but in school they were the big naked, inodorous kind.

Early works

But my artistic attempts never came up to the standards I set for myself. My piece called *See the Big Cow* demonstrated either a flare for humor or science fiction. Or perhaps it was just a lack of drawing proportion, anticipating the elongated figures of El Greco—if he were painting cattle rather than saints. In another bucolic scene, I committed an error my mother would fall prey to in one of her early paintings. I neglected to hitch the hay wagon to the horses. The burden on the farmer, however, appears to be lessened by the fact that the distance of his ride is limited by a fenced-in corral.

Q is for Quizzes
As a competitive little teacher's pet, I loved the quizzes where we would show our understanding by drawing lines with crayons between objects and the letters they started with, or spell dictated words I had practiced with Mama. What I loved even more was the glory of an A at the top of the paper. Anything less brought on my jealousy of the A-getters, a moping session and often-parental disdain.

R is for Radishes
Only the kindergarten class had its own outside courtyard. Here we had our garden where we grew radishes in order to understand the concept of farming (with perhaps a little botany tossed in). What I learned was that eating whole radishes makes your mouth prickle and your eyes water.

S is for Scary Stories
On rainy indoor-recess days, my third-grade teacher Mrs. Newman found a way to get my exuberant self out of her jurisdiction. She sent me out to other classrooms to tell ghost stories. I was given a hall pass and traveled with great pride through the shiny corridors to other rooms, even to those hallowed upper-class ones upstairs where the library was. After a short introduction by the teacher, I would dramatically relate horror stories that sprang from the darker corners of my imagination and from the creepy scenes of the Disney movies that had traumatized me. My greatest accolade from the desk-bound kids was their looks of fear as I described in great detail the horrors of witches, ogres, ghosts and all that might go bump in their lives.

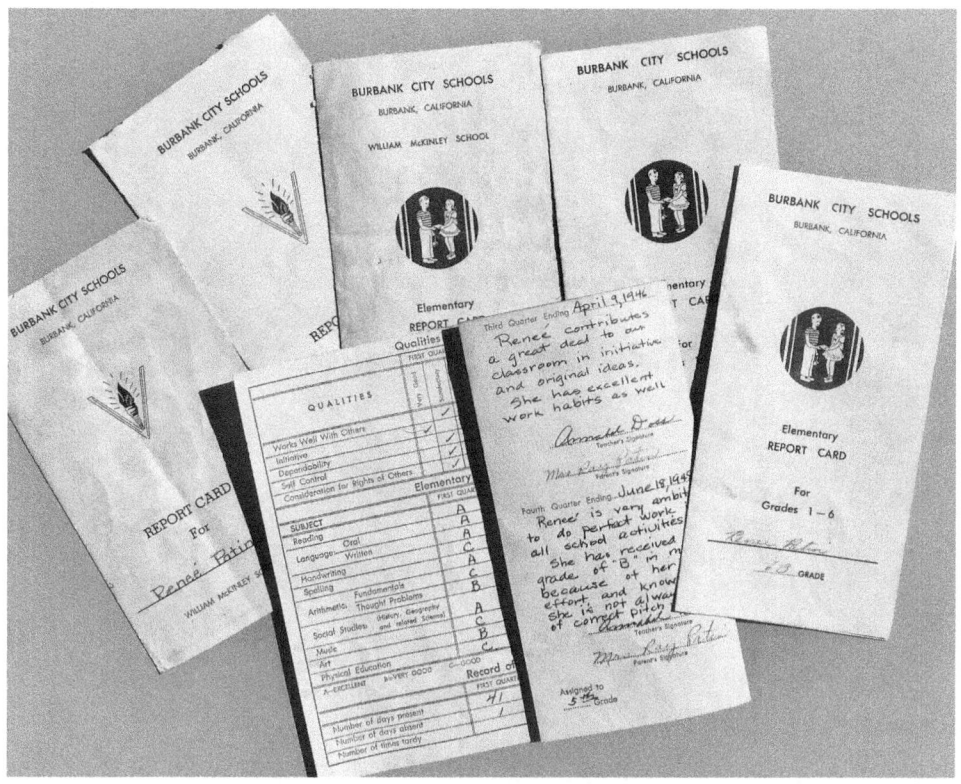

Third grade C's in Handwriting, Arithmetic, Music and Physical Education

T is for Tune Carrying

I hated music as much as ball games. My tone deafness and raspy contralto proved impediments to any possible singing career. Calling my renditions "pitchy" would have been a kindness. In third grade, a special music teacher with a forgotten name came into our class once a week. But even with her limited appearances she managed in one fell blow to put a severe dent in my musical appreciation. This was the painful time she demonstrated her displeasure at my unintentionally creative rendition of "My Country, 'Tis of Thee" by slamming my head into my desk mid-note. At least that's how I remember her action. I remained with my tear-streaked face hidden, the patriotic tuneful strains of my classmates' singing adding fuel to the fire of my humiliation.

Apparently in fourth grade I tried to make up for my vocal ineptitudes through academic aptitude. This led to a rather odd disclaimer on my report card. It looked as if Miss Doss was justifying a not-really-earned grade. Maybe I charmed her, my favorite teacher, through my writing prowess for which she lit the spark as we shall see in the "W is for Writer" chapter.

> *Renée is very ambitious to do perfect work in all school activities.*
> *She has received a grade of "B" in music because of her interest,*
> *effort and knowledge. She is not always sure of correct pitch.*

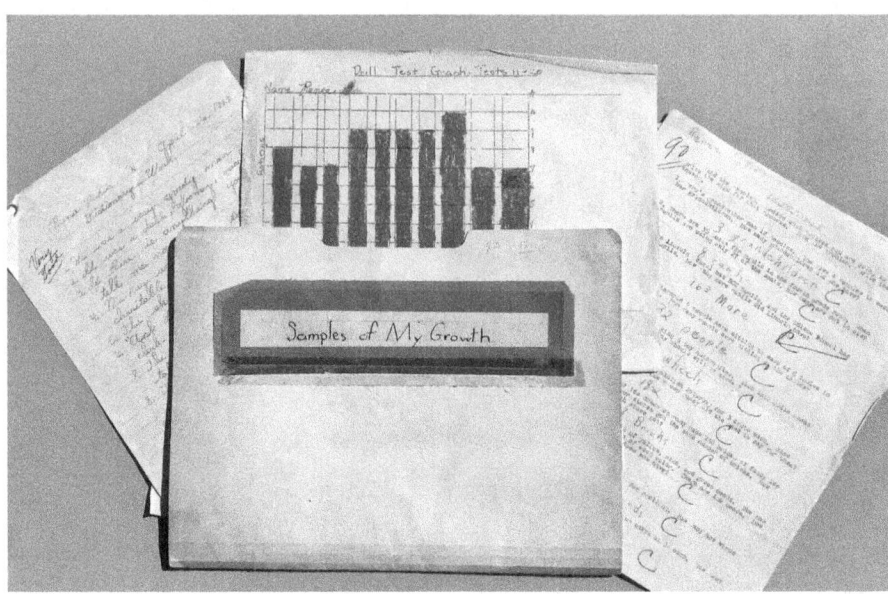

A not-so-model pupil's progress

U is for Unsatisfactory

As I continued on my early academic journey, my parents kept a close watch on their pupil's progress. They dutifully went to all the open houses where the fruits of my labor were left upon my desk for their examination. They saved everything including my report cards which weren't always stellar. I collected quite a few "U" marks for unsatisfactory behavior on report cards that were otherwise filled with academic accolades. Boredom? Excessive enthusiasm? My parents would show some pleasure at the A's, but home in on that bottom deportment section with its rare E for excellence, a sprinkling of satisfactory S's and the dreaded U's in self-control.

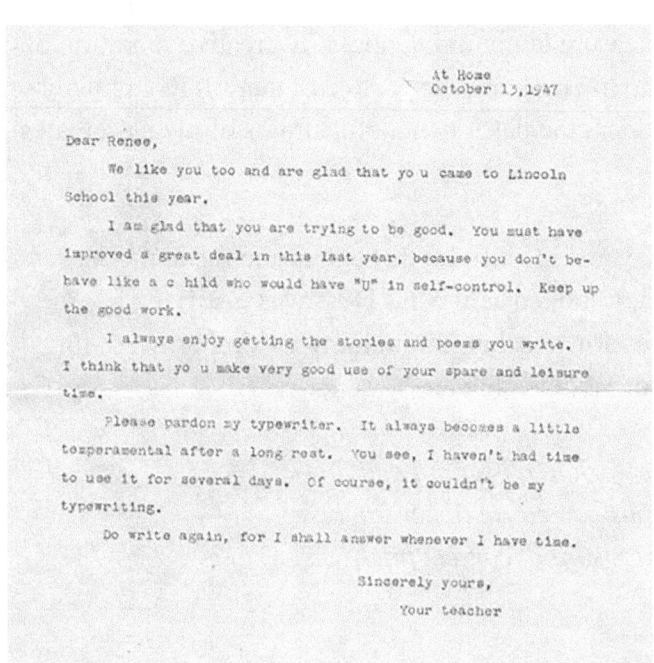

Dear Renee

Apparently, I was aware that any history of U's would proceed me when I transferred from McKinley to Lincoln. A letter I saved from my fifth-grade teacher Miss Lee—who became Mrs. Sanal midyear—assures me that she would not hold my U's against me.

I am glad you are trying to be good. You must have improved a great deal in this last year, because you don't behave like a child who would have "U" in self-control.

V is for Valentines

With the kitchen table covered in paste made from flour, white paper doilies, red ribbons and construction paper, Mama and I would create sticky valentine cards for every member of my class. Sometimes we just bought those tiny cartoony ones with flimsy envelopes.

Then on the morning of February 14, or the closest school day, we kids would deposit our greetings in a red and white festooned box. Later, while the teacher distributed the valentines, I sat apprehensively at my desk, fearful of receiving too few greetings from the popular kids or unwanted ones from the riff-raff.

Young love

 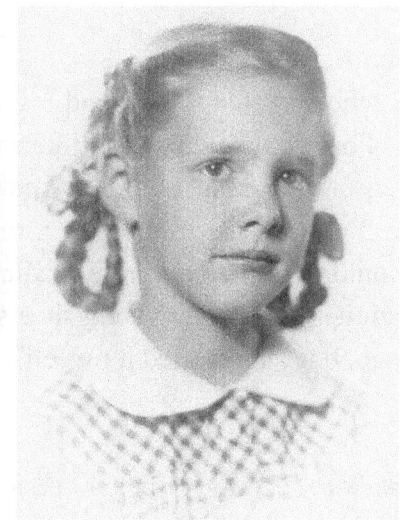

Natalie and I. Guess who influenced whom in her coiffure?

W is for Wood, Natalie

Natalie Wood went to Lincoln Elementary School when she was in the fifth grade and so did I. I didn't know her, but I had seen her in *Miracle on 34th Street* and *Scudda Hoo! Scudda Hay!* Her celebrity fascinated me, but I never got up the gumption to get her autograph. My 1949 annual portrait and my diary entry for January 5 showed how closely I would follow her every move:

Dear Diary,
Natalie Wood whares jeans to school and doesn't even roll them up. She's a movie star too. Mama won't let me whare jeans to school.

Envy dripped.

Getting shod forties style: the sign and the fluoroscope

X is for X-Ray Machine
Every summer before school started, Mama and I went downtown to San Fernando Road to Red Goose Shoes. There I would climb up onto the pulpit-like wooden machine called a fluoroscope to have my feet x-rayed, thereby ensuring a perfect fit for my new brown oxfords. It had viewers for me, for Mama and the shoe salesman. I was mesmerized by the x-ray image of my newly shod toe bones. I guess shoe experts thought kids couldn't give an accurate account of how the footwear felt. Certainly, they weren't concerned about radiation. Some clever young shoe shoppers inserted keys and coins under their feet to add interest to the image, but I never tried it myself.

Y is for Yodeling
When it was time to walk to school—or better yet, to play—Mary Jane and I would hail each other across the fence with Tarzan calls. They were loud enough to be a rude wake-up call for unsuspecting neighbors. I was able to parlay this talent into my own version of yodeling for my classmates. All I needed to do was shout "Ooowwlld laaaadyee" and then embellish it with some ear-splitting trills emanating from deep in my throat. This and my Woody Woodpecker imitation had them gathered around me in adulation—or so I imagined.

Pinocchio tempted away from school to the actor's life

Z is for Zealous

My first foray into the halls of learning soared beyond my very high expectations. I was a zealot about learning, about achieving, about finding my place in the spotlight. As the forties came to a close, and I entered more advanced halls of academia, I still tossed myself with zeal into my schoolwork and most especially into my extracurricular tomfoolery. Although I may have been tempted, like Pinocchio, to follow the actor's life of La La Land, it would be the academic's life for me.

9
War on the Home Front

On the Home Front

It was December 1941. I was three and Christmas was coming. Then the Japanese bombed Pearl Harbor on December 7, and America went to war. Life on the Home Front would change drastically. But, for me, the Day of Infamy was just one of the things that went on in the periphery of my headlong rush to experience all I could as fast as possible. After all, there were letters to Santa to "write."

During the four years that we were at war on two foreign fronts, I continued to dance to the comforting rhythms of routines choreographed by grown-ups. In the morning, I listened to the clink of the Carnation homogenized milk bottles deposited in the little indoor/outdoor metal compartment cut into our kitchen wall.

Curbside service

Daily bread

Later in the day Mama and I might go out to the curb when the Helms truck driver blew his tinny whistle after spotting the big blue H in our front window. I loved the aroma and display of baked goods when he pulled out the smoothly gliding wooden drawers. And I crossed my fingers that Mama would add something sticky sweet to her bread order.

I screamed for ice cream

My afternoons were spent in anticipation of the glorious chimes heralding the approach of the Good Humor truck coming up Parish Place, and I would run out to stop him. If my parents came with me, the always cheery driver, all in white, would salute Daddy and tip his hat to Mama. The height of my day was when he opened the thick icy door with a flourish, and I got to choose from the frozen treasures inside. My decision was always between a 50-50 Popsicle, a confection of orange popsicle stuffed with vanilla ice cream, or a chocolate-covered vanilla bar called an Eskimo Pie. For me, it was chocolate every time. I would first contemplate the beauty and anticipated taste of the bar. Then I would lick a little design in the dusting of frost on the shiny chocolate. Next was the impossible challenge of trying to savor it slowly and make it last forever without it melting down my arm.

Almost butter at your fingertips

Changes that were enforced during the war were just more routine for me—just the way things were supposed to be. Sometimes we didn't put butter on our bread because butter was oily, and fats and oils were needed to fight the war. I had no idea how. Instead of butter we had oleomargarine—"oleo." I got to knead the white gooey stuff with a packet of red dye to turn it yellow in order to make it look more like real butter. Mama would save her bacon drippings and scrap to donate to the cause.

I understood that Mama needed ration stamps to buy things like meat, sugar or cooking oil because we were at war. When we went to the store, I watched her reach into her purse and take out a rubber-banded wad of ration stamps along with her money. I knew that food and other things were being sent far away to the fighting troops, and it was rationed—or divided up—at home so everyone would get their fair share.

Ration books and those valuable stamps

Growing things and canning them made us feel patriotic

We bought fewer vegetables and fruits because almost all the families on the block had Victory Gardens and fruit trees. Mama, Daddy and I tended rows of more lettuce and tomatoes than we could ever eat, and mutant fuzz-covered squash grew beyond usefulness. In our steam-filled kitchen, I helped Mama can the fruits and vegetables in glass jars sealed with shiny metal lids in boiling water. The lids made good bird deflectors to hang in our peach and apricot trees. Much of the lettuce was eaten by my pet tortoise Toby until his unfortunate demise in an attack by a neighborhood dog.

I cried for Toby, but for not the chickens we ate after raising them in a coop in the backyard—even though I named a few and appreciated their occasional eggs. We also ate rabbit, though not my pet Thumper, named for Bambi's buddy, who would twirl cartoonishly whenever we let her out of her cage. I did wonder, though, at my parents' explanation of her being sent to live on a farm due to the ever-growing front teeth that Daddy was always filing.

 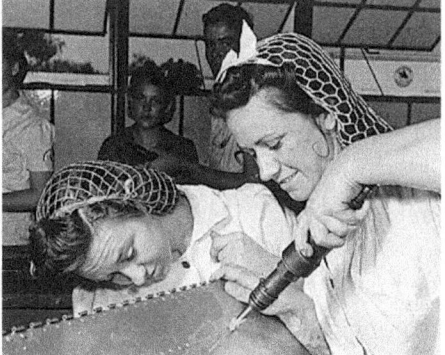

Rosies at work

To save on material and show a no-nonsense spirit, Mama's fashion was more severe. Inspired by Rosie the Riveter, she bound her hair in scarves and snoods like the women working in the factories, often called "Rosies," who replaced the men who had gone to war.

Women on the assembly line

Rationed stockings with seams and a liquid stocking solution

Nylons become a scarce luxury because their material was needed for parachutes. Mama covered her legs in a special leg makeup and used an eyebrow pencil to draw seams like those on real nylons that were rationed. She donated her rubber girdles because war tanks and trucks needed rubber. My pretend toilette applied in a boudoir I designed under a covered card table benefitted from the makeup that was left in her discarded bottles and stubs of brow pencils.

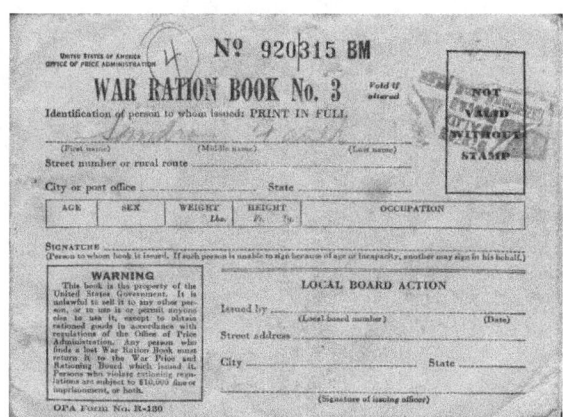 

Gas and rubber were in short supply

When Daddy drove the green Plymouth, he needed a ration book for gas. He put an "A" sticker on the windshield of the car to show it wasn't an essential vehicle. On the side that faced inside the car were tips on how to aid the war effort by saving the rubber on your tires.

Wartime international relations for kids

Changes on the home front affected kids, too. We couldn't get the plump pink pillows of Dubble Bubble Gum because the ingredient needed for face-sticking bubbles came from where we were fighting in the Pacific. Christmas tree bulbs weren't as shiny because the tinsel coating was needed for weapons. We made balls of metal foil from cigarette and gum wrappers. When the balls got big enough, we'd take them to a station where they were weighed, and we were paid so many pennies per pound, so the metal could be recycled into ammunition, tanks and bombs. I showed my victory spirit by buying and patriotically pasting war bond[1] stamps into little books. It was a way to save money and help fight the war.

I missed the Japanese friends I used to play with when I went to visit my godparents Kelly and Roy in my old Glendale neighborhood. I wasn't told that their sudden disappearance was because they were sent to a relocation camp. In our classrooms and halls, propaganda posters were posted teaching us how to identify and fear our enemies.

---

[1] War bonds were a way to make money for the war effort by having citizens invest in bonds of all values that earned a modest interest. Over the course of the war, 85 million Americans purchased bonds totaling approximately $185.7 billion.

Hitler　　　　　　　　Mussolini　　　　　　　　Tojo

The enemies

We could identify buck-toothed Hideki Tojo, leader of the Japanese (we shortened the nationality name to its most insulting one-syllable version). Adolf Hitler, the German führer, was the epitome of evil with his ridiculous mustache and madman scowl. And there was the other fascist, the Italian Benito Mussolini with his defiant chin and potbelly. We used the posters as stereotypical models for acting out war stories. Mary Jane's parents used them to decorate her bedroom—not exactly lullaby material.

We stretched the corners of our eyes and stuck out our teeth to mimic the enemy Japanese. With great trepidation and solemnity, we kept our right arm stiffly held out straight and our left finger over our upper lips to simulate Hitler's mustache. We then made sure no one was in earshot before exclaiming the dreaded "Heil Hitler!" This was often accompanied by a goose-stepping, stiff-legged march.

One of our allies was England, and Churchill was its leader

Newsreels were filled with footage from the front. Often, we saw Winston Churchill, the rotund, cigar-chomping Prime Minister of Great Britain, one of our allies. We thought we were clever when we turned our Nazi salutes into V for Victory signs made famous by my babyhood doppelgänger. We saw the English people whose homes were bombed and the children who were sent to the country for safety. But the royal family stayed in England, and even Princess Elizabeth, who became Queen, helped the war effort and learned to be a driver and mechanic.

Kilroy was everywhere

Just to be sneaky, we drew the dreaded Nazi swastika symbols on the playground, saying if anyone asked, that they were Navajo signs because we'd heard that similar design is on their rugs. Our graffiti repertoire also included the ubiquitous "Kilroy Was Here" sign that the GIs used to make their presence known wherever they had been.

The dreaded swastika

The war in the air

I could identify the P-38s that flew over the house as I played in the backyard. And I recreated what I saw on paper. They were made at nearby Lockheed Aircraft where Mary Jane's mother worked so that "Aunt" Dell had to take care of her.

Lockheed P-38s being made and under cover

At one time the whole plant was completely covered in camouflage, so any invading Japanese planes would think it was a rural neighborhood. The employees worked and parked their cars under camouflage netting, and the few folks who could afford to fly arrived and departed under cover.[2] Camouflaging to fool the enemy was a frequent site around Burbank. It was like the painted landscapes of skies and mountains that I saw stacked up at Warner Bros. or the movie sets at Columbia Ranch. I knew these, too, were made to fool folks.

---

[2] The original terminal at Lockheed is now called the Hollywood Burbank Airport although its legal name is the Bob Hope Airport. Once again Burbank takes second place in the shadow of show business.

Lockheed's parking lot and passengers under cover

What didn't look real were the actual pictures from the war. When we went to double feature movies at The Loma on San Fernando Road, we had to sit through the Pathé and Movietone newsreels filled with battle scenes. The black and white images seemed as remote and unbelievable as the movies they preceded.

President Roosevelt calmed a nation's fears

Sometimes I felt fear about the war coming to Burbank. Those guys from the posters were as scary as any monster Walt Disney could create.

Knowing we were disguised by camouflage by day and blackouts[3] at night helped calm my fear of an enemy invasion. I was also calmed by President Roosevelt's "Fireside Chats" which I listened to lying on the carpet next to the cloth-covered speaker of our floor model radio.

---

[3] In fear that the Germans or Japanese would use the lights to identify cities, all exterior lighting had to be extinguished, and blackout curtains placed over windows.

For safety's sake: gas mask and air raid warden's helmet

Hanging in our garage next to the pile of saved *Life* magazines was a gas mask and a helmet. It was scary to think about the kind of disasters that would necessitate Daddy's having to don the trappings of a Civil Defense Air Raid Warden. It helped that Daddy was helping to keep monsters away. He put on the helmet that showed he was a neighborhood warden in charge of making sure we all had our blackout curtains pulled tight so that the enemy couldn't see our lights inside. He had a gas mask in case the bad guys came equipped with poison gas. It made Daddy look very strange.

Daddy, at 35, was too old to be drafted which meant he wouldn't have to go into the service. He continued working at The Walt Disney Studios where they were making lots of films to help fight the war. One of the cartoons he animated was *Donald Gets Drafted* where our duck hero is involved in military life that is less fun than what he had seen on the recruitment posters.

The art of war

The Screen Cartoonist's Guild put out a pamphlet of cartoons called *Service Ribbin'* to boost morale for the soldiers fighting the war. The cover of the February 1944 issue shows a G.I. at his easel, his rifle stuck by its bayonet into the ground by his side and a Japanese bomber flying over his head. The enemy is shown criticizing his technique with machine gun fire. Above his signature the cartoonist who used only one name, Carmichael, thanks the Guild for the sketch book and Christmas card. I hope he made it home okay. Daddy's contributions featured comic scenes in India and on a tropical island.

Daddy also worked on a short for the United States Office of War Information called *Point Rationing of Foods,* an explanation of how the system of share and share alike worked. I preferred the adventures of Private Snafu who did everything wrong and whose name I was told meant "Situation Normal: All *Fouled* Up" in military slang. It was a wildly popular series of black and white cartoons teaching G.I.s what not to do—like in *Booby Traps* of 1944.

Signs of service

Our day-to-day life was filled with service men and women in uniforms. Sometimes we would drive into downtown Los Angeles to Union Station to greet the relatives from Louisiana who were going off to war. Their boots echoed on the tile floors as they were marched through the vast, echoing waiting room.

Soldier Dick with Gerry, Fran and Mama–and at Fort Ord

When we went to Culver City to Mama's girlhood house, my grandparents had a banner in the front window with three stars showing they had three sons in the military. A gold star would have meant they had lost someone during the war. My uncles Bob, Dick and Jack all came home unharmed, so all the stars were blue.

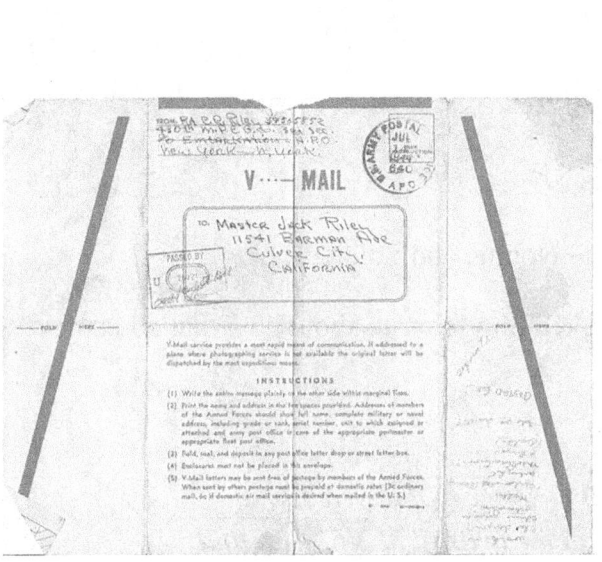
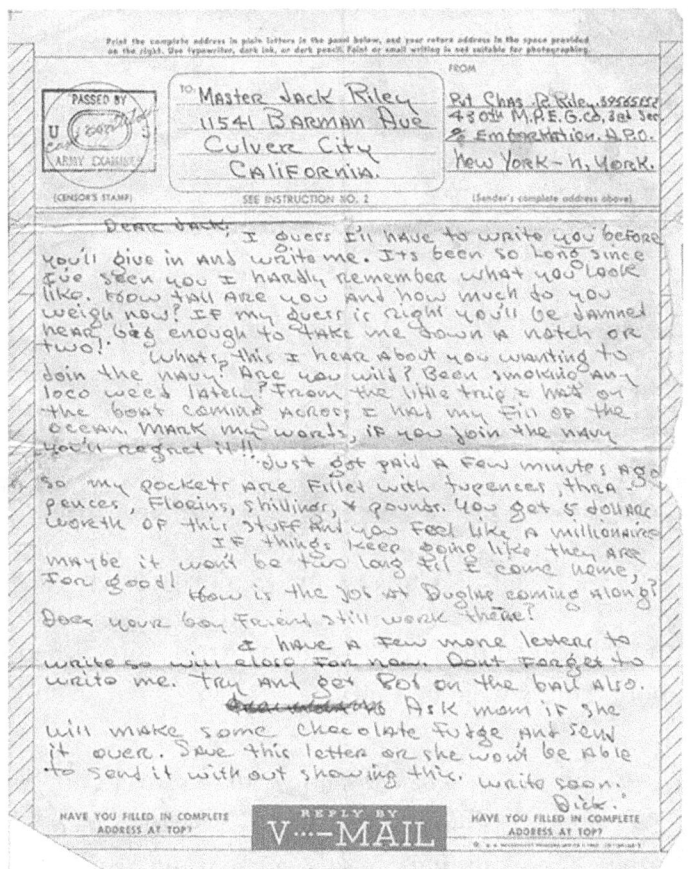

Dear Jack

Dick was in General Patton's Army in Europe. He wasn't in the fighting because he had a bad ankle from when he was a kid and jumped off the roof of the schoolhouse and it wasn't fixed because he was afraid to tell his father what he had done. He was an MP. I knew that it stood for military police and he was very proud of his job guarding the mean German prisoners. He brought back German military souvenirs and gave me a shiny iron cross with a swastika on it. He gave his brother Bob a German Luger pistol. He sent a V-Mail (V for Victory) letter to his younger brother "Master" Jack with some brotherly joshing and a little advice:

> *What's this I hear about you wanting to join the Navy? Are you wild? Been smoking any loco weed lately? From the little trip I made on the boat coming across, I had my fill of the ocean. Mark my words, if you join the Navy you'll regret it.*

Culver City: Sailor Bob with Pop and Nonnie and Soldier Jack

So Jack joined the Navy—and the Army, too! When I asked him to write about how that all came about, here's what he said:

> *You asked if I was in the Navy. Yes, for a short time. The war was over in September of 1945. I didn't turn 18 'til October of that year. So, the military in all their wisdom decided to draft me in April of '46. They told me to report to the induction center at Fort Macarthur at San Pedro. I entered a gymnasium type room with about 100 other poor souls. A Chief Petty Officer walked up and down the rows of naked sad sacks waiting to be evaluated. I guess I had a nice butt because he stopped and asked me if I would like to go into the Navy. I said yes and was the only one he chose. I went to San Diego and went through 13 weeks of boot camp. By this time, they got the news the war was over, so they told me to go home. Then when Korea heated up, they called me back into the Army.*

Bob was in the Navy too, and didn't leave the States. So, it looks as if the Riley boys did their part to keep America safe for democracy.

Uncle Linn on leave and the photo he sent from the front

When Aunt Gerry married Uncle (John Howard) Linn, he was in the Air Force. He went to the South Pacific and sent me a picture from Leyte of the poor Filipino kids being fed through a barbed wire fence. On the back he wrote, "Are you eating your food, Renée?"

Two months after V-J day, when he was about to come home, Uncle Linn wrote me a long letter as if I were much more mature. He described life in the Philippines where he bargained for a straw purse he sent me, explaining he traded it for three bars of soap which meant a lot to the Filipinos who wanted to keep clean under very bad conditions. He looked forward to telling me more in person about other "dirty hot places in the jungle" where he had been. I can only imagine what he must have experienced that he wasn't including in his letter and never did talk about with me.

Celebrating V-E Day

In May of 1945 the Germans surrendered, and Victory in Europe was declared. Mary Jane and I copied the grown-ups' jubilant celebration with a march around my backyard banging metal pots with wooden spoons. I commemorated the event with a crayon picture of a peaceful scene of a soldier celebrating on the front and of me doing the same on the home front.

Four months later, a week after I turned seven, we dropped the atomic bomb on Japan, and another dreaded enemy surrendered. We hailed V-J Day with little American flags waved from the top of the jungle gym Daddy erected with a folding wooden stepladder attached to our clothesline pole.

By September the war was over. Newsreels were filled with joyful, optimistic scenes of rebuilding instead of devastation. In Burbank, blackout curtains and camouflage came down. At Union Station, we greeted servicemen returning home to Louisiana rather than going to war.

The Rodger Young Village Quonset hut housing

On the way to Los Angeles we could see the funny tunnel-like Quonset huts that sprang up in Griffith Park. They housed the returning service men and their families who soon got to work creating a generation of Baby Boomers. In Burbank, Japanese-Americans returning from internment camps were housed in travel trailers.

For me the end of the war meant that the V for Victory hand signs I had been flaunting now stood for celebration rather than hope. As peace returned, many wartime routines came to an end to be replaced by new ones that would now frame my childhood. Thanks to Uncle Linn, I now had a real grass skirt from Hawaii in which I could perform a hula of thanksgiving.

Victory hula for the camera

10
Old Kids on the Block

Wonder

If I had influence with the good fairy who is supposed to preside over the christening of all children, I should ask that her gift to each child in the world be a sense of wonder so indestructible that it would last throughout life…

Rachel Carson, *A Sense of Wonder*

My childhood wonder was not dimmed by the hardships of the Home Front. How lucky I was to have been tapped by a magical wonder wand. The good fairy, or whoever determines these things, gave me parents filled with wonder—a mother who loved to share make-believe worlds and a father who created fantasy worlds with a pencil. They saw to it that my years growing up were filled with all manner of delights, both real and imagined.

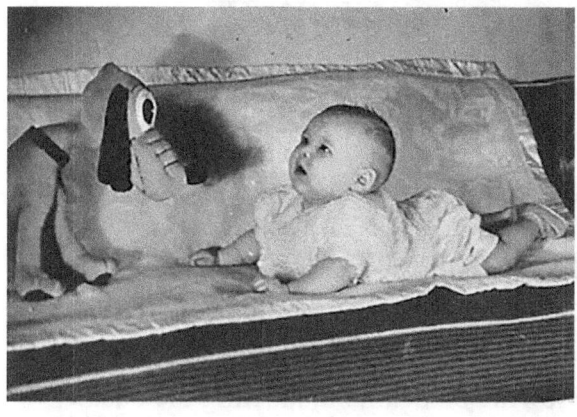

Potsy and her play pal Pluto and his shadow

Some say an only child is a lonely child. Not this kid. From my very beginnings, I was constantly entertaining and delighting myself with my imagination as my best friend. My babyhood buddy was Pluto, a nod to where Daddy went to work. My plush pal was about my size, cushy and yellow with a gigantic black nose and ears to match. Unlike humans, he never made noises that I was expected to understand but instead listened to my babbles without misinterpretation. Plus, he allowed my affectionate mauling, never made fun of my extra poundage nor protested my tendency to steamroll over him.

Mama and Heidi

Another canine companion with whom I was compatible was my first dog Heidi, a dachshund, who, though not stuffed like Pluto, was presented to me like a surprise toy in a bag of groceries. I named her from my book *Heidi,* the story of the very good little girl who alone with a grumpy grandfather lived in the idyllic Swiss Alps where I would one day live too. Heidi was a good sport about being put to bed in a doll's bed under a doll's quilt and tolerated my dressing her in doll clothes. She even garnered a blue ribbon at a doggie dress-up contest for her ballerina ensemble. She enthusiastically joined me in all sorts of adventures including watching in fascination when we borrowed ducks from Nan and Bob's across the street. The ducks' job was to eat the snails out of our ivy beds. Heidi's barks herded the flock as they waddled and quacked across Parkside Avenue, then immediately set to work to click, clack and crunch their escargot delicacies.

My friend Heidi

Heidi was a friend and confidant and a fascinating object of my curiosity. She amused me for hours, and I pictured her many activities in an early work of art, paying homage to her antics if not the spelling of her name. I showed her sitting up, a trick she could maintain for admirably long stretches. I also captured the pose in a photograph taken with my Brownie box camera, labeling the back: "Hidee Patin." Always patient, Heidi allowed the litters from our inappropriately named cat Beautiful to nurse her during her frequent sessions of false pregnancy. The kittens even got their fill of doggie milk while she sat up.

Come play with me

I also enjoyed intimate friendships with non-canine friends who were always on call from where they lived in my imagination. I chatted with them, had tea with them and enjoyed their company in the steady stream of roles I assigned to them.

The most special of these imaginary pals was Yehudi (pronounced Yeh-hood-y). I'm not sure about the origin of his name. Probably I told Mama about the elf-like fellow who accompanied me in my meanderings, whereupon she named him. She may have thought the name sounded playful, sort of like "You hoo!"—the greeting she and the neighbor ladies used to announce their visits. Anyway, I remember Yehudi by my side as I went off on backyard adventures. He sat next to me on the wooden plank of the swing Daddy rigged up on our back patio. I would vigorously pump and pump my short legs to go as high as I could while sharing my exhilaration with my funny-named friend. He, Pluto, Heidi and my dolls Nancy, Mary Rose and Jo March were perfect players in my pretend scenarios.

Mary Jane growing into a proper young lady

But there came a time when I had to plunge into the much more complicated world of real people playmates. My three closest buddies on our block were Mary Jane, Lorna and Joanie. Since my memories of childhood relationships tend to be seen prejudicially, I called upon them to get their impressions of our wonder years. Our tales reveal childhood fantasy, jealousy, lying, daring, guilt, aggression and other dramas from playtime worthy of the other side of the Sign.

The Bennetts of Burbank

MARY JANE

Next to the Parkside Avenue wing of our house, beyond the snail-ridden ivy, was our next-door neighbor's asphalt driveway of which I was very jealous. In a neighborhood deprived of sidewalks, it was long and roller skateable, while ours, though a smoother cement, was uselessly short and slanted, hardly worth the trouble of finding my skate key and clamping the metal skates on properly. The desirable driveway was owned by the Bennetts—Emma who was a secretary, and Sid who worked for the Los Angeles County Department of Weights and Measures checking the accuracy of scales.

Sid and Emma's daughter Mary Jane was ten months older than me, and, when we met at the age of three, became my lifelong best friend. Her driveway wasn't the only thing I envied about Mary Jane. She had bouncy blond curls, a coiffure created through the application of white rags ripped from sheets and strategically placed all over her head in a rather startling display that she wore most of the time along with her utilitarian overalls. Our memories reflect the way we were and are:

MJ: Remember the Christmas when our mothers bought us both the same doll?

R: Yeah, we were about four or five. I found mine on an expedition through Mama's closets. She had hidden it because it was supposed to be from Santa—further convincing me you were right, that he didn't exist. I was punished, and it was touch and go whether I would get the doll.

MJ: You got it though. Yours was dressed in blue, and mine was pink. I named mine first and chose Rosemary, matching the rosebuds on her outfit.

R: And I was left with the name Mary Rose who was dressed in an inferior blue. She soon lost her lovely curls due to my curiosity as to what was below the wig of curls that I had ruined with my mothering ministrations. The poor doll had a scalp marked with glue and nails marring what was supposed to have been sculpted hair. I'm afraid my affection for Mary Rose was tainted by guilt over my Christmas crime and her inferiority.

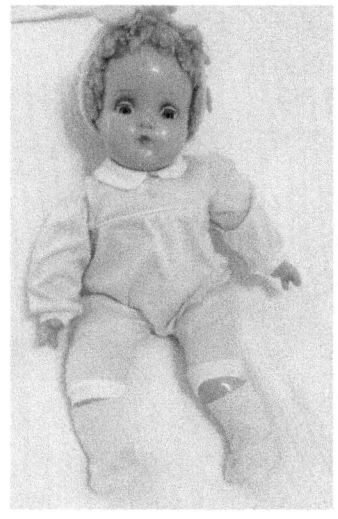 

Rosemary now   Mary Rose then

MJ: And I still have Rosemary in my bedroom. Still in pink, still with her blond curls.

R: Mary Rose is no longer around to remind me of when I was naughty, not nice, precariously close to Christmas. All I have is a photo of my dressed-to-impress godmother Kelly holding me in her gloved hand. I am impishly hiding behind my temporarily bewigged baby doll.

MJ: Remember how we'd go down to the horse stables on Riverside to the pony rides? I always got on the slowest horse and you'd ask for the fastest. Then you'd cry because your ride was over, and I was still going happily around the circle all calm and ladylike.

R: You were always so prim and proper, more adult. Your room was girly, not covered with toys like mine. Your birthday parties were so much more grown-up. We sat at a big carved wood dining table on upholstered chairs and had nut cups at our places and ate fried chicken, peas and mashed potatoes. And we had to use our manners.

MJ: You had big parties in your backyard or the park and your parents made us oilcloth bibs with our names on them for when we ate your fancy cake and they made funny centerpieces and lots of games. I liked it better when it was just you and I playing around our houses.

The Nancy Drew Bridge at the Disney fence

When we got older, we wandered all over the neighborhood finding venues where we could act out our fantasies. Down by the back lot of The Walt Disney Studios, near the water tower where they would put the set used in *Zorro,* we had what we called our Nancy Drew Bridge. It was a walkway across a culvert, but to us it was the scene of mysterious goings-on inspired by the Carolyn Keene novels and our fantasies of what was underfoot on the Disney side of the fence. A bridge is still there, graced by a not very mysterious stop sign.

Sometimes when Mary Jane and I played, it was less like pretending, and more like work. Take, for example, our Bentin Press. It was our two last names combined, Bennett and Patin. We wrote out all the neighborhood gossip on Daddy's punched animation paper and tied it together with red ribbon and sold it to the neighbors. I think there was only one issue—not enough gossip, I guess.

MJ: It was probably too much work, though I made you do the writing. Seems like we always had a new enterprise, like the time we set up shop on your red brick walkway to sell stuff we had scrounged from the neighbors' trash cans. And you and I got into a fight and tipped our entire change-making box into that ivy of yours. Your mother was furious, and we got a "damn it to hell!" because we had "borrowed" her wrapping paper and geranium plants to supplement our meager junk collection and she had to go around to the neighbors to get them back.

R: We did have a lot of fights. It seems like every day I ended up crying and we went home. The worst was when you made me hang by my knees from Nan and Bob's back porch rail and poured Coke in my mouth to watch it come out my nose. We had our worst fight ever after that. I hit you with a whisky bottle and you hit me with a toy iron. We must not have had done much harm, though, because I didn't even need any Mercurochrome or a bandage of honor.

MJ: And we are still friends.

R: And we still argue.

MJ: But without weapons.

JOANIE

In matching hairstyles, Joanie (left) and Renée strike a pose

Across the street on the Parish Place side was Joanie's house where she lived with her parents and dog Lucky. Her parents called themselves Pat and Pete because they didn't like their real names. Pete was a businessman. To me this was a much more acceptable occupation for a father than the cartoon business.

Patin Productions' perfect family commercial: Pete, Joanie, dog Lucky and Pat

Joanie's family was the ideal family, the kind I saw in the movies. In fact, when my father started his own studio making animated commercials and needed a live action shot for the typical American family, he chose Joanie's family. He filmed it at the house next door to Joanie's though because he liked its "moderne" glass brick door decoration. As Pete's business grew, so did their house. They even built a fish pond and the only swimming pool on the block, much more jealous-making than Mary Jane's driveway.

Joanie's bedroom was filled with fun activities, and she always had great play ideas. She did all those crafty projects in the kids' magazines like making dioramas in shoe boxes and people from popsicle sticks, and she had stacks of kits for crafting and boxes of games. There were even games laid out on her linoleum bedroom floor. Once when we were playing one of those games, I must have expressed my need to win inappropriately or maybe even swore, because Pat called in from another room to caution me about my language.

The pollywog pond with daredevil young pipe-walker and atmospheric horse

Joanie was one of kids on the block who frequented the pollywog pond in the wonderful wilderness between Riverside Drive and the river (or river bed, depending on the time of year). The field is now occupied by the Roy E. Disney Animation Building. But then it was where we acted out jungle or western movies and paddled about in the suspiciously sourced water that came in from a huge galvanized pipe, probably from The Walt Disney Studios across the street. We collected pollywogs (tadpoles) in jars to raise and watched them grow legs and turn into tiny jumping frogs—those that made it.

Here are some of the things Joanie listed when I asked about her most vivid memories from life on the block:

- Heidi galloping through my ivy and disappearing in the green leaves between leaps
- The fireworks Russ next door brought back from where he worked on the bomb at Los Alamos
- Barbecues on the street and listening to a teen neighbor talk with her boyfriend on the party line[1]
- The sound of Mary Jane's and my yodeling like Tarzan at the top of our lungs as we called each other over our shared fence
- Trading Nancy Drew books and then acting out sleuthing scenarios with Lucky Strike cigarette wrappers as clues
- Practicing those detective skills trying to find the hidden money around the house on Parkside where Mabel Monahan[2] was murdered

---

[1] More than one house was "plugged" in on a line at the telephone company, and you could listen in while covering your breathing or giggling with your hand over the receiver.

[2] Elderly Mabel Monahan was slain and robbed in a house down the street and caused us kids all manner of speculation before the bad guy was arrested.

Joanie had the disadvantage of being two years younger than me. She suffered for her junior status, and Mary Jane and I took advantage of it shamelessly. We took it upon ourselves to become her resident grammarians. Whenever she said, "I aren't," we would give her an "Indian burn," the ethnic derivation of which I am unsure. We would grab her wrist with two hands and twist the skin in opposite directions until she cried. Amazingly, either because of or despite our painful English lessons, Joanie grew up to be a successful writer. Here is what she wrote about a time when playtime turned terribly wrong.

> *Our neighborhood was the perfect place to grow up. In nearly every other house there were kids within a year or two of other kids in the neighborhood. At my place we played in my own little house in the backyard. It had been a wooden shipping crate for a Lockheed plane engine and was a woodshed when we moved into the house. Daddy cleaned it out, then he cut out windows, put on a door and a ladder so we could climb on top.*
>
> *Renée and I made up clubs and invited each other to join. The one that is clearest in my memory is The Black Widow Spider Club. I don't remember what we did in our club, but I remember the initiation that Renée invented.*
>
> *I had to run up the grass cuttings pile that her father had in the backyard. It was a tall stack of dead grass. I managed it OK, but then I had to roll on a barrel. I tried but didn't do well. When Renée went in for lunch, I practiced but fell off, and my arm twisted behind me. I walked home, across the street, but didn't start crying until I was in the middle of the street and my mother heard me. I spent Thanksgiving at St. Joseph Hospital with two metal pins in my arm.*

That night my parents took me to St. Joseph Hospital across from the Studio. As we walked into Joanie's darkened room, I first saw a girl in a white metal bed whose head was all in bandages because her jaw was broken by a horse when she'd walked behind it at the stables on Riverside Drive. Joanie was lying in the other bed with a big plaster cast looking very sad, and I knew it was all my fault. Many years later I learned that our neighbor who worked in the movies made an autograph book for Joanie when she was injured due to my orders. It was signed by movie stars like Ronald Reagan and the director Cecil B. DeMille. But despite the fact she received this boon from the other side of the Sign, it didn't assuage my guilt over my ignominious initiation ritual, or the Indian burns.

LORNA

Lorna (right) at her house ignores Renée's attitude

If you walk down the block past Joanie's, you'll come to Lorna's big brick house and dramatic curved driveway. Lorna's house had all sorts of fascinating accoutrements ours didn't. On the back porch, there was the Arrowhead drinking water in a huge bottle a deliveryman placed upside down on a metal rack. And in their bathroom were beautiful chrome accessories like the little compartment with a door that twirled open and closed to hide the toilet paper.

The Netten household also had the most enviable of additions, a teenage sister, Gerry, who actually went to high school with Debbie Reynolds. Gerry was five and a half years older than Lorna, and didn't deign to play with us little kids, but I admired her and the contents of her teenage boudoir whenever Lorna and I could sneak into it.

Lorna's father Lorne was from Canada and was a very kind, happy man and the bearer of Joanie's get-well autograph book. He was a gaffer, the head electrician, at Paramount Studio in Hollywood, a real studio, not a cartoon studio like where my father worked. Lorna's mother Mae was exactly the way mothers were supposed to be, cushy and cheery. Each morning Mae would march around the table to music on *Don McNeill's Breakfast Club*[3] broadcast on the radio. She always made me feel welcome as if my presence were a great amusement and joy to her. She made us wonderful lunches and introduced me to the intricacies of seed wrangling in watermelons and pomegranates on their lovely terrace overlooking what I thought was a movie star-worthy backyard.

Lorna was an ideal playmate who shared and played well with others. In addition to the driveway and big sister, Lorna had workbooks to study phonics, a pursuit I found quite mysterious. We learned words by sight. And she got to have her tonsils out and eat ice cream afterwards. We spent many hours planning and acting out imaginary scenarios at her house or mine. We never fought (with or without weapons) and I caused her no broken bones.

---

[3] A long-running national radio show that would play the theme music and invite listeners to march around the table.

Let's pretend: lovely Lorna tolerates Renée's pretty pose

Lorna still has the joie de vivre and amused/bemused sparkle that she inherited from Mae. During our many reminiscing sessions over the years her blue eyes have retained a child-like twinkle and there seems to be a giggle about to bubble up and burst out at any moment. Here are some memories from Lorna followed by how I remembered our playtimes.

L: At our house we played pretend games, like using marbles to create an orphanage. I remember using our fingers on the carpet to create the buildings.

R: She had a beautiful smooth beige carpet and we would run our fingers against the pile and "draw" on it to make a blueprint of the orphanage. Then we designated the big marble shooter as Mother Superior who would parade her orphan marbles into their dormitory, dining hall or other areas we had created for them.

L: We both had big wooden dollhouses. You would bring yours in your wagon down the block, so we could have them side by side. We would call them apartment buildings and decide who got which rooms for their apartments.

R: Lorna's father made hers and hand painted tiny tiles on the roof, and it had a stairway and intricate woodwork. My grandfather made mine, and it wasn't as fancy. We would empty all the furniture out of our houses and take turns picking the pieces we wanted. That and the interior decorating took so long that we didn't have time to play with our apartment dwellers before I had to wheel my house home.

L: You came to my fourth birthday party. I think it was just you and me. We had cake outside on our porch. At Christmas, we went to those wonderful parties at Peg and Len's, and one Halloween our dads dressed up like ladies. They had blond wigs, dresses, high heels, and they wandered around the neighborhood.

R: I remember the playhouse Lorna's father built in their backyard. Unlike Joanie's converted crate—that I loved despite its rusticity—Lorna's house was very fancy with electric lights and a Dutch door. It seems we had to do a lot of preparation there too—like deciding who we would be and how we would dress up.

L: Daddy brought home a big thick book like a telephone book filled with pictures and information on all the actors and actresses at Paramount. We would study it and have long discussions deciding which movie star we would be and what roles we would play.

Jo and I in outfits by Maxine of Burbank

R: Lorna and I each had Madame Alexander dolls from the book *Little Women.* She had Beth, the lovely, sweet one who dies. Mine, appropriately, was the awkward, tomboyish future writer, Jo. I still have her. I took better care of her than I did Mary Rose. She still has her hair in a net and her original long dress. And in a doll's trunk I have the clothes Mama made for her, many of which matched mine that were also created in the house of Maxine. From tutu to negligée and wedding dress, from outdoor attire, to school clothes, Jo was ready for any pretend play Lorna and I could fantasize. I loved the clothes so much that I drew them the way I had Heidi. Apparently, I was pleased by my fashion plates, but found my representation of Jo lacking.

L: I think you explained "the birds and the bees" to me. And you also cut my bangs once when we were playing.

My fashion plate renderings

R: I hope Lorna didn't take my procreation explanation as fact because I'm sure I made it up or it was something Mary Jane told me. Or perhaps Lorna was remembering Daddy's audio-visual instruction that we will learn about later. I forgot the haircut. I did it to myself a few times too. I know I did it to my dolls and to Heidi's tail fur to put under the doormat for good luck. Something I'd read. Growing up with the kids on the block was indeed filled with wonder. It is from them that I learned many of my first lessons. Some of the lessons were as painful as jealousy

Playmates in plaid—Renée, Joanie and Lorna
at the pollywog pond

or bodily harm and others were as magical as a shared enterprise or an imaginary adventure. Everything was new. Everything was a discovery. Each day seemed to last forever, and it seemed forever before we would be grown-ups.

Now, at a time when days and years flash by at a frightening speed, I am thankful to the good fairy who presides over children. Her gift has helped me unpack some of the baggage I've gathered from my grown-up journeys and return to the wonder of playing on Parish Place.

11
Grown-Ups, Relatively Speaking

Potsy's *Little Prince* book

Once when I was eight years old, my godparents, Kelly and Roy, gave me a magnificent book called *The Little Prince*. It's filled with lessons about grown-ups and their fascinating foibles as seen through the eyes of a child. Here's how the book begins:

Once when I was six years old I saw a magnificent picture in a book, called True Stories from Nature, *about the primeval forest. It was a picture of a boa constrictor in the act of swallowing an animal.*

In the book it said: "Boa constrictors swallow their prey whole, without chewing it. After that they are not able to move, and they sleep through the six months that they need for digestion."

I pondered deeply, then, over the adventures of the jungle. And after some work with a colored pencil I succeeded in making my first drawing.

Here's a picture of the narrator's first drawing. What do you think it looks like?

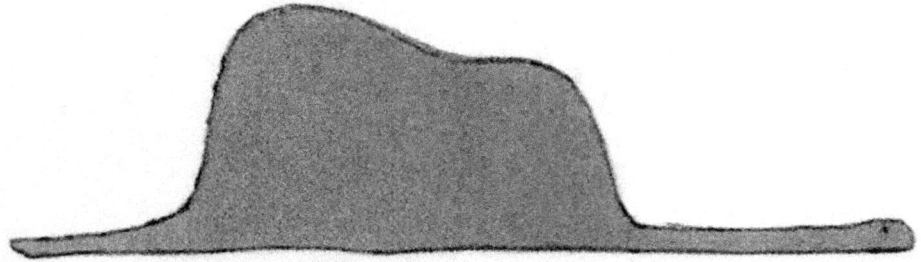

What the narrator drew for the grown-ups

Imagine the frustration of our budding artist when he showed this drawing to the grown-ups asking whether it frightened them, and they answered,

Frighten? Why should anybody be frightened by a hat!

But the boy's drawing was not a hat. It was a boa constrictor devouring an elephant. Because the grown-ups could no longer see the wondrous world a child sees, the narrator of our story drew another picture. This time he showed the elephant standing patiently inside the boa constrictor.

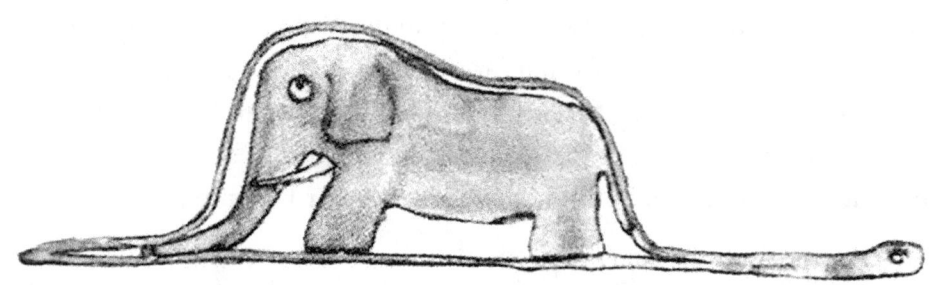

The narrator's second drawing

The grown-ups' response, this time, was to advise me to lay aside my drawings of boa constrictors, whether from the inside or the outside, and devote myself instead to geography, history, arithmetic and grammar. That is why, at the age of six, I gave up what might have been a magnificent career as a painter. I had been disheartened by the failure of my Drawing Number One and my Drawing Number Two. Grown-ups never understand anything by themselves, and it is tiresome for children to be always and forever explaining things to them.

Saint-Exupéry's portrait, plane, prince picture and boa constrictor on old fifty-franc note

In the book our narrator grew up be a pilot just like the book's author, Antoine de Saint-Exupéry, who was a French national hero, author and pilot. He disappeared over the Mediterranean on a WWII mission. When the book's fictional aviator crashed his plane in the desert, he met the Little Prince who, seeing things clearly as only a child can, immediately understood the drawing of a boa constrictor devouring an elephant. Having traveled from a faraway asteroid, the Little Prince proceeded to tell the narrator of his confusing encounters with grown-ups from king to businessman, geographer to drunkard and other baffling characters. Sometimes we grown-ups seem just a little silly as seen through the eyes of a child. At the end of the book, our narrator lamented,

I have lived a great deal among grown-ups. I have seen them intimately, close at hand. And that hasn't much improved my opinion of them.

Nana and Potsy

DADDY'S SIDE

One of the most watchable grown-ups in my life was my grandmother, Therese Patin, or Nana to me. She starred in the bottle-warming scene in Chapter 1 and later appeared in Chapter 3 holding her baby son Ray. Even though she was terribly old—well into her fifties when I was a kid—Nana still had a lot of the child in her. She passed on to me her tendency toward the dramatic and her passion to devour all of life to the fullest. I loved her greatly and followed in her steps shamelessly.

Gregarious and very proud of her appearance, Nana is shown in Daddy's movies primping, posing and pontificating in her not quite Southern/not quite French accent. She was alive with intriguing sounds like the crackle of electricity as she combed her thick gray hair and the scritchy-scratch as her nylon-stockinged feet settled into her pumps. She could never wear flat shoes due, my mother explained, to foreshortened Achilles tendons that rendered her unable to walk flat-footed after years of exclusive high heel walking. Although she always walked upright and posed proudly, Nana's bones creaked when she laboriously stooped over to pick up a piece of lint or a crumb from the carpet (an unsolicited task to which my mother took great exception).

Pretty in pumps

Mrs. Patin all primped up

Nana was a widow before I was born and visited us often on Parish Place. She slept in the hide-a-bed in our dark little den that smelled of nubby grass paper wallcovering and the film and art materials Daddy worked with there. I loved to climb into bed with her and listen to stories of her Durand ancestors' antebellum[1] life near what Nana called "Petit Paris." From time to time she returned to Louisiana to visit her large family scattered around the Bayou Country. She had them convinced that her son Ray taught Walt Disney everything he knew. When she returned, she brought my cousins and me sugar cane stalks that felt like stringy bamboo when we sucked the super sweet sticky liquid. I relished the little white, wrinkly bag of licorice drops she called by a very un-PC name. And I learned how the candy store man added some roasted pecans as a *lagniappe*, a local term for something added as a bonus or extra treat.

When Louisiana relatives came to visit us in Burbank, Nana became their tour guide. I would sit beside her in the front seat of Daddy's car as she narrated a trip highlighting the homes of celebrities that she didn't seem to think were any grander than her son's. The tour always ended in Forest Lawn Cemetery in Glendale where we gaped appreciatively at genuine copies of Leonardo's *Last Supper* and Michelangelo's big *David*—complete with big fig leaf. Nana pointed out the exact replicas of European churches like the celebrity wedding chapel called Wee Kirk O' the Heather and the Little Church of the Flowers where many years later Walt Disney's funeral was held. His ashes are interred not far away near the Freedom Mausoleum.

---

[1] Antebellum–before the war, usually meaning before the Civil War when life was genteel and there were slaves to make it so. It was Scarlett O'Hara's time before they lost Tara.

Vinnie and Wally pose with their first-born, Dick

Sometimes Mama, Daddy and I drove thirty-five seemingly endless miles from Burbank all the way to Long Beach. This is where Nana lived with her daughter, my equally vivacious Aunt Vinnie, and her husband Wally Shannon, a mild-mannered accountant, along with their four boys. It's funny how both Vinnie and Ray, with their French/Spanish heritage decided to mix the game up a little by marrying an Irish lad and lassie.

The Shannon boys left to right: Dick, Jeff, Pat and feisty Brian, the youngest

When we finally arrived at the Shannons' little clapboard house set among the oil wells on Signal Hill, I would hide in the bottom of the back seat of our Plymouth so that my cousins would be devastated thinking my parents had come without me, and then act delightfully surprised and relieved when I popped up. I did it every time and doubt the trick had the dramatic impact for which I hoped. Nana, however, would mock ecstatic surprise before serving jambalaya or a Thanksgiving dinner to all ten of us at the grown-ups' and kids' tables that filled the tiny front room. It was just as well that Jeff, Brian and I, the three younger scamps, were isolated as we played with our food and each other with great abandon.

Tough trio: Brian with handcuffs and Jeff with ball flank their cousin

While the grown-ups drank bourbon and argued (except for Wally and Mama), I played with Jeff who was three months older than me, and Brian a year younger. Dick and Pat, the older sons, acted as if we didn't even exist. We played cowboys where Jeff was Roy Rogers and I was Dale Evans and Brian could be whoever was left over. When we played house or hospital Brian had to be the son or the patient, but we always let him call himself "Bob Green." When it was time for us to settle down, Nana might propose a game of cards. On the rare occasion when she wasn't beating us, she became surly, and I learned my first French as she peppered her disgust with phrases that included the word *merde*.

Nana always insisted on a French pronunciation for French words like brassiere (brah-zee-yair). Daddy liked to point out her little linguistic slips like calling our Venetian blinds "vanishing blinds." She wasn't aware that the French she spoke with her Louisiana family was quite different from that in France as her French hadn't changed much since the French settled her home state. But I loved learning French from her. One of the many legacies she passed on to me was an ear for and a lack of fear of foreign languages.

Nana loved laughing at our antics. She cackled when she laughed, hiding her dentures, as cousin Pat described, with a coquettish Geisha girlish gesture. Her hilarity was highest when she was winning at cards. It was much later that I learned about her alleged arrest for playing cards in an apartment house that didn't allow such suspicious activity. It is also said that in her later years she would take the bus on a daily fifteen-mile journey from Long Beach to Gardena, walking in her high heels from the bus stop to the casino for some legal card playing to supplement her income from her Social Security check and my father.

Each summer Nana took Jeff, Brian and me to The Pike, the fun zone at the pier in Long Beach. Her beaming amusement at our maneuvering of the bumper cars greatly enhanced our enjoyment. Perhaps her high heels or the dignity of her station as the mother of the world's greatest animator kept her from joining us on the rides, but she sure looked as if that's exactly what she wanted to do.

Nana would have been up for any role in my cast of characters. She tended to overact and was always highly entertaining. But she didn't dramatize her final illness. She hadn't even let us know what was going on with her until one Sunday when I was on a break from my senior year at UCSB. We stopped in Long Beach to visit her on the way home from Lido Isle and saw that she was very sick. Her breast cancer had spread. Daddy decided she would come live with us.

Maman

When she got weaker, we took her to St. Joseph's, the big Catholic hospital in what was the strikers' eucalyptus grove across from the Disney Studio entrance. I went to see my grandmother who had been such a star performer in my life. I read "The Lord's Prayer" to her from her French prayer book as she lay dying. And I kissed her goodbye.

My father's mother taught me many lessons. She's the reason French is my second language. She's the reason I toss myself into everything with as much abandon and flair as I can muster. I don't sneak off to gamble in Gardena, but I do love games, resisting the tendency to swear in French when I am losing. And I may have cackle-laughed a little when Jeff and Brian and I reminisced over her joy in our far from grown-up shenanigans.

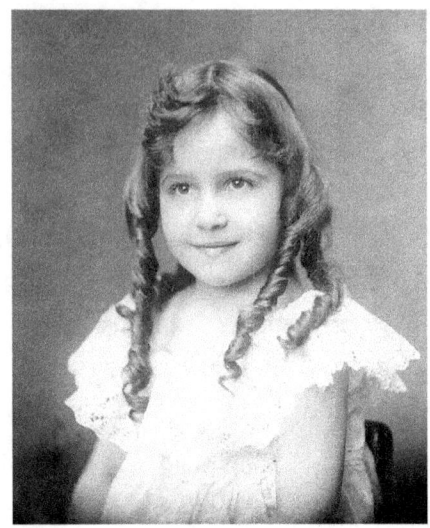 

Nonnie as a girl and as I knew her

MAMA'S SIDE

Mama's mother was named Ida Bitts Riley, but to me and most of my cousins, she was Nonnie. She was a jolly, jiggly, dimply model of what a grandmother should be. She possessed a more rounded version of my mother's beauty and shared with her a lack of pretension and a knack for hiding her true emotions.

The dreaded Los Angeles Orphan Asylum

Nonnie may have acquired her stoicism as a young child of divorced parents (a late nineteenth century rarity) who, when her mother couldn't support her, put her temporarily into the dreaded Los Angeles Orphanage. Whenever we took the 20-mile drive from Burbank to Culver City to visit Nonnie we always passed that huge menacing asylum on top of Boyle Heights, the Los Angeles neighborhood where my mother was born. My parents' warnings that I might end up there if I didn't behave must have left an impression as it became the inspiration for Lorna's and my orphan marble reenactment.

Our social studies lessons about the farm did not teach me to spell it

I loved visiting the farm-like homestead where my mother grew up. It was like a living social studies lesson. I followed Nonnie around as she performed the many chores that kept her constantly in motion. A great treat was to "help" her feed the cows and chickens. On Mondays "we" did the laundry in the shed outside the back of the house. I watched as she grated a bar of Fels-Naptha soap into the top of round-barreled washing machine and loaded a big family's dirty clothes to be agitated, then scrunched through a ringer. She pinned them on the lines behind the house, the ones near the animal pens shown in Mama's painting. I sat at the oilcloth-covered kitchen table and watched Nonnie sprinkle and wrap the freshly dried laundry then iron it on the mangle.[2] With apparent ease she catered to the demands of her husband and children and joined with gusto in the uproarious gatherings of their ever-expanding numbers.

At Nonnie's house, I could stand off to the side like the Little Prince watching the Riley relatives in fascination. There was always high hilarity, much to the discomfort of my shy mother whose inevitable squirming prompted even more non-stop kidding by her brothers, father and husband.

The ongoing show provided by my mother's family was even more entertaining than the Fun House at The Pike. Uncle Jack described the family as "basically a gang of hillbillies from Kentucky who were pretending to be civilized, living a bohemian existence and saved from the poor house by some natural born talent."

---

[2] Nonnie's mangle was a mechanical laundry aid that pressed the dampened clothes as they were hand cranked through hot rollers.

Introducing Nonnie and company

My father captured the life of Rileys in a film shot around 1931. It begins with the clan emerging from the house in a parade through a vine-covered arbor. The matriarch comes first, in an overcoat, blowing her nose, followed by her children. They make their entrances in descending age, exhibiting a variety of attitudes and states of dress, from the boys' bathrobes to my mother's self-tailored plaid suit. "Baby" Jack comes last, imitating the slow motion he had seen on the silver screen. In the finale, the ensemble approaches the camera two by two as if for a curtain call. Nonnie and my mother come last, chatting and perusing what was probably a fashion magazine.

Daddy draws Gerry smoking and scootering

Aunt Fran was off and married to her first husband, Lloyd, but Aunt Gerry, only fifteen years my senior, was often home, staying in the little house in back. I was mesmerized by her sophistication and status as a college coed. Particularly appealing was the fact that she smoked a corn cob pipe and commuted to classes at UCLA on a putt-putt scooter.

Gerry had to leave college during the war. She worked at nearby Hughes Aircraft where they needed women with small hands. Her job was to work on the assembly line for airplane wings, reaching blindly through the machine gun holes to ratchet up the wiring.

Aunt Gerry becomes "Rosie the Riveter"

The patriarch of the family was John Clinton Riley, called Clint by his friends, but Pop by his grandkids. With his white hair and mustache, he looked like one of those English actors who always take the role of majors who served in India. He served as the very model of manliness for my uncles, as a disciplinarian for the whole family and an object of fear for my mother.

Portrait of Pop

The landmark Hollywood Hotel demolished in the fifties

Pop's father was a carpenter who worked on the famous, but long gone, Hollywood Hotel.[3] Pop was a carpenter too, and all three of his sons followed him into the business. Since I often was looking at my grandfather and uncles from a very low angle, I remember how their shins were always bruised from scampering around construction sites.

My Riley uncles were rough and tumble fun. I loved being around them and watching their very male tomfoolery. I would follow their every word while nestled into the lap of handsome Uncle Dick where I examined the distinctive mole on his chin that I labeled his "rotten spot."

---

[3] Located on the site where the Academy Awards are now held, the Hollywood Hotel, built in 1905, hosted the greats of stardom such as Rudolph Valentino and Louis B. Mayer, one of my grandfather's big bosses.

Pop celebrates Jimmy, the cocker's, birthday

My father created many madcap movies featuring my grandfather cavorting with different members of the family. Watch as he poses with one of the many black cocker spaniels called Jimmy, dog and man in celebratory attire, man's glasses now on dog.

Madcap comedy featuring men and dog

Many scenes featuring the Riley men are like something out of the Keystone Kops.[4] One scenario involves their tearing apart a convertible jalopy apparently to solve a malfunction. The far from expected—or desired—outcome is the discovery and extraction of a large dog that performs a stellar role as "dead dog."

---

[4] The Keystone Kops were wildly popular comedy teams whose films were often shot near where the Rileys were performing their own hilarious hijinks.

Clint, Bob and Jack perform a gun-toting action scenario

The Riley men were avid hunters. The smell of gun oil pervaded the little knotty pine-paneled room where I was sent to nap on the boys' bottom bunk. In an action-packed movie that might be called *The Mighty Hunters*, Clint and the boys go hunting with a great deal of finger and weapon pointing. The results of their efforts are seen in lingering close-ups of a horned toad they have been stalking and the droppings of a larger prey they have missed.

Uncle Jack taught me the dangers of guns when he decided to use his finger at the end of the barrel to test the power of his BB gun. My mother took great exception to the fact that I, at about three, was standing in front of him, but I thought the experiment and his subsequent arm cast were just fine and dandy. After all, I wasn't hurt like the time at the Rileys' when I learned the power of an electric fence. I had tried to climb the shocking enclosure in order to pet the cow called Glamour Girl.

Later, at the family cabin he had built in Big Bear, Pop taught me to shoot a chest-thumping rifle and how to catch a sun-basking lizard by whistling and petting its back with a string lasso that would nab him. The lizards fared no better than my pollywogs. They met their end in jars, accidentally cooked by the same mountain sunshine they had been enjoying.

When I was about eight, I was the victim of my grandfather's brand of fun laced with a mean streak. Nonnie and Pop were taking care of me in Burbank while my parents drove cross-country to Louisiana. Pop suggested that I go into the den and crawl into the firewood cupboard. Despite a fear of the child-devouring black widow spiders that dwelt there, I did as I was asked. I was deep into the cupboard when I was scared out of my wits by the approach of a huge, roaring monster. It turned out to be my grandfather who had stuck his head into the other entrance to the cupboard from the living room and was playing "boo." His laughter at the success of the trick was drowned out by my hysterical screeching. Perhaps this answers the mystery of why my grandmother always called my grandfather "O'*Roar*ke."

Riley short subjects: *Jack and Dick Argue* while *Fran and Lloyd Pass the Roll*

Daddy's movies feature my relatives at a movable feast of family encounters. He captured daily domestic scenes like Jack and Dick in a mock ruckus and the family celebrating holidays. At Thanksgiving, he zoomed in for close-ups of the diners as they tried to ignore the camera in their faces. My father usually had a theme for the shoot like the fascinating passing of a dinner roll. This long scene culminates in my Aunt Fran's oral sharing of said bread with her first husband, the unpopular Lloyd.

Comic relief: *Uncle George, the Tree-Climbing Monkey*

One of my father's cinematic triumphs featured my Great-Uncle George, married to Pop's sister. In the film, I am shown at about three feeding a peanut to Uncle George who is down on all fours. He grabs the goober and scampers up a tree where he perches on a branch to perform his denture-less monkey imitation. They say Uncle George liked the bottle and that's why he acted crazy, but to me his antics were pretty cool and no crazier than those of the rest of my adult relatives.

The lives of the Riley clan and their offspring provide movie-worthy stories of successes, sorrows and even a scintilla of scandals. Watching them was fascinating fodder for my insatiable curiosity.

After their six boys and girls went off to raise their own children (seventeen in all), Nonnie and Pop set out in an RV to explore the USA. Eventually they stopped roving and settled near San Diego where at age sixty-eight, Pop's heart gave out and O'Roarke's roar was silenced. Nonnie was left with twenty years of merry widowhood. She was always active with one or another of her kids and their kids and eventually great grandkids who visited and were always having parties—often to fete her. Here are snapshots of some of those last parties:

Happy octogenarian

Nonnie, the caped octogenarian gets a kick out of my reading from the picture book I prepared for her. Or maybe she is reacting to my hairdo seemingly inspired by Moe of Three Stooges fame.

Nonnie at ninety

In the wheelchair she hated and called Mehitibel, the ninety-year-old matriarch is surrounded by her six children posing in reverse birth order: Jack, Dick, Gerry, Fran, Bob and Maxine. The boys were all builders while the girls all built families and worked at periodic professions and domestic duties.

Nonnie was always working hard and surrounded by lots of grown-ups, including a very demanding husband. But I loved and felt loved by her and basked in the joy she had in life that I was to learn belied the hardships she suffered. When she was ninety-three she grew tired of living.

Her ashes are scattered in the Pacific that provided beach escapes from the Culver City homestead.

Preteen Renée, Daddy, Kelly, Mama, Jack, Nonnie and Pop pose on Parish

As the forties drew to a close, so did Daddy's movies. He put aside his amateur cameras for professional ones that recorded the commercials he created. And I began to cast aside most, but not all, Potsy-isms in order to enter the fifties as a species perhaps even more bizarre than one of the Little Prince's grown-ups: a San Fernando Valley teenager.

12
Sex Lessons and How I Learned Them

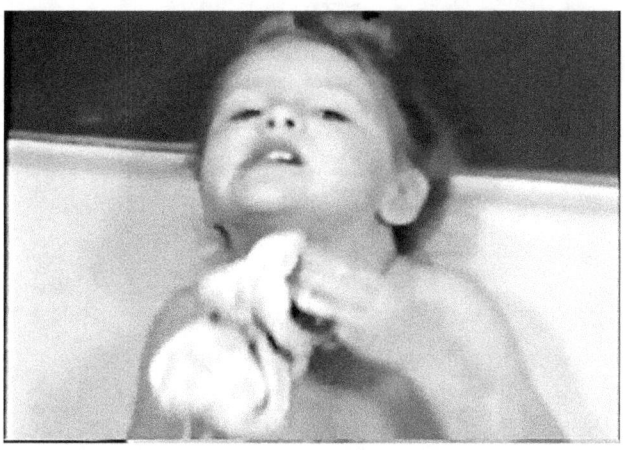

Potsy, age 3, at her toilette

The curriculum for my lessons in sexology was composed from a crazy quilt of sources. Here are a few of the seminal teachings I managed to learn.

1. Boys and Girls Are Different

It happened when I was about three. I was sharing a tub in their Long Beach bathroom with my cousins Brian and Jeff when I was intrigued to observe that between their legs the boys had silly little teapot spouts bouncing about in the bubbles. According to Nana, who was performing our ablutions, the jiggly part is called a "go-go." I was OK with the knowledge that girls have nothing in that area worth naming.

2. My Girlie Area Has Its Own Fascination

Twinges that there was something special about the place where I should have had a go-go arose during later domestic scenarios. These were enacted in the backyard of Freddy, Mary Jane's other next-door neighbor. As our elder at age ten, Freddy played the part of the dutiful husband to Mary Jane and doting father to six-year-old me. Our tranquil home life was always interrupted, however, when the improvised script called for me to suffer an unspecified medical emergency. This crisis would necessitate Freddy's alteration from father to doctor. No matter what my diagnosis, I made sure that Dr. Freddy's examination never required disrobing. By six I had learned the secret sanctity of my still unnamed girlie parts.

One happy family

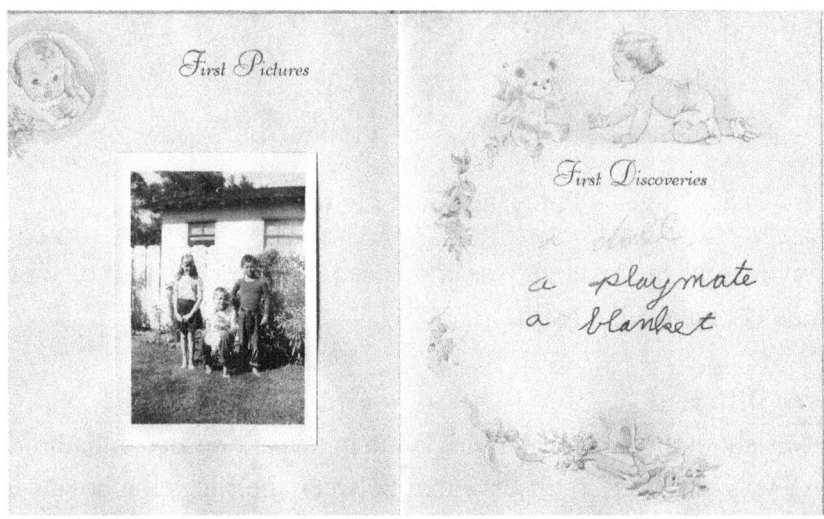

Nancy's doting family in her baby book

3. To Make a Baby You Need a Mother Who Is a Lady and a Father Who Is a Man

On a visit to my house, Jeff and Brian were handy for a lesson in the mysteries of family pre-planning. I took advantage of their gender and assigned them roles to play in raising my drink-and-wet[1] doll, Nancy, whose imaginary development I documented in her own baby book. They performed admirably. However, due to a total ignorance of their necessity, several crucial steps were eliminated in our procreational play.

4. Go-Gos Don't Always Look Like Teapot Spouts and Go by Other Names

My first reaction to seeing an erect adult penis was the same as the one I had toward my cousins' jiggly bits. I laughed. It looked like a pink palm tree toy that the man was animating on his lap. Mary Jane explained that the man in the car asking directions shouldn't be acting like that, and that we'd have to tell Mama. Between Mary Jane, Mama and the police, I learned, at the age of eight, the correct name for the appendage, but continued to find it rather amusing.

---

[1] Unfortunately, my knowledge of female anatomy was not aided by the location of Nancy's "wet" feature in her lower lumbar region.

  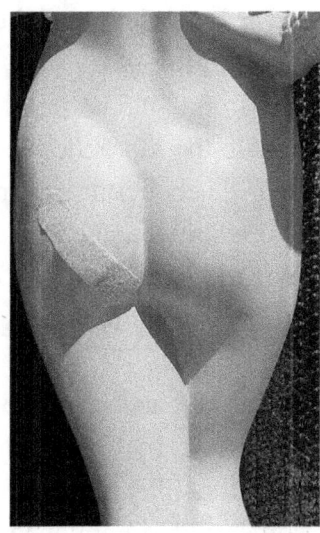

Model and art

5. There Are Parts That Are Best Kept Hidden, Some More Than Others—Unless They Are Art
This lesson began with the gift of a 26" nude statuette of Mae West.[2] According to my Aunt Gerry the piece was a present from George Jessel[3] to my great-grandfather Riley because he worked on the Hollywood Hotel. Or the sculpture was given to my grandfather Riley (according to my mother) because he worked at MGM. Anyway, after it came into our family, it was kept in a specially designed niche in our Parish Place bathroom. With a burgeoning sense of modesty, I would turn Mae booby-side in whenever I was expecting guests. My father, who valued art and humor over propriety, covered a chip in Mae's painted derriere with a Band-Aid to add interest to her booty-side view while her more spectacular features were turned toward the wallpaper.

The presence of Mae in our home led to an understanding that some otherwise best-hidden body parts can be revealed if they are art (an exception being the previously mentioned fig leaf on the reproduction of the statue of David at Forest Lawn).

It was with this understanding of the nude in art that I studied with interest the double deck set of playing cards I found in Daddy's den. They featured photos that his friend Tom Kelly took of Marilyn Monroe in two alluring poses upon red velvet. The artistic value of the special edition set was lost on Mary Jane and me as we slammed down our cards in our highly competitive card games. Years later I learned of the financial value of the decks we treated so harshly.

---

[2] An overtly sexual film star of the thirties known for her bawdy double entendres. There is a life jacket named after her for obvious reasons.

[3] Called "America's Toastmaster" for his many gigs in that role, "Georgie" Jessel was a vaudeville and movie entertainer who seems to have no ties to Mae West, the Hollywood Hotel or MGM.

6. My Quest for Knowledge of the Mysteries of Reproduction Was Not Going to be Satisfied by Academic Explanations

The art objects around the house did more to further my sex lessons than my father's audio-visual attempt to explain the reproductive habits of humans. In an effort to enlighten the prepubescent neighborhood girls about our impending roles as baby-makers, my father gathered us together in our living room for a "birds and bees" discussion that best befitted his manner of communicating. It was the Walt Disney production called *The Story of Menstruation*. It was designed to answer any questions we might have as we entered the age when not knowing this stuff might get us in trouble.

If the animated film featured any explanation of the act that leads to conception, it was either too subtle or drowned out by Lorna's and my giggling. I saw no relationship between my nether regions and the instructional illustrations. My only take-away was a fallacious understanding that fallopian tubes were some kind of appliance I would have to wear in order to create a baby.

7. Puberty Happens

It happened when I was twelve. I was sitting behind the wooden half door of a stall in the Girls' restroom at Jordan Junior High. Something was wrong, and I had no idea what it was. I thought the spots on my panties could have happened when I rode my bike to school. When I got home, Mama explained my coming of age milestone. It felt more like a millstone. Rather than a sense of pride, I worried about what was yet to come. I wasn't so sure I wanted to go through any more rites of passage.

A different kind of shadow

"Those days" when I had to attach that humongous pad to the metal clip on the twisty, pinchy elastic belt were mortifying. I knew everyone following me through the halls was pointing at the telltale bulge under my skirt. It was a confusing new development in my path toward becoming a grown-up woman. Too embarrassed to discuss the practical side of this new development, I looked to my trusted source—the ads in my teen magazines. But the confusion was just compounded.

Some of the ads, like the one called "Not a Shadow of a Doubt with Kotex," just added to my doubt. I wondered if I was the only one who didn't feel lucky to need their product for what we dubbed "that time of the month." The beautiful scenes portrayed the "period" (or "curse" as I also learned to call it) as if it was a lovely romp in the meadow on a spring day or an activity for lovely ladies who lunch, or even something Mama and I could share in the matching dresses she made for us.

Other Kotex ads with the equally subtle title "Are you in the know?" featured catchy multiple-choice quizzes on trendy teen topics like dating, dance routines, or camouflaging freckles. The reader was led gently into the final quiz that tastefully touted the merits of the brand.

How to get "in the know"

Tampax also used the advice approach such as an article about how you were chained down during that period on the calendar if you were using pads instead far less cumbersome tampons.

Some of the ads were downright scary like the one for The Belt where an older woman tells a teen that if you use a tampon, you'll lose your virginity. Was this as true as what I was told about getting pregnant from toilet seats? Very confusing. In the end, neither advice from magazines nor from Mary Jane led to my feeling at all comfortable during THAT time.

Why didn't boys have to suffer the humiliations of puberty? But wait! Look at what we girls tittered about in the cafeteria. Our topics of the day ranged from Rick's squeaky voice to Stanley's unfortunate bump "down there" during a sock hop in the gym. It seemed that "maturing" was a cross to bear for both genders.

Better watch out!

Unchained malady

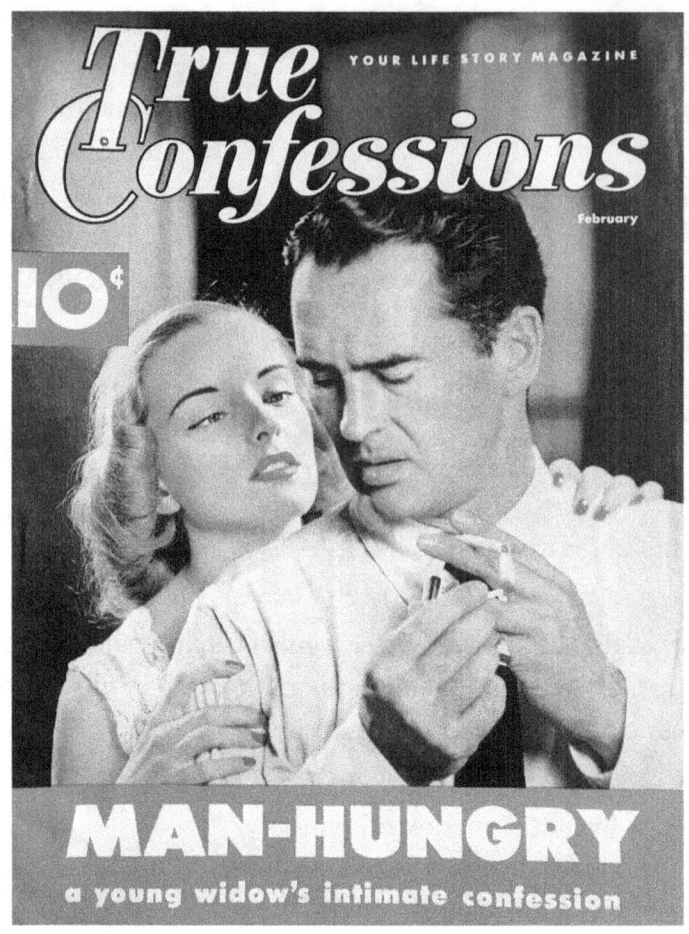

Sex education text

8. Sex Education May Be Acquired Through a Variety of Texts
Literary lessons in sexual maturity came knocking one summer afternoon in the form of a nice looking young man selling subscriptions to *True Confessions* magazine. Mary Jane agreed to help the polite fellow in his quest to return to his homeland in Israel. So, we took advantage of Mama's separation from her purse and borrowed the money for a two-year subscription. The rest of the summer was spent lying on my backyard lawn where I, the better scholar, read Mary Jane stories of wayward women whose sweaters were too tight and who snuck off to roadhouses to perform acts that were never described. I didn't know what a roadhouse was, but both it and the acts sounded titillatingly nasty.

Magazines weren't my only sex education texts. As if they had not already contributed enough, the Shannon cousins once again furthered my body of knowledge when one of them left a *Boy Scout Handbook* within easy perusing distance. The passages about a certain forbidden pleasure and unwelcome nocturnal dampness were fascinating though raised intriguing questions about boys' mysterious anatomies.

Secrets of feminine wiles

9. Successful Seduction May Be Achieved Through Feminine Wiles—the Definition and Application of Which May Remain Mysterious

One Saturday while Mama attended her lampshade-making class, I decided to try my wings at enhancing what the girls in *True Confessions* so successfully flaunted. I intensified my lipstick from a Pepto-Bismol shade of Pixie Pink to a seductive Tangee crimson that I had seen advertised as practically guaranteed to make me kissable. I exoticized my eyes with Mama's painful eyelash curler and a block of her cakey mascara. Having uncomfortably crammed her falsies into my Teenform training bra, I donned my tightest red angora sweater. Then, in as voluptuous a pose as one could assume atop a Schwinn, I pedaled throughout the neighborhood past the homes of potential young gentlemen callers. The quest was not worthy of the preparation, garnering nary a "Hubba hubba" wink nor wolf whistle let alone romance. Apparently, the objects of my affections were engaged in whatever it is that preteen boys found more intriguing than preteen girls.

 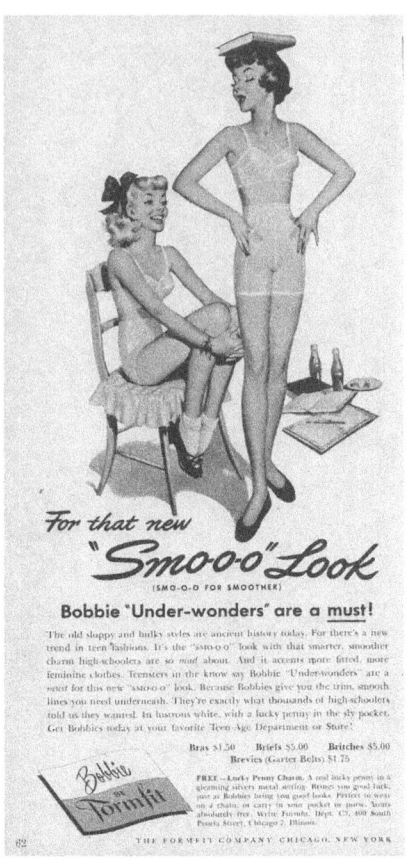

What's a girl to do?

Even before I felt the first flutters of hormonal butterflies, I received messages from my reading material, movies and slumber party conversations that I needed fixing if I was going to set out on a crusade to find the holy male. I followed the magazine ads religiously to learn how to become a beguiling teenager. After all, I'd seen the ads announcing, "She's Engaged, She's Lovely, She Uses Ponds!" I assumed that I wasn't lovely if I wasn't engaged. Maybe cold cream would help me snag Mr. Wonderful. Perhaps I needed Bobbie Under-Wonders for that "smarter, smoother charm high schoolers are so *mad* about." I even considered that sporting a pair of shoes named for my successful-in-love friend might help me meet the boy of my dreams.

How boy meets girl

Mary Jane's beau as child actor and teen dream boat

10. Mary Jane Knows

I knew, though, that it wasn't shoes that made Mary Jane an object of desire. Not only was she nearly a year older than me, but Mary Jane's sexual evolution was enviously rapid. It seemed forever that I had been listening to her as she proudly announced each budding bodily change from the coveted need to wear a bra and deodorant, to leg shaving and other unmentionable hygienic processes I longed to perform.

I watched a stream of boys gather round her house, knowing she had learned far more from *True Confessions* than I had, even though I had done the reading. When her suitors narrowed down to one of the most popular boys in junior high, the dishy child actor Johnny McGovern, the very one who played Red Ryder's[4] Little Beaver, I thought I would die from jealousy.

---

[4] From 1938 to 1964, Red Ryder rode his steed Thunder through the comics accompanied by his sidekick Little Beaver. When the comic strip became a radio show, Little Beaver was voiced by Johnny McGovern (now John Wilder) from 1947–50.

Bathing beauty
(with a little reinforcement from Mama's lingerie drawer)

Tale by tantalizing tale, ad by amazing ad, I was let in on the secrets of sisterhood. But I knew there was a deep trove of information that Mary Jane and the magazines weren't telling me. This sex thing was much more complicated than friends or relatives or literature were letting on. Despite, or perhaps because of, the lessons I had been afforded, I would enter adolescence not a great deal further advanced in sexual awareness than the babe in the bathtub—with a longing to return to that splashing good time.

13
Dear Diary

First dear diary

It has the look and feel of a museum artifact viewed in a glass display case, perhaps the preserved possession of a late great author or artist. Layers of fuzzy stuffing and cardboard stiffener fan out from the scuffed oxblood-colored faux leather cover. "Five Year Diary" embossed in gilt, matching rococo embellishments and a tarnished zipper lend an air of importance.

Though the document is indeed old, it would have no value to museum curators let alone flea market and eBay browsers. But it has great value to me. What I read between its faded lines brings laughter and sadness and cringe-inducing awareness. And I begin to understand the kid who wrote it and how she became me.

On January 3, 1948 at age nine, I began to follow the format of a Five Year Diary where one writes a short paragraph on the same date for five different years. Let's look at that first diary page, unedited except for a couple of spelling and punctuation changes. Some names are slightly changed to protect those who still feel innocent enough to be protected.

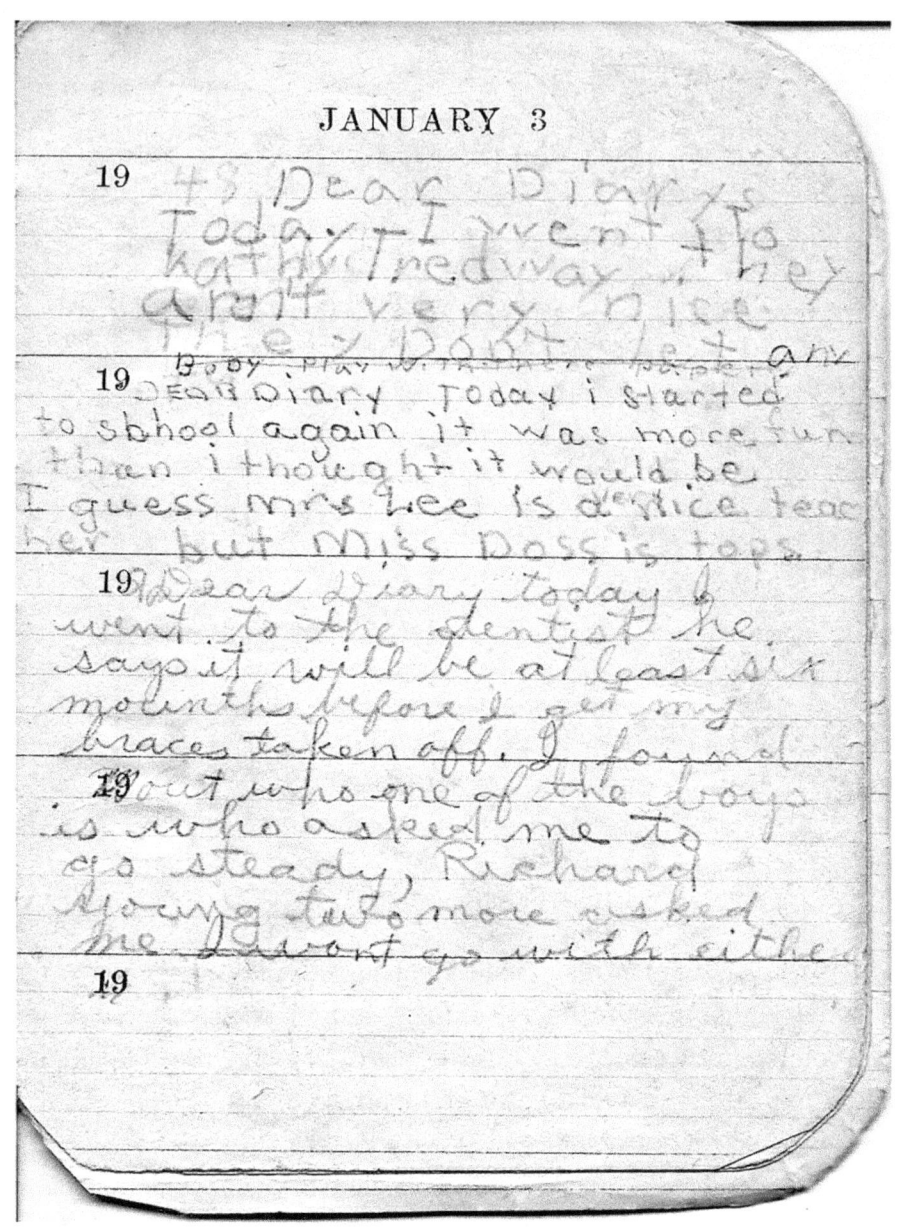

Neighborhood drama

January 3, 1948

Dear Diary,
Today I went to Kathy Treadway's. They aren't very nice. They don't let anybody play with their puppets.

This contretemps was a heavy blow for a self-styled future famous entertainer. The magnificent professional marionette stage took up a big portion of the Treadways' playroom. The curtains were rich red velvet and you could pull braided golden cords to open and close them. Lavishly painted backgrounds of indoor and outdoor scenes stood at the ready to inspire puppet play plots. I was dying to get my hands on the tangle-prone strings of those beautifully-detailed royal and peasant puppets. Eventually I did, and I went on to upstage the Treadway girls by producing shows that the neighborhood was invited to enjoy for the price of a hand-written ticket.

1949

Dear Diary,
Today I started to school again. It was more fun than I thought it would be. I guess Mrs. Lee is a (very - inserted above the line) *nice teacher. But Miss Doss is tops.*

Here's the dilemma. I loved my fourth-grade teacher Miss Doss. I felt it was therefore being disloyal to her to write a favorable first impression of my fifth-grade teacher Mrs. Lee. As it turned out I loved her too, and, like Miss Doss, paid her the compliment of an invitation to Parish Place for a special mama-made dinner.

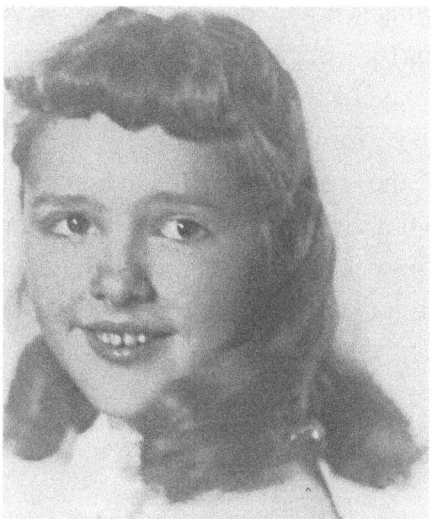

Before braces

In 1951 as a seventh grader at David Starr Jordan[1] Junior High School, I poured out my cursive innermosts in defiance of the one paragraph per year rule. I can imagine an increasingly introspective preteen recounting the vagaries of her love life on the same page where a year or so before she wrote in block letters about her play day. The childish earlier entry must have felt like the intrusion of a bratty younger sister.

Let's get honest. I did not enter junior high as a model of adolescent attractiveness. No poet would compare my freckled face to jewels and flowers. No artist would immortalize my maidenly beauty. Jose Reyes of Hollywood gave it a good stab on my annual portrait, but even with the dramatic sweep of my curlered tresses, I was far from comely. Orthodonture was imminent.

---

[1] A very California choice of name, Jordan was an American ichthyologist, educator, eugenicist, and peace activist. He was the founding president of Stanford University.

1951

Dear Diary,
Today I went to the dentist. He says it will be at least six months before I get my braces taken off. I found out who one of the boys is who asked me to go steady, Richard Young. Two more asked me. I won't go with either.

According to my January 3 entry, I had just discovered the identity of a boy who asked me to go steady, a puzzling sequence of events. But though often brutally honest in the pages of my diaries, I fudged a little on this submission. I'll explain.

I was referring to the day I was leaving school when what to my seventh-grade eyes should appear but a pride of the most magnificent lions (or Cougars as our mascot was called) in Jordan Junior High's social hierarchy. These were the cream of the ninth-grade male crop—all gathered in one formidable cluster, slouching sexily against and performing acrobatic tricks on the metal pipe banister at the school's back entrance. As I passed, they roared a chorus in mock flirtation, jeeringly asking me to go steady. My face, which I knew was not flirt-worthy, burned with humiliation as I hurried by them. At a time when my twelve-year-old self-esteem was at its lowest and the priority to find a male admirer at its highest, the experience was too traumatic to confide even to my dear diary. Thus, the casual mention of the name of one of my taunters.

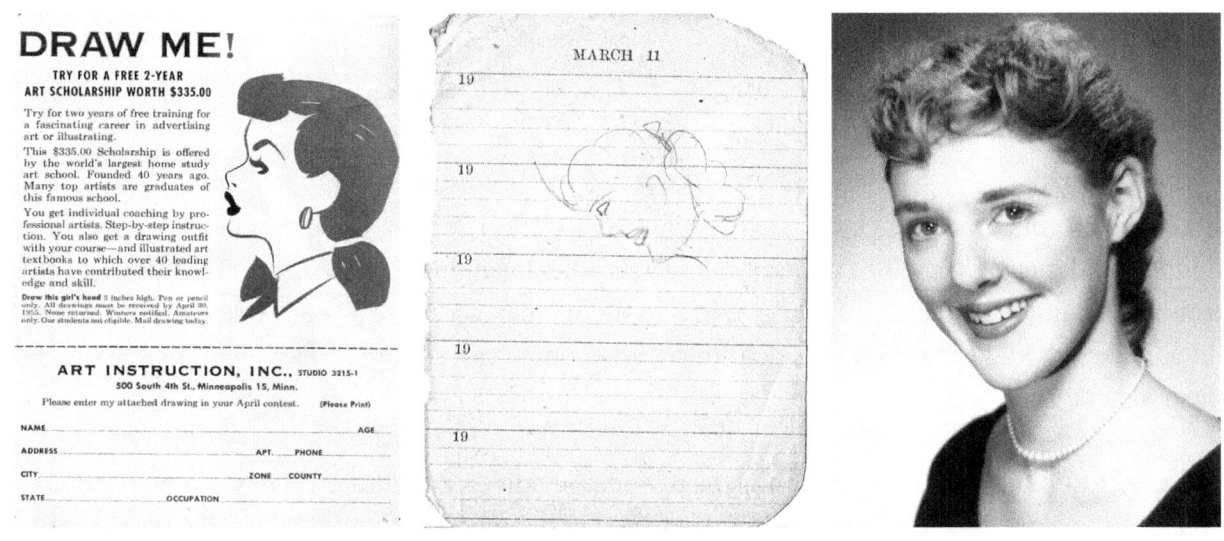

Wishful doodling and wish fulfilled

On March 11, instead of writing, I drew a portrait of how I wished I looked. It was a first attempt to copy a profile that I hoped would earn the prize of an art scholarship. I never made a final drawing nor entered the contest to follow in my father's art correspondence school footsteps. Ironically my little diary trade school sketch bears a sight resemblance to how I would look in my high school graduation portrait, four years hence.

Dear Diary,
I think I'm boy crazy 'cause I want a boyfriend so bad.

I was indeed obsessed with the hunt for male companionship. I perused all advice on the art of the chase and the popularity that would enrapture and capture my quarry.

Renée Diane, the huntress

Further evidence that I had become preoccupied with the opposite sex fill the three months of entries before I tired of my first diary. Almost daily I recounted the attentions or lack thereof from four seventh grade boys. I will violate the sanctity of the diary confessional and share a few of these courting chronicles. With a little fleshing out, the twists and turns of my road to romance might make compelling soap opera plotting.

January

Dear Diary,
…Today we danced in gym. I found out who my true boy friend (right now) is, Ronnie

The disclosure in my diary that Ronnie was my current one and only fails to explain what epiphany caused me to "find out" who my true boyfriend was. It sounds like a sort of pronouncement from on high. Apparently, there was more than the squeaking of our socks on floor wax as we box-stepped around the basketball court.

The art of the chase

Truth be known, I saw any twinkle in the eye of a male teen as a step toward the realization of my dream—Going Steady—the ultimate prize in the dating game at Jordan Junior High in the early fifties. It was like grabbing the brass ring on the courting carousel. And a brass ring was actually a sign your relationship had arrived at the steady stage. The oversized ornament resembling an auto part was fashioned by Jordan boys in metal shop and not designed as finger jewelry. It was to be worn on a chain around the neck where its clanging weight created sought-after bruises.

My first dating escapades were more of a roller coaster than a carousel as seen in some of the excerpts from my diary.

February

*Dear Diary,
…I am sorta mad at Ronnie because he didn't treat me very well and didn't give me his jacket. I sorta like Rodney again.*

March

*Dear Diary,
…I wore Ronnie's jacket today and all the girls are jealous.*

The next best pre-steady trophy was the motorcycle jacket. In San Fernando Valley teen culture, this super-masculine article of apparel was a token of commitment just short of going steady. No gift of sable could match the feeling of cherished femininity that came with the donning of this oversized garment smelling of leather and whatever had been imbibed or touched by its owner.

Alas, Ronnie and Renée's road to romance was not a smooth one. The promissory jacket was returned, and our journey toward the coveted ring was interrupted. My head was turned toward other suitable suitors, but with time, my thoughts turned—though sporadically—back to Ronnie.

March

Dear Diary,
…I like Ronnie again and am not mad at him any more. I like Rodney but Ronnie better.

Dear Diary,
…Tonight, Clyde called me. He told me he liked me. I love him. Also Billy called.

Dear Diary,
…Rodney had me do something for him after school. I hope Clyde didn't see us.

Dear Diary,
…Clyde didn't see us (thank heavens). He rode home with me tonight. We talked for about an hour out on the driveway. I am so mad at Ronnie. He just found out today that I don't like him.

Dear Diary,
…Tonight, Janet called. She asked me to ask Ronnie to meet her.

The entries in my seventh-grade diary stopped abruptly in March, and my ardor for Ronnie, Rodney, Clyde and Billy eventually faded like the pages of the diary on which I told their stories. I don't know the outcome of the Janet and Ronnie story. But I do know that—though I didn't report it to dear diary—I briefly wore Rodney's ring and had the chest bruises to prove he had replaced Ronnie as my steady squeeze.

 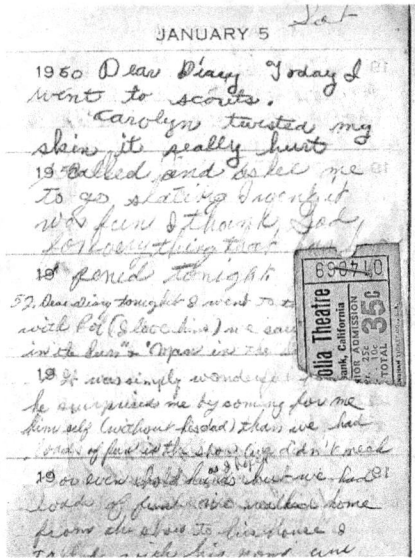

Diary #2

My next diary was a sweet, lady-like volume, a gift from a distant cousin in Louisiana. On the embossed white and gold cover is a picture of a hoop-skirted, poke-bonneted damsel, her serene stateliness a stark contrast to the whirlwind of eighth and ninth grade activity I poured out on the gold-edged pages.

In addition to improved grammar and penmanship, my daily reminiscences also become more varied. The love quest drama continues, but the revolving door of actual and yearned for boyfriends spins a little less frequently. Days are assessed on a scale of "awful" or "boring" to "loads of fun" or "wonderful." Social occasions, most especially actual dates, are documented in detail, sometimes accompanied by memorabilia such as a double feature movie ticket stub (Burbank's Magnolia Theater, 35 cents).

Entries in the little volume continue throughout 1952, and the twists and turns in the plot of my romance novel continued. When I learned that nerdy Billy had obtained a Chevy convertible, I would "find out" that he was my one and only forever true love.

Dear Diary,
Tonight I went to the show with Billy (I love him). We saw "A Place in the Sun" and "Man in the Saddle." It was simply wonderful. First he surprised me by coming for me himself (without his Dad). *Then we had loads of fun in the show. We didn't neck or even hold hands as I had hoped,* (inserted between the lines), *but we had loads of fun. We walked home to his house. I talked with his mom and dad while he washed his hands. Everything was just grand. I ~~love~~ like him very much. I don't care how popular he is or cute. I still do.*

I began to do all the teen type things I learned about in magazines. Of course, a must-do was to be au courant with the Hit Parade.[2] A favorite shopping foray was for new 45 records bought after listening to them in a glass booth at Wallichs Music City on Sunset and Vine in Hollywood.

I played the little records with big holes over and over behind the closed door of my bedroom. I wallowed away the hours sympathizing with the loneliness of Don Cornell, swooning with The Four Aces and crying at the agony of Johnnie Ray.

Come cry with me

---

[2] A list of the top recordings—often presented on radio and later on television

Renée with Danny at a lakeside outing

Dear Diary,
…Today we went swimming at Eleanore King's mansion. Her husband runs Technicolor. Danny and I had loads of fun running around the place. It's huge.

Danny was the son of one of my parents' animator friends, so he didn't count as a real date. Danny's family and mine went to the mansion because the wife of another Disney coworker was the personal secretary to Eleanore King who had been an actress. Her husband was the founder and head of Technicolor. We explored their (to me) palatial estate, swam in the pool, romped on the elaborately landscaped lawns and imagined how we would live a show biz millionaire's life.

We were most impressed to learn that Eleanore's daughter Cammie played Scarlett and Rhett's daughter, Bonnie Blue Butler in *Gone with the Wind.* She was the voice of Faline who I thought of as Bambi's girlfriend. The fact that I met none of these illustrious residents did not prevent years of recounting my visit to their home.

Treks to the other side of the Hollywood Sign were the highlights of my social calendar. The best were the occasions when Mama let me join Jordan girlfriends for a parentless Saturday outing to the movies on Hollywood Boulevard. One of the girls' mothers was the designated driver who got us there and then was expected to disappear. My mother was never the chauffeur because she didn't know how to drive. After Mary Jane took Driver's Education at Burroughs, she taught Mama how to drive.

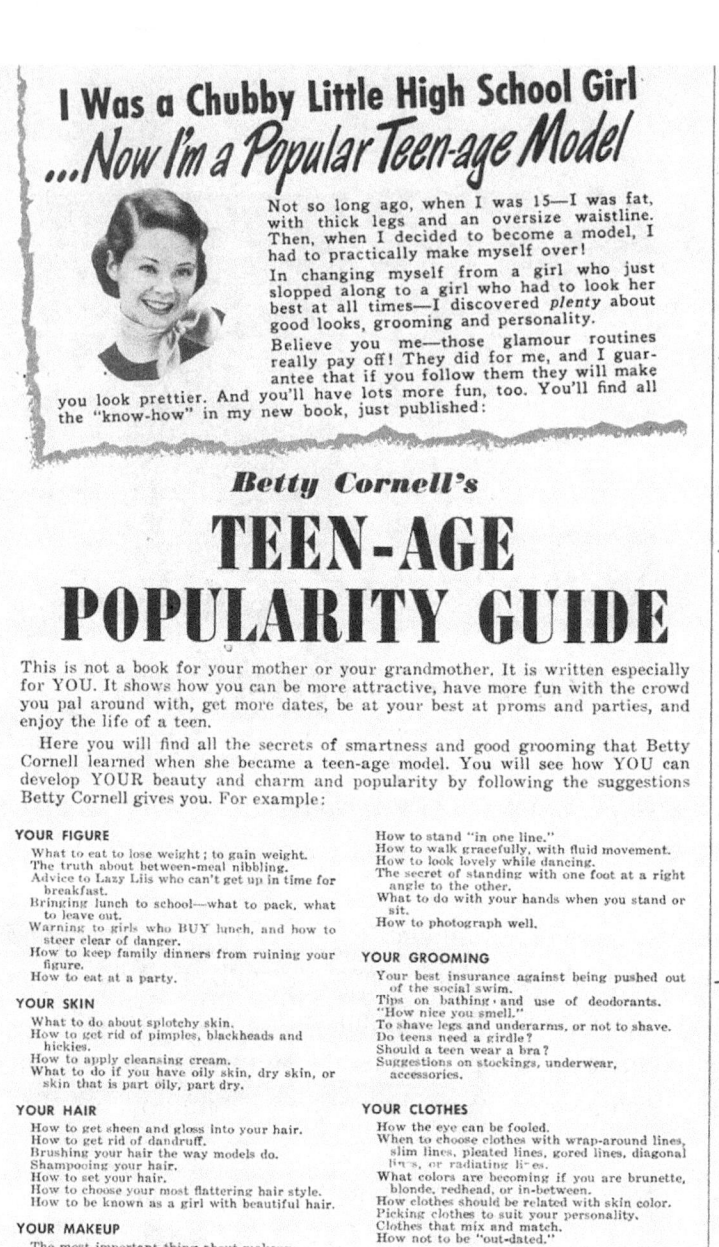

The path to popularity

Super special was when that gaggle of girls fell into the "popular" category. I longed to belong to this superior caste. I was convinced that the way to join them was to follow their lead in fashion and manners. I must do nothing that would make myself different. I would struggle into a waist-cinching and aching girdle, pointy bra (the cup size now barely a size over the training size), preferably cashmere sweater with detachable white Peter Pan collar and scratchy horsehair crinoline under my full circle skirt. I left the house in high hopes I hadn't forgotten a detail that would make me worthy of their company. I feared I would come up short.

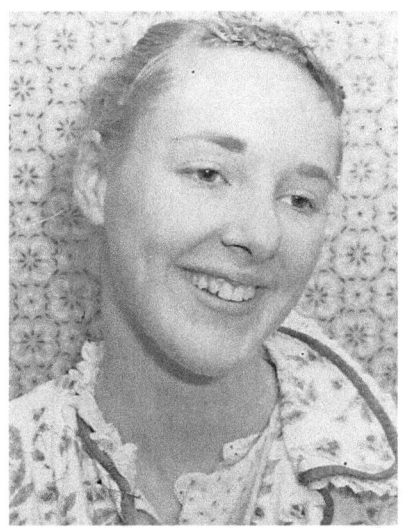

Bangs bobby-pinned, teeth straight

Ironically, the highlight of my junior high social career—my pinnacle of popularity up to that moment—involved a trip to Hollywood when I looked my worst.

Dear Diary,
Tonight I was initiated into Detas (a select club for Jordan "in" girls). *We had to go to Bobs in pin curls and with no lipstick. At Bobs we rode around the lot in wagons and sang and danced for money. The parking lot attendants asked us to leave so we went to Hollywood where we went up and down the boulevard and everyone we came to we'd sing to, dance and act up for money. Our group of eleven girls made $4.82. I am now a Deta. I sure had loads of fun.*

Even allowing for inflation I'd say that our little troupe was more interested in performing random acts of attention-attracting silliness than money collecting. The point, of course, was not to enhance the coffers of our junior sorority (named before we were familiar with the Greek alphabet). The object was to be noticed and prove our undying loyalty to the secret sorority. Becoming a Deta meant I was a novitiate in the A-listers club. I would belong.

Radio days

Dear Diary,

...Mary Jane and I went to the Lux Radio Theater which was "Girl in White" with none other than my favorite actress June Allyson. She is awfully tremendous even more so than I expected. It was loads of fun.

Mary Jane, who was a Deta before me, was now seriously dating her practically famous actor, and we watched him broadcast radio shows at CBS or NBC that both had headquarters on Sunset Boulevard in downtown Hollywood. The super special treat was to go to the Lux Radio Theater to see famous stars reenact plays and movies. The theater was so named, not because it was luxurious, but because the show was sponsored by Lux Soap.

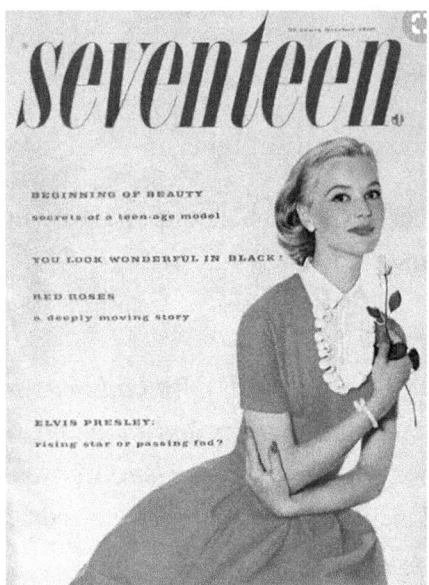 

            Teen ideal   Pouting teen, curl down

But not every entry in my diaries described brushes with fame in La La Land. Many of my musings were more suitable for the advice columns of teen magazines. For me, junior high was a very prickly, confined chrysalis in which I was undergoing a metamorphosis from an awkward junior high kid to a glorious high school butterfly like the ones I saw in *Seventeen* magazine. The transformation was often painful as seen in the increasingly introspective nature of my submissions that were sprinkled with a mist of angst. But for now, let's save these musings for the "V is for Virtue and Vice" chapter.

My moods, as reflected in lawn picture poses throughout my teen years, vacillated as rapidly as Potsy of the two faces. My pouty curl in the middle of the forehead morphed into the many coifs that would follow as I prepared to enter the halls of higher learning. We'll see if high school brings less diary-worthy agony and more teen ecstasy.

14
Fast Times at Burroughs High

John Burroughs High School under renovation in 1955

September 14, 1953

Dear Diary,
Today was my first day at Burroughs. It's all so big and all the kids are so big. I'm just wild about my French class.

Ah, high school! It had been my dream ever since I watched from my bedroom window as clusters of teens glided chattily by on the way down Parish to the big school at the corner of Clark. I fantasized myself as one of those carefree young women, strutting into an ivy-covered, Corinthian-columned senior high school. As I embarked on my senior high voyage, I dreamed of becoming a high schooler with no "junior" attached to the name; a confident, tiny-waisted, bouffant-skirted, bobby-soxed, perkily-ponytailed model of teen perfection.

Burroughs JUNIOR High's most famous alum (before she was Debbie)

On opening day, I walked the mile down Parish Place to the corner of Clark Avenue, and turned the corner to enter the halls of John Burroughs Senior High.[1] The setting wasn't exactly the impressive temple of learning that had filled my yearnings. Maybe there were ivy and columns when the school was the junior high attended by Burbank's own Mary Frances (later Debbie) Reynolds whose eminence as a Burbank girl was hinted at previously. She went on to Burbank High, our arch rival. But now the two-storied school had been transformed into a senior high school and modernized into a sprawling, streamlined campus.

Far from perfect, I felt very unsure and unattractive. Butterflies fluttered in my stomach as I stepped tentatively into the lobby with its glass cases of trophies and plaques bearing the logo of the fierce fighting Burroughs Indians.[2] I was immediately vacuumed into a vortex of hyper-energized teenagers. I cowered in the crush of those kids I had imagined would become instant friends. Some of the boys were huge and even had a hint of mustaches. Giggling girls, heads bent into little huddles, shared confidences in secretive tones, glancing around to see if anyone beyond their inner circle heard them or, hopefully, noticed them. They were flawlessly attired in glamorously curved sweaters with silk neck scarves, shoes and purses that matched.

I was now a big high school girl and felt so small. And so scared. I didn't know even one of these raucous older kids who all seemed to know each other. I watched them excitedly and loudly catch up with classmates they hadn't seen since June. They yelled greetings over the sound of the clanging lockers that lined the slippery looking hallways leading to the first-floor classrooms. I knew I'd never be able to operate those combinations as easily as these old-timers who threw in one article and retrieved another in one dexterous swoop. I'd never be one of those laughing, chatting semi-adults who twirled gracefully onto the staircase and mounted it to pursue subjects upstairs in classes I'd never be able to tackle.

Gone was the apprehension over whether I'd be popular and have a boyfriend. All I wanted now was to find and then disappear into my first class where there might be some kids I knew from Jordan, one of three junior highs that sent their graduates to Burroughs for tenth grade.

---

[1] Named, like Jordan, for a naturalist/activist. Even then California was actively green.

[2] Yes, it's California, but California of the fifties. Sixty years later the mascot will be protested, changed and then changed back.

The John Burroughs foreign language department

After that first jittery day, my times at Burroughs High went from fearful to bearable, and sometimes zoomed by exhilaratingly fast. I discovered the refuge of the classroom, and French I in particular. French had a logic that brought calm and order to the fearful tangle of my teenage monkey mind. I discovered I was good at it after all those mini lessons Nana gave me. Speaking another language didn't seem totally foreign, and I wasn't afraid to open my mouth to wrap my tongue around those silly sounds. I immediately liked Mrs. Benson who guided me through all the vocabulary and conjugations of three years of French, and even tutored me in French IV, not offered at our three-year school. In her Language Department photo, we see her comrades admiring a bullfight poster while she, chin in hand, appears to be admiring her colleague—or a joke he just told. The Latin teacher seems to be balancing a pan of paella on her lap.

Chanteuse at age 16

Mrs. Benson taught me the words to "La Vie en Rose," the 1945 torch song[3] written and sung by the French national treasure, Edith Piaf, who was forty when I presented my rendition on top a piano at a school assembly. She died eight years later. As a sixteen-year-old, I had not experienced the many tragedies that led to her soulful singing. But I tried to imitate the quiver-throated guttural gusto of the tiny troubled woman the French called "The Little Sparrow." I'm afraid my comic send-up was far from tragic and met with much welcome laughter and applause. I would recycle my chanteuse act many times in the future. And I had a new dream to add to Hollywood stardom: travel to France!

---

[3] The expression for a song of love and loss and sadness comes from carrying a torch for someone or keeping the love aflame for a rejected love.

Midnight oil

Unlike junior high, I actually learned to like the classes in high school, particularly the ones that didn't involve numbers or group showering. On the back of a photo my father took of me doing my homework in our dining room he wrote, "Taken late in January, too late for Renée to be studying, by her 'late' father."

Daddy is in the kitchen behind me listening and contributing to a call-in radio show and drinking Jim Beam bourbon. I am in pajamas and robe, hair set in pin curls, wearing the glasses I began needing after a bout of measles when I was nine. I am looking up a word in my *Webster's New Collegiate Dictionary* or perhaps my *French Junior Classic Dictionary*. At my side sits the Royal typewriter at the ready for me to enter whatever it is I am up late completing for the next day.

The cane bottom dining room chair in which I am pillow-propped is in the same reddish maple as the hutch behind me where Mama displays some of the antiques from stores she can't pass without a visit. The results of her night classes are throughout the house. She has re-upholstered anything that can be stuffed. Lamps are adorned with frilly shades she crafted. And scattered over the floors are splashes of colorful rugs created from scraps of wool used in the sewing of both of our wardrobes plus outfits worn by my dolls. She belonged to a group that hooked and braided rugs. With his ever-ready wit, Daddy quipped that he was relieved she was a braider and not a hooker.

It was a lovely home, and I was proud of it, inviting a widening circle of girlfriends to visit or spend the night. Yes, I had friends. I belonged. I became one of those senior high cognoscenti who gather in groups, sail the halls with ease, and know their combinations.

1954 Phi Lons—Mary Jane and I in front row, second and fourth from left

The social scene at Burroughs was much improved from Jordan's. Most importantly, I had a new suffix on my name: Renée Patin, Phi Lon. Yes, I was accepted into the elite (and "illegal" at Burroughs) "passionate lovers of wine" sorority. We were told the secret meaning and believed it though none of us, to my knowledge, drank wine. What we did do, if memory serves, was go to meetings and discuss things such as wearing the same thing on certain days to make sure our secret membership was known to all.

In my first year as a member, I joined my "sisters" for an official photo at a professional photography studio in downtown Burbank that documented our lives and immortalized our accomplishments. We would have had several "business meetings" deciding on our outfits, or really our neckwear as we always wore tight sweaters and a gray pencil skirt for our official photo. In my junior year, we eschewed the Peter Pan collar for the more sophisticated string of pearls.

1956 Phi Lon Photos—Mary Jane, front left—where's Renée?[4]

After primping in the crowded dressing room, we carefully chose our places near our best friends, and then were regrouped for aesthetic reasons by the photographer. He then went behind his camera stand and directed us in our poses: hands clasped in laps for the sitters and to the side for the tall standers,

---

[4] Middle row third from left.

big smile, eyes forward. After he got all the shots he wanted, we were told to relax into our craziest positions. With great hilarity on our part and much encouragement from the photographer, we attempted to remain adorable while displaying our talent for high comedy. I managed a rather fetching elbow twist in my senior year, belying the impression in the formal portrait that I was too shy to look at the camera. I was probably admiring how well a girl in the front row filled out her sweater as opposed to my flatter profile.

Peer envy was a frequent intruder on my self-confidence. There was always someone whose very existence made me feel inferior. Take Stephanie, for example. There she sits bottom row, second from right in her Peter Pan collar and in another shot, she sits be-pearled in the top row at the right. Stephanie was our designated idol. She could do no wrong. She had been the student body president at Jordan while still remaining nice to us lesser beings. In our discussions of her stellar attributes, we all agreed she was glorious perfection. Well, maybe those tiny veins in her nostrils kept her from being absolutely perfect, but we had to look hard to find that almost hidden flaw.

Mary Jane remained my de facto best friend, but our social lives whirled in different circles. My constant best chums were Eva May De Pew who sits next to Stephanie in the 1956 Phi Lon photo, and Mary Wheeler, a member of the rival sorority Fifinellas, the meaning of which remained a secret to me. Both were office holders and award winners and all-around leaders of those of us who needed to be led. I was proud when they all extolled our friendships when signing my yearbooks.

Memories—Native American style

Stephanie, Mary Jane, Eva and Mary held places on my highest pedestal, the one reserved for those girls who had not only looks and honors, but also boyfriends. Yes, patient reader, my hunt for trophy male prey continued on into high school. As I pursued my academic career, I also followed my dream of attaching my name to that of one of the choicest dreamboats, preferably one with a red and white letterman jacket and lots of photos of accomplishments in the *Akela*[5] yearbook.

---

[5] Perhaps named for a symbol of wisdom like Kipling's wolf in the Mowgli stories or for a leader in the Cub Scout program. Or perhaps it just sounded Indian.

Clubs

The purpose of the John Burroughs Lettermen's Club is to promote all sports. Members participated in the Blue Crutch Drive and in the Awards' Banquet. Top: Brian Heming, Gordie Davis, Dave George, Kent Volding, Jim Smith, Bob Stoll, and Dick Mackey. Second row: Joe Gargaro, Gary Jolley, Gary Brewer, Paul Bazan, Al Ehring, Bob Catalano, Rod Sanneman, and Tom Heath. Bottom row: Bob Dow, Dave Burton, Bill Elias, Joe Paggi, Jerry Persinger, Dick Gillis, Chuck Fisher, and Max Melch. Mr. Kiefer is faculty chairman of the group.

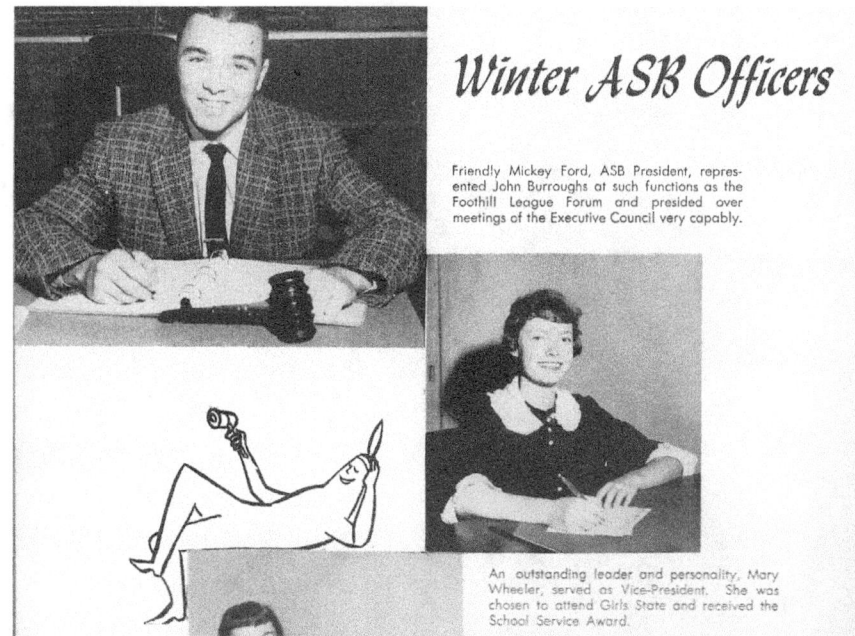

Winter ASB Officers

Friendly Mickey Ford, ASB President, represented John Burroughs at such functions as the Foothill League Forum and presided over meetings of the Executive Council very capably.

An outstanding leader and personality, Mary Wheeler, served as Vice-President. She was chosen to attend Girls State and received the School Service Award.

The *Akela* academy of awards

Opening the yearbook today is like letting loose a Pandora's box of all the stories I told myself about my inferior social standing. The year I graduated, the book divided the students into cutesy but enigmatic Native American categories enlivened by a feathered character who was a cross between the Pillsbury Doughboy and Casper the Friendly Ghost. There was a section called "Hunting Grounds" featuring, appropriately for us seekers, the highly sought-after athletes. "Big Chiefs" showcased class officers including my friend Mary and her hunky boyfriend Mickey who were stars of the class that graduated a semester before mine.

The "Z" Club's increase in membership and numerous activities have made it one of the most outstanding clubs on campus this year. Members are: Top row; Ruth Snowbarger, Karen Watkins, Dorothy Balker, Sue Whitney, Carolann Hall, Gail Schueltge, Arlene Dewey, Patsy Boyd, Lynne Richardson, Wanda Remy, Carolyn Sleeper, and Sandy Foster. Third row; Carole Shipley, Juanita Daily, Barbara Autry, Pat McCall, Judy Tjomsland, Jeanette Stallard, Sondra Bohan, Sue Sutherland, and Lorraine Genisauski. Second row; Madelon Cooke, Gail Loudon, Nikki Lane, Jan Cosby, Pat Dubell, Renee Patin, Charlotte Walker, Betty Kuka, Mary Bolin, Naida Travers, and Kathy Lentine. Bottom row; Carole Pacal, Diane Nassif, Steff Cooke, Penny Kirk, Susan McCleery, Mary Wheeler, Cindy Brown, Martha Mallery, Linda Clegg, Caroline Arroyo, and Kathy Street. Mrs. Straley serves as faculty advisor to the group.

The "Z" Club

Then there were the "Redmen" defined as the "working classes" in a variety of activities including clubs. I was pictured in the "Z" club[6] for career-oriented young women. There were photos of the "Warriors," the seniors among whom I am pictured (second row from bottom, on left) accompanied by the fact that I was "college prep," followed by a scattering of undistinguished memberships which I attended sporadically and remember not at all: "Z" Club, Girls Athletic Association, Girls' League Social Committee.

Akela accolades

---

[6] Sponsored by the Zonta Club of Burbank, whose volunteers work for empowering women.

Alas, despite Mary and Mickey's best efforts at introducing me to a variety of blind double dates, not one of the scions of Burroughs aristocracy ever dubbed me as their consort. Perhaps it was my academic proclivities, or my freckles and inability to tan, or my big feet. Or maybe my trying too hard to make up for not feeling worthy repelled, rather than attracted, their affections. Though I was a member in good standing of the most popular girls' group, I always considered myself on the fringe, in the shadow, a reflector of the light cast by the all-stars. I may have crooned about seeing life through rose-colored glasses, but offstage my shades were tinted blue.

Oh, I dated. Mostly older men, eighteen-year-olds and junior college students like Billy, whose attentions I had reciprocated sporadically since meeting him at swimming lessons before I entered junior high. Our romance would end rather traumatically, however, as detailed in entries in my 1954 diary. My writing shows an emerging Francophile with a need for more grammar lessons and an affinity for the exclamation "gee."

Dear Diary,
…Got my grades today for the semester and was pretty proud of them. An A in French and the rest B's.

Tonight I went to Billy's graduation with his family. It was really nice.

Gee, it certainly would be nice if I could get some sort of acclaim when I graduate.

Dear Diary,
…Went out with Billy tonite. We saw "The Long, Long Trailer" with Lucille Ball.

The most awful and yet not so awful thing happened at Bob's. Sam from geometry parked right next to us on my side and he was acting as if he liked me. Here I go again getting my hopes up. Gee, I was really embarrassed.

Dear Diary,
…Went to the show and to Bob's avec Guillaume ce soir.

Je n'amuse pas (sic—need work on the reflexive verbs) *The battery went out in Bob's and we had to be pushed out—gee was that embarrassing! I think that'll be the last time that I'll be going out with him— I hope.*

The dreaded Patin lamppost

It was. Billy was history. Greg took his place. He's the one who put a paper bag over the too bright lamppost in the front of the house in order to romanticize our curbside vehicular goodbyes. Knowing that my strict father accompanied by his bottle of Jim Beam were waiting for me in the kitchen doused any passion I might have brought to our farewell activity. And when Greg failed in his attempt to round the bases during a rendezvous in Stough Park, he decided I was not worth the effort. Looking back, I wonder if HE was worth the effort if that's all he wanted.

Dear Diary,
...Well, I guess it's over between Greg and I (sic—need work on English objective pronouns).

I'm awfully sorry about what I did last nite. I certainly hope I profit by my mistake. I guess he just took me up there to see what I am like.

Oh well, there are plenty of other fish in the sea. I'm just disgusted with myself though.

The lovely Mary Frances Reynolds

I judged my adolescent self in a harsh light. Not just against the glow of the Burroughs' elite, but also against the luminescence emanating from the teen stars on the other side of the Hollywood Sign. I saw myself in their shadow. Who could match the dewy desirability of my childhood classmate Natalie Wood or the perennial perkiness of our hometown girl, Mary Frances Reynolds? Debbie, as she would come to be headlined, entered a beauty contest because she wanted to win one of the prizes, a blouse. When she became Miss Burbank of 1948, she won the blouse and a movie contract with Warner Bros. and for a time went to Burroughs High because it was near the studio. Ah that fame would anoint me so effortlessly!

Car hop and starlet

Perhaps if I had continued with drama classes at Burroughs, I, too, could have landed a movie contract. I, too, could see my photo posing with Burbank dignitaries in formal gowns. I, too, could pose on my very own Thunderbird at Bob's. I, too, could sing and dance and emote on the silver screen. Oh, I dabbled a bit with showbiz, setting my sights on the act of becoming a star rather than the art of acting. But after failing to land a lead in the first play I tried out for, my ambition faded. A job as set builder did provide a rather dramatic role, however. I had been using a hammer's claw to remove a brad from a backdrop when a clumsy slip gashed my non-tool-holding hand. I worked the accident for all it was worth, dripping blood and tears and gasping in pain I didn't feel all the way to the nurse's office, and on to the doctor for a disappointing butterfly bandage in lieu of stitches. That was when I gave up my quest for stardom for good with only a scar on my middle finger to remind me of what might have been.

Pre-prom portrait with poodle

My senior year afforded other opportunities to satisfy my dramatic urges. First there was the Senior Prom, the Cinderella event I had been imagining in elaborate detail, along with my wedding, for years. Most crucial was that my formal be a gown worthy of the importance of this glamorous gala. I didn't want one of those tulle confections that looked as if they were repurposed from *Swan Lake*. The couture creation Mama and I designed and she sewed would be unique. I chose layers of sea foam green and white embroidered organdy. The ensemble even included an optional sea foam green organdy duster. For me it was a dream dress fit for a queen.

White faced and gowned, not quite ready for my close-up

Unfortunately, the queen I resembled was the white-faced Elizabeth I. The cause of my startling appearance was a case of hives brought on by the stress of graduation tests and activities. Mama's attempt to cover the offending red welts with makeup resulted in my unusual look in the photo Daddy took of me in my gown. I am posed in a cloud of organdy perched on the armchair featuring upholstery of Revolutionary War scenes. It was a favorite photo op location as seen in my pre-prom candid.

With the addition of an orchid corsage on my mottled wrist, I was ready to set off for the evening's festivities. Daddy promised he would turn off the blaring light post if I would come home before 1:00 AM. To the best of my recollection, the venue was the tropical faux palm paradise of the Ambassador Hotel's Cocoanut Grove nightclub. It was so romantically spectacular it could have been a movie set—and it actually often was.

The dress and the date

The big night—just not at the Cocoanut Grove

That is until I found my Senior scrapbook, sent to me along with boxes of family memorabilia by the current residents of 540 South Parish, who found them in an attic I didn't know we had. It was there I found the unimposing little program from the Hawaiian-themed affair (and every detail from graduation week) and learned my prom was held in my birthplace, Glendale, at the Civic Auditorium.

After an initial frisson of fear at being the laughing stock of my peers or in danger of passing on an infectious disease, I decided to tell the truth about my condition rather the more exotic excuses I had been inventing. I actually managed a good time despite maddening itching and twin pains from my never before worn dyed-to-match sea foam green heels and the awkward dance position necessitated by my date's height.

A night in Paris

Much more memorable was the no date/no dance Senior Graduation Party called "The Farewell Cruise" that took place the following week at the Moulin Rouge dinner theater in Hollywood, "Showplace of the World." I gloried in the French theme and the show called "Paris Toujours!"

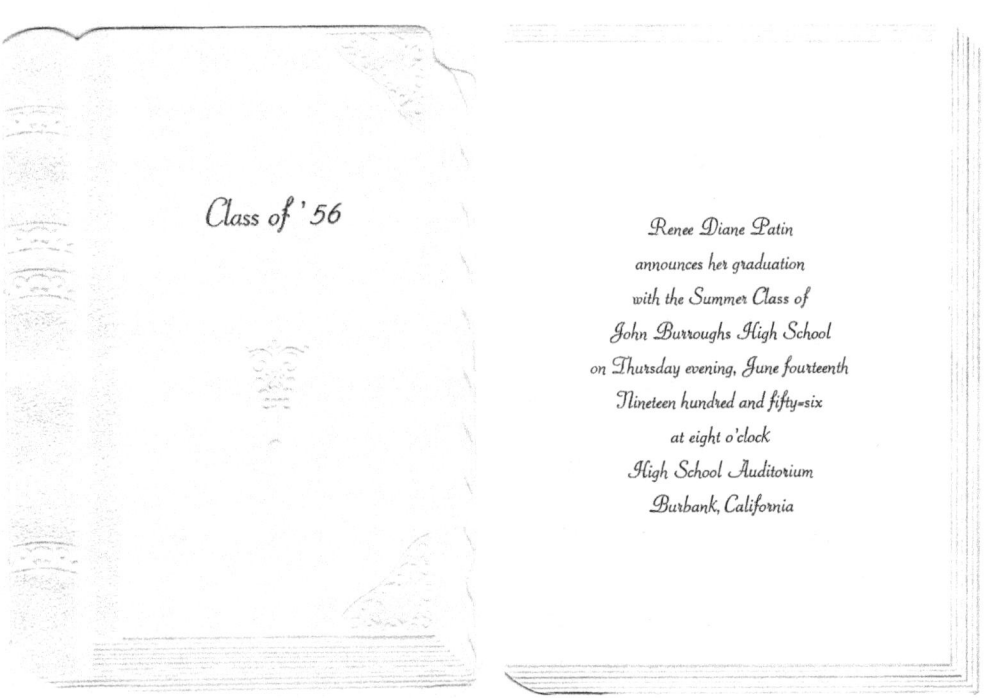

Pomp and Circumstance

The whirlwind of senior activities culminated in my performance as valedictorian, the anxiety over which had been a prime contributor to my hives. I scanned the audience for my parents but was only able to spot Mama's hat that bore a remarkable resemblance to my mortarboard.

I waited for the choir to finish a song based on the poem "Creation." The piece was ironic because it was written by James Weldon Johnson who was known for writing about his African American culture and was active in the NAACP. My audience contained no black students or families or faculty.

Patin Pride

At the rousing end of the choir's performance, it was time for mine. I stepped out on stage and up to the podium, no longer cowed by the microphone as I was in elementary school. After a long dramatic pause, I intoned in my most stentorian tones, the first lines of Mr. Johnson's poem they had sung:

> *And God stepped out on space,*
> *And he looked around and said,*
> *I'm lonely –*
> *I'll make me a world.*

Then I added, paraphrasing Browning: And in this world "if you get simple beauty and naught else, you get the best thing God creates."

The speech extolled the virtues of beauty, a lofty and rather broad subject that I doubt had any lasting effect on the future of my fellow graduates. But, as with my prom attire, it came in very handy for college repurposing—as a term paper.

Clinging to our mock diplomas, my classmates and I excitedly exited the Burroughs auditorium for the last time, no longer constrained by the step-pause-step of our "Pomp and Circumstance" procession. I searched the family-filled lobby for my mother's hat and was overjoyed to find her along with my beaming, congratulatory father. He had arrived late from his studio in Hollywood but hadn't missed my oratory debut. My gratitude, joy and pride helped me forget his lateness entirely.

My accomplishment was celebrated at a dinner at The Smoke House, the lodge-like eatery established in 1946. It is a special occasion place—dark, leathery, clubby—where I loved the garlic bread and the real snow that decorated the entrance at Christmas time. It was the perfect spot to revel in the ending of high school and share my dreams of college to come.

Part II Becoming

15
A is for Academia

Problem? Call a grad

And so there we have Potsy's BEGINNING in the shadow of the Sign, culminating as a seventeen-year-old with a high school diploma. We now move a few steps away from the shadow to a discussion of Renée's path toward another milestone—BECOMING twenty-one. Many of the events and influences that led to this auspicious event—documented with a college diploma—were spent in the halls of academia. We shall, therefore, harken back to our description of her grade school days and present alphabetically the factors that prepared Miss Patin to enter—ready or not—the world of BEING a grown-up.

Daddy made it to my high school graduation, but he didn't make it to his. He had to leave Poly High before his senior year, so he could use his art to supplement the Patin family income. Ironically he used that art to extol the importance of the high school diploma. In one cartoon he illustrated how a Poly High grad can help unburden the world and all its problems. Now 30 years and countless cartoons later, he was a successful animated film producer whose income would put me through five and a half years of university.

The college dream

I had fantasized about going to college. Although Mama and Daddy never had that opportunity, I did have my Aunt Gerry as a model coed during her brief UCLA scooter-commuting days. When I was eleven, Mama and I took the bus to The Loma in downtown Burbank to see the movie *Mr. Belvedere Goes to College.* Longingly ever after, I imagined myself as a college coed cavorting adorably around campus with my raccoon-coated and beanie-topped classmates.

Seven years later, Daddy packed our Studebaker with my freshman finery, and we drove the 100 miles to my first home beyond the Hollywood Sign. I was to join the Class of 1960 of UCSBC. The school that would become my alma mater actually began in 1891 as the Anna Blake School. It was taken over by the state in 1909 and became the Santa Barbara State Normal School of the Manual Arts and Home Economics, which then became Santa Barbara State College in 1921. In 1944, the college became a part of the University of California—UCSBC. Then, while I was a student in 1958 the school became the official University of California campus it is today—UCSB.

My university matriculation was less traumatic than my kindergarten enrollment when I threw a tantrum because my mother didn't physically roll me in. Now my slight pangs of disorientation were drowned out by the strong beat of anticipation for all that awaited me in my new independent, almost grown-up life.

The prestigious Princeton Review in its annual rankings of U.S. colleges and universities often lists UCSB, as it is now called, among the Top Ten. Unfortunately, this is their list of party schools. Some, like the chancellor, say that the Princeton party ranking actually reflects the overall happiness factor among the students.

It's not that Santa Barbara isn't a great school academically. It is. You can be happy and scholarly too. I was, and years later feel my undergraduate education was mighty fine indeed. Some of our teachers were really famous. Look at Aldous Huxley, a certifiable academic, the author and lifestyle pioneer who wrote *Brave New World.*

Aldous addresses alumni to be

Huxley's yearbook photo showing his weak eyes closed against the California sun and hair wisping in the sea breeze is a snapshot of academic Santa Barbara in the late fifties and sixties. It was pure intellectual illumination laced with countercultural seeds blowing in the wind.

Students who imbibed in something other than NoDoz to chemically balance their educational endeavors found a role model in Huxley who wrote about his hallucinogenic trips in *The Doors of Perception*. Others of us—with varying levels of success and happiness—pursued academic accomplishments and party pleasures with more legal performance enhancers. I didn't know then that while my father was working for Walt Disney, Aldous Huxley was too. He tried and failed to write a script for an *Alice in Wonderland* movie. Perhaps if I had, I might have chatted with our distinguished visiting professor about his perception of Alice's wonder trips. More about Mr. Huxley later.

There have been many more distinguished professors, several of them Nobel Prize winners. Long lists of accomplished alumni in all areas can be found online. We can even boast of show biz folks. Oscar-winning actor Michael Douglas graduated from UCSB, and Gwyneth Paltrow was a student. The list of distinguished alumni even includes a world-famous artist whose romantic company I was to share during my university days.

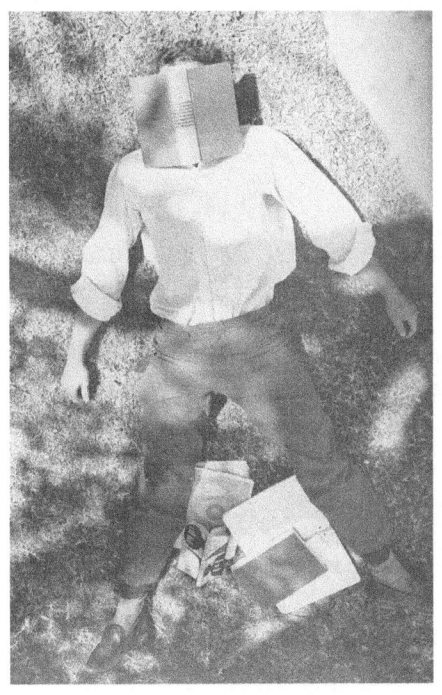

Study break

Although my name does not appear on any of these lists, stories from my four years of college may be of some interest, if not for biographical enlightenment, then perhaps for cultural/historical entertainment. In the unlikely possibility that a biopic is produced about my college career, it may lack the cinematic hijinks and drama enacted by Clifton Webb and Shirley Temple, but I would not have written my script any differently. Looking back is like viewing a movie of youthful Renée speeding from place to place, experience to experience, all the while learning the lessons that will transform her from teen to twenty-one-year-old.

16
B is for Beach

Between classes

What could be more quintessentially Southern California than going to school by the sea? Here's what was great about a beachfront education:

1. Crashing waves were a siren song to escape the stress of studying. As a rather intense eighteen-year-old, I could calm my monkey mind looking out from my dorm at the kaleidoscope sea: the shiny carpet of sapphires in a calm ocean, the translucent shades of jade and turquoise when the sun shone through breaking waves or the grey green drama of its turmoil and sudden changeability—like my moods.

2. You could surf between classes.

3. Surfer boys were nice to look at as they carried their boards seaward to "hang ten" riding a "gnarly" wave sandward.

4. You could celebrate your final final exam, as I did each semester, by changing into jeans and running down to the beach for a tumble in the sand like a kid making snow angels.

5. If, like me, you had a boyfriend who made you laugh so hard you wet your pants, and you happened to be climbing down the bluff to a beach party, you could cover up the contretemps by just continuing into the water as if that's exactly what you had in mind, though you were dressed in pedal pushers, sweatshirt and tennies.

Here's what was not so great about going to school on a beach at UCSB:

1. Too much heeding the siren song to contemplate the sea or indulge in between class-surfing could lead to grade point average wipeouts.

2. Santa Barbara beaches confusingly face south, so we didn't look out to sea for a romantic sunset on the western horizon.

3. The oil that is being pumped on all those faux islands offshore is part of the Santa Barbara Channel oil seep. Gooey black feet combined with the fragrance of deceased marine fauna and rotting sea flora were incompatible with amorous ambles on the sand.

4. The beach setting was perfect for collegiate camaraderie. Unfortunately, UCSB might end up on the wrong Princeton Review list, and one could gain an undeserved reputation as a party girl.

5. Beware of invitations to watch the submarine races.

The Patins pose on the Santa Barbara shore

When my sea-loving father sent his only progeny off to be educated by the sea, he was well acquainted with the location. According to his album pictures, he romped with his sister Vinnie, her suited boyfriend and, I think, their bundled-up mother on the beach in Santa Barbara in the twenties. In one photo where he wears a tie on the beach, he even gave homage to the town's Spanish heritage by using the word *tambien* for "also."

Scenes from the movie: *Beach Blanket Baby*

If there is a gene for beach-loving, I got mine from my father who never missed a chance to dip his toes in sand and sea, whether it be Santa Monica or Santa Barbara. I doubt if said gene is site specific, but a seafront location was a big factor in my choice of universities. I have loved the sea since my first visit to Venice Beach when Daddy made a movie of Mama and me frolicking on the sand. He etched the title of the episode in the sand, embellishing it with seaweed.

First favorites

In my baby book, under "First Outings," my mother wrote: "Always wants to hear the story about a little girl (named Renée Patin) who went to the beach. Playing at the beach being her favorite pastime."

Thirty years after my father and his entourage explored the Santa Barbara coastline, I made Santa Barbara my academic home. I savored the sea in the Patin tradition, though dressed a bit more casually. The going sometimes was tarfully sticky, and the waves were often rough, but I still think I was a mighty lucky kid.

17
C is for Campus

The UCSB campus location then and now

It's been more than sixty years since I left Burbank to begin my climb up the tower of academia. My residence was a brand-new women's dormitory on the two-year-old campus of the University of California at Santa Barbara College. If you look at the photo of UCSB today, you can see my dorm in the far upper left corner, across the road from the wave swept shore.

My classes were some of the first held on the former Marine Corps Air Base in Goleta, twelve miles from Santa Barbara. The base is pictured above during the war in 1944. You can see the same point of shore and the neat rows of barracks that would become the University's first classrooms.

1957 Santa Rosa modern

My dormitory was one of the first buildings erected just for the university. I loved my new residence with its modern Frank Lloyd Wright inspired Aztec-meets-Pacific style, so different from the columned and vined East Coast dorms I'd seen in movies. It didn't bear the name of a wealthy benefactor, but instead was called Santa Rosa Hall, named for one of the Channel Islands that we could see from the beach just steps away.

Daddy (who was greeted by shouts of the mandated warning, "Man in the hall!") and Mama moved my college-worthy possessions and me into my room. We three agreed it was a mighty spiffy space for my first home away from home. The sleek sunny room, decorated in the fifties autumn palette of beige and burnt orange, was in sharp contrast to my Burbank bedroom of sixteen years with its blue polka dot wallpaper and chalk white built-ins that still held my childish toys and treasures.

My new home made me feel that I could take on a new personality: Miss Cool Coed. I felt myself transform from a high school girl to an almost adult in my almost apartment. I pictured myself lounging on the couch upholstered in nubby faux fabric plastic with a bolster from which a bed cleverly trundled. No more would I spend late nights doing homework at the dining room table. Now I would study at my own sleek Danish modern desk with a gold-brushed aluminum gooseneck lamp—not the green glass-shaded number I'd been led to believe was standard student lighting.

Now, instead of the sight of the Disney water tower, I would have a soupçon of the sewery scent of the Goleta slough as a landmark heralding my proximity to home. And I had RAs (Resident Assistants) instead of my father to ensure my compliance with the curfew.

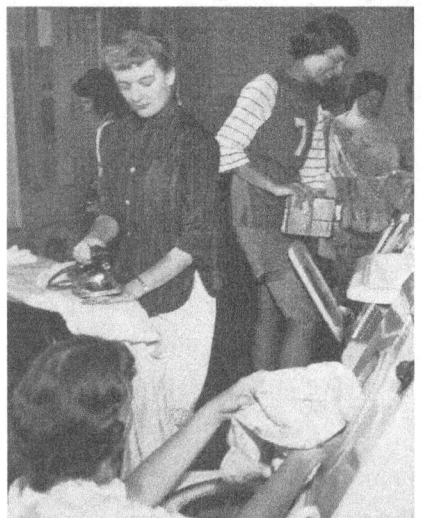 

The dorm where the same coed irons her hand...and examines her mail

I learned how to sign in and out at the streamlined desk in the lobby, to gather much anticipated mail, and share the sparkling bathrooms and laundry rooms.

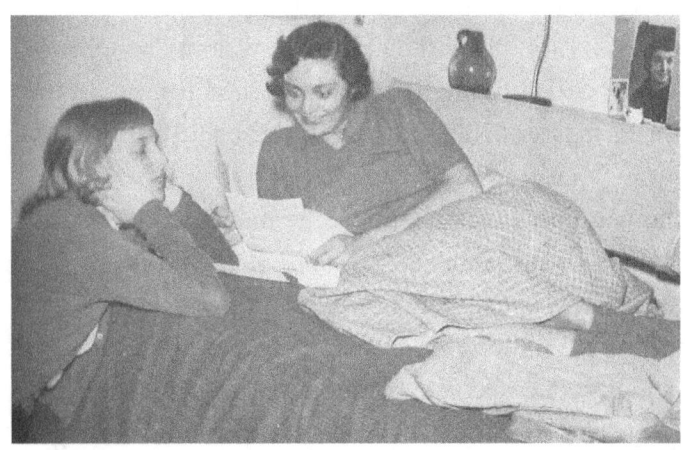

Coed confidences

Each time I succeeded in smoothly navigating one of these independent living skills I saw myself in the mirror as someone who might just begin to belong to this world. I remember long talks with my roommate Mindy, my close Burroughs friend who also followed our friend Mary to UCSB. We lay on our trundle couches comparing notes on our freshmen comfort levels. It turned out that I would seldom use the room for studying, preferring the late-night isolation of the laundry room or one of the little glass-fronted niches off the lobby designed to entertain visitors on the streamlined couches.

One of the many scenic campus dwellings, the home away from home.

Yearbook caption: "One of the many scenic campus dwellings, the home away from home"

Each breakfast and dinner Mindy and I crossed the campus to the dining hall, a rundown clapboard venue repurposed from an officers' mess, where she worked. It was located among former barracks that had to pass for housing until more dorms could be built. These were the tree-named residence halls (Toyon, Laurel, etc.) where the accommodations were less modern, but cozy.

Often shiny-skinned young men could be spotted roughhousing in a game of touch football in front of their residence, making for a very pleasant walk for us young ladies from across the campus. After the meal I would socialize with other dawdlers while Mindy cleaned up the area and removed her cafeteria lady hairnet. If we had breakfast, we would go off to classes to the recorded ten-minute warning chimes ringing out from on top of the library. After dinner we would follow the path to the library or back to Santa Rosa Hall, hoping for a not-so-chance encounter with a gentleman barracks dweller.

A few years ago I attended a Golden Gaucho[1] reunion. Over the years that have passed since I first stepped foot on the new campus, it has changed almost beyond recognition. Now I feel like an urban archeologist when I return, trying to dig up memory ticklers from my past. On my drive-through I became hopelessly lost in the maze of streets. This jumble of buildings was not the stomping grounds of my youth. I tried to get my bearings while stopped at a crosswalk, waiting for a wildebeestial stampede of students on wheels to pass by on their migration to classes.

Golden get-together

---

[1] See "G is for Gaucho" to learn about our UCSB mascot. The "golden" adjective for our reunions from the good old days implies that we are now in our golden years.

Lowering my window, I made like Proust with his Madeleine cookie and sniffed the VapoRub scent of the eucalyptus trees lining El Colegio Road. I wanted to conjure up remembrances of times past when that fragrance and a hint of jasmine provided a background to seemingly momentous encounters.

Then: El Colegio Road 1959   Now: campus on wheels

After several roundabouts of Mesa, Lagoon and Ocean Roads, I found a parking structure, and set off on foot. Alert to the swishy whir of bikes and clickety clack of skateboards that threatened to overtake me, I set off down the great mall dominated by a 61-foot campanile housing real, not recorded, bells. I was determined to find landmarks from the campus we had crisscrossed without benefit of wheels in days of yore.

My father was always proud to tell his artist friends that I went to a university designed by the world-famous architectural firm Pereira & Luckman. They created modern buildings that were far ahead of their time like the LAX theme building and CBS Television City. What he failed to mention was that there were about six of these permanent showpieces when he was putting me through college. The rest of our learning took place in decrepit wooden military buildings.

Fifties collegiates on foot pass a barracks classroom with library beyond

UCSB students of today and yesterday gather at their center

I finally managed to uncover a scattering of our buildings that stood like not-so-charming reminders of a bygone era. I paused by the old Student Union—where big men and women on campus determined our fate, and we minions enjoyed long, deep tête-à-têtes over coffee or hamburgers and Cokes. I wondered whether passersby or the student who parked a bike on the lawn had any idea of the historic significance of the squat little building of yesterday dwarfed by the high-rises today.

Yesterday's Student Union dwarfed by today's campus

Barracks: not all halls of learning are ivy-covered

At the far end of the mall, tucked in a corner, I found the barracks where as a student I used to climb the outside rickety stairs, hurry down the buckling linoleum hallway to enter the classroom where I jiggled myself into a desk/chair contraption and opened my notebook binder to record words of wisdom emanating from the front of the class.

Nearby I entered the library. Recognizing nothing, I approached a reference librarian whose white hair gave me hope she would have compassion when asked if this was the same library where I studied in the late fifties.

"It's over there," she answered pointing toward a wall.

"Farther down the mall?" I asked as if I were acquainted with the area I had just trudged.

"No," she replied consolingly. "It's on the other side of the wall. It's condemned, couldn't be retrofitted. They're tearing it down."

Behind the tarp and keep-away tape covering a chain link fence I found the hub of my academic and social pursuits. Its rubble could no more evoke remembrances of research and study dates than the crumbles of Proust's cookie.

I left the ruins of the old library, found a bench far away from the youthful hubbub, and leafed through the papers in my reunion packet. Some considerate soul who understands the selective forgetfulness of septuagenarian alums had inserted the words of an irreverent hymn to the school. Sung to the tune of Cornell's Alma Mater "Far Above Cayuga's Waters," it captures the school spirit of us pioneers who paved the way. It's called "UCSB (at G)."

Far behind Goleta's Airport
High above the sea
Stands our mighty Alma Mater
UCSB – (at G)

We are not from Westwood Village
Nor from Berkeley's Pomp
You will find us ankle deep
In Goleta's swamp

Santa Barbara at Goleta
Gad! How we love you
High above the roaring ocean
Almost in the slough

Santa Barbara at Goleta
Gad! How we love thee
Rally 'round our shabby barracks
Slosh on to victory.

18
Ð is for ΔΓ

Renée Patin, Delta Gamma

Nothing, absolutely nothing, had ever been this important. I was rushing to get into a house. This was Greek speak for going through a weeklong selection process called "rush" where a sorority or "house," would choose me as a member, thus adding a Greek letter suffix to my name and prestige to my persona.

In 1957, there were only eight sororities housed in mini-mansions scattered around downtown Santa Barbara. For me, each house had a caché, a personality and ranking based on the scuttlebutt I'd gathered about it and its members.

I'd heard that Walt's daughters, Diane and Sharon, had been Kappa Alpha Thetas. I'd enviously examined magazine photos of these girls who were a few years older than me as they accompanied their father on his magical adventures. I mean, didn't he practically build Disneyland for them? I liked the idea of calling myself their sorority sister.

The Theta House complemented by a retro roadster

The one-time Pi Phi house

Then again, my high school friend Mary was a Pi Phi. That would be fine too. Their house up on Santa Barbara's "Riviera" looked mighty inviting.

Delta Gamma was another "top" sorority under consideration. I ignored the saying that the reason they had an anchor symbol was because they "went down." I believed instead the other stereotype, that they were the wholesome, brainy, cute girls.

Together Mindy and I, who had spent a semester as roomies in the dorm, set our eyes on living in one of those prestigious houses. We endured a Panhellenic obstacle course, trying to maintain our presentability while sashaying from sorority house to sorority house. Each day we scrambled to fewer houses according the invitations we received and accepted each morning. The events became more elaborate throughout the week, sometimes requiring prim and proper white gloves, great for disguising sweaty hands. The idea was that through enjoyable socializing we would find a match. For this socially fearful "rushee," it was agony. I suffer from a lifelong syndrome that manifests whether meeting a potential gentleman caller, partying, job applying or basically being with other human beings I don't know well. It's like I am parading in a beauty contest and falling several judge points short of the crown.

For me, the sorority girls emitted an iconic aura like A-list celebrities. They were gorgeous, more mature, more sophisticated and smarter than I could ever be. Sure, there were times at each event when I sensed a modicum of success convincing these higher beings that I was just the girl they were looking for. But mostly I was aware of a sweaty upper lip and the conviction I was spouting inanities and committing all manner of unsorority-like misdemeanors. I imagined I had spots from an unidentifiable substance on my totally inappropriate ensemble, crumbs of the lovely tea cake stuck between my teeth and all the blemishes "my flesh was heir to" (as Hamlet—who never had to go through rush—moaned). In my mind the process was no less agonizing than the "slings and arrows" he suffered in his soliloquy.

Each morning I fearfully approached my cubby at the student union to learn if any sorority had decided to ignore my blatant flaws. On the morning after the final night of rushing, with the three "top" houses remaining, my box held one bid. It was from Delta Gamma. My joy was tempered by having been dropped by the Thetas and the Pi Phis and learning that Mindy had no invitations. Was it because of her difficult home life or her financial situation? All these concerns became irrelevant when the following summer she fell in love and married a young minister, leaving UCSBC behind her.

My dream of a sorority membership, if not love and marriage, or movie stardom, was now a reality. I would be presented like a white-clad debutante to parents and public at an affair called Presents (PREE-sents) at the Santa Barbara Women's Club behind the Mission.

Pledges pose prettily[1]

Greek badges of belonging

For a semester, I stayed in the dorm and wore the tiny white pledge pin over my heart—never when not wearing a skirt—and kept my grade point average above 2.5 so that I could be initiated as a full-fledged "active" member, earning the honor to move into the house and don the DG anchor pin.

---

[1] Second from left. The dress was white eyelet.

Me and my HillmanPride of ownership

The first thing I did upon becoming official was to affix ten decals to spell D-E-L-T-A G-A-M-M-A on the windshield of my Hillman Minx. I loved the sporty convertible my father gave me as a birthday present. I was proud of its sleek lines and very trendy shade of avocado green, slightly subtler than our refrigerator. The Greek letters were just what I needed to add to its caché. It wasn't until it rained, and I needed wipers, that I learned that the suggested method of affixing the decals was inside the car. For a while I had quite a creative alphabet dance adorning my windshield.

DG alumnae like Miss Burgess, with her sensible shoes and Camel chain-smoking habit, taught me how to behave in a manner befitting my new affiliation:
- Don't walk in public without shoes.
- Never walk with a cigarette or have it in your mouth without your fingers on it.
- Place each item (except your elbows) on the dining table in its proper place and handle utensils appropriately.
- Butter your bread in delicate bits daintily separated from the baked item out of which bites are never taken.

Renee Patin
Spring President

Sorority success

When rush week came around, and I was on the "in" side, I had great compassion for the hopefuls coming through our house. Judging that some were not quite up to snuff was as painful as being judged. I knew what it felt like to be dropped.

For my senior year, I was elected president of our chapter, adding yet another suffix to my name and identity. I conducted Monday meetings, and performed the century old traditions such as initiation. It was hard to maintain a presidential demeanor, however, when some of the initiates were so tearfully moved by the emotion of their induction that their mascara leaked two Halloweenish black smudges onto their white blindfolds.

Joe's today (just like yesterday)

The same jitters I felt going through rush returned fifty years later when I attended a class reunion happy hour for golden age alums. I approached Joe's, the oldest restaurant in Santa Barbara, with trepidation. Our old haunt still bears the resplendent neon sign that lights up lower State Street. At least something was older than us senior imbibers! It was with great relief that I spotted the silver curls of my fellow DG Barbara sitting in one of the original thirties wooden booths where we had both enjoyed our dating days as undergraduates.

We played the game of which former classmate was lurking behind which much-more-mature body. "Isn't that…?" "Wasn't she a Zeta?" Then we shared whatever true or not-so-true biographical data we'd gathered. It took just a certain twist of a smile, flick of a gesture or sparkle in the eye to erase the gray hair and wrinkles in order to recreate the classmate we had cavorted with in our day. Upon reuniting we identified each other by different memories. Some remembered my long ponytail. Others knew me as a rather serious French major. Then there were those who recognized me as Renée Patin, Delta Gamma president. After the initial game of placing the personality, we learned how different our life stories were from Greek dramas and dreams of our college years.

After compulsory mingling, Barbara and I traded tales from the Delta Gamma house. We talked about how very different sorority life is today and how so much that seemed fine then would be politically incorrect fifty years later. Take for example a song we loved to sing about ourselves that rhymes Delta Gamma with our DG mascot doll Hannah who "has a figure like a baby grand piana." The song is now part of history. We agreed that though things have changed, and our anchors are a bit tarnished, our golden years shine brighter because of the memories and lessons from those days of yore.

19
E is for Entertainment

In the spotlight—real and imagined

For a very long time, I believed I was destined to entertain the world. I longed to play before rapt audiences, perhaps reprising my starring role as a grocery store manager as described in Chapter 8. I pictured myself in elaborate costumes, curtain calling to the roar of the crowd beyond the footlights. Or I would become a movie star whose Oscar-winning performance earned a slinky walk down the red carpet in the glare of those klieg lights I saw beckoning from the other side of the Sign.

DG Theme Night, front, second from left, letting my waist-length hair down

My role as a university French major was at odds with my childhood self-image as the world's most famous silver screen star. However, because I had enough of my father's entertainment gene, and little enough of my mother's shyness, I still loved the spotlight. The kid who did the hula to celebrate war's end, imitated Woody Woodpecker and sang from a piano top still had a place in my personality.

Delta Gamma provided the ideal stage for my thespian pursuits. During rush week, I wrote and performed skits for the parties where we entertained to entice girls to join our ranks. Our most special night was Theme Night where we honored our anchor symbol with a Hawaiian motif. We gathered prickly palm fronds from under the trees in our front yard to create an island paradise. We glamorized ourselves in sarongs and leis, accoutrements not difficult to find in the fifties when tiki-torch-lighted luau pool parties were the rage.

And now a word from our sponsor

Most of the girls had legitimate talents that they lent to the evening's entertainment. I didn't have such talents. But, as a transplant from La La Land, I had learned that if you can't be it, act it—comically, if possible. I provided the commercials, perhaps a nod to my father's job producing animated television advertising. I remember one I performed for an indigestion remedy where I demonstrated my talent of alliteration by wailing, "Peter *Pain* punctured my pancreas!"

DG also allowed me to hone my (albeit offtune) musical comedy skills at Barbary Coast, the annual carnival in which we showcased our acts to audiences rendered either more or less appreciative by sneaked sips of beer.

Crowned in a royal version of *Carmen*

In our stuffily intimate little DG tent, I starred as the ever-lamenting queen in an opera we composed very loosely to the music, if not the libretto, of Bizet's *Carmen*. In our version of the "Toreador's Song," I redundantly bemoaned the departure of my king, played by tall Sally Arnold.

> *You are leaving*
> *And I'm left grieving*
> *Because you're leaving,*
> *I'm left grieving*

I was backed by a cast of costumed courtiers who merrily announced the chorus.

> *Now he's away and we can play*

This is followed by the interminable final scene where I die of unknown causes only to revive repeatedly.

> *Look what you've done*
> *You have spoiled all my fun.*
> *I think I'm going to die*
> *No! I'll cryyye!*

The Moulin Rouge in Goleta and Paris

On the occasion of another year's Barbary Coast event, our act was inspired by the 1952 movie *Moulin Rouge* starring Jose Ferrer. In our anything-goes-if-it-is-French version, I, *bien entendu*, emoted my oft-reprised Burroughs High rendition of "La Vie en Rose" to a chorus of can-can girls.

The yearbook photo of our evening's offering asks, "Is it true what they say about French women?" At this point in my French cultural education, I had no idea what was said about *les dames françaises.* But I was well acquainted with the Hollywood Moulin Rouge after our high school graduation party there, and I was always ready to emote my *chanson français.*

French women—*ooh la la!*

My talents came to the attention of none other than the famed arts critic Henry J. Seldis.[1] Here's what Mr. Seldis's photo caption writer wrote about *me*...and our act:

Presenting a Franco-Goletan version of the Gay Nineties, the Delta Gammas entertain Barbara (sic) *Coast crowds in their Moulin Rouge pavilion.*

Shown here are can-can dancer, Mary Lou Spitsnaugle, honky tonk pianist, Dorcas Vanian and soubrette Renee Patin. There it was, my name in print. Could my name in lights on the other side of the Sign be far away?

Soubrette Patin piano-posing
in print

---

[1] He was writing for the *Santa Barbara News Press* before his renown as the *Los Angeles Times* art critic and author.

Moulin moments

Today as I write in my little office, the walls are covered with my mother's paintings. One of her palettes hangs over my shoulder, and on it hangs a child's watercolor palette I bought at a flea market in Provence. The paint set served as a prop for a movie moment when I became an artist like my parents. The setting was a friend's Oscar costume party in 2001, the year *Moulin Rouge*[2] was nominated for an Academy Award. Many of the ladies, like my "date" Gretchen—whom you met earlier—were can-can girls. But not I. No, with my kiddy palette hanging from a brush stuck in my pocket, I played the rôle of the painter who brought fame to the Moulin Rouge, Henri de Toulouse-Lautrec himself! I won the grand prize, not an Oscar, but a dinner at Maxim's in Paris–transportation and lodging not included.

Palette on palette

---

[2] The one with Nicole Kidman, not the great one with José Ferrer on whom I modeled myself.

20
F is for Fashion

Although my entertainer persona glowed with self-confidence, my fashion savvy was not so bright. As a student who considered non-conformity the number one fashion faux pas, I searched for wisdom essential to dress for collegiate social success. Here for your enlightenment and amusement is my version of a *Fifties Fashion Handbook* whose advice I would have devoured religiously and followed assiduously.

A HANDBOOK FOR THE WELL-ATTIRED FIFTIES COLLEGIATE

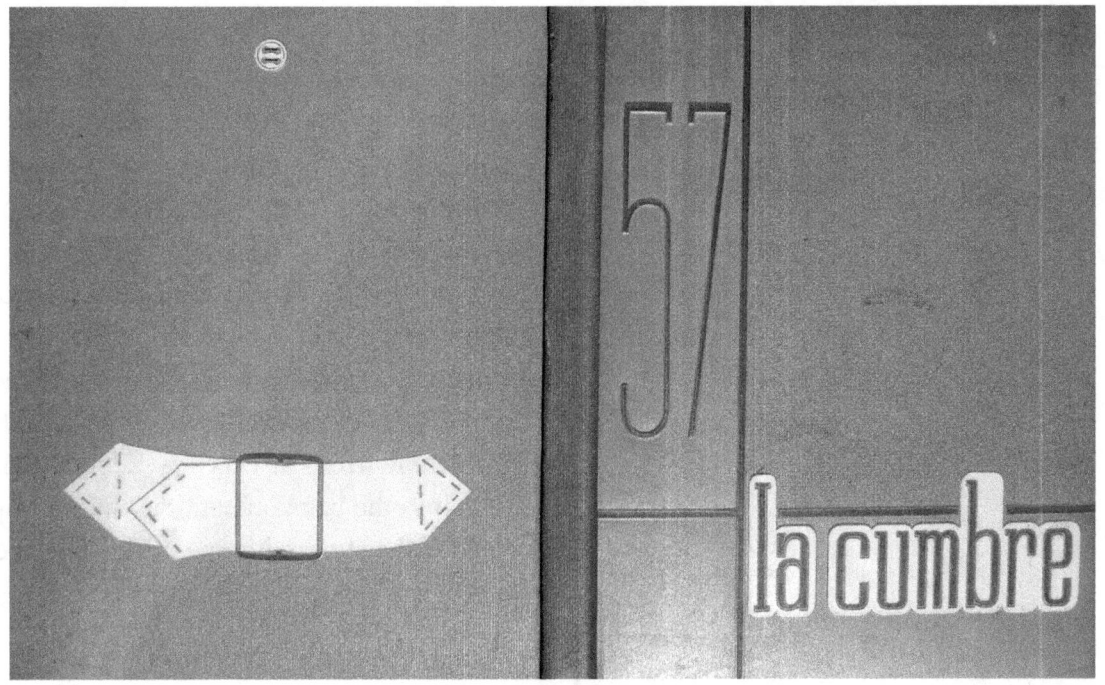

Yearbook fashion statement

QUESTION: What is symbolized by the images on the back cover of this UCSB yearbook?

ANSWER: Ivy League Fashion

The back cover of this fifties yearbook portrays a trend so important that it rates pride of place. The drawings are of two elements that characterize a collegiate look started 3,000 miles away at a select number of East Coast vine-covered schools.

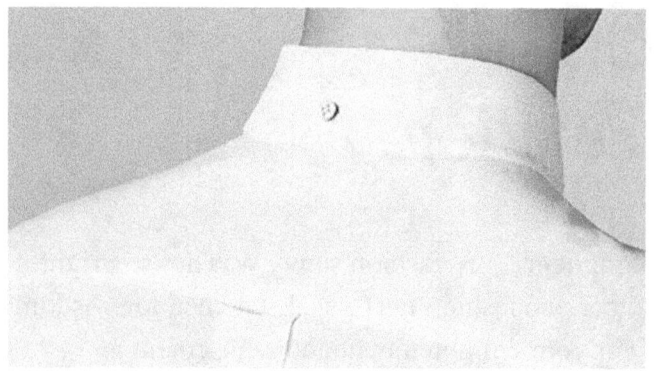

The back button

The upper image on the yearbook back cover is of the shirt collar back button. This accoutrement is designed to keep a tie perfectly in place and not, as one might imagine, to prevent nasty collar curling mishaps. It now serves as a signal to those who view the wearer from behind that he or she is à la mode.

The button-down collar is so all-pervasive that the era's number one cutting edge comedian entitled his cerebral album *The Button-Down Mind of Bob Newhart.* You will also note in the photograph above the subtle signature "locker loop" at the top of the box pleated panel that gracefully finishes the look.

The back belt

The lower image on the yearbook cover is of another no less vital fashion element, the back belt and buckle. This vestigial item, not to be confused with the utilitarian pants-upholding belt, is found on gentlemen's rear trouser quarters. It also appears on women's skirts and even embellishes caps and other accessories as a sign that the buckle bearer is in the know. Some have said that a buckle left undone is a sign of one's availability. It is also said that the joke in the fifties at very Ivy League Yale was "a belt in the back" meant having a drink in the back of the store with one of the salesmen at J. Press, the famous on-campus clothing store.

Wear stripes!

Stripes are an Ivy League apparel must. With the Four Freshman to serve as models, the true Ivy Leaguer knows that the stripe is a de rigueur pattern for campus wear. Note the joy and sex appeal of the well-buttoned and striped UCSB attendees. The author, a college sophomore in the photo to the left, demonstrates the power of striping.

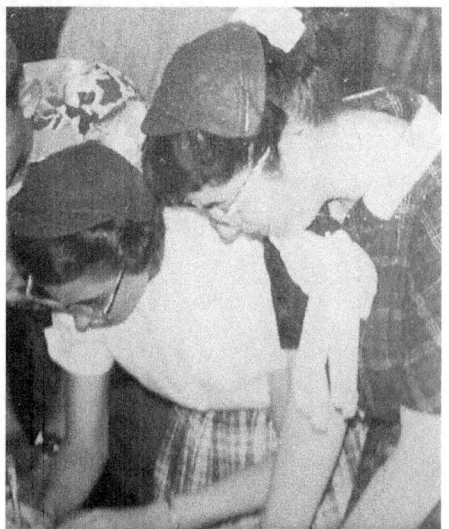

Mad for plaid!

Another must-have pattern inspired by clean-cut guy group quartets is plaid. The pattern adorns a broad range of garments from trousers and Bermuda shorts[1] to pleated skirts. As you observe students on campus, you will note that many of the most successful and fun-filled students are clad in plaid. Even unfashionably beanied freshman sport plaid.

---

[1] Although it seems unnecessary to mention it in a discussion of proper campus attire, a word to the wise is in order. Shorts are not worn on campus, Ivy League or not. Young women on campus wear skirts with hems below the knee, never pants of any league.

Fashionable footwear

Both male and female students enjoy the comfort and attractiveness of a nice pair of oxfords, named for the Ivy League-like university in England. A popular style is the saddle oxford, a white leather shoe with a contrasting quasi-equestrian embellishment in the shoelace area. Also fashionable are the fuzzy-surfaced white buckskin oxfords called "bucks." A word of caution here. The buck bag, used to slap white chalk onto the shoe for cleaning purposes, tends to whiten whatever is within the cloud created by the shoe-cleaning chore.

You may be asked to join a classmate in his or her (hopefully small and foreign) automobile and will want to dress appropriately. Passé is the raccoon coat that Mr. Belvedere wore in the movie version of college couture. The Ivy League garment of choice is the car coat,[2] preferably in camel-colored wool or polished cotton. The mid-thigh length jacket is fastened with nautical accents consisting of rope and peg toggles—again, not necessary for function, but critical for form. Headgear might include a jaunty newsboy cap—in plaid or wide wale camel corduroy with an on-trend back button or buckle appendage.

Automotive attire

---

[2] Also called a duffle coat based on its naval roots. The coats were supplied to the British Royal Navy in the late 1800s. Authentic versions need horn or wood toggles, originally designed to be attached to rope or leather loops to protect against cold weather at sea. So, it is also called a toggle coat. The attached hood could even be worn over a naval cap.

Formal frock evolution from freshman to senior ballroom appearances

Gentlemen will find a suit or coat and tie appropriate for both formal and semi-formal wear. A nice white dinner jacket and black tie is always acceptable for more formal fashion occasions particularly at the Rockwood Women's Club or The Biltmore's Coral Casino Beach and Cabana Club.

Women have a variety of fetching gowns from which to choose. Here you will note a progression of acceptable styles displaying an increased degree of sophistication. In the photos above, the author[3] demonstrates two fashion principles: 1) A gentleman is equally admirable in suit or dinner jacket, but handsomeness and boutonnière help. 2) A woman can wear the same formal twice, even one repurposed from her mother-made high school prom gown. (Though she runs the risk of other frothy frocks in white eyelet on the same dance floor.)

The Merry Widow and how she got that figure

A last word to the ladies: formal wear may be enhanced by a merry widow foundation garment named for the fashionable figures flaunted in a 1905 operetta of that name.

This important—even functional—foundation garment is designed to give you the wasp waist and maximum cleavage of Belle Époque damsels who had to endure the agony of boned, cinched, vice-like corsets to produce their hourglass silhouettes.

---

[3] The author would like to caution young ladies not to attempt, as she often did, a last-minute coiffure clipping of the bangs before embarking on a formal evening.

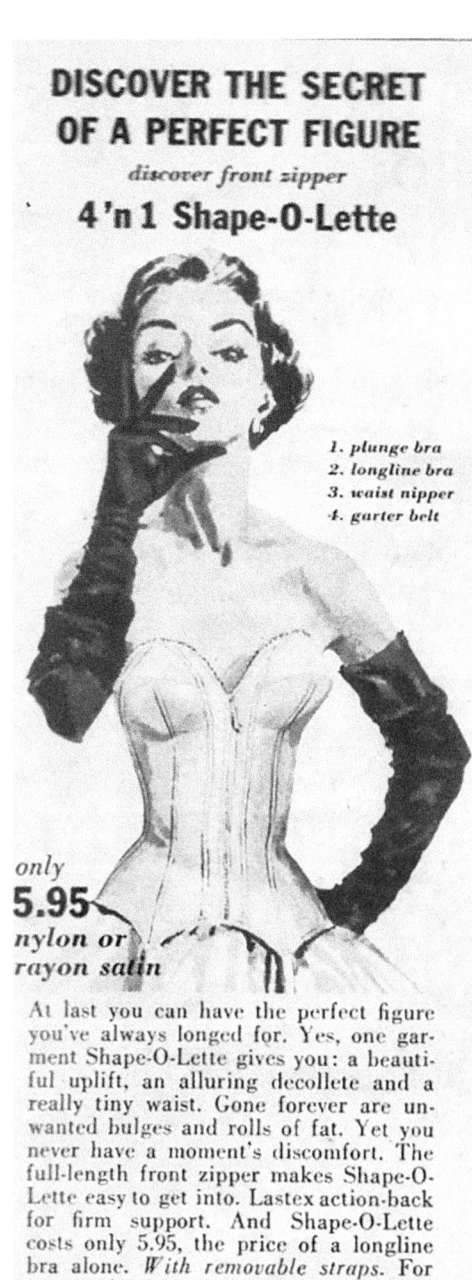

Discover the secret

Your modern waist-length unmentionable is designed for the sleeker fashion of the fifties and allows you to "discover the perfect figure you have always longed for." Yes, one garment gives you "a beautiful uplift, an alluring décolleté and a really tiny waist."

If you should perchance experience just a little agony under that scratchy formal frock, remember your merry widow not only gives you the confidence of movie star glamour, it also doubles as a garter belt to hold up those essential nylon stockings.

So, be merry, be proper, and wear Ivy League. You too can live your dream as a successful university man or woman— at the height of fashion.

21
G is for Gaucho

When I enrolled at UCSBC, I added another appellation to my ever-growing repertoire: Gaucho. I was already well schooled in mascots named for heroes of the range. At Burroughs High, we were the Indians. Then I became a Vaquero, Spanish for cowboy, at Glendale Junior College where I spent a semester waiting for housing in the UCSB campus dorms. So, to me, a South American pampas rider didn't seem that strange a standard bearer for my new university.

Looking back, I realize I had no idea what a gaucho looked like. But my father was aware of the horsey heroes of the Andes. He had seen Mickey Mouse star as one in 1928's *The Gallopin' Gaucho*.

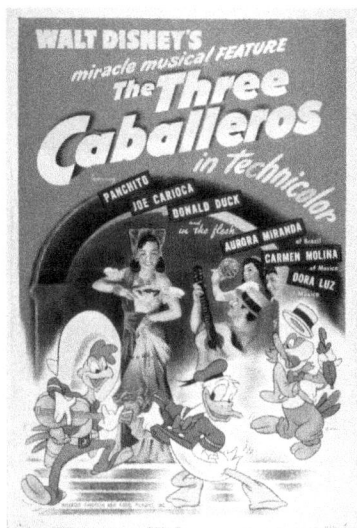 

Disney goes Latin

My father also knew that his former boss had been in South America from a letter he received when he asked for his job back after being laid off following the strike. On *Fantasia* letterhead stationery, Walt's right-hand man in the Animation Department said that:

Walt returned from South America yesterday and, of course, we are all very happy to see him. He looks good and had quite an experience down there. Just what the program regarding South American shorts will be, none of us know at this time.

Later Daddy was hired back, and maybe he worked on *The Three Caballeros* with the little "gaucho boy" or *Saludos Amigos* that featured *El Gaucho Goofy*.

Real gauchos and gaucho-inspired fashion

Yes, Walt Disney was inspired by gauchos. And so was fashion. Maybe you remember the gaucho-inspired couture, like those culottes in the sixties and the jaunty flat cowboy hat?

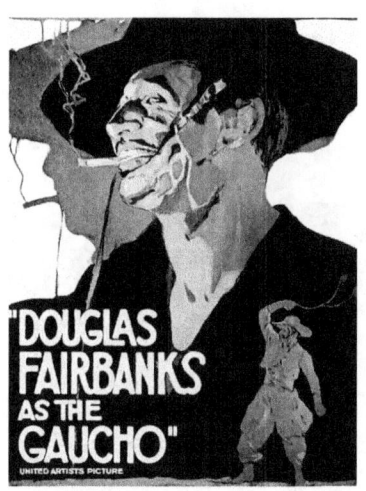 

Douglas Fairbanks in mascot-inspiring twenties roles

It's hard to imagine a rough and tumble football coach being so inspired by the gaucho mystique that he would choose one as the mascot of his mighty team, but that is what happened. It all began in 1936 when Coach Theodore "Spud" Harder[1] decided his highly successful Santa Barbara College football team, the Roadrunners, needed a stronger mascot than a spindly-legged bird. According to his son and namesake (Ted, not Spud) who was my classmate, Spud had seen a movie called *The Gaucho* and was really impressed by the swashbuckling role played by Douglas Fairbanks. He felt the macho gaucho was a perfect representative for the athletic efforts of the school, so he polled the student body and they voted to make the name change. As is the way of creative college students, the gaucho likeness morphed, combining Mr. Fairbanks's gaucho role with that of Zorro, until today we have the mighty Olé, the masked hero of the UCSB Gauchos.

---

[1] UCSB's Harder Stadium is named for Coach Harder.

Yes, this is the mighty, masked mascot of the University of California at Santa Barbara. Today UCSB fans cheer on the mustachioed Olé, imploring him for a Gaucho victory—or perhaps a selfie.

Looking back on my student days, I don't remember thinking of Fairbanksian swashbucklers when I heard cries of "Go Gauchos!" All around me the word "gaucho" was attached to everything from festivals to food. Would a hungry traveler stopping in Goleta at a favorite campus snack stand wonder if the beef in the El Gaucho Burger was specially lassoed by South American cowboys?

Olé

Try the El Gaucho Burger!

A masked gaucho's salute at a fifties homecoming

I must confess to a certain lack of school boosterism. Oh, I went to a few games when I was invited or when a current boyfriend was on a team. And I even cheered when I knew what was happening. But I don't recall a costumed gaucho frolicking about La Playa Stadium, our temporary field at Santa Barbara City College, across from the harbor. A gaucho is a hard guy to create in crepe paper as seen in this masked, saluting gaucho in our homecoming parade.

I did wonder why we couldn't have a more nobly strong and heroic mascot. Our mother school at Berkeley were Bears, and our sister school UCLA appropriately chose the mighty Bruins. Couldn't we have been Grizzlies instead of Gauchos? Even with his mask, Olé, our flat-hatted hero, is about as menacing as the Hamburglar or Elmo, to which he bears a resemblance. At least we didn't end up with the Banana Slug—the mascot of upstart UC Santa Cruz.

UCSB boosters boast of a fine athletic department with honors in many sports, but the school is not really renowned for its athletics. There was a moment, however, when we actually drew national media attention on ESPN. It was when the custom of tossing tortillas[2] onto the basketball court and shouting "Olé!" resulted in the ejection of the coach. What would Spud say?

Now that I am a Golden Gaucho, I feel quite affectionate toward our caped crusader. As the daughter of a Disney animator, I rather fancy a symbol that is a cross between a cartoon and silver screen star. I'd love to toss out a few tortillas and sing the short but scintillating rallying cry.

Olé, Olé, Olé, Olé
Gauchos, Gauchos!

---

[2] A safer replacement for the dangerous Argentine bolas or balls that students would fling on a string.

At a Golden Gaucho reunion brunch, I eavesdropped on a conversation at a nearby table where two of the movers and shakers from my era were meeting with a business-attired woman who was either a reporter or selling them something. All I could understand was the word "statue." I asked Barbara when she arrived if she knew what it was all about. She told me there is a committee dedicated to erecting a Gaucho statue on campus where proud families of students and alums can pose for pictures—sort of like the bronze Joe Bruin statue at UCLA and triumphant Tommy Trojan at USC.

The problem is that nobody could agree on how to portray Olé as attractive enough so that folks would want to pose with him. But we Golden Gauchos are a pretty creative lot. I was sure that one day there would be an almighty Spud-worthy monument beckoning all posers to pay homage to the glory of the great galloping Gauchos of UCSB!

The Gaucho as seen by an Argentinian sculptor

Not too long after that overheard conversation, I learned that UCSB Gauchos now have an official Gaucho statue created by Argentinian sculptor Teresa Farga de Corominas who named her work *Gaucho Argentino*. The bronze likeness of a handsome, proud man of the pampas graces the plaza at the Mosher Alumni house and is one of the most popular photo op spots on campus. Olé!

22
H is for Hollywood Calling

Where Daddy worked

In the process of perfecting the persona I presented to my college classmates, I was aware that my Hollywood connection added a certain sparkle (or cachet). Though I knew that I lived in the shadow of the wrong side of the Sign, I could still tell stories about forays over the hill to Tinseltown. And, then of course there was always the fact that I was the daughter of a producer—albeit of animated commercials—whose studio was in that fabled town.

Hollywood—that city of stars over the hill from Burbank—was a big influence on my formative years. As I pursued my academic career, I got to know this fabled film factory on a more intimate basis, even working there on college breaks.

When Daddy set up his animation studio on Sunset Boulevard, I was proud to call him a Hollywood producer. Nana's boy had come a long way from the tiny Holly Drive guest apartment in the hills near the Hollywood Sign.

The road to Ray Patin Productions began in 1947 when Walt for the second time informed my father that his services were no longer needed. Donald Duck would have to survive at the pen of another animator/story man. I learned the meaning of the word "freelance" when Daddy didn't have a regular job. He drew cartoon strips and made pitches to local businesses to hire him to make animated television commercials or "spots" for the new medium of television. His budding business was located in our house. Once my mother was confused when she saw an envelope addressed to the PROD Family among other mail sent to 540 South Parish. The mystery of why the name Patin should suffer such a mangled spelling became clear when we realized Daddy used our address when he started Ray Patin PRODuctions.

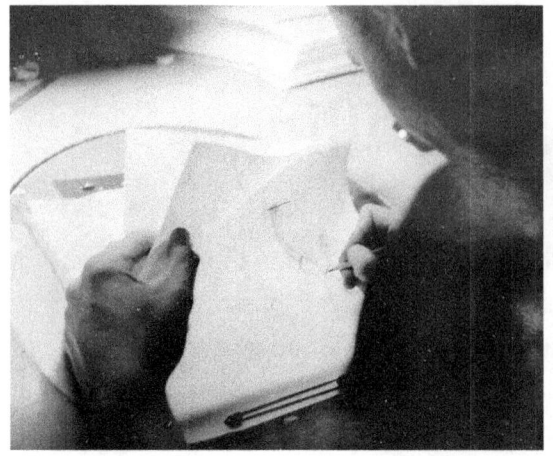 

At the drawing board and the camera stand

I watched my father at work in our den, gyrating his mouth into the attitudes of his characters, drawing and flipping cartoon characters in different stages of motion, and painstakingly inking the outlines of his drawings on the back of clear celluloid "cels." He needed 24 of them for each second of film. In an era before color TV, he filled the inked outlines with different shades of black, white and gray paint from the jars lined up in the den closet.

Milford Muddle

Out in the garage next to his tool bench and *Life* magazine collection he built an animation camera stand and photographed each cel. Then he threaded the developed film onto a Moviola machine and hand cranked it back and forth to see his drawings come alive. His first commercials featured an everyman called Milford Muddle who, through a series of Disney-worthy mishaps, learns the wisdom of getting an auto loan through Security First National Bank. Another jolly animated character gets a boat loan through Detroit Bank and Trust.

In 1951 as I was finishing junior high and contributing my angst to that of my parents, my father took out a loan of his own. It was a mortgage on our house to finance opening his first studio. A few years later he would be successful enough to buy his own boat.[1] I don't know if he needed a loan.

---

[1] See "N is for Nautical Interludes."

Want a boat? Get a loan

He set up shop on the other side of the Sign on an industrial side street, just across the far western border of downtown Los Angeles, a location he could technically call Hollywood. Behind the building, rickety wooden stairs wound up to the boulevard where he put his mailbox, so he could use Sunset Boulevard as his address. He hired a little staff of other out-of-work artists, many he had known at Disney. They worked at the animation tables Daddy had painted a thoroughly modern shade of acid green.

The producer at 6650 Sunset Boulevard

Eventually more advertisers came calling, and my father hired more animators, background artists, photo and sound technicians (all male) and inkers and painters and office staff (all female). He moved the chartreuse furnishings to 6650 Sunset, in the heart of Hollywood within view, if buildings didn't block it, of the "right" side of the Hollywood Sign.

Same tricksters, different photos = Patin payroll

Ray Patin Productions was one of many small production studios that were scattered around Hollywood. It was not a big building, and certainly not a famous landmark[2] but, through the magic of manipulation, Daddy was able to produce a photograph of his imaginary, perhaps hoped for, cast of players. He had pictures taken of himself and his employees in three different configurations, moving around and striking different poses in each. He then stitched the photos together, repeated and shrank them, and voilà—the headquarters for Ray Patin Productions became a monolith.

---

[2] Except to rock and roll fans who seek out the location of Sunset Sound where the Rolling Stones (perhaps while staying at the Holly Drive house), the Doors and more recorded.

Early TV ad producer appears on early TV

It may have been technological tomfoolery that super-sized his headquarters and staff, but it was talent and a lot of hard work that turned Ray Patin Productions, incorporated in 1955, into a super success. As more and more families watched their floor model cabinet TVs in their homes or through the windows of furniture stores, the demand for selling on the new medium grew. *City at Night,* a Los Angeles TV show, toured the studio and interviewed my father as he consulted on storyboards and explained the art of animation. The program conveyed his passion and the electric enthusiasm that ran throughout his staff.

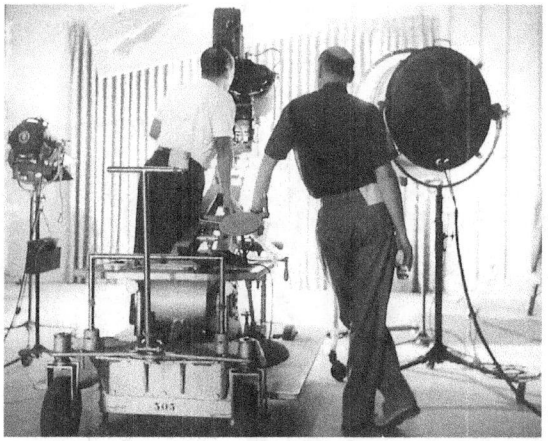

Lido at the Crossroads of the World

He set up another studio across the street at the Crossroads of the World, the one visited in Chapter 6. He called it Lido Films after the marina where his boat awaited his visits. Now he was just like a "real" producer—though his studio and his boat may have been a bit smaller.

The rooms vibrated with upbeat, creative folk quipping between animation and painting desks. The air was filled with scents of pencil and eraser shavings, paint and that acrid, perfumey film.

Men at work

Daddy's studio churned out reels of animated ads. They sold everything from cereal and cake to beer and toilet paper (a daring TV first).

Ads for ads

More ads for ads

The artwork created by Ray Patin Productions artists was groundbreaking. Now it is "retro" and coveted by collectors, seen in auction house catalogs and books on the art of animation.

Blacky and Dirty Sludge

One of the more successful was the gangland style Bardahl Motor Oil commercial. It featured Blacky Carbon and Dirty Sludge who came to be known as "The Grime Gang."

Unlike my mother, who was dying to work in the all-female ink & paint department, I was allowed to work at Ray Patin Productions. I started during school breaks at fourteen and continued to work there on and off through college. At the reception desk, I learned how to press the proper buttons on the dial telephone and talk into the little speaker so that my father and his staff were connected to the right callers.

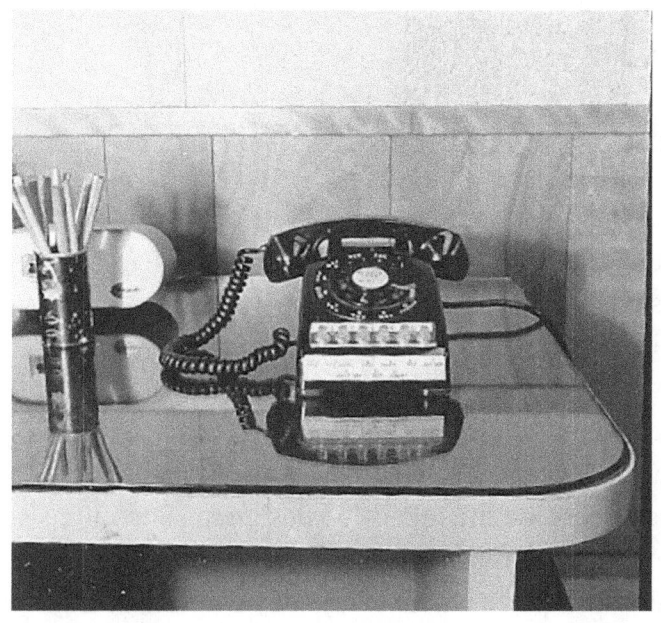

Ray Patin Productions communications center

I acted as gatekeeper to visitors like out-of-work actors handing me their 8" x 10" glossies in hopes of landing a commercial, or ad agency men in suits who'd flown in from New York for a meeting. Under the tutelage of Vinnie's husband, Uncle Wally who was the accountant, I totaled the key punch cards the staff used and learned that my father was paid $25,000 per year! We were rich!

For me the trip over the hill to the right side of the Sign meant traveling between teen and grown-up land. Working on the right side of the Sign gave me a new self-image that I liked a lot. The tinsel dust cast an imaginary coating on all my rough edges. I lunched in the ship-shaped coffee shop at the Crossroads of the World, perching prettily on a stool waiting to be discovered by a passing producer. Once, as I dashed around the neighborhood performing my goforette duties, I popped into the Caroline Leonetti modeling school down the street to sign up. I had often passed the lovely fountain outside with the saying written on ceramic tiles: "To the young in heart—May they dream their dreams and find a guide for their tomorrows."

I walked up to the receptionist's desk saying I wanted to become a model. She will never know how important her kindness and advice were to me. Instead of just saying I wasn't model material, she told me that I had other talents and encouraged me to use them in another direction. I would need to find other "dreams for my tomorrows."

Ray Patin Productions artist at work

I did achieve one dream for a while. I dated, with his blessing, one of my father's animators, the one with the movie star looks. He lived in a medievalesque Spanish-style home in the Hollywood Hills where he kept his arms and armor collection including full suits of mail and some mighty scary weaponry. In keeping with his hobby, he indulged in the art of fencing. He may not have been a gaucho, but in my imagination, he was my own swashbuckling hero for a time.

23
I is for Imagineering®

Mary Jane and Renée at "The Happiest Place on Earth"

If I had known when I first fell in love with Disneyland that there is a career where you can pretend and play and create for a living, I would have changed my major to whatever it took to become an Imagineer.

Imagineers are the folks who design the attractions that continue to bring to life Walt's extraordinary vision of a place where everybody can feel young and families can play together.

I have adored Disneyland from the time it opened when I was in high school. My first visit was a double date with Mary and Mickey and his friend Larry whom I longed to call my boyfriend. We drove down the 5 Freeway from Burbank to Anaheim until we could spot the Matterhorn attraction. Inside we hopped on the train that went around the park, monorailed over it, steered the Autopia course in imitation of the drive we had just taken and let Mr. Toad scare and delight us on his Wild Ride. We forgot about being blasé teenagers. We became little kids delighting in the marvels of all we encountered as we rushed through the incredible "lands." Forever after, I longed to join the attractive college students who were actually getting paid for playing in paradise.

Wistful shop girl enters drug business

First, I had to master a skill that was needed in The Happiest Place on Earth. I decided retail was appropriate—and one of the few part-time opportunities available to kids. My entry into the world of retail had been a position as a gift wrapper during the Christmas season. The location was Lakeside Pharmacy, the drugstore to the stars in Toluca Lake near Bob's Big Boy. Ever watchful for a celebrity like the ones whose autographed portraits surrounded the store, I succeeded only in sighting Lee Marvin. He was the tough-voiced actor infamous for the lawsuit that led to the term "palimony." Bob Hope, who lived around the corner, must have had his drugstore orders delivered. From the drugstore business, I built up a long retail résumé including Bullock's department store in downtown Los Angeles where I fitted optimistic women into too-small bathing suits. This post was followed by a variety of establishments from dime stores to gift shops.

In my junior year at UCSB I finally landed my dream job at Disneyland with help from the father of a sorority sister who had known my father when he worked for the Studios.

School of submarine mermaids

My new post actually earned bragging rights for my grandmother Nana who, with great élan and exaggeration, was telling the Louisiana relatives that her son had risen from almost running The Walt Disney Studios to becoming the most famous, practically Academy Award-winning producer in Hollywood. Now it was my turn. Since swimming was the only sport I performed even half well, I had hoped to become one of the mermaids who, for a short and rather dangerous time, swam around the Submarine Voyage attraction. The fact that I was not chosen to lure guests with a wave of hand and tail did not interfere with Nana's boasting of my awesome aquatic Submarine Voyage act to her rapt relatives down south.

Animator at work

Instead of becoming a sea siren, I was hired as a cel seller—a job description that I was sure would land me on the TV show *What's My Line?*[1] My duty was to explain to grown-ups, whose kids had failed to drag them to more interesting attractions, how animation is done. I would tell them all I knew from watching Daddy and his animators at their special rotating light board flipping and drawing pages. Then they could buy original cels from Disney movies mounted on printed backgrounds.

---

[1] The long-running, and oft-reprised, prime time TV game show (1950-1967). A panel of celebrities guessed the occupation of regular folks and identity of voice-disguising celebrities.

The Magic of Disney Animation attraction at
Disney's Hollywood Studios in the Walt Disney World Resort

Today at the Disneyland Resort and Walt Disney World Resort, visitors can learn all about animation at multi-media interactive animation centers. Those Imagineers, visionary though they are, probably couldn't have anticipated the nostalgic thrill they would provide for this elderly visitor with visions of her father dancing in her head.

Back in 1958, my little animation center was a simulated shop in a Parisian street scene scented with the lavender that guests could scoop into little sachets. This was the Art Corner, located in (soon to be yesterday's) Tomorrowland. To fit the bohemian theme, I attired myself artily in a uniform of black Capri pants and tomato red smock, accessorized with a floppy black tie and beret.

1950s Art Corner, Tomorrowland

My corner of the Corner was quite different from the fifties futuristic look of the rest of the building where visitors taking a respite from more active attractions could explore arty exhibits. They even had a *Blue Boy* and other classic reproductions on the wall.

Despite my Gallic charm, engaging erudition and sales savvy, some patrons balked at the prohibitive prices of the artwork that ranged from 75 cents to $1.50 and had a gold seal with the words, "This is an original hand painted celluloid drawing actually used in a Walt Disney production." Many opted instead for the ten-cent sachet of lavender. If they had only known the price of the rejected souvenir in today's market!

Even though my work kept me behind a counter rather than basking on a wet rock, I loved every minute of my summer-long stint. I had the run of the park on my breaks and could hop on any ride with my Magic Kingdom Pass. My first choice was the Jungle Cruise where a good-looking college boy ended his spiel with, "And now, the most dangerous part of our journey, the return to civilization and those California freeways. Talk about a jungle!" I didn't manage to tempt a gentleman caller from the plethora of alluring ride operators. My romantic life that summer was devoted to a handsome caricature artist who drew the likenesses of his subjects across from my animation station. Our bliss was perfect until both his wife and I learned he had greatly exaggerated his single status.

My magical summer at Disneyland was over fifty years ago, and I still savor every minute I'm there and at the Walt Disney World Resort. One very special time was when Mary Jane and I celebrated my sixty-eighth when Disneyland offered free entrance on birthdays.

Magic for all ages

As always, I began my visit with a train ride around the park. When the engine chugged into the station, I saw its name, *Ward Kimball*! I flashed back to our family visits with the Kimball family and to how Ward was such a child in man's clothing as he played with his life-sized railroad. In that moment, I was again Potsy in the caboose of that train. It was magic—thanks to the Imagineers! Walt said, "It's kind of fun to do the impossible." That's just what he did when he created "The Happiest Place on Earth."

24
J is for Joint

Santa Barbara may have been labeled a party school, but I certainly was not a party girl. If I confide to you that as a coed, I hated joints, you may wonder what it was that I found so despicable.

Joe's joint

Was it Joe's, the joint on State Street where gallivanting groups of Gauchos slithered into side booths or hopped onto leatherette barstools for an evening's revelry?

Or it was the occasional clandestine joint savored during an idyll in Isla Vista, the independently-spirited enclave next to the campus?

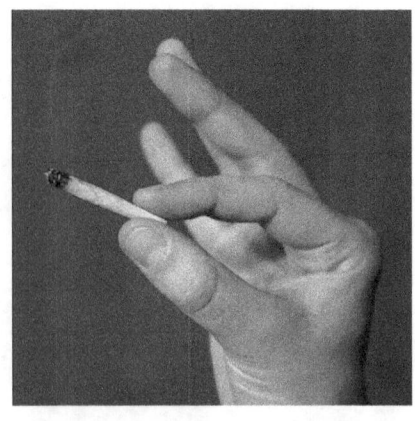

Smoky joint

No, dear reader. We will examine an entirely other genre of joint. For mid-century modern Greeks, a "joint," was a social affair where a sorority and a fraternity got together for joint fun and frivolity. A sorority invited a fraternity to their house for an evening of coffee, cake and camaraderie, and sometimes a fraternity invited a sorority to join them for other kinds of fun and games we will discuss later. Sometimes there were joints with two fraternities and two sororities. These were called "four-ways," and, if they still exist, no doubt go by a different name. We'll begin with joints held at the DG house.

Joint fun?

Here is a picture of a joint that took place with the Delts in our DG living room during the late fifties. The looks on the faces of my roommate Judy and the crew-coiffed, bow-tied boy in the foreground reflect something other than joint jocularity. I was no doubt wearing a similar expression, hovering somewhere in the background in my "dressy sport" attire (skirts or dresses and heels for the girls, coats and ties for the boys). I would be in a huddle with like-minded sisters who also dreaded joints, feeling uncomfortable amidst all the testosterone and bluster. Joints were required, and we were fined if we didn't go. Otherwise I would be upstairs trying to finish a paper for Philosophy 101.

What you were supposed to do at a joint was merrily mingle and engage in gay repartee with the guests. Flirting was expected, and the most successful joint participants finished the evening arm in arm at Joe's— or perhaps in Isla Vista. I'm not sure because I was never one of those fortunate ones. I found chitchat agonizing. Not too many frat boys were enthralled with my scintillating discussion of nineteenth century French poets or German Abstract Expressionism.

There was a moment, however, at each joint when I actually enjoyed myself. One of my friends, perhaps prompted beforehand, would call upon me to do my Edith Piaf imitation. With feigned reluctance, I came forward into an imaginary spotlight, filled my lungs with gusto and belted out my comic/seductive rendition of "La Vie en Rose." I would smack my lips salaciously on the word "moi" and scan the room, landing my heavy-lidded eyes on an attractive frat boy as I gargled the throaty "r" in "rrrrrrrose-eh." In that wink of time I loved the joint and all its participants as they laughed and applauded my oft-repeated chanteuse-y charade.

I may have claimed that I was uncomfortable at social interactions because I was shy, but that wasn't true. My fear was not of people. It was of people not finding me adorable and desirable. My social insecurity was a manifestation of a lifelong A-getter syndrome. Watching those klieg lights from over the hill in Tinseltown gave me a hunger to be a star, not a bit player.

The yearbook caption says, "One of Kappa Sig's many joints."

Joints hosted by fraternities were often TGIFs[1] held on the beach or a patio at their house. These occasions offered another remedy for my joint jitters since at a TGIF, a beer keg replaced the coffee urn. I soon discovered the lesson that my life-of-the-party father had long ago learned: "Liquor is quicker." The trickle of cold amber fluid loosening its way through my system was the elixir that soothed my social anxiety. It also helped that the dress code was casual sweatshirts and pedal pushers. No need to agonize over my ensemble. And I needn't worry about small talk. Our interchanges involved basic topics like whose turn it was to top off paper cups of brew or whether you loved the song playing on the record player or, if you were lucky, what you'd be doing later.

Joshing about joints

This was the house of the Delts. The yearbook caption for the all-black image on the left reads "Delta Tau Delta Function," and hints at the reputation of their social offerings. Their joints were sometimes a little wild, but not out-of-control-total-toga-hijinks like in *Animal House*.[2] It's probably just a coincidence that the Delt mansion was located on the site of what is now the Santa Barbara Zoo.

---

[1] "Thank God It's Friday"

[2] Directed by John Landis who, a few years after I graduated from UCSB, would be an endearingly frustrating class clown in one of the junior high classes I taught.

Steps to what was the Delt House, now on Santa Barbara Zoo grounds

The house was located near the Bird Refuge on Cabrillo, the boulevard lined with skinny sky-high palms paralleling East Beach. Once, during a rather loud function at the house, I accepted an invitation from one of the brothers to go wading. Looking forward to getting away from the clamor and peacefully dipping my toes in the moonlit Pacific, I followed my host across the street. We scrambled over a wrought iron fence and through grass that I expected led to the sand. Instead we arrived at a stone bench where he had me sit. He then affixed two lighted candles into wax he'd dripped onto the armrests. I guess he felt they added a more romantic note as he sat beside me. An innocently romantic interlude ensued. When we left to return to the Delt house, I saw the bench backrest for the first time. On it was carved a single word, "Waiting." Our little expedition had not been to "wade" hand in hand along the sea. I had been chosen to "wait," communing by candlelight in the Santa Barbara cemetery.

I don't know if the Delts regaled all the unsuspecting girls with the same "wading" versus "waiting" ritual. My companion and I never had a repeat rendezvous, and no one ever told me they had experienced the same romantic moment.

Today my only fear of joints is of an orthopedic nature. But I will always remember that night when a dreaded joint affair was transformed into movie-worthy magic.

2016: Renée still waiting (note the candle)

25
K is for Knowledge

Store of knowledge

Today, to my dismay, there are many empty shelves in my store of knowledge. This diminishing inventory is most apparent when I fail to come up with the correct question to a *Jeopardy* clue. Time was I could impress myself immensely yelling the responses at the TV before the contestants could press their buzzers.

In the seventies, I passed the *Jeopardy* test and was all set to knock 'em dead with my knowledge. But the show, hosted then by Art Fleming, was temporarily canceled. They lost the opportunity to have me as a contestant.

I actually won the game show *Crosswits* where celebrities assist you in coming up with the answers to fill in a crossword puzzle. Fred Grandy, Gopher on *The Love Boat* and former congressman, was a big help. Phyllis Diller and Vanessa Williams, who didn't quite get the game, were more amusing and decorative than helpful. I loved my grand prize of a trip to St. Thomas and a side-by-side refrigerator and barbecue grill. Unfortunately, I was living on a boat[1] at the time…but I get ahead of myself. The proceeds from selling the fridge and grill went to pay for a trip to New York to see the show when it first aired.

I was less successful in winning *Tic Tac Dough* with Wink Martindale. I remember he had a little mirror hung at the entrance to the set, so he could double-check his sparkling smile and glistening coiffure before going on stage. My losing the game was due to not knowing the location of Deadwood, the final resting place of Calamity Jane and Wild Bill Hickok.

I could blame this knowledge lapse on being allowed to graduate from college without having taken a geography course and on my United States history class where, as far as I know, there was nary a mention of the legendary lawless South Dakota town.

---

[1] See Chapter 43, "Marriage Afloat and on the Rocks"

But the truth is that my academic aspiration was not the acquisition of knowledge for game shows or any other purposes. I didn't have a burning passion to become whatever a French major becomes. I had no dreams of being asked to conjugate irregular French verbs for rapt audiences. My collegiate goal was to have gone to college. I studied to earn the grades that would allow me to call myself Renée Patin, Bachelor of Arts extraordinaire. Any knowledge I picked up in lectures, studying for tests and writing term papers was a by-product.

I majored in French because A's in high school French had come easily to me thanks to Nana's plying me with Louisiana French phrases. I learned to understand, speak and analyze the language of love. I learned to write it and appreciate who wrote it best. And I learned some facts about France and its culture. I wrote scholarly theses on subjects and in diction only a professor could love, like "Flaubert: His Hatred of the Bourgeoisie and his Religion of Art."

I was an English minor because I have loved to read since learning that there was something beyond *Dick and Jane.* I studied the highlights of the prose and poetry of my own language and wrote scholarly regurgitations of what I heard from and thought would please my instructors. I recycled old material like my Disneyland sales spiel that became a piece defending animation as art for my Art of the Film Class (A+) and I jazzed up my high school graduation speech into an erudite essay on beauty (A)—subjects that didn't exactly provide a turn-on for party pitter-patter.

Yes. I was an A-getter. My roommates might have used egghead or nerd to describe my study habits. Most of them were elementary education majors and kidded me about my esoteric subject matter and habit of hitting the books a little too hard. I was always the last one up studying way into the night, tossing back NoDoz pills with coffee. I honored their request to burn my midnight oil outside our rooms so they could sleep. When I lived on campus in the dorm, I studied in the laundry room surrounded by lost linty socks and the smell of Tide detergent.

Santa Barbara store of technology with happy DG typist

In the DG house, I studied downstairs in the kitchen accompanied by the off-and-on humming of the refrigerator that the cook had filled with tiny glasses of orange juice for a breakfast that wasn't far off.

Until I convinced my father that his money would be well spent on my hiring a typist, I pounded out my term papers on my typewriter placed on a folded towel to muffle the awkward clickety-tap of my keys. I used glossy, thick erasable paper (before the invention of Wite-Out or IBM Selectric self-correcting typewriters). Mary Jane, ironically, was currently studying to be a business and typing teacher at UCLA, yet another bit of knowledge she could lord over me.

Rush to knowledge:
UCSB students register before digitalization

Each semester I scrambled with the scholars crowded around the table in the gym in search of courses that would satisfy our requirements for graduation. My fear was that a class would be full or that I would get a particularly demanding professor. But I always managed to come up with a heavy course load that required heavy study time.

I spent many hours studying in the library. I loved scouring the stacks for research books that smelled of the glue and varnish of their bindings. The heavier the tome, thinner and mildewier the pages, and smaller the type, the more successful I felt in my scholarly pursuits. I studied there for tests until the information swarmed in my head that bumped onto the blond wood table. Then I would leave the glare of the overhead fluorescents to retreat for a nap in the little dark room provided for coeds' study respites. Livelier breaks were with scholarly suitors.

Yearbook caption for professor with Blue Book: "I always wondered what was in these things."

Did I gain any knowledge from all this research and test taking? Of course I did, not that I remember it all. For midterm and final tests, I filled scores of those robin's egg-colored, lined composition Blue Books with knowledge learned over a semester and solidified over a late night's cramming. But looking down from a not-so-ivory tower, I know that not all knowledge I gained in academia was included in the prescribed curriculum.

Just like the stores where Mama and I did our special shopping, my store of knowledge has many departments. The inventory continues to deplete and grow in each department.

Ray Patin's teen cartoon about gaining knowledge despite distractions

Although my parents didn't go to college, I thought they knew everything. They instilled in me the importance of learning. They also showed me that learning can be fun. We tested our knowledge on radio game shows like *It Pays to Be Ignorant, Take It or Leave It* with its prized 64 Dollar Question[2] and the *Bob Hawk Show* where contestants earned the letters L-E-M-A-C (backward spelling for the sponsor, Camel cigarettes) for each correct answer. "You're a Lemac now!"

Young Ray's cartoon about knowledge gained from a high school graduation

---

[2] No, there are no zeros missing from the top prize on the show. Later when it was on television the ante was upped to $640. And of course, *The $64,000 Question* was part of the fifties quiz show scandals.

Here is some knowledge outside the curriculum that I took away from my college education:

1. Knowledge is not just information that can be looked up on an app, or back in the day, in an encyclopedia.

2. I am not what I know.

3. Knowledge doesn't equal wisdom. Hard knock knowledge is as valuable as that learned from lessons.

4. A college major does not always indicate a career path.

5. To prove that my quest for knowledge has not been in vain, I will now paraphrase Shakespeare.

Hamlet: "There are more things in heaven and earth, Horatio, than are dreamt of in your philosophy."

Me: "There is more knowledge in heaven and earth than I can dream of in a lifetime."

Epistemological Epilogue

Let me conclude with a treatise on knowledge that I can only wish I had written, and that you may be glad I didn't. It is a song from Gilbert and Sullivan's 1879 comic opera *The Pirates of Penzance*. In this scene, the pompous Major General performs a humorous rat-a-tat rap touting the vast range of his knowledge.

> *I am the very model of a modern Major General,*
> *I've information vegetable, animal, and mineral,*
> *I know the kings of England, and I quote the fights historical*
> *From Marathon to Waterloo, in order categorical;*
>
> *I'm very well acquainted, too, with matters mathematical,*
> *I understand equations, both the simple and quadratical,*
> *About binomial theorem I'm teeming with a lot o' news,*
> *With many cheerful facts about the square of the hypotenuse.*
>
> *I'm very good at integral and differential calculus;*
> *I know the scientific names of beings animalculous:*
> *In short, in matters vegetable, animal, and mineral,*
> *I am the very model of a modern Major General.*

Never mind finishing the whole thing. It is not required reading and won't be on the final. But, you never can tell. It could be a final *Jeopardy* question.

26
L is for Light Fantastic

The romance of the dance

So my college quest for A's, rather than knowledge, left little time for the more frivolous activities such as joints and, the most dreaded of all, dancing.

The term "to trip the light fantastic" for dancing was already a comic cliché when I was a little girl. The phrase meaning to dance lightly and nimbly goes all the way back the seventeenth century poet Milton. By the time I was twelve and watched Walt Disney's Cinderella and Prince Charming twirl dizzily around the palace dance floor, I knew I would never be either light or fantastic at ballroom dancing. But I was also puzzled. I didn't understand how Cinderella became such a naturally graceful dancer while she was toiling for her mean stepfamily. I hardly toiled at all and had a lovely family. But I already knew I was not meant to win any dance contests, let alone princes.

Perhaps if we were to probe the hidden depths of my physical and psychological development, we would find several causes for my lack of lightness on my feet.

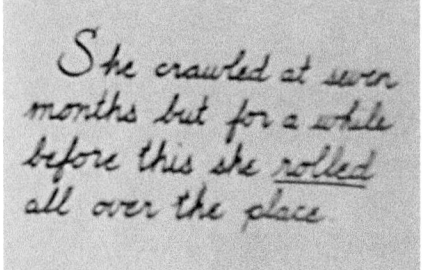 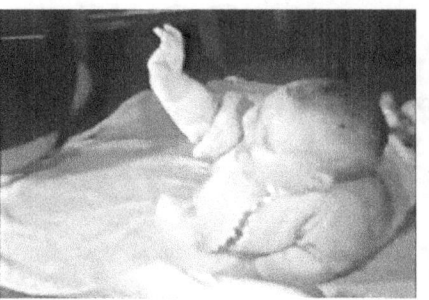 

Movie: *On a roll!*

I was born with hip dysplasia,[1] a condition I share with highly-bred German Shepherd dogs. The first sign may have been my tendency to roll to my destinations rather than crawl. Then there were the contortions that I bragged to my friends were the result of "double joints."

Patin paschal portrait—note the stance

I was completely unaware that I had anything out of line except when I was told to point my feet outward instead of inward due to "pigeon toes." A comic family Easter portrait shows my awkward avian stance. By the way, what may to some look like mother-daughter forties maternity outfits were actually the fashion, not part of the comedy. Daddy's "purse" is his ever-present movie camera case.

So, it followed that my inherent lack of physical grace put the "trip" in "tripping the light fantastic." I was well aware that I was several steps shy of the stylings of Fred Astaire and Ginger Rogers whom I'd watched on the silver screen cutting an elegant rug in *The Barkleys of Broadway.* For those whose dancing days are more recent, "cutting a rug," a term for a couple dancing well together, comes from the 20s and 30s when jitterbugging couples danced so hard, carpets appeared to be "cut" or "gashed."

---

[1] The faulty hip has now been replaced.

My father was a good dancer, a talent he no doubt honed in the Avalon Casino along with his buddy Leslie Arthur. Leslie and his wife Rosemary tangoed gracefully well into their seventies.

My parents would "cut the rug" around our living room, too. But they did not pass their terpsichorean talents on to me. I have a painful memory of the time when I was about eight and Daddy took me in his arms to dance to a recording of Les Brown and His Band of Renown. As he led me around the living room, he became increasingly impatient with my stumbles and stingingly remarked that I had no rhythm. My graceful, athletic father's remark became another reason for disdaining dancing.

Perhaps if I had seen what my father wrote about his own dancing, I would not have taken his remark so seriously. Remember the letter my father wrote about the rumble seat date that practically froze my mother and her siblings? Well the rest of the letter describes an outing that turned far more romantic. He tells of their first dance with great honesty, confessing feelings of inadequacy as an older man of twenty-five trying to dance with a girl of seventeen. He ends with a

The dancing Arthurs

wonderful line drawing of the two of them where the lines are so rhythmical that they almost seem to dance.

Ray and Maxine date and dance

There followed later a very enjoyable night at Ocean Park when we were kids again thrilling at the breath-taking, death defying scintillating Chutes; posing for those marvelous dime portraits and then topped it all with our first dance together. I did my darnedest to keep on my toes and off of yours. I truly enjoyed that dance–you were so patient with me and all. Someday, perhaps, after a few sessions like the one in the Ice house canyon lodge, I'll be able to limber up those old legs and trip the light fantastic as I used to do. You might call number eight a puzzle picture, but it's meant to be a "Symphony of Lines." After making miles of pencil lines at the Studio, it's a natural tendency for us all to see what we can do with the least lines possible. Sometimes the results are pleasing. Other times they are quite puzzling to those uninitiated in the lineal "Rhythms."

So even fathers who seem to be so light on their big feet had trepidation about dancing with a partner of the opposite sex. I dreaded the times when our junior high gym teachers Mr. Lloyd and Miss Simpson would combine our classes and let us satisfy our budding hormonal urges by dancing in the gym. Worthy of a debutante cotillion, our teachers entered from their opposing locker rooms leading their shoeless charges onto the slippery hardwood floor with its menacing cougar logo designed pro bono by my father. We would then stand and stare at each other, eventually following instructions to find partners. My heart would pound and my upper lip would shine with sweat as I anticipated the half-hour we sock-squeaked around the gym.

The yearbook elucidates the Burroughs dance program

Another hindrance to my enjoyment of dancing with my fellow adolescents occurred when they played slow dance records like "Chances Are" by Johnny Mathis or Elvis's "Love Me Tender." I was filled with fear that the proximity of our position would lead to unfortunate protuberances emanating from my partner. I affected a bent-over posture that elicited correction from Miss Simpson.

Our high school yearbook, with its peripatetic Indian logo, shows the variety of personalities a dance might take from games to athletic jives to slow dances. The popular dance events are listed as The Sweetheart, the Huddle Hop, and thank goodness for me, the Backwards—or Sadie Hawkins Dance—where girls invited boys. My repugnance to perform cheek to cheekfulness was painfully brought to the forefront at the graduation prom when I danced the night away with a self-invited escort whom I'd met in my drugstore job days and was a foot taller than my 5'3".

The dreaded slow dance

When I entered college, I learned, much to my discomfort, that dances were the accepted, even anticipated, mode of making and deepening friendships with the opposite sex. As you might assume from my continued quest for a gentleman caller, I went to the dances.

Musical mixing

Dancing was the activity of choice for "mixers." Here the idea was to make new friends and perhaps make a date. There is a junior college yearbook photo that pictures my friend Eva and me in some kind of musical mixing activity. Eva, in front, looks blasé, secure in the knowledge that she is endowed with natural dancing skills. Sashaying behind her, my smile says I am enjoying myself, but inside I am saying, "This beanpole better not ask me to slow dance." When Eva and I took PE classes together in social dancing, my self-esteem and grade point average were challenged when I received C's. Eva got A's.

UCSB rug-cutting fifties style

Recently when I told a friend I was writing about my dislike of dancing, she countered, "But you were a sorority girl!" She's right. Not only was dancing a stereotype of sorority life, it was a reality. I yearned to be invited to the dances (especially by someone of campus repute) but dreaded the actual dancing (especially with someone who knew the steps to all the dances including the Latin versions). I preferred less formal affairs like the ones at the Montecito estates of successful fraternity alumni or at the Circle Bar B Guest Ranch north of town. At these venues, there was a chance for a glass of wine to loosen libido and limb. The dancing was looser too, less by the book. Although we were too sophisticated for the "Hokey Pokey," which I was just beginning to master when I graduated from high school, we indulged in fast dances where my awkward gyrations might be mistaken for creativity.

The Mar Monte when I was dancing in its ballroom

The Coral Casino Beach and Cabana Club the year I was born

But, alas, most of the dances were formals held, alcohol free, in fine ballrooms all around Santa Barbara. Most popular were the grand hotels like the Mar Monte (now the Hyatt) on Cabrillo and the super posh Coral Casino Beach and Cabana Club at the Biltmore Hotel (now Four Seasons).

Before tackling an evening of dance and romance, I would adjust my just-coiffed hairdo, perform a toilette applying the little makeup I wore and dutifully don appropriate ballroom attire—often the fabled recycled high school prom dress. By the time I got to the venue of the evening, my attitude would be adjusted, and I would dance smilingly, banter scintillatingly and pose prettily.

Fish and formality in the fifties

Under bright lights and the scrutiny of chaperones, we mingled musically en masse like a swirling school of mackerel. Like the whirling waltzers at Cinderella's ball, we danced to live music mostly the way our parents and grandparents had danced. This all was before the frenzied dances of the sixties—the ones with the silly names and pantomime gestures and partners who didn't touch. Maybe I was just before my time?

C'mon baby. Let's do Christmas!

Always with the times, if not ahead of them, my parents' Yuletide greeting in the sixties showed they were aware of—if not practitioners of—The Twist. Their trendy collage/card was a far cry from the romantic snow-dashing couple of their first Christmas greeting.

Cutting a Kenyan rug

Now that I am beyond my time of worrying about my dancing skill set, I actually enjoy tripping, if not the light fantastic, a few steps here and there—like the rhythmic swaying and shuffling to drumbeats in Kenya—and dancing like there's no one watching in my living room.

27
M is for Music

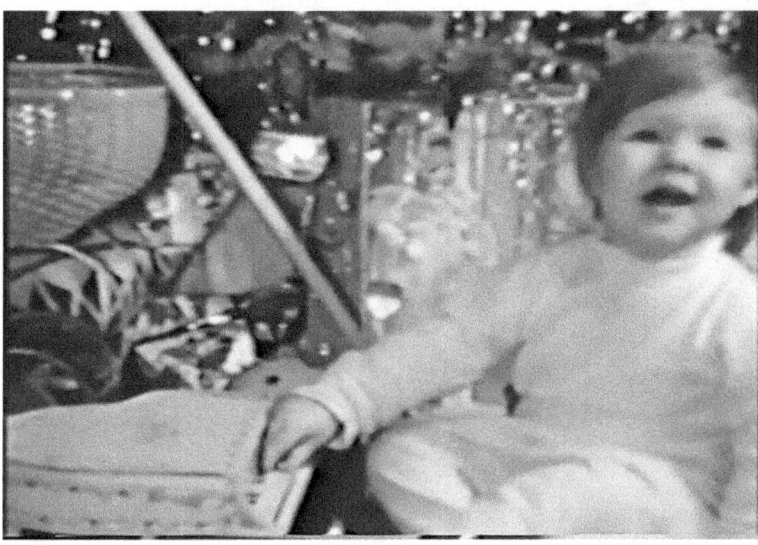

Potsy's first notes

My musical talents are right up there with my aptitude for dancing. In fact, my ear might be called tin by those who can tell such things. And my singing talents are amusing at best. The lack of any courses in music after junior high and discouragement of my attempts at university musicology might be to blame. But I think I was just, as Lady Gaga might intone, born this way.

When I was two months of age, my father described my singing voice on one of the titles he made for his home movies of me: "Renée coos now. She is a deep-voiced contralto." At two I posed at the keyboard of my very baby grand piano. When I was three, Daddy created our Christmas card from a linoleum block print. It imagined a prim and proper me tickling the ivories of the pump organ in our living room. The portrait belies the fact that I would never have sat still long enough to pose so prettily, nor could my short stubby legs have reached the pedals necessary to pump out sound even if I did know how to play. Which I did not.

Despite these optimistic nods to my musical proclivities, my repertoire is limited to posing with, rather than playing, musical instruments and to the rather dubious comedic singing career detailed in previous chapters.

Renée today posing at a key-covered piano in a Portuguese palace/hotel

It's not that I wasn't exposed to great music. After all, I saw the thirties movies Daddy animated to musical scores like the Oscar-winning series of *Silly Symphonies* where Donald Duck was introduced along with innovations in Technicolor and the multiplane camera. I saw *Make Mine Music* in the forties when so many animators were out fighting the war, so they used clips from other films put together to music.

Music in motion

Animated music

My father was one of the animators who set in musical motion the mushrooms that danced to *The Nutcracker Suite* in *Fantasia*. Gerry remembers a time when she was a teen and we were living at the Culver City house while ours in Burbank was being built. Daddy introduced her to *The Nutcracker Suite* and how the distinguished Leopold Stokowski conducted the score to which he animated the mushrooms. And he probably didn't tell her he based their antics on The Three Stooges.[1] I could identify with cute little Hop Low, the dancing mushroom who was always missing steps—and captured all the audience's attention with his silly stumblings.

Learning from music

I learned the instruments of the orchestra by listening to *Peter and the Wolf*.[2] I still imagine the birds of Peter's forest when I hear twittering from flutes, and I feel the menace of the wolf from the eerie blare of French horns. And I memorized the song about that other wolf, the big bad one in *The Three Little Pigs*. The song was "Who's Afraid of the Big Bad Wolf?" and sometimes we substituted Hitler's name for the furry beast. And I could belt out a mean "Heigh-Ho, Heigh-Ho, it's off to work—or home from work—we go" from *Snow White and the Seven Dwarfs*.

---

[1] A wildly popular comedy trio known for their vaudeville and movie silly slapstick. There were actually six stooges over the years 1922-1970, but mostly it was Larry, Curly and Moe.

[2] Made into a fifteen-minute animated short by Walt Disney, it was part of the *Silly Symphony* Series.

Our cultural cabinet of curiosities: *Scheherazade* and Spike's Slickers

My parents' taste in music was disharmonious. Mama's favorite record was Rimsky-Korsakov's *Scheherazade* with Sir Thomas Beecham conducting the Royal Philharmonic Orchestra. The dazzling interpretation of the tale of the seductive storyteller of *The Arabian Nights* suited my mother's love of fairy tales.

Daddy's preferences were more outrageous. He loved Spike Jones and His City Slickers. The wacky ensemble punctuated their arrangements with sounds of gunshots, whistles, cowbells and uncouth human vocalizations. Horn honking, voice gurgling and hiccupping made their arrangement of "Cocktails for Two" something less than romantic. And their "All I Want for Christmas Is My Two Front Teeth" was a 1948 yuletide favorite. Ours was not a salon of cultural elitism.

The only instrument in our house was the aforementioned antique organ. But it was more for interior decor and Daddy's whimsy than chamber musicales. As a joke my father relabeled the fading knobby "stops" that were supposed to indicate musical terms like "piccolo" and "dolce" to read "chocolate" and "vanilla."

Mama, Daddy and I never did learn to play that organ. It's not exactly an instrument fit for an upbeat session of tickling the ivories. "Chopsticks" loses its spice when you have to pump air into the notes that always came out sounding like a dirge.

The house organ and stops

Renée's song

I began my singing career at about six or seven. The occasion was a talent show held at Camp Blue Jay near Lake Arrowhead where my parents and I were enjoying a rustic vacation in the pines eighty-four miles from Burbank.

The setting was casual enough that I didn't feel the fear of failure instilled by my McKinley music teacher/tormentor. My song choice, evidence that I inherited Daddy's silly gene, was the enigmatic "Mairzy Doats."[3] To rehearse my number, I sequestered myself in the laundry hut near our cabin, a favorite haunt for a boy named Jimmy and me. While we washed and rewashed rags with a bright red cake of Lifebuoy soap, I rehearsed my rendition of the ditty's gibberish. The night of the performance, I rushed up on stage and burst forth with all the force of my whiskey voice:

> *Mairzy doats and dozy doats and liddle lamzy divey*
> *A kiddley divey too, Wooden shoe!"*

Then, with a sly gap-toothed grin, I sang the final words of explanation:

> *If the words sound queer and funny to your ear, a little bit jumbled and jivey,*
> *Sing "Mares eat oats and does eat oats and little lambs eat ivy.*
> *A kid'll eat ivy too, wouldn't you?"*

After a modest bow, I basked in the roar of the crowd—well actually polite applause from a scattering of campers who had been looking forward to a chalk talk by my cartoon-drawing father. But the recognition of my talents, real or imagined, set me off on a "career" of my own backward brand of musical comedy as evidenced in my high school and university days.

---

[3] Written and composed in 1943, it was first played on radio by Al Trace and his Silly Symphonists. The song by the Merry Macs reached No. 1 on the pop charts in March 1944.

The piano stylings of
Miss Mary Jane Bennett

Back in Burbank, the music coming from Mary Jane's living room next door was of a more classic caliber. She really could play the piano and went to lessons with Miss Hoke on Riverside Drive. I went to those recitals where I watched Mary Jane and sometimes Natalie Wood, who was a fellow piano student. The parade of players seemed to last forever while I sat politely on a stiff-backed dining room chair and endured ennui and envy over Mary Jane's talent and proximity to an actual movie star. And their recital dresses. And their curls.

We were about nine when Mary Jane decided I should learn to play "Ghost Riders in the Sky" on the piano. She would provide the necessary lessons for a quarter per lesson. We sat at her shiny black piano topped with a metronome and a miniature white bust of Chopin. Crowded side by side on the wood bench that opened to store her music, she tried to teach me the basics. After a few too many painful but ineffectual finger positionings, we decided I should give up any dreams of piano virtuosity. Whereupon she declared I was tone deaf, and the lesson concluded with our daily tussle.

As my musical tastes and hormones matured, my ear turned to heart-rending ballads to which I could croon and swoon in what I thought were passionate sing-alongs. I pictured myself in a movie scene side by side with the popular kids at Bob's declaring my love for a top forty hit like Nat King Cole's "They Tried to Tell Us We're Too Young," the lyrics of which I knew by heart. In my scenario, I would put a nickel in the jukebox[4] and snappily punch in the number and letter of my selection. Then together we would harmonize, sway and swoon with the crooner and maybe even "cut a rug" at which I would now excel.

Teen tune time

In junior high I perfected an act where tune carrying wasn't a prerequisite. This was the popular art of lip-syncing onstage to a record played offstage, a sort of fifties karaoke with groovy moves. In one stellar variety show performance we memorized the words from one of the magazines where they were all printed out for us. Then we mimed "Jukebox Saturday Night," The Modernaires' tribute to Glenn Miller[5] that features cameos by the top vocalists of the day.

---

[4] Tabletop or floor model music machine. Remember "Don't Stop Believin'" blaring from the jukebox and abruptly stopping at the finale of *The Sopranos?*

[5] The epitome of a big band leader in the forties, Glenn Miller disappeared during a flight while entertaining the troops in World War II.

Don Cornell croons

My role in "Jukebox Saturday Night" was mouthing[6] the words of Don Cornell. Dressed in male attire, I dramatically slid on stage to join the quintet of songsters in swirly skirts and tight sweaters. I knelt on one knee in the spotlight, stretched out my arms, and "became" the smooth star with matinee idol looks.

Spring Sing

At UCSB our musical highlight of the year was Spring Sing. We would all dress alike and regale the audience in Santa Barbara's outdoor theater with a medley of choral selections. My sorority sister Barbara remembers watching the Delts with flaming torches held high winding down the mountain trail to the County Bowl. Our star attractions were Judy Johnson and Kathy Gerard who sent their soprano voices soaring into the moonlight.

Unfortunately, my tin ear and wobbly contralto were not of a caliber to join the chorus. I would always assume the role of narrator. But I was thankful for on-tune voices like Judy's and Kathy's, not only for adding beauty to our presentation, but also for helping me out as DG president. My presidential duty was to start the singing of grace before dinners in our formal dining room. I needed only to tinkle my knife against my water glass and one of them would start us off on the right key and I could join in with my well-practiced mouthing.

---

[6] Now referred to, usually derogatively, as lip synching, though there are contests where the art form is rewarded.

28
N is for Nautical Interludes

Setting sail

My education at a beachfront university was part of my ongoing love of the sea, and when that education became overwhelming, my escape was to get out onto the sea in a boat. I guess I was a little like that seaman whose "Call me Ishmael" introduction to *Moby-Dick* I echoed as my own. He said, "Whenever I find myself growing grim about the mouth; … then I account it high time to get to sea as soon as I can."

It was my father's affection for boats throughout my growing years that brought me my affinity for nautical interludes. From the time he arrived on the Pacific Coast, my father dreamed of boats. He was a teen when he made a drawing of boys in sailor hats aboard a patched together sailboat just big enough to hold the two of them. As a caption he wrote:

> *Where'll we sail to first, Jim, Borneo? The West Indies? Oh I dunno.*
> *It's so close to supper time, what say we just sail across the pond and back?*

My father's prose may have had a hint of Ishmael who also said, "As for me, I am tormented with an everlasting itch for things remote. I love to sail forbidden seas, and land on barbarous coasts." Happily, Daddy's days at sea were far calmer than Ishmael's.

Forties footage: *Artists Ahoy*

Ray finally did get to play the role of a skipper in one of the rare times he appears in one of his own films. He took the helm on a schooner voyage to Catalina with Mama and friends from The Walt Disney Studios.

He again filmed Kae Sumner, the tall jitterbugger. She hammed up a scenario where she couldn't get her movie camera to work. This melodrama is followed by shots of another ink and paint lady sucking on a lemon, in hopes to prevent seasickness. The exotic locale where they went ashore was the Isthmus at the other end of Catalina Island where they wore leis and paid for their drinks in shells.

Movie Melodrama: *The Spurned Animator*

Daddy was also able to indulge his nautical and cinematic inclinations in the not-ready-for-prime-time playlet he produced while "working" at the Hyperion studio. In it he overacts his pride and joy watching animated footage he drew featuring Donald Duck aboard a sailing ship. He then, with great anticipation, shares his production with his fellow artists. The sad saga concludes when one of his peers deems the work so stinking bad that he needs to clip his nose.

The movie continues with the footage that the dejected artist had so proudly projected for his peers. It is a pencil test for the 1939 Disney short film *Sea Scouts*. In the cartoon, we see animated drawings of Donald Duck as an arrogant admiral. He endures death-defying moments flying in the rigging as his crew (played by his nephews Huey, Dewey and Louie) attempts to bring him down.

Pencil test: *Sea Scout Stuff*

Donald's nautical role followed in the wake of another screen star mariner. Mickey Mouse performed his 1928 breakthrough role in *Steamboat Willie*, whistling aboard his watercraft. So, my father was part of a fine Disney tradition when he actually became the captain of his own sea-going vessel.

Mickey at the helm

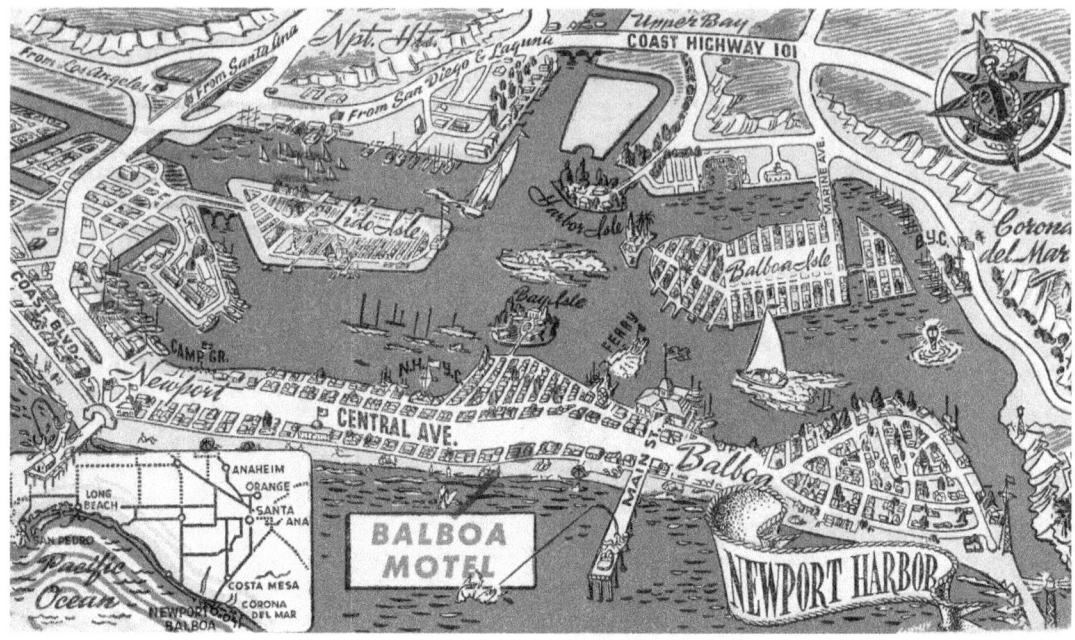

Newport Harbor in a post card for the old Balboa Motel

In the fifties and sixties, when he was directing rather than doing animation, my father realized that all work all the time was making him a dull boy, and that it was time to play. Our playground was Newport Harbor.

The *Trinket* and the *Goose*

Our plaything was the *Trinket,* a 26-foot wooden cabin cruiser. She was docked on Lido Isle around the corner from John Wayne's 136-foot converted minesweeper, the *Wild Goose*.[1]

---

[1] Unreliable sources claim that when John Wayne stormed up the sands of Iwo Jima in the movie of the same name, he did the storming on a beach near Lido Isle in Newport Harbor.

"Messing about in boats"

*Believe me, my young friend, there is nothing–absolutely nothing–
half so much worth doing as simply messing about in boats.*
                                Rat to Mole in Kenneth Grahame's
                                         Wind in the Willows

Daddy enthusiastically drove fifty-five miles from Burbank to Newport to mess about in his boat almost every weekend. He was accompanied by my less than enthusiastic mother. For him it was a reprieve from the demands of running a studio. He loved just being on board the *Trinket* and messing about, catering to her many demands. For mother, it was the same routine she had in Burbank, only performed in a cramped cabin while being jostled by a scary sea in which she was unable to swim.

Balboa's famous ferry

I loved Lido Isle. It was a great place to bring my latest boyfriend and a fertile ground to hunt for new ones. I looked forward to the teen mecca of nearby Balboa Island and particularly enjoyed the ferry that made the fifteen-minute trip from the island to the mainland Fun Zone. It was just enough time to set my smile beguilingly and hand over my quarter to a shorts-clad toll taker.

Fun and games aboard the *Trinket*

Another potential fishing spot for dates was the fuel dock where we stopped before heading out to sea. I would pose seductively on deck anticipating a glance from the fuel pumper whose bronze godliness was a match for the ferry boys.

Ray and family enjoy nautical interludes

When guests came aboard, Daddy donned his captain's cap and, echoing his mother's automotive guided perambulations, conducted tours of the affluent waterfront highlights. He waved to port or starboard narrating information about Shirley Temple's honeymoon cottage, Madame Modjeska's[2] private island home, Jascha Heifetz's[3] lawnscaped spread designed by Frank Lloyd Wright, and the

---

[2] Polish born actress famed for her tragic Shakespearean roles, died in Newport Beach in 1909.

[3] Russian born violinist considered one of the greatest of modern times.

Maxine at play in port

two houses that were created from one after a nasty divorce. The locations for these celebrity landmarks would change, and their stories' authenticity may have been in doubt, but it was a tour worthy of a guide with a Hollywood-sized imagination. He always pointed out the Sea Scout base, a waterfront headquarters for this nautical division of the Boy Scouts of America. I thought it was for my benefit as there were some mighty fine fellows—not ducklings—in attendance. But Captain Ray may have been remembering his days animating Donald Duck at sea.

The dock at Avalon on Catalina Island today

We often sailed twenty-six miles across the sea to Catalina, my father's long-time favorite isle. I was thrilled when we left the breakwater and the harbor's five miles per hour speed limit. Then Daddy could open the engine and let the *Trinket* skip atop the ocean swells. Two hours later the engine's roar and body jarring motion came to a sudden calm as we entered Avalon Harbor. Circling under the pier, Daddy would yell up at the harbormaster to request a mooring. Then we were led to one of the rusting buoys where we'd grab a rope attached to a float and tie up.

Sometimes Mary Jane joined us, and we took advantage of the best Avalon had to offer. We slathered on Johnson's Baby Oil spiked with iodine to enhance our tans and white zinc oxide to protect our delicate noses. We slithered into our latest bathing suits and tooted the air horn for a shuttle launch to venture ashore. At the pier we'd climb up onto the dock and make our way over the wood planks to Crescent Avenue that still follows the little sand beach on one side and bars and other establishments on the other. Our summer fun consisted of looking for likely male companionship, fighting over miniature golf or tennis and maybe a movie at the Casino.[4] Unlike my father in *his* teens, our antics never landed us in jail.

One lazy afternoon we stayed on board to work on our tans and play canasta on top of the cabin, an activity that aroused my father's ire. "Get in the dinghy and have fun, damn it!" he shouted at us. We still quote his admonition that when at sea you should do seafaring stuff.

La Paz: *El Viejo y el Mar*

Not too long ago I came across a statue in La Paz, Mexico. I loved the piece that spoke to me of my lifelong love of the sea. It is called *The Old Man and the Sea.* The figure is about my age now, staring out to sea, wearing a paper hat and standing at attention in a paper boat. The poem attached written in Spanish by the sculptor Guillermo Gomez Macias is in the voice of the old mariner. He sings of his childlike dream of sailing the seven seas. I thought of that other great poem called "Sea Fever."

> *I must go down to the seas again,*
> *to the vagrant gypsy life, To the gull's*
> *way and the whale's way where the*
> *wind's like a whetted knife;*
> *And all I ask is a merry yarn from*
> *a laughing fellow-rover, And quiet*
> *sleep and a sweet dream when the*
> *long trick's over.*
>
>   John Masefield

---

[4] My parents, who had danced there in their youth, had no fear we would gamble in the Casino. No games of chance are offered there. They were outlawed in California by the time the landmark structure was built.

Like my father and Ishmael and the old mariner and John Masefield, I have always had sea fever. It was not just the gypsy life and the laughing fellow-rovers that made my nautical interludes an important sea change from UCSB. It was the sleeping and dreaming too. Like my father, I found peace at sea away from the pressures of chasing success. On the *Trinket,* I snuggled into the narrow Naugahyde bunk in the cabin that smelled of varnished mahogany and slept to a lullaby of creaking wood accompanied by the clickity-clack snacking of crustaceans on the hull. Here I could dream rather than strive. It's highly unlikely that my sea reveries could have foretold that twenty years later my only home would be a boat that my husband[5] and I built and sailed from Newport, California to Newport, Rhode Island.

But that's a story for another chapter.

---

[5] Neither a frat boy, amusement ride operator, ferry toll taker nor fuel pumper.

29
O is for Old Santa Barbara

1939 Ray Patin production: *An Outing to Santa Barbara*

Patin family sea tales go way back, and so do tales of Santa Barbara, my first home outside the shadow of the Sign. But my first experience there has a Hollywood flare. When I was eight months old, I starred in a movie shot on location in Santa Barbara. It was written, directed and produced by my father.

Despite his bovine buffoonery and the beauty of both my mother and the Mission, I was not impressed. They could not get a smile out of their little darling. Now when I visit as often as possible, the town makes me smile a lot.

Santa Barbara is less than a hundred miles from Burbank, but in its serene beauty, a world away from La La Land. Not that the town hasn't had its share of show biz. The American Film Manufacturing Company, or Flying A Studio, was one of the largest movie studios in the country, rivaled only by Hollywood. Flying A made more than a thousand silent films such as *The Dyspeptic* that takes place south of the border "In the Land of the Tortilla."

Hollywood in Santa Barbara

Royalty in Santa Barbara

The several-block spread had horse stables and a glassed-in studio for interior shots. The photo of the old studio was taken October 13, 1919 when King Albert of Belgium was visiting Santa Barbara and was invited to tour the studio. If you look closely, the man standing up exiting the car is King Albert. Two city policemen are standing on the sidewalk.

Flying A Studio today

Flying A closed in 1921, but you can still see what is left of the studio at the corner of Mission and Chapala. Today an architecture firm occupies the site. Their sign is suspended on chains from the Flying A sign marking the glories of a Tinseltown that almost was.

Montecito Inn then and now

Adding to Santa Barbara's claim to movie-making fame, Charlie Chaplin and friends built the Montecito Inn in 1928. Montecito, Santa Barbara's affluent suburb to the east, is still a retreat for celebrities looking for homes far from the madding glare of La La Land. Their posh estates and those of their East Coast old money neighbors are hidden behind gates and eucalyptus trees, leaving us visitors to guess which is Oprah's or Ellen's.

Sixteen years after I was first carried there for a Patin family outing, I was impressed enough to make Santa Barbara my future alma mater. Now, with a warning that I have a memory on every corner—and in the spirit of my forebearers—let's take a quick tour of my temporary home.

The California Riviera

We'll begin our tour on Cabrillo Boulevard near the dramatic sight of the Bird Refuge on our right and the Montecito Country Club and the Santa Ynez Mountains beyond. Along that mountainside is the area the locals call "the Riviera." Here winding roads at different heights make curve-conscious drivers who've driven it think of the Corniche Roads of the Cote d'Azur.

Cabrillo Boulevard then and now with taller trees

We will stay below that neighborhood of precariously perched homes on curvy roads. Instead we will head west along the seaside boulevard named for Juan Cabrillo, the first explorer of the coast we are admiring. Between the sand and us, standing tall like a surrealist's painting of malnourished guards on duty, are rows of Mexican fan palms. Some are 100 years old and reach almost 100 feet high, defying reality with their towering skinny trunks and silly tufted headdresses.

Relaxing under the palms

It's amazing to look at old postcards of the same street when the "beards" of the stubbier, younger palms almost hit the ground. No, that banjo-strumming fellow relaxing under the palms is not a former boyfriend. Flower Power came after I graduated.

As we head north on State Street, we begin to see more and more quintessential Santa Barbara architecture. There is a feeling of harmony as if the downtown were designed as a movie set in Seville—which it kind of was. After a disastrous 1925 earthquake destroyed most of downtown, Pearl Chase—a grande dame whose name graces the palm lined park along Cabrillo that she endowed—was largely responsible for the movement that still keeps the buildings in the style of colonial Spain: low earth-toned stucco, red tile roofs and lots of Spanish tiles.

The Santa Barbara County Courthouse

Take time to wander through the magnificent County Courthouse where we once held Spring Sing on the steps. Duck into the nearby arcade called the El Paseo. I loved wandering through the bougainvillea splattered courtyards to the Tecolote Book Shop. It was the classic consummate bookery with its broad creaky floorboards and thick wavy window glass that filtered sunlight onto tables and shelves of often-musty books. I still love the Tecolote Book Shop, now relocated to Montecito where it continues the true book shop tradition begun in 1955—without the creaks and mustiness.

DG house yesterday

A few blocks away we arrive at the location of the long-gone Delta Gamma house. Our tour ends here at the corner of Arrellaga and Anacapa streets. It was called the Colt House because it was said to have been the winter retreat of the Colt family, maker of the Colt 45 six-shooter and other firearms. The 100-year-old house was a two-story Victorian, but not the fancy kaleidoscope-colored, curlicued kind. It sat in a quiet tree-shaded upper east side neighborhood of downtown Santa Barbara and is now replaced by a semi-Spanish business building.

All that remains on the site from our DG days are descendants of the palms we deconstructed in order to create our luau theme party during Rush Week.

Many of the original homes in the quiet neighborhood, including a posh bed and breakfast, The Simpson House Inn, do remain, set back from the low golden sandstone walls. If you look carefully, you can still find the iron hitching rings and posts to which carriage horses were tied.

Today an office building sits on the site of the old DG house

Daddy was appalled at the house's shabby contrast to Santa Rosa Hall where he had paid so much less for so much more. I proudly showed him and Mama around the upstairs where eighteen girls crowded into five rooms tangled with a spaghetti of extension cords. Barbara says it was a miracle that the girls, who almost all smoked, didn't set the place on fire. Doris, who grew up to head the Delta Gamma National Council, remembers how we were crammed into that "rabbit warren" and the furor when Marge hung out laundry from the front windows. "Miss Burgess was there in a flash, telling us it looked like a tenement."

I thought the house was mighty fine indeed. Around Burbank most of the buildings over 50 years old were torn down to make way for modernity, and I had never lived in a two-story house before. I felt very grown-up living semi-independently in the house with such solidity, security and caché.

In my senior year, I, as esteemed president, cut the pink and blue ribbons and turned the earth with a bronze-painted spade to inaugurate the building of a new house. I later placed a time capsule into the stone facade of the soon-to-be new UCSB chapter house of Delta Gamma. It was an ironic turn because, while I was enjoying the shabby, but not chic, residence my father disdained, he was still paying supplemental fees for building the lovely Southern-inspired mansion I would never inhabit.

The Gamma Kappa Chapter of Delta Gamma

The former president who broke ground for its construction returns in 2015

The new DG house still sits gracefully on Picasso Road in Isla Vista, a half hour beyond downtown Santa Barbara. Isla Vista now is the unofficial home to many UCSB students including fraternities and sororities.

Welcome to Isla Vista, but stay away if you're going to create Halloween havoc

At the time of our groundbreaking ceremony, Isla Vista was a tranquil little settlement. You'll hear more about what used to be my little bohemia next to the campus in "R is for Renée Reanimated." But if you visit "IV" today, be prepared for a slow slog through streets named for Spanish towns and bigwigs, and for things favored by collegians such as *Sueno* (sleep) and *Sabado Tarde* (Saturday afternoon). Just go with the flow of bikes and skateboards and backpacked youths zig-zagging through a topsy-turvy townlet. It's like an urban design created by freshmen from magazine cutouts tossed in the air and glued down wherever they helter-skelterly scattered.

There have been some less than tranquil times in Isla Vista. In 1970, it was in the news for the burning of the Bank of America building during a Vietnam War protest. Also, more than fifty years ago Isla Vista began a long and increasingly problematic tradition of out-of-control community Halloween parties. Recently the university, law enforcement and other powers that be decided this was a tradition that had had its time. Alternative activities were offered, and streets closed down to non-resident, rabble-rousing revelers. Peace returned.

Rover

It's time to return to Santa Barbara to find our own peace and quiet. We might stroll in the ocean breeze among the palms along Cabrillo Boulevard or relax in one of El Paseo's courtyards. We're sure to find serenity at the Mission of my babyhood movie where my parents tried unsuccessfully to amuse me. On the way, we must pay a visit to Rover, the handsome dog who has lived at the corner of Mission and Garden for over a hundred years. He guards one of the five houses built by railroad magnate William H. Crocker. We need to see if his current owners have dressed him for a special occasion. I'm not sure about Potsy, but I know that grown-up Renée was thoroughly amused when she found him decked out in his Valentine ensemble. I loved it, and him, as much as I continue to love Old Santa Barbara.

30
P is for Picture-Making Pains

Drawing #1 *Elephant Devoured by Boa Constrictor*

Although I did not inherit my artist parents' talent, they did pass on a love for looking at art—sharpened during my days at UCSB. This is despite a rather rocky introduction to picture-making. Remember the artistic anxieties suffered by the young narrator in *The Little Prince?* He was thwarted in his artistic development after failing to make grown-ups understand his drawing of a boa constrictor devouring an elephant.

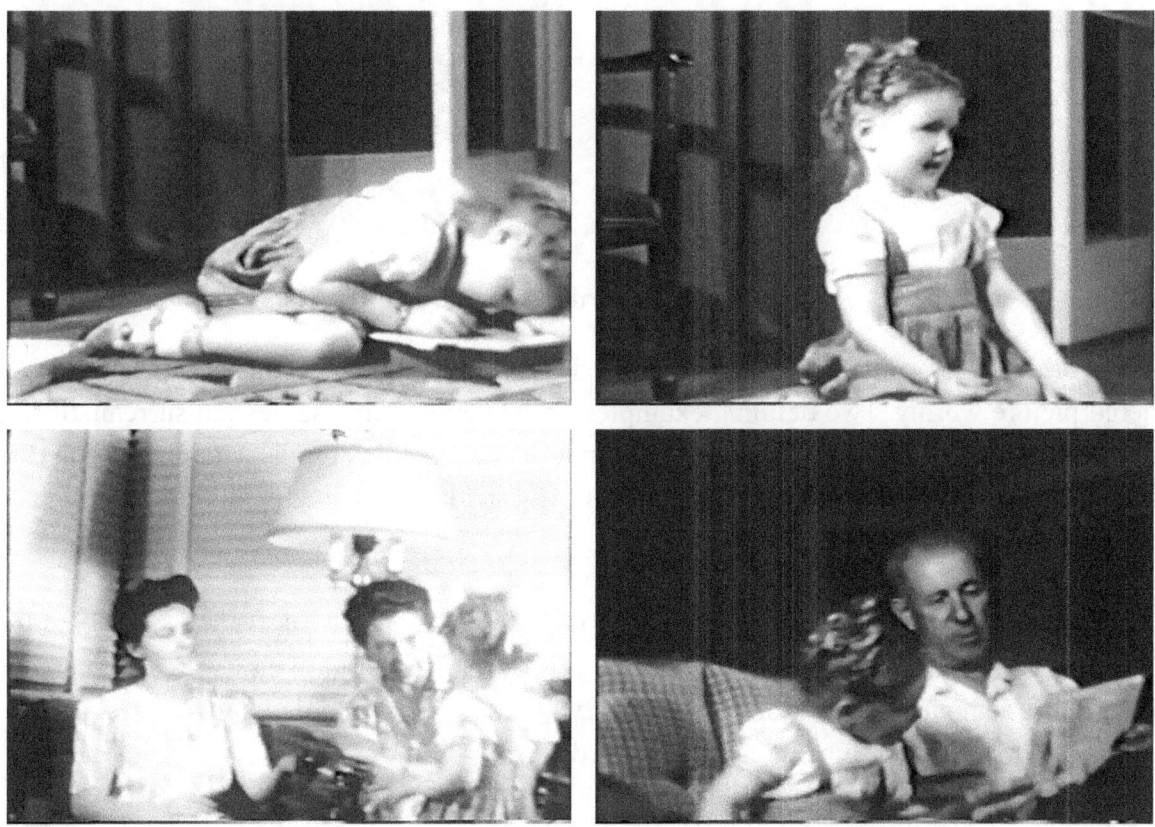

Documentary: *The Tale of the Thwarted Artist*

When the story was first read to me, I was much too young to understand that *The Little Prince* is about adults who, not being blessed by Rachel Carson's fairy, lose their sense of wonder. But I did understand the boy's difficulty understanding the thick-headedness of grown-ups. I, too, made early attempts to be understood through art. One such effort was recorded, not in print, but in film shot by my father when I was about the age of St. Exupéry's narrator.

The movie opens with my dramatic entrance running headlong through the door to plop enthusiastically on the carpet, anxious to create my masterpiece. I obediently try to follow my artist/father/director's orders not to have my eyes so close to the paper, an order that seems to dim my enthusiasm somewhat. I then take my drawing first to my mother and godmother Kelly (who gave me *The Little Prince* book). They make a valiant attempt to decipher whatever it is I want them to appreciate. I next take my drawing to my godfather Roy, whereupon—perhaps in order to avoid another misinterpretation of my art—I proceed to chatter while sketching on his rather large chin. So, my creative career paralleled that of the narrator who concludes his story of art unappreciated with, "That is why at the age of six, I gave up what might have been a magnificent career as a painter."

Pictures by the artist as a young girl

My early works were narratives depicting idealized characters of my age engaged in activities I considered picture worthy. Two defining examples of the genre emit a somewhat surrealistic aura reminiscent of Bosch or Dali. We see a girl in blonde Sadie Hawkins braids leading a flying dog along a path lined with walking trees. She appears to attract head-turning bemusement or fear from a purple suited gentleman stroller.

Then we have the piece entitled *See the Girl Play with Her Dill*. The work features a girl in blonde curls—or fuzzy hoodie—who, also in defiance of gravity, carries her doll clone by its identical coif/headgear. This one includes narration by the artist who obviously struggled between "b" and "d" consonants and the vowel choice in the tricky word "doll."

A second grader's chromatic analysis chart

Since both my parents were artists, they could provide me on demand with sheets of animation paper upon which they had drawn outlines of pictures to color. But I preferred the rough pulpy pages of coloring books. I loved spreading out a thick new book and my crayon array. The primo box was the tiered presentation of 64 shades including the exotics like *Gold Ochre, Burnt Sienna* and the no-longer-politically-correct *Flesh.* I pondered over the perfect shade and whether to make light subtle strokes or press hard, taking the risk of breaking a color stick behind its wrapper, thus rendering it useless and unloved. Still high among my favorite things is to open a new box of Crayolas to reveal the array of colors, smell their intoxicating aroma and test out their hue.

I tried to confine my markings within the lines, an admonition from my father, and to avoid purple, a color Mama detested. I attempted without success to perfect the technique Mary Jane taught me where she very lightly applied color, then gently rubbed it into a smooth lovely pastel effect. I did nothing lightly or gently.

A model rabbit

I filled the buff-colored blank pages of photo albums with my original pictures. I made a visual documentation of what I learned in school and what went on in my vivid pretend world. From time to time one or the other parent would offer suggestions on my artistry. We even have an example of my father's addition of a huge ghostly gray Thumper-ish rabbit to aid me in my rendition of an Easter scene.

There were times when I thought I could advance from crayon drawings and become a painter. I gathered a tablet of lovely white paper, a tin of watercolors with cartoons on the lid, a skinny brush that fit inside and a glass of water. After arranging my materials on lots of newspapers spread on the kitchen table, I dipped my brush into the water and then into a circle of color. Soon the water and the tin and my painting and I all turned into a muddy brown mess. One or the other parent might offer instructions to better my technique. But, a perfectionist even at a young age, I did not enjoy working at something that did not bring immediate success. I had seen *The Blue Boy* at The Huntington Library not far away. I knew I would never be a Gainsborough. Or a painter Patin for that matter.

As I occupied myself with other-than-artistic pursuits, Mama enjoyed more time at her painting. At her drawing board in the sunny lanai, she began to paint all day, every day—her grown-up palette, tubes of paints and brushes on a stand beside her. The whir of the sewing machine ceased. The rugs, carpets and upholstery were left unchanged by her handiwork. I enjoyed watching my mother surrounded by paintings at different stages as she worked in her rapid, almost frenzied fashion. Bit by bit she began to ask for my comments, and I began to see through her eyes. Unlike Daddy, whose cartoony art I deemed to be just what he did at work, I was proud of Mama's pictures that visitors could see and admire.

Masterpiece by Maxine

My mother's paintings began to hang around the house, replacing framed prints of master artists that had hung there, perhaps to further my art appreciation education. In the hall, there had been a picture of a very old man in a huge golden coat and funny silver hat. Now Mama's picture of her Culver City family hung there. And over the fireplace in the living room, a country cottage by Maxine Patin took pride of place away from a picture of ballerinas in fluffy tutus. I didn't know that the displaced prints were reproductions of art created by Rembrandt and Degas.

It wasn't until much later that I realized that these prints hanging around the house and the originals I had been taken to see in museums might have inspired my father's claim to fame in the fine arts. An article in the *Sunday Chicago Tribune* written in June 1945 explains how this all came to pass.

The Blue Boy by Gainsborough   *The Blue Duck* by Ray Patin

It's called "Off-Hour Creations of a Famous Studio." The author, Floribel Muir, describes how one day in 1938 some of Walt's boys gathered around my father's desk and watched him use a special kind of colored crayons that look like oils or pastels to transform Donald Duck into Gainsborough's famous *The Blue Boy*. Ms. Muir went on to describe what she called the "impish burlesques" of the great masters that my father and a couple of fellow animators went on to create.

The Walt Disney Gallery of Old Masters was born. Walt saw the boys' work and said they should make it into a short film, but they never came up with anything that their boss found movie worthy.

Man in Oriental Costume
(*The Noble Slav*) by Rembrandt

The Noble Snob
by Ray Patin

Dancers Bending Down
by Degas

Two Dancing Ducks
by Ray Patin

The titles of some the mock masterpieces my father created reflect the classical as well as comic facets of his artistry: *The Blue Duck* after Gainsborough's *The Blue Boy; Donald Macdonna* inspired by Leonardo da Vinci's *Madonna; Tahitian Ducks* after Gauguin's *Two Tahitian Women on the Beach; Donald's Whistling Mother* from James McNeill Whistler's *Arrangement in Grey and Black No.1 (Mother)*; and, mirroring pieces in our home gallery, my father gave us *The Noble Snob,* a take-off on Rembrandt's *The Noble Slav* and *Two Dancing Ducks* in the manner of Edgar Degas's *Dancers Bending Down.*

At seven I wasn't aware of my father's pantheon of quackeries. But he later talked about the project. His faithful renderings were published in our favorite weekly magazine, *Life,* in April 16, 1945. On the cover was General Eisenhower, who the following month accepted the surrender of Germany, ending the war in Europe. The art is in black and white and doesn't name the artists; instead it discusses the importance of Donald Duck, who had made his debut ten years before. Nevertheless, Daddy was proud of his work. He would get a big kick to know that his pastiches became postage stamps in Sierra Leone in 1995.

Mr. Benchley admires the Disney Gallery of Old Masters

The works started as a lark by my father and his colleagues actually finally made it into a film. While filming *The Reluctant Dragon,* Robert Benchley[1] toured all over The Walt Disney Studios. In one scene, he entered the office of Ward Kimball (of train fame). While looking around, Mr. Benchley stopped to admire the gallery of duck works.

---

[1] Famous in the 1920s-40s as writer, humorist, actor and filmmaker, Benchley was a member of the Algonquin Round Table of sharp-witted New Yorkers.

Despite my parents' talents, my drawing and painting skills did not develop much beyond my depictions of *Girl with Dog* and *Girl with Dill.* I was not always as lucky as the aviator when I shared my art with others. When he grew up, he showed his Drawing #1 to the little prince who understood immediately that it was not a hat, but a boa constrictor devouring an elephant. Sometimes to see clearly, we need to look through the eyes of a child. Now as a grown-up who still loves looking at the art of others, I keep my scribbles to myself and confine myself instead to expressing myself through words.

Although my artistic development remained dysfunctional, some of the spirit of my parents must have rubbed off into a lifelong passion for art. When I took my first college art history classes I was fascinated by how different painters throughout the ages and across borders saw the world so differently. I was in awe of their ability to express what they saw in so many ways. I felt proud that I could so easily identify the painters on the slides the professor showed us and proud of the A grades on my papers and in the courses. My parents, too, were proud of my grades, but never had any expectations of my entering the world of art.

Then I fell in love with one particular painter. And my passion for painters took on a new meaning.

31
Q is for Queens

Who's not the fairest?

Queens topped my childhood list of scary things that go bump in the night. My fear was no doubt due to a premature viewing of *Snow White and the Seven Dwarfs* featuring the ever most powerfully scary Evil Queen who for a long time was the monster under my bed.

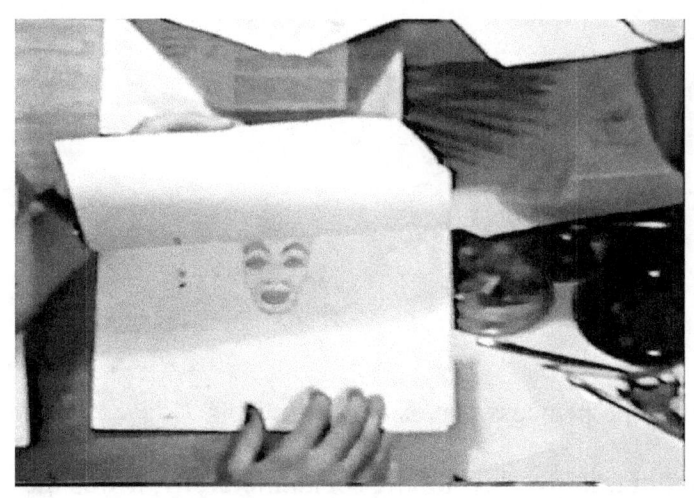

Footage from the never-produced film *Snow White Animators at Work*

This was silly, really. I knew that the Queen was just a bunch of drawings. I had seen her actually being drawn in one of my father's mini movie melodramas. It was the story of his fellow Hyperion animators competing for the best rendering of the Queen's malevolent mug. Reminiscent of the nose clip-producing film of my father's failed *Sea Scout* sequence, this saga concluded with the animator throwing his unappreciated work in the trash can.

It came to be that my perception of boogey-woman queens persisted throughout childhood. After many sessions listening to my record of Ginger Rogers in *Alice in Wonderland,* my royal repugnance was reinforced. Her very head was in danger from the chronically enraged Queen of Hearts.

Jack the Queen-maker and his loyal royal pages

I knew, of course, that being a queen was a desirable thing. I listened with Mama to the radio show *Queen for a Day* where Jack Bailey granted needy housewives just about everything they could have ever desired. Later we watched the show on TV.

And I knew there were non-pretend queens who were probably not evil at all and didn't demand that the heart be excised from their fairer offspring or the decapitation of visitors to their realm. The week I was born, the new queen of England, Elizabeth, sporting long gown and white fox fur cape was on the cover of *Life* magazine. She smilingly waved to the camera, fingers pointed inward, as she passed saluting subjects. She had unexpectedly become queen when her brother-in-law gave up the throne for the woman he loved. Her namesake daughter, Princess Elizabeth, would follow her as queen as well.

I was fascinated by Elizabeth and Margaret, whom the media dubbed "the little princesses." I poured over pictures of the sisters at pomp and play. They were shown with royal perks of their very own like their just-like-grown-ups playhouse and roadster.

Servants parade the regal litter while the princess waves at her subjects

The queen may have been glamorous and brilliant, but, in my developing social hierarchy, it was the princesses who were the stars. Often featured in my fairy tales, they had the important qualities like frothy dresses, sparkly crowns, and kindness to forest animals and to little people. Though it often took finding a prince to become one, the princesses always had the best accoutrements like the swirliest dresses and minions who transported them throughout their kingdom in fancy coaches.

Queen Mary and King Mickey

My fear of queens had faded by the time I went to high school. I had watched Mary Frances Reynolds rise from queen to movie star. So, my fear was replaced by awe and admiration. Then, in high school, the green-eyed monster raised her jealous head when my close friends Mary and Mickey were chosen as Prom Queen and King. I tried not to show my envy as I joined the other lowly prom-goers in cheering the triumphant couple. They entered resplendently with their court and gracefully danced before us, she in her emerald green satin gown modeled on a creation Audrey Hepburn wore in *Sabrina*.

Mary Jane came closer than I to being crowned. She appeared on a sort of junior version of *Queen for a Day* called *Glamour Girl*. It aired in 1955 and began by announcing it was filmed in Hollywood, "the glamour capital of the world." It promised to bring out the princess that was hidden in every woman. Not quite a woman, Mary Jane was taken to Max Factor, a famous beauty studio on Hollywood Boulevard where they did her hair and painfully plucked her eyebrows. She wore a beautiful pink dress that she got to keep and wear at her senior prom (where she wasn't, by the way, the queen). I mitigated my jealousy over Mary Jane's winning the show by telling myself she was just chosen because Jack McCoy, the host of the show, lived across the street. She had babysat Jack McCoy's baby[1] so he arranged she would be chosen.

Honor to the queens

---

[1] In the house that had been occupied by Ivan Ditmars, a musical director for game shows and then Robert Shield, an actor best known as TV's *The Judge*.

DG queens on their royal float thrones

In the collegiate society, the queens were the A-listers, lovely to look at and desirable in character. I felt a species apart from these campus queens featured in their own section in the pages of the *La Cumbre*[2] yearbook. Note the introductory page to the 1957 "Royalty" section displaying the tiara, trophy and trappings of those chosen as the fairest in UCSB-land. These highnesses of Homecoming posed in regal serenity on their own portrait page. And in the Homecoming parade, the queen and her court waved regally from atop of their frilly floats like animated wedding cake toppers.

Military sweethearts

Another opportunity for crowning was the formal gala known as the Military Ball sponsored by the ROTC (Reserve Officers' Training Corps). The queen of this event was chosen from the Colonel's Coeds, the bubbly fresh-faced female representatives of the Corps who wore their red corduroy jumpers on Thursdays and served as hostesses for the aspiring military men.

---

[2] The Spanish word means the "peak" as in the mountains that surround Santa Barbara where there is also a mall and country club of the same name. It also implies a pinnacle of excellence.

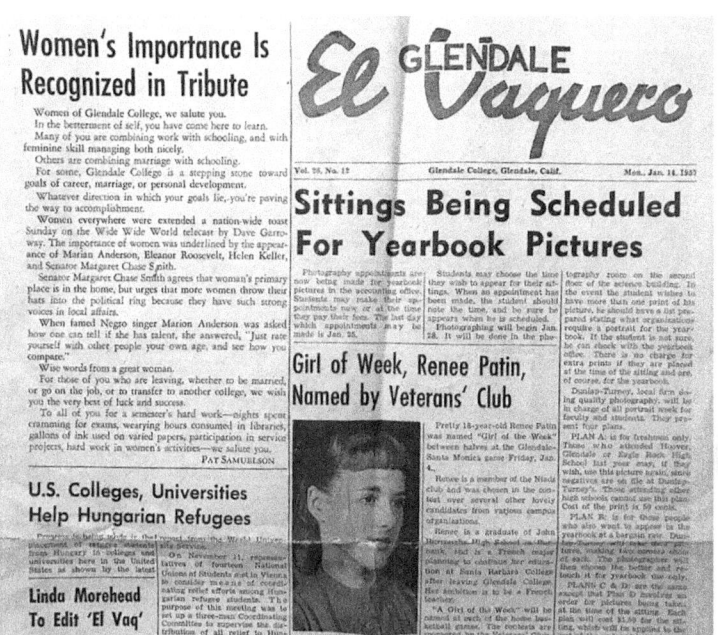 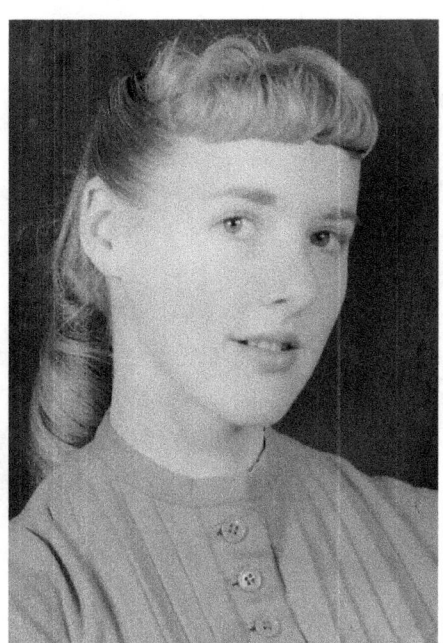

Glendale College Girl of the Week, age 18

I was not a Colonel's Coed. The closest I came to being a military favorite was when the Veterans' (Korea) Club at Glendale Junior College sponsored me to be their candidate for Girl of the Week. My dating one of the veterans at the time may have entered into their nomination. The attendees at a basketball game voted on their favorite nominees. Before the tip off I stood in the lobby, greeting the fans and touting my vote-worthiness in what must have been a captivating fashion. Or it may have been my particularly lovely coif featuring bangs created with the overnight aid of a Kotex sanitary napkin pinned in place to poof out otherwise stick-straight hair. The ponytail required more conventional curlers. I doubt it was due to my hairdo, but I was voted worthy of the honor bestowed at halftime—without benefit of a crown. The announcement of "Pretty 18-year-old Renee Patin" becoming Girl of the Week was published in the venerable *El Vaquero,* next to an article on the importance of women.

So, I was never crowned as queen of any event. I saw myself as far from campus courts as from those of England and fairy tales. My self-image did not include what I considered monarch material. I saw myself as acceptably attractive. Girls chosen as queens seemed like another species—girlier girls than I considered myself to be. I was content to have played a comic royal role in a Barbary Coast operatic production.

Musicale royale   My parents in touch with royalty

But there was one little nod toward royalty in the Patin family—my father's unsung role as a queenly sort in one of his live-action commercials. It is an ad he produced with Stan Freberg, the all-around funny man, author, recording artist, animation voice actor, comedian, radio personality, puppeteer and advertising creative director. His comedy albums of satire and songs were highly popular. I had loved him, but did not know him as the voice of Cecil, the Seasick Sea Serpent on *Beany and Cecil*, a TV puppet show I watched religiously.

In the commercial Mr. Freberg is playing on a candelabra-topped piano for the amusement of what appears to be the back of Queen Marie Antoinette. (But it is actually my father whose queenly behind is visible to the viewer.) In the middle of a stately minuet, Freberg breaks into a wild rendition of one of his wonderful wacky songs. At the conclusion of the ditty, the elaborately bewigged queenly presence turns toward the camera. Now, through the magic of film editing, the queen is again Stan Freberg. My father's role as a royal rear end must have delighted my fairy tale-loving mother who attended the filming, and whose own appearance as a queen in her later years is featured in Part III.

As it is, let's just say that if my parents' artistic talent wasn't inherited, their creativity at reinvention was. I could be whatever I wanted—as taught by my father, the Queen.

32
R is for Renée Reanimated

The UCSB student body as seen by illustrator Dick Phipps in our 1958 yearbook

Even as a small school, UCSB offered a wide choice of roles to play. As I clambered up the ladder of the academic ivory tower, I reanimated myself into a different Renée on each rung. I acquired the faces of far more than the good and bad personas of my Potsyhood. I considered myself terminally unique and frightfully important. And I felt like the tiniest of guppies in the vastest ocean. I knew I was riddled with flaws at the same time I was accepting accolades. I was like the model sheets my father followed so he could animate the many moods of Donald Duck.

I weighed my attributes by comparing Renée vs. Everyone Else and found myself superior to many and inferior to most. Depending on my audience, I acted the role of the academic or the actress, the leader or the led, the pursuer or the rejecter, the shrinking violet or the chit chatter, the lady or the tramp.

I found one mask comfortable—sorority girl. As a duly-initiated Greek citizen of UCSB, I found it difficult to imagine the social lives of those UCSB residents who didn't affiliate themselves with a sorority or fraternity.

The world as seen by a Manhattanite

I suffered from a sort of xenophobia toward non-Greeks. It was kind of like Saul Steinberg's famous *View of the World from 9th Avenue* cartoon on the 1976 *New Yorker* cover where he pictured the rest of the world from the perspective of a Manhattanite.

It is embarrassing to confess that I viewed Everyone Else on campus through the lens of the initiated. It was hard for me to fathom that the unfortunates whom we designated GDIs (God Damn Independents) had any hope of full lives without being in a "house." I later learned that many of these perfectly happy enrollees professed blissful lives because of not being in a silly sorority or fatuous fraternity.

1957 first year as Delta Gamma—right page, third row from bottom, third from left

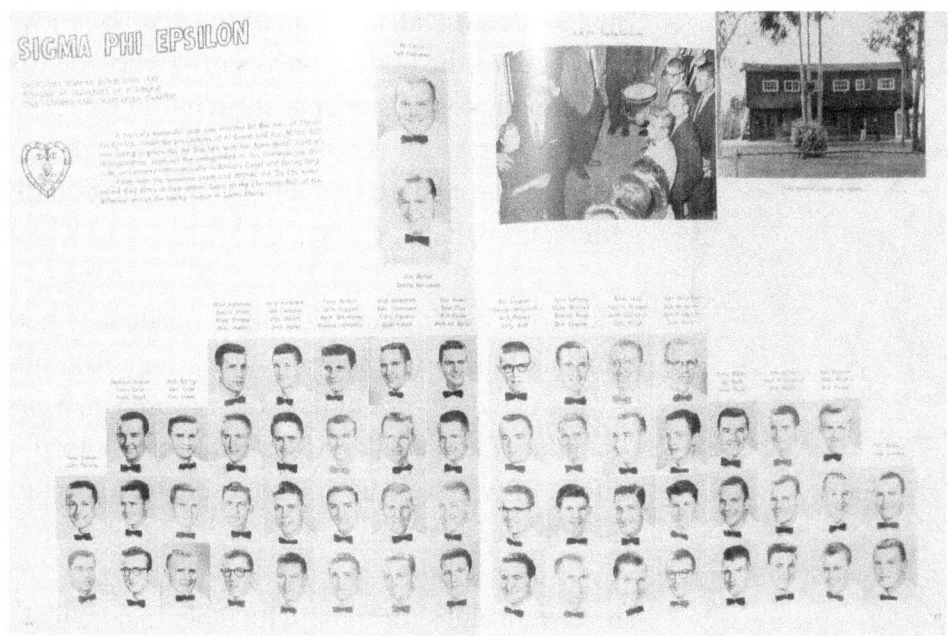

The Sig Eps and their Isla Vista house

Our *La Cumbre* yearbook certainly recognized our status as "Greeks" on campus. Each year it devoted two pages to smiling members of each sorority and fraternity. Looking much alike, we posed at Gilberts of Goleta Photography in the same sweater or jacket and tie passed from member to member.

Everyone Else

RESIDENCE HALLS

The other half

The Residence Halls section of the yearbook is introduced by a photo of the bottom halves of "Everyone Else" followed by group photos of students clustered in front of their dorm drapes. Cypress proved itself a barracks with personality by posing in casual garb including sweatshirts boldly emblazoned with their GDI status.

Aside from affiliations with one's residence, there was an abundant buffet of other non-Greek organizational offerings to which students could lend their presence. Many even had Greek letter names like Alpha Mu Gamma for foreign language majors, of which I was one but eschewed its club, thus never learning the mysteries behind the name.

There were clubs for those with other majors like the Muse-ettes for music majors and several, like the Elemeds, for elementary education majors, who were the highest proportion of female students. This was because UCSB had started as a normal school, not implying that abnormal students were not accepted, but that it was a school for teacher training.

Some students affiliated with the arts. Others chose a military affiliation like the Scabbard and Blade for the uniformed youth of the ROTC. The sailors organized into a club, but surfers didn't. It's hard to picture them on the sand, cross-legged on their boards, following Robert's Rules of Order while the waves beckoned behind them. There were also unorganized organizations like the scholars who hung out in a special collections area of the library or in the venerable Reserved Book Room. And the bridge players held seemingly continuous meetings in the east wing of the Student Union.

Rally Committee: Judy in the center, middle row; I'm two places to the right

But my picture of myself did not include signing up for clubs. I lent my presence to only one other non-Greek group, the Rally Committee, the one that put the "rah" in school spirit. I joined at the behest of its leader, my roommate Judy who unlike me, found it possible to be in a sorority and also shine as a very big woman on campus. My diminished sense of rah-rah made me less than effective within the organization, and my attendance was spotty. I think we discussed festive decorations and school spirit apathy.

I also wore the white outfit and white bucks and socks of a proud member of the Spurs.[1] These were sophomore women selected for their grade point average. But if there were meetings, I didn't attend, nor did I make it for the group picture. Many members went on as juniors and seniors to membership in Chimes or Crown and Scepter, the organization that honored academic excellence in upper division students. I didn't. Judy did.

The Spurs with Judy in the front row, second from right.

La Cumbres 1957-1960

The clever creators of our yearbook still tickle my funny bone with their skewed view of campus extracurricular activity. They often snuck in mock organizations. Looking back, I realize how much fun it would have been to be part of that yearbook staff who took a more lighthearted view of campus life than I did. Here are some of them:

---

[1] See "G is for Gaucho" for clarification of the equestrian significance of the organization's title.

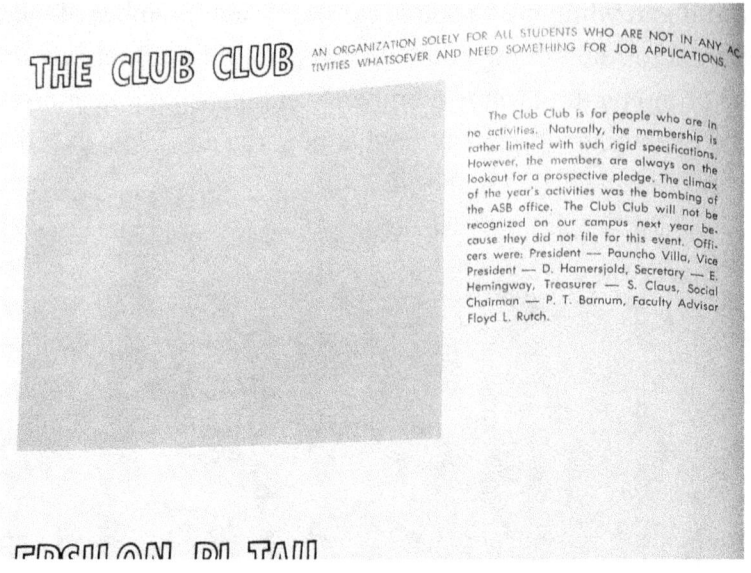

The Club Club:

An organization solely for all students who are not in any activities whatsoever and need something for job applications.

Rho Rho Rho (pronounced Row Row Row like the boat song):

The national honorary fraternity for upper division students in the sanitation engineering department of the harbor division of applied arts.

The Goleta Sophists:

A spirited philosophical group directed at orienting the non-creative individual. By October they had twenty-five 'interested people.' (The Sophists[2] shun the word "pledge" fearing association with another campus element.)

While I played the role of campus coed in a sorority, I had another venue in which I became a very different persona. This little hideaway was Isla Vista. You may remember visiting this campus community on our tour of Old Santa Barbara. For me, there was magic to this little settlement next to the campus. The few streets were unpaved. Chickens and an occasional cow roamed the open fields. There were a few very basic dwellings and only a hint of the apartment sprawl that now dominates the landscape. Businesses came and went: a rustic market, a gas station, and Nebi's, a corner café that served a very limited menu.

In Isla Vista I was reanimated. There I no longer was playing my DG role of a prim and proper president who served on the "Standards Board" passing judgment on members whose morals might have demonstrated a little loosening.

---

[2] Sophists, not to be confused with the Elemeds, were a special kind of teacher in ancient Greece.

My own loosening came when I drove the half hour into Isla Vista. I left behind the restraints of sorority life. There was a little hint of the naughty in the hamlet that lay beyond the properness of Santa Barbara. There I felt twinges of the bad little girl with the curl and shed my A-getter, good girl. I fraternized with budding bohemians who imitated the Beatniks currently establishing their anti-establishment. I'm not sure if others called Isla Vista the "Left Bank," but, as a Francophile, I did. I envied what I considered the on-the-edge lives of the scattering of independent spirits who lived there.

Saving for the good life

My role as a bohemian in Isla Vista was but one reanimation that I would undergo in college and well beyond. I loved artsy and philosophical discussions with the scruffy residents of one particular former fisherman's shack and with one boy in particular. He was a painter, and I fancied myself his muse. He was probably the clever one who wrote "Jesus Saves" over the shack's unusual wallpaper designed from Green Stamps.[3] You'll meet him in "X is for XOXO."

---

[3] A method of saving for products that could be redeemed at stores. When I was a kid, my mother gave me the task of licking the stamps and putting them in the books. It was a sticky chore until I discovered wet sponges.

33
S is for Smokes, Spirits and Suds

The magic of a great smoke

In college, most of us smoked. My first inhale was choke inducing, but I soldiered on to join those who indulged. I blamed free samples distributed on campus for my habit. I was hooked by a Lorillard tobacco company representative. His lure was his male magnetism and a mini pack of five Kent cigarettes, the ones with the Micronite filter (the "healthy" feature later found to contain a virulent form of asbestos).

Pat, the roommate who followed Judy, says that I required her to descend from our cozy presidential sunroom each school morning in order to warm up my Hillman Minx and light up my cigarette. She said it was fair exchange for a ride into campus. That's a pretty embarrassing reminder of something I had forgotten—the assignment, not the smoking.

I didn't think of myself as "bad" when I began lighting up. No one could say I was akin to those nasty high school slouchers who gathered in their odorous corner in front of Burroughs. They feigned a detached coolness, cigarettes adangle in their pouty mouths, eyes aslant like James Dean, as they exhaled toward the Burbank skies. Their smoke signal (coincidentally the name for our school newspaper) proclaimed them as the badasses of Burroughs High.

Here are some of the core beliefs about tobacco that floated around my impressionable head:

1. Cigarettes are suave.

Look at all the brand names that hint of European sophistication, even aristocracy: Kent, Marlboro, Raleigh, Chesterfield, Parliament, Pall Mall, and Viceroy.

Nana in the middle with the smooth smoking M. Francois

I'll never forget when I was about thirteen, and we were paid a visit by a confusingly-connected cousin from Paris. He was a super suave, highly handsome actor named Jacques Francois. The thing I remember most about his many sophisticated attributes was the cigarette that balanced on his languorous lips and the lidded eyes behind the cloud of smoke. He was so very French, I determined, that he could even exhale through his nose and blow smoke rings. I fell immediately in love.

2. Celebrities smoke.

Advertisements were filled with their handsome faces side by side with a pack of cigarettes. Unfortunately for our picture story, but perhaps fortunately for society, I'm not allowed to show these ads. The cigarette companies could not give permission because of the 1998 Master Settlement Agreement that resulted from lawsuits brought by individuals against tobacco companies for the damaging effects of cigarettes. The Agreement changed and limited how tobacco products are advertised, marketed and sold to youth. There are no longer misleading ads extolling false benefits of smoking—especially those aimed at young people such as I was when I took up the habit.[1]

Movie stars like Ronald Reagan, Frank Sinatra, Lucy and Desi, Joan Crawford, and John Wayne, Olympic athletes, even Santa were pictured in full color and quoted on the benefits of a great smoke. This meant that if I lit up, I too, could be sprinkled with stardust and have a more fabulous life like theirs or like the romantic couples whose rollicking was enhanced by cigarettes.

---

[1] If you want to see some of these unregulated ads, search Google for "Fifties Cigarette Ads" and "Vintage Ad Browser." You'll also find them on YouTube under "Fifties Cigarette Ads."

For more on the history of how the MSA came to be, search Google for "Master Settlement Agreement."

3. Smoking soothes.

I looked forward to that half hour drive to and from school to savor my Kent. A cigarette to calm me down was a welcome companion when I studied late into the night.

4. Tobacco isn't bad for you.

Look at all the doctors—often in white coats and giant reflectors strapped to their foreheads—who guaranteed its benefits in the ads. Even healthy babies cherubically attested to smoking safety. There were amazing headlines about how a puff on a certain brand guards against "throat scratch," or the brands that more doctors and dentists smoke than any others, and even "the smooth taste expectant mothers crave."

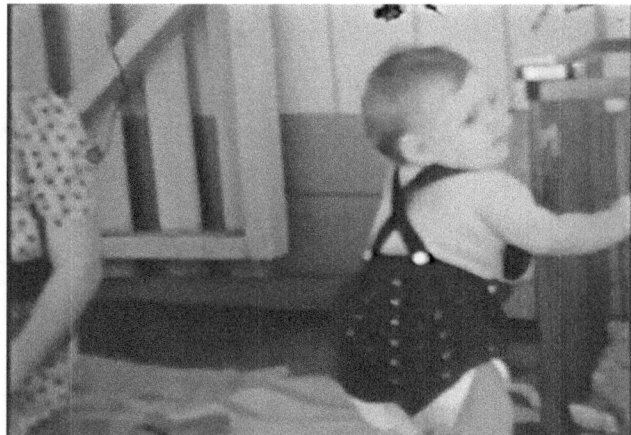 

Droopy drawers? A cigarette is just the answer

I was actually one of those babies photographed with a pack of cigarettes. In one of Daddy's mini-movies, I starred as a hefty ten-month-old with droopy diapers crawling toward my playpen upon which is perched an enticing pack. My joy at attaining my crinkly goal was ad-worthy.

Maxine lights up

5. Parents do it.

My father was a chain smoker. He was never without a pack of unfiltered Luckies, and our wastebaskets always contained those packs with the red target. At first packs were green, but they changed to white during the war when the green dye had chemicals in demand for the effort. His pockets were always filled with a mixture of tobacco and eraser shreddings that he trailed wherever he'd been, especially during the lean days when he messily rolled his own on a little machine he kept in the den. Little oval brown cigarette burns dotted his clothes, furniture and anything placed near where he had been drawing, reading or relaxing.

Mary Jane's mother did it. Mama didn't smoke, but my father managed to film a rare moment when she tried. The occasion was a Riley family Christmas gathering at Nonnie and Pop's Big Bear mountain cabin. He zoomed in for a close-up of probably her one and only moment of weakness brought on by several yuletide toddies and goading brothers. His camera lingered on his lovely thirty-something wife as she inhaled and doubled over choking.

6. Smoking is something to sing and shout about.

A top Billboard hit in 1947 was Phil Harris[2] singing "Smoke, Smoke, Smoke (That Cigarette)" whose lyrics hint that someone knew cigarettes were not a health benefit.

> *Smoke, smoke, smoke that cigarette*
> *Puff, puff, puff and if you smoke yourself to death*
> *Tell St. Peter at the Golden Gate that you hate to make him wait*
> *But you just gotta have another cigarette*

As a kid, I memorized and mimicked the radio ads for cigarettes. I could imitate the diminutive bellboy who, in the finest of hotel lobbies shouted, "Call for Philip Morr-ee-us!" I knew that L.S.M.F.T meant "Lucky Strike Means Fine Tobacco." (Not, as the bad Burroughs boys chanted, "Loose Straps Mean Floppy Tits.")

---

[2] American comedian, jazz musician, orchestra leader and singer. He was on the radio with Jack Benny and on TV with his wife Alice Faye.

Cigarette sorcery

I don't know if my father produced any of the animated smoking commercials that are now banned. But I did find some artwork in his archives advertising a brand that shall remain nameless. It features Puffo, the magician—definitely appealing to kids—doing a trick with cigarettes popping out of a hat and the brand spelled out in smoke puffs.

7. My charm factor would be greatly increased with a cigarette in my hand.

As a coed, I thought a cigarette held gracefully between two extended fingers gave me a certain *je ne sais quoi*. Following DG rules of never walking with a cigarette or removing my hand from it while smoking, I learned a tricky cigarette-lighting maneuver of striking a match and switching hands, all while never letting go. I added my own flourishes to the lady's art of smoking whenever a polite gentleman of interest offered to light my cigarette. It was a gentle guiding touch on his hand and a slow simmering, eye rising to meet his. I doubt it was this gesture that attracted my husband-to-be ten years later, but, soon after we married, I quit the habit except for what I inhaled second-hand from his chain smoking.

Ray Patin Productions TV commercial for happy hour

Spirits, too, were part of our daily ritual. My parents' evening cocktails-for-two was a familiar one. Every day after Daddy got home from the studio, I would hear from my room the ritual sounds coming from the kitchen: the crack of the metal ice tray handle followed by the clink of the cubes and gurgle/splash of the enticing elixir filling two tall glasses. I knew that my parents had poured their first bourbon and 7 Up highballs. I watched as the spirits raised and then lowered their own spirits and learned to time my disruptions to avoid the latter.

Happy hour on board

Jim Beam bourbon bottles always accompanied us on sojourns to the *Trinket*. As soon as we removed the tricky tarps and boarded the musty craft, Mama and Daddy would agree that "the sun is over the yardarm somewhere" (nauticalese for Happy Hour).[3] Out came the harvest gold and sunset orange plastic insulated tumblers. In plopped ice chipped from the block we'd lugged from the Newport Beach icehouse, topped off with the precious liquid of tranquility. With the boat still tied up, they settled into folding chairs on the afterdeck and toasted the safe journey from Burbank with the cocktail flag on the antenna wafting in the Newport Bay breeze.

---

[3] On sailing ships of yore, when the sun seemed to be above the topmost crossbar (yardarm) on a mast (around 11:00 AM), the officers and crew of a sailing ship got their first issue of rum. The *Trinket*, a powerboat, had no sails, thus no yardarm.

Animators' night out

Back in La La Land, Mama and Daddy dressed up in hat and gloves for her and suit and tie for him to spend evenings at watering holes whose names reflected the popularity of fancy cocktail concoctions. In the San Fernando Valley, they frequented The Tail of the Cock and The Pump Room, pricey and dimly lit restaurants that catered to "the industry" (anybody connected to the Hollywood scene). In 1947, my parents were photographed at The Pump Room with Pat (whose pompadour made up for her hatlessness) and Hal King as they celebrated the anniversary of Volus and Susan Jones in the middle. The evening would later be heavily lubricated with liquor, but for their photo the diners posed primly with uncustomary cups of coffee.

Fraternity title page and beer stein

A UCSB yearbook page that introduced fraternity life featured a poker table laid with cigarettes and an array of beer steins. We Greeks had our own personalized steins with coats of arms for each house. Suds, sand and surf were the magic mixture for merriment at our Goleta beach parties. I remember some words from a ditty of unknown origin that we sang with great gusto to celebrate our drink of choice:

> *My teeth are dull.*
> *I cannot chew.*
> *It comes from opening cans of brew*

Odes to suds by Ray Patin Productions

I liked a cold swig of beer once I got used to the bitter bite. But there came a time at a Kappa Sig party when I sipped my first glass of white wine. I discovered the balm that soothes all social anxiety and forgot all the times I watched grown-ups suffer the effects of overindulging.

On many a date my imbibing made my apparently loosened libido an easy mark for a lusting lothario. I particularly remember going to the parentless home of a Montecito "townie." He seemed very posh, with a first name that sounded like a last name. He plied me with my first martinis from which I learned the speedy effect of drinking gin and vermouth as if it were a cold brew.

My lesson in the art of cocktail slipping was but one I picked up in my collegiate studies of smokes, spirits and suds. I learned a great deal from sources not listed in the UCSB catalog. Next, we'll look at some of the teachers of a curriculum better befitting an academic institution.

34
T is for Teacher

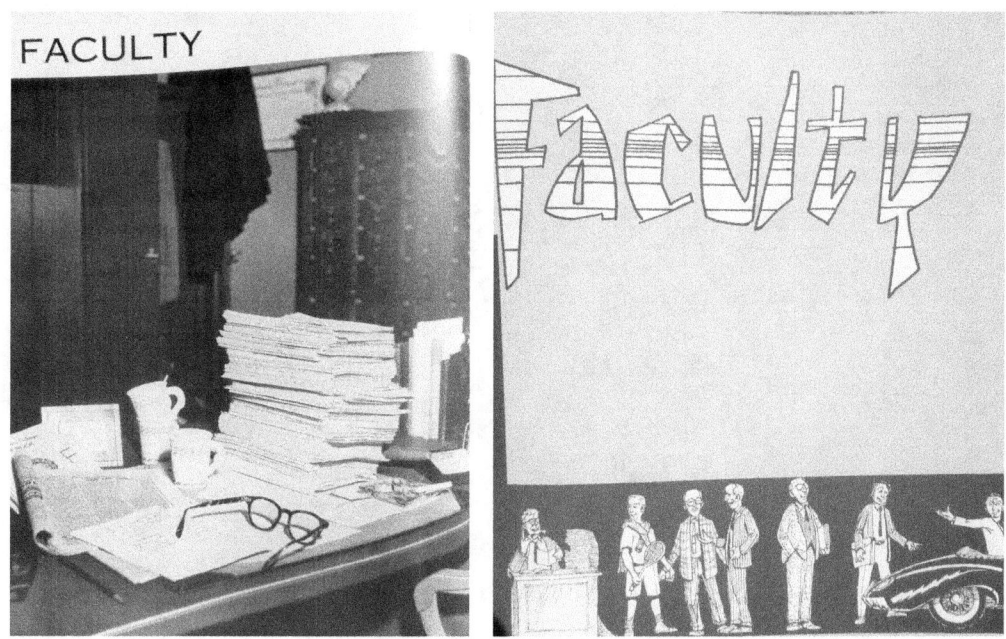

How we students viewed the faculty

In 1957, the faculty section of the *La Cumbre* was introduced with a photo of a desk filled with Blue Books, horn-rimmed glasses, coffee and cigarettes—no beer steins. A Blue Book marked with the dreaded F shows the fruits of a professor's labor. In the 1958 yearbook, Dick Phipps and his satirical pen posed our instructors in various professorial and leisurely guises fanning out from another Blue Book stacked desk.

Our student body was small at about 2,000. In a time before social media, word of mouth assessments of our little faculty spread fast. We enjoyed grading our teachers on their level of erudition, entertainment and overall coolness. We talked about who we "had" like items on a menu. "I had Dr. Blank. He's OK, but boring." We warned each other about teachers' grading proclivities as in "Don't get Smith. He never gives a girl more than a C." This probably wasn't entirely true. Sexism was rampant on campus and everywhere else, but we had no names for it, and there were no movements to combat it. I had no reference to think it wasn't just the way things were. I felt it in the dating game and saw it in the faculty. All my teachers were male except for teacher training and physical education.

An education on paper

As I look over the transcript listing the college courses I undertook, I have forgotten the names of most of the academicians who spent hours preparing to illuminate me, countless sessions imparting pearls of wisdom and hours more reading my Blue Books to discover if they had been at all successful. I admired my teachers and loved the picture I had of myself as a bright young thing in the presence of professors I could call "Doctor." Some of the French teachers even had us stand for them. But, for this student, my teachers' status as dispensers of knowledge was less important than their power of grade granting—preferably A's.

A yearbook picture of our little English Department

My all-time favorite teacher was Dr. Hugh Kenner. He's sitting in the photo in the middle of the front row as chairman of the English Department posing, appropriately, in the library "stacks." I sat mesmerized in my little chair/desk taking notes as he gushed forth fascinating facts about the masterpieces of modern literature. He talked with the cotton-muffled pronunciation that resulted from losing most of his hearing after a bout with influenza as a child. I remember writing in my notes what I heard him say about "damn novels" until I realized he was discussing "dime novels." Dr. Kenner could even make me understand and love something as obtuse as

James Joyce's *Ulysses* on which I wrote one of my catchier term papers, "The Contrast Between Bloom's Consciousness and that of Stephen Based on Sartrean Existentialism." My esteem for Dr. Kenner was boosted when he found my dissertations A-worthy. Vivid in my memory is the time I felt particularly desirable upon meeting an eligible Delt who remarked, "I hear you got an A from Kenner." Ahh, adulation!

Artistic arrangement of free spirits in suits

For their yearbook group portrait, the teachers who turned me on to my favorite subject, art history, arranged themselves in an artistic diagonal design on the stairs of one of the former base buildings instead of in the courtyard of their new art building.

Polyglot professors: Sartre look-alike back row, right and the real Sartre, inset

The teachers in my Foreign Language Department were a motley crew of continentals. The German and Italian female teachers in the front row on the right may recently have emigrated from the country whose language they taught. Dr. Murray on the far right in the back row looks as if he has just come from a sidewalk table at the Deux Magots in Paris and was channeling Sartre.

Corrections

I remember Dr. Murray always took the time to write pages of notes on the first drafts of my Seventeenth Century French Literature term papers. He carpeted the cover page of my dissertation on the world-view of the fabulist La Fontaine with scholarly notes and appended more pages of notes inside. I got an A thanks to all the work he put into the first draft.

My very bright roommate Judy surmised that her academic achievements were due to an education in Hawaii and Las Vegas where they taught the basics, not the progressive education to which we Californians were subjected. Judy was among the few and finest English majors chosen for Aldous Huxley's seminars on "The Human Situation."

Judy remembers staying at the home of the Provost whose daughter was a DG. She told me that when the great Huxley came to visit, he used her bathroom, and with his limited eyesight mistook Judy's hairbrush for a nailbrush. And that is why Judy, and I by distant association, can claim an intimate connection to the great thinker. Judy also remembers the time she and her class attended one of the great man's lectures in the Arlington Theater after which they waited for Huxley to join them. They finally found him backstage enthusiastically engaged in a discussion of psychedelic drugs with a cleaning lady.

Homer, Rousseau and Hemingway celebrated at homecoming

Huxley was so popular on campus that the Pi Phis dedicated their 1960 homecoming float to him and named it for his most famous book, *Brave New World*. Sadly, there is no record of the Pi Phi's homage to Huxley.

The theme for the parade—proof that revelers can be scholarly while celebrating our team's homecoming game—was "Gauchos Salute the World of Books." The Sig Eps won both the Sweepstakes and Theme Prizes with their *Odyssey* float. A hulky Sig Ep in a fake beard (our boys didn't sport facial hair) represented Ulysses. On the prow of the float the Gaucho (UC) Bear, a short-term mascot, represented one of the lesser known of Ulysses' trials. Even the Industrial Arts Club, not known as bookworms, saluted the great thinker, Jean-Jacques Rousseau, with a stack of high-minded tomes. And the Kappa Sigs honored Hemingway's recent bestseller *The Old Man and the Sea*. The confusing figure of a tiger shark and motto "Spear Those Tigers," are an allusion to the Tigers of Occidental College who were indeed speared in the homecoming game.

Although I admired and sometimes idolized my teachers, I didn't want to be one. That is, until I did. It was by default that I realized I had no clue how to launch a career related to my French major or passion for art history. And the chance was remote that I, who never took a drama class, would become an overnight movie star. Reluctantly I approached my father to announce I needed to spend an additional year and a half in graduate school to obtain a General Secondary Credential that would let me teach any subject in grades seven through junior college. He was furious. He wanted me to become a diplomat or United Nations translator or even a foreign import buyer.

Congenial college of educators

But Daddy came around, and in my junior year, alongside liberal arts classes, I began education courses like Pupil Personnel and Counseling and the one from which I might have benefited, Adolescent Growth and Development. I found the subject matter a little too factual, lacking the imagination my upbringing valued. I had to learn to speak the lingua franca of the Education Department, those playful souls who posed for the yearbook gaily chatting in desks like the ones that would be occupied by students we were learning to teach.

After having spent a few years as a teacher,[1] I appreciate my instructors even more. I see that their zeal for sharing their subjects endowed me with one of my greatest gifts: a hunger for learning and a thirst for sharing and teaching what I have learned.

The 1949 Lincoln faculty that lit the flame flanked by principal, custodians and crossing guard.

___

[1] See "Potsy in Grown-Up Land"

35
U is for Under the Sign

1957 Art Directors Club Gold Medal presented to Ray Patin

Not only did my father not envision his only daughter as a teacher, he also never considered her to be his heir as head of Ray Patin Productions. Girls just didn't do that kind of work in the late fifties. When I look back on how my father was affected by the glare of success under the Sign, I wonder if the effects would have been the same on me.

As my career days approached, Daddy was at the height of his. Awards lined the halls of the studio. The Prod family became the proud family. Now when I filled out school information cards, I put "Producer" in the blank for "Father's Occupation."

Yuletide greetings from TV land

The upbeat, whimsical art produced by his studio was groundbreaking and showcased the spirit of successful creativity that ran throughout the studio. Their annual Christmas cards reflected that spirit and played on America's love affair with television in an era many called its Golden Age. The cover of one card shows Santa with a sleigh filled with characters from Ray Patin Productions' commercials. Inside we see the chimney he is approaching where stockings are all hung with care—on rooftop TV antennas![1] The greeting is, "Best wishes for an even brighter TV Picture."

---

[1] Yes. We all had antennas on our rooftops. Some sets had indoor antennas called "rabbit ears" that needed constant adjustment, sometimes necessitating metal coat hangers and aluminum foil.

Watch the changing images on the screen

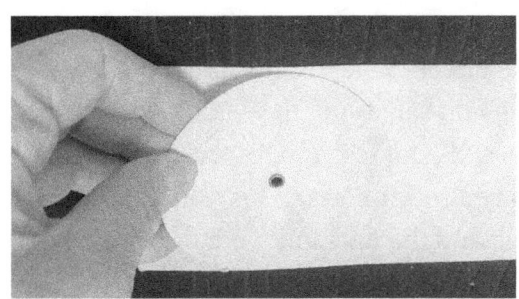

A creative way to "channel surf"

In another card, signed by all the staff, Santa is watching television. The picture can be changed by rotating a wheel on the back of the card. In one frame it says, "From the guys and gals at Ray Patin's," another reads "A Christmas Spectacular" and yet another bears a familiar phrase from radio days, "And now a word from our sponsor."

Pretty good commercial, eh?

The studio's most lastingly lauded production was the Jell-O "Chinese Baby" commercial. This is the one where a baby is trying to eat grape Jell-O with chopsticks. Having seen the child's dilemma, her mother brings a spoon "invented for eating Jell-O." The last line, with a background of tinkling glass chimes is, "Pretty good commercial, eh?" A prophetic self-compliment judging from the slew of awards the spot garnered.

Today you can watch the commercial on YouTube. Just type in Jell-O Chinese Baby. It is often tinted yellow by viewers who, in a lively forum, object to its "racist" intent. As a Louisiana-born boy who spent his life proving he didn't adhere to the racism against African-Americans he saw as a child, my father would find the criticism puzzling, if not maddening.

Perhaps my resurrected father would be confused by modern reactions to his commercial, but he would find one TV portrayal of the advertising world right on target. The show *Mad Men* took place during the time when he had his studio and is a mirror of the Madison Avenue milieu in which he moved. The show's title is an abbreviation of *Mad*ison Avenue ad men. These men—hardly ever women—of the street, synonymous for ad biz, were my father's clients. They're the ones who wooed the sponsors, and they chose who would make the ads. Courting and satisfying the Mad Men became as much a part of my father's job as creating the commercials—and a lot less fun, especially after the buzz from the ever-flowing booze wore off. If you've ever seen an episode of *Mad Men*, you've entered the smoke-blurred, alcohol-splashed society where the cigarette and the cocktail were the pleasures *du jour*. The sleek liquor cabinet was a sort of altar to the gods of chic chicanery.

Bottoms up! The Musso & Frank Grill in Hollywood

My father spent long wet lunches courting clients at The Musso & Frank Grill on Hollywood Boulevard around the corner from his studio. The specialty there is the classic martini still served the way it was to F. Scott Fitzgerald, Raymond Chandler, William Faulkner—and Ray Patin.

Brennan's, New Orleans

When Daddy hit the road to peddle his services to the agencies in New York, New Orleans and elsewhere, the meetings were always more copacetic after a shot or two or more.

Ray Patin Productions: ladies who paint

While my father climbed the ladder of success in Hollywood, mother was becoming more and more confident as a painter in Burbank. But she wanted to go over the hill to work at the studio joining the ladies who painted the cels. Probably it was just old-fashioned husbandry that made my father want my mother at home. For a man who had brought himself up from less than prestigious beginnings, it was a badge of honor that his wife didn't need to supplement an income that was starting to increase.

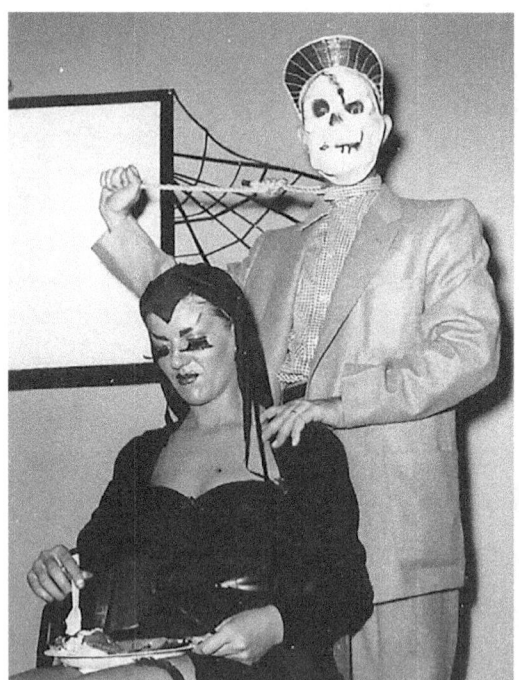 

Cartoonists' capers at "The Thing"

Not only was my mother not invited to work at my father's studio, but she wasn't invited to its grand Halloween extravaganza called "The Thing"—inspired by a popular horror movie of the time.

 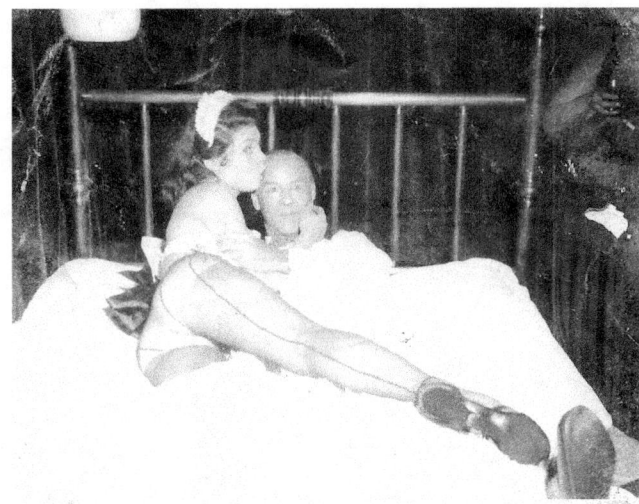

"The Thing" with Ray and guest

Did Daddy keep her away because he felt the shenanigans were a little too racy for his naive wife? My Burroughs friend Mickey, who worked part-time for my father, reported that the risqué phantasmagoric spectacular was a howling success.

Animators' appreciation

The boss as seen by his workers

But the thank you note for the party from the staff may have revealed the true nature of the boss/staff relationship. Their long hand-drawn scroll features a scantily clad, caped caricature of my father as a haughty, wrinkle-faced taskmaster. In an obsequious line at his feet before him, his artist staff created bowing self-portraits from their fingerprint blob artwork.

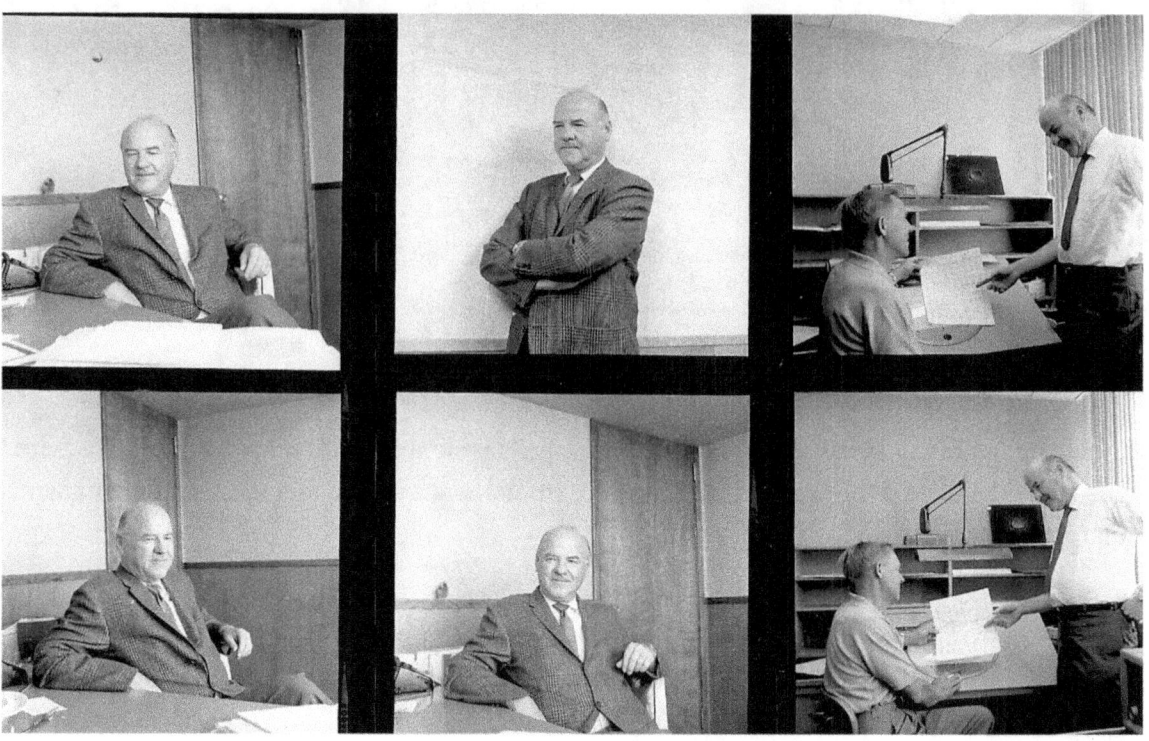

The boss how he wants to be seen

Merry Christmas?

I can imagine my father's silent seething over his employees' depiction of him. He must have seen the handwriting on the wall when his staff presented him with a Christmas card showing a Santa threatening to strike. The art was comical, but the message was not exactly joy to the world. It began, "Pity the worker called SANTA. He has no overtime CLAUS or a steward to grant a grievance or champion his cause." Ironically, my father was a member and interim president of what was called the Commercial Film Producers Association who negotiated with the Screen Cartoonist's Guild, his employees' union. That's the guild my father had gone on strike to be able to join as a Disney animator, and he had served as its president in the previous decade.

Mr. and Mrs. Patin and another Art Directors Club Gold Medal

Mother and I knew things were becoming difficult at the studio. Daddy's bad days were reflected at home where we were often the objects of his frustrations, especially when happy hour became less so. Her job was to perform the duties of the boss's lady. She was the lovely worshipful wife when he received his awards in New York and the gracious hostess to his friends and clients.

But I did see what was happening at the studio when I worked there during school breaks. I was there a month after my graduation from UCSB when Daddy's trusted vice president and heir apparent took key personnel and left to form a new animation studio. A lot of my father's spirit was knocked out of him with this crushing blow. The minutes of Ray Patin Productions on July 14, 1960 show that the former directors of the corporation were out, and new officers were in. They were my father and family he trusted, Uncle Wally, and I as secretary/treasurer. My job was to keep the minutes of the infrequent meetings of the new board of directors.

Ray Patin Productions on Animation Alley

That same year Ray Patin Productions moved to a new ultra-modern studio on Cahuenga Boulevard near that other cartoon factory, Hanna-Barbera Productions, in what was called "Animation Alley."

I never worked at the new studio, but I visited often so I could use the new electric typewriter for my graduate school papers. I had been replaced by a very professional full-time receptionist. She plugged calls into the modern PBX machine and kept intruders from climbing the curving stairway to my father's office.

New studio with receptionist positioned near the stairs to her boss's lair

Sometimes when I came home from college and visited the studio, Daddy was sequestered in his upstairs aerie, taking a long nap behind locked doors after an extended cocktail lunch. Once I saw the bourbon bottle in his desk drawer and his closet filled with untouched brown bag lunches that Mama had made. Perhaps this is why Daddy kept Mama away from the studio where there were things he didn't want her to see.

I knew he drank a lot. I thought that's just what grown-ups did. Once he showed me how shaky his hand was, the one that held the pencil. He told me it was from the drinking, as if he were warning me of what booze could do. I also saw how he used Mama's Max Factor pancake makeup to cover his red nose. Each time I was with my father, he seemed to be more weighed down by the burdens of the mad, mad ad world. Mama and I were confused by and afraid of his moods. The man who made everyone laugh with his cartoons, jokes and antics grew sullen and sarcastic. I watched for a certain tightness in his lips, a tiny flick of the tongue or tic of a jaw muscle as signals that I should tread lightly. My mother quietly shared her concerns with me and not so quietly with my father.

Alone at the top

My father's career under the Sign was threatening to destroy the man who lived in its shadow. But wait! In "Ray Redux" we will see how Ray not only survived, but triumphed, over the tribulations of TV and Tinseltown.

36
V is for Virtue and Vice

By the time I graduated from college, my path toward virtue had taken some twists and turns. It's not that I plummeted into a life of vice, but I stopped listening to all those voices that helped me see life with the innocence of a child.

By Jiminy, it's my cricket conscience!

It all started with Jiminy Cricket. The wee critter in top hat and tails was my first arbiter of virtue and vice. I was five when I saw the movie *Pinocchio* and learned the consequences of not obeying your better bug. I was already familiar with crickets in a non-moral sense. Their wing rubbing screeched their presence hiding in the dark corners of the Parish house. I even saw Jiminy in repeated viewings of Daddy's strike footage. There he was on a picket sign moralizing to Disney just as he did to Pinocchio and to me: "Taint Cricket to Pass a Picket."

I chose Jiminy as my first conscience—though I wouldn't have assigned such a grand term to that wee small voice in my head. I knew I should do what was commanded by grown-ups. For example, from watching *Pinocchio,* I knew lying was wrong. It was the boy/puppet's stumbling block, and among the vices I sought to eschew. Mary Jane's prevarications, though they didn't lead to nose lengthening, did get her mouth washed out with soap.

Then Santa came to town and he became my higher power. Ol' Saint Nick's warning was as dire as Jiminy's. I had to watch out and not pout, a demeanor to which I was prone. I really believed he knew when I was naughty or nice. He saw me the day I found a doll intended as a Christmas present in Mama's off-limits closet, or the time I ran away from home to the next block. I became increasingly aware of ways I was naughty and ran the risk of less than my usual bonanza under the tree.

 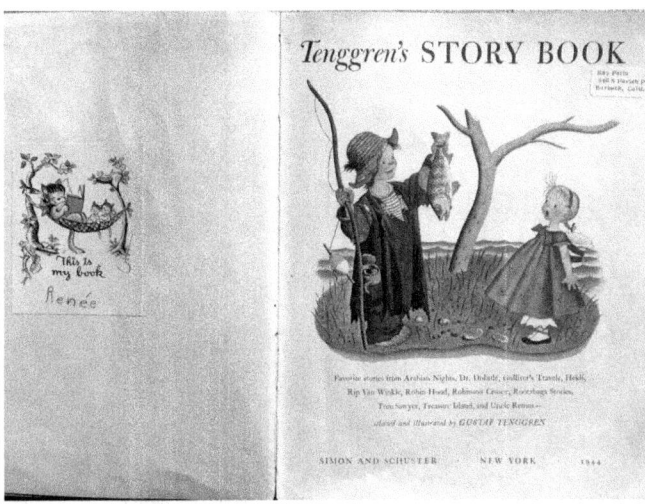

From the libraries of Renée and Ray Patin

My parents were not religious. As a child, my mother may have picked up a smidgen of spirituality from her Christian Science grandmother, but the Rileys were not churchgoers. Her religious path was never a topic of our conversations. Instead of Bible stories, she provided me with other models that I could strive to emulate or evade. These were in fairy tales. The vivid accounts of unspeakable trials that beset those who did not obey gave me pause. I had no idea that the pictures in my *Tenggren's Story Book* were illustrated by the artist who was the chief illustrator of *Snow White and the Seven Dwarfs* and the other Disney pictures that also served as parables teaching how to lead the good life.

Magical angels

From an examination of her art, my mother might have seemed religious to those who didn't know her. Angels often appear hovering over a scene, giving it a sort of magical mood. Remember the boy and girl angels flying over Culver City in her early painting of the Rileys? But what looks like a heavenly host were closer to the fairies of her childhood tales than to Michael, Raphael and the rest. Mama didn't look to angels for spiritual succor any more than she did the Mexican churches she collected and pictured in her paintings. Like the Victorian houses we'll see later, they appealed to her for their magic castle-like look.

A collection of churches under a painting of churches

Now I lay me...

However, I did manage to receive the basics of religion appropriate to a well-brought-up little girl. I was aided in this endeavor by a little book published the year before I was born called *Prayers for Little Children—and Suggestions to Fathers and Mothers for Teaching Their Children to Pray.* I remember the book sitting on my shelf and thumbing through the pictures of an idyllic religious family. I could recite "Now I Lay Me Down to Sleep" but didn't really think I would die before I awoke and had no conception of the soul I was asking God to take. By the looks of the battered little book today, I was doing either a great deal of praying or using it for other more profane purposes.

The bells of San Gabriel

I didn't receive religious training from my father either. He had lapsed away from the Catholic church of his upbringing. But in 1928, when he was looking for ways to make money from his art, he began a series of booklets describing the eighteenth century Catholic missions that dot California. Each booklet features a finely etched rendering of a mission on the cover. He abandoned the project, however, when his research led him to believe that the Spanish missionaries mistreated the native peoples who helped build the missions. His sense of virtue spoke louder than his business sense.

Despite my lack of religious training from my parents, I came to the conclusion that there was ONE who was so all mightily powerful that he could even tell Jiminy and Santa and my parents how to be virtuous. When I was about eight, I made the decision that I was not paying enough attention to this God whom I kind of equated with Santa Claus. I decided I would become a nun despite the fact that my family did not attend any church, let alone St. Finbar's, the Catholic church down the street where Nana went when she visited. Somehow, I concluded that self-sacrifice was a prerequisite for this career choice, and that it must be holy in nature. I found a Bible stuck next to the encyclopedia set in the living room cupboard. In the sanctity of my room, I knelt abjectly, as I had seen in my little prayer book, and set out to read the entire tome with its tissue-thin, gold leafed pages. I vowed to stay in place until the end despite the pain in my knees. My chosen entry to enlightenment proved too uncomfortable, however, and I gave up halfway through the who-begat-whoms in Genesis. I still thought I might like to be a nun—if I couldn't be a movie star.

As a fifth grader, we had released time to attend Christian education classes taught in a private home across the street where our ecumenical activities would not be interpreted as crossing the line between church and state. We sat at tables set up under a picture of a blond, long-haired, wispy-bearded Jesus. I got the idea Jesus Christ was to God as Jiminy Cricket was to the Blue Fairy who told him how to get Pinocchio to be a proper little puppet. They even had the same initials.

More formal Christian training culminated in my parents and I being baptized together at the Episcopal Church in North Hollywood when I was twelve. The impetus to this surprising event was from my godmother who thought I was in need of upstanding church attendance. Our attendance was limited to holidays. I went on to be confirmed. My parents did not.

Teen temptress or tomboy?

Slouching toward teenhood, my prime concern was identifying who the heck I was and who I wanted to be. I tried on various masks, sometimes worrying whether there was a higher power approving the new me, sometimes forgetting him/her/it entirely. Was I a temptress or a tomboy? Was I a good girl or a bad girl? Confusion reigned over clarity.

In junior high I attended YWCA[1] camp where we were required to confess our love of Jesus to a counselor. Depending on what you said, you got a blue scarf for beginners, red for more serious confidences and a treasured white scarf for the ultimate in devotion. The scarves were called rags, and the girls were called raggers. What I confided to the counselor must not have had the required devotional tone as I never became a ragger of any color. My raglessness did not affect my standing among the campers who appreciated my campfire ghost stories if not my religious fervor.

---

[1] Young Women's Christian Association

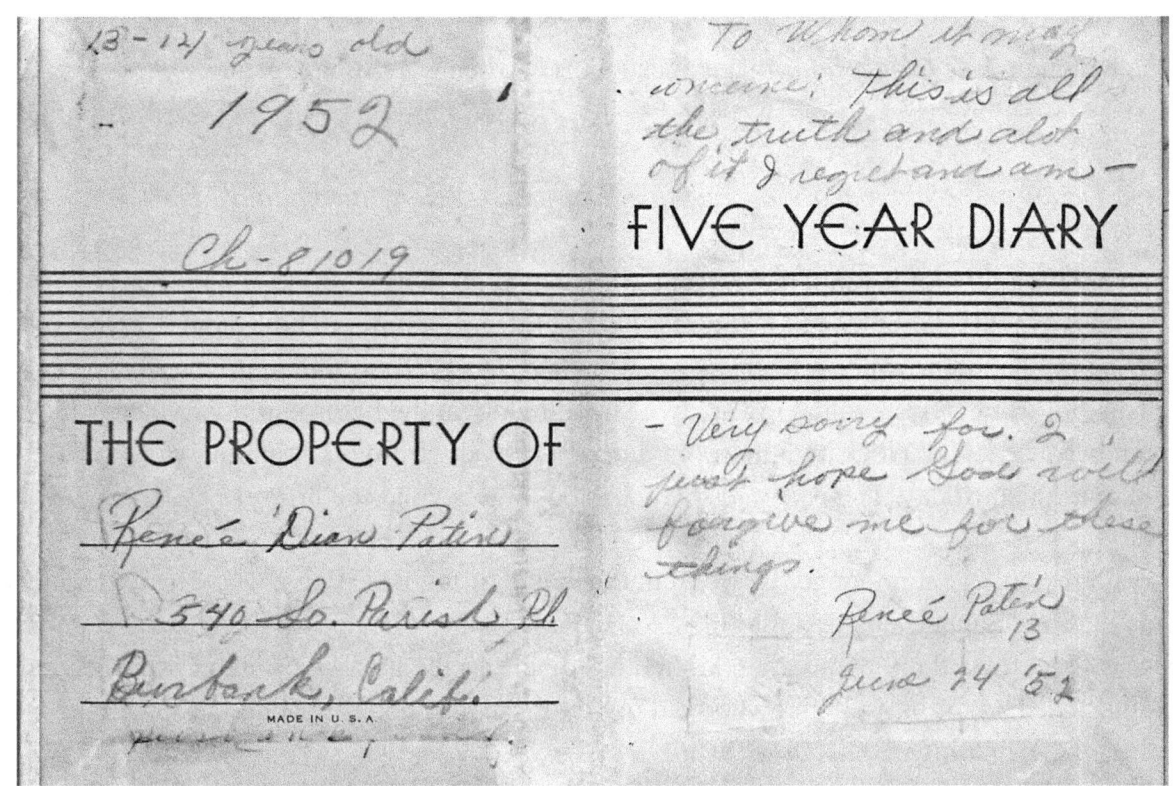

To whom it may concern…

The diaries that documented my teen years often dripped with guilty confessions of my misdeeds and apologies to God as I had learned to conceive of him from the Episcopalians.

On the opening page of my 1952 diary—after entering my name with a creative spelling of my middle name, Diane, and age, 13—I poured out my soul's ponderings to any interloper who might read my diary.

To whom it may concern:
This is all the truth and a lot of it I regret and am very sorry for. I just hope God will forgive me for these things.

On the following page, I felt the call to write a letter to God:

Dear God My Heavenly Father,
I feel as if I know you very well as I talk to you every night.

Thank you so very much for all the wonderful things that you've done for me. And please if it is your will forgive me for the bad things.

Much Love,
Renée

I had read enough *True Confessions* magazines to know when I was going astray.

Dear Diary,
...Tonight Daddy and I had a heart to heart talk. I sure hope I don't turn into a J.D.

J.D. is an abbreviation for juvenile delinquent. I knew that my hormonal urge surges were causing me to act in ways that might lead to incarceration. There was the time in high school I removed the screen from my bedroom window to sneak off with Andy, the undesirable renter boy from across the street. This fall from grace resulted in Daddy's knocking down the bathroom door where I hid after my return because it had a lock and my room didn't. The welts from his spanking were visible on my thighs in gym the next day. The pain and shame lasted long beyond the bruises.

When I entered college, I no longer believed in the magic of the Blue Fairy who granted Pinocchio life as a real boy.[2] Santa Claus was for kids. No heavenly father dictated my behavior. My moral compass was set toward my own father. I dared not displease the man whose hopes for me were as high as those he had for himself and who held my future in his hands. Though the spankings were a thing of the past, I still feared his displeasure.

The virtue of *Faithful Study*

My father's moral code was strong as were his expectations that I would follow it. After all, he was born right after the end of the Victorian age and raised by parents who had lived under its code of virtue. My father's sense of right and wrong was established early. In Chapter 3 we saw the *Truth, Love and Courage* award-winning drawing he created when he was eighteen. At the same age, he drew a cartoon with his beloved ocean as a theme. He pictured the gallant vessel *Faithful Study* steadfastly plowing through rough waters where less virtuous ships like *Bad Habits, Negligence, Laziness* and the ill-fated ship *Etc.* have floundered. The safe harbor is labeled *Vacation,* an indulgence my father rarely afforded himself—except for those weekend nautical interludes in Newport.

---

[2] Though in the original Collodi story he had to survive a hanging and having his feet burned off as well as the guilt of having Geppetto arrested for child abuse.

The vice of wrongful romance

During his dating days, Daddy drew a tale of love gone astray. What vices might be involved to elicit the double exclamation marks in the lightly-penciled caption, "NO!—and that's final!" Does the suitcase mean an engagement or elopement (or even worse) to cause the distinguished gentleman to deny the couple their desires?

At the same age as my father, I too expressed thoughts on virtue vs. vice, but in words rather than pictures. My medium was a 16-page paper for Philosophy 135 called "Sartrian Existentialism, Man's Fate in the Modern World." Here is some of my overblown prose:

> *God is dead. Man is a nothingness going toward the impossible...But is man completely alone? Doesn't he have a grounded code of ethics to which he can turn for answers? Again, the answer is negative. It is the individual who creates and maintains his own values...We cannot turn to a single essence as a standard of model for our behavior; but one must not rule out a unique ethical responsibility for the individual.*

Yuk! No wonder Sartre wrote of the nausea we feel when we realize we are alone without a cricket, jolly gift-giver, parent or even a deity to be our guide. Sartre's Left Bank ponderings fit well with the bohemian spirit I fancied myself to be when I escaped to Isla Vista. My new discoveries about right and wrong meant I no longer needed fairies or their tales or Christmas legends or God or my father to prescribe my sense of virtue and vice. I was my own harshest judge. The Renée who left the shadow of the Sign could be whatever she chose. My existence preceded my essence. I would be an Existentialist! Sartre could be my god. I adapted his wisdom for mine, and even—as seen in my Sartrean-based paper on James Joyce—I would adapt it for other classes.

Praying in Provence, France

It has taken many years to regain the childlike ability to listen to all the voices that come from a higher, often magical, place. I have heard them in mosques in Morocco and Turkey, temples in Taiwan, grand European cathedrals, on the African Savannah, in a Christian chapel in France decorated by Jewish Chagall, sitting alongside buddhas lining the halls of an esoteric hotel in Provence, and stopping by early California Spanish missions near where I live now. I often hear the whispers that remind me to stop and see the wonder and be grateful for a little moment of virtue without a thought of vice.

Remember when I found Ward Kimball's train at Disneyland? You may have noticed that on its shiny headlamp, emblazoned in gold was my old voice of virtue, Jiminy Cricket. I hadn't known as a child that my parents' friend with a steam engine in his backyard was the creator of my first conscience. I came alive with childlike delight at the sight. And I think I just may have heard a still-small chirping in my ear when I spotted the wise old cricket leading the way, his golden top-hatted silhouette emblazoned on the gleaming red headlamp.

37
W is for Writer

Favorite stories and books

Yes, the tale of Jiminy and Pinocchio influenced my spiritual journey. And it was telling tales that began my career as a writer. Mama loved storytelling. I'm sure I was a great excuse for her to indulge in her fantasies as I sat rapt on her lap while she read to me. Under my baby book heading "Favorite Stories and Books" she wrote, "Three Bears (Dears) and made up stories about Renée Patin and Teddy Bears." It was the earliest indication of my own lifelong love of reading and writing (and a tendency to invent my own language).

As I matured, I demonstrated my love of the storied bears. My illustration of the tale's climax features the surprised intruder as she contemplated the best bedspread on which to lay her lovely locks of gold.

Potsy's picture

Fiction on film: *Drama on the Rocks*

My father was a great storyteller. His humor, imagination and gift of expression were talents that besotted young Maxie. He even made up scenarios for Mama and me to perform for his camera. One action adventure is set in the rocks of Laguna Beach where my mother, dressed in a fetching suit with matching beanie set jauntily askew, casually leans against a boulder to check her manicure while I hide in plain view. The dramatic finale occurs when I jump upon my unsuspecting parent whereupon we walk off the set congenially as she chides her husband the cameraman—perhaps requesting a retake.

Shakespearean advertising

At The Walt Disney Studio, Daddy wrote several scripts in which Donald Duck acted out his animated talents. And when my father had his own studio, he wrote award-winning television commercial copy and ads for Ray Patin Productions that were worthy of Shakespeare such as:

> *Oh can of beans,*
> *Within my means*
> *I findeth not*
> *The ways to sell thee.*
> *Turn not to poetry turn to pro's*

With such subtle puns on his professionalism and prose, my father's writing talent could not be disputed. Could my future in writing be far behind?

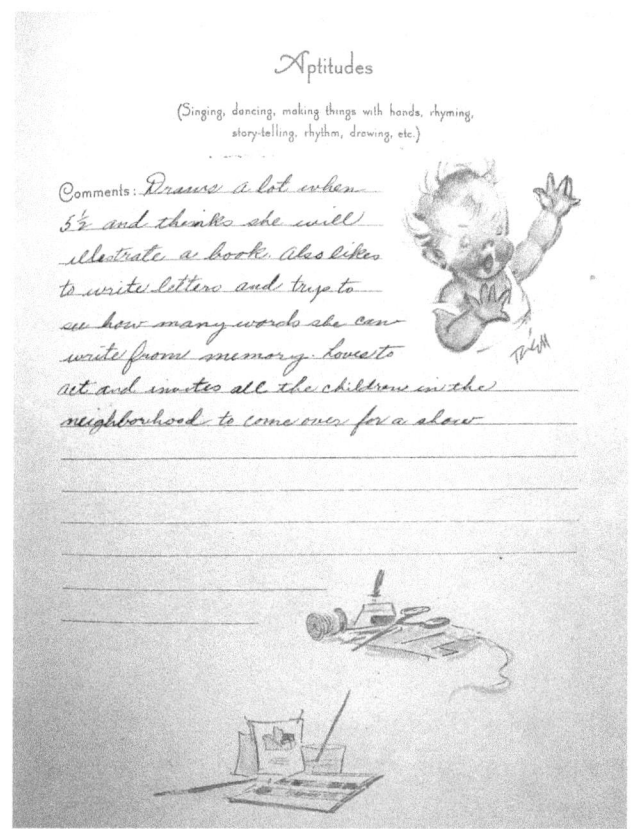

Aptitudes

My mother was still writing baby book entries when I was five and a half years old. Here's what she wrote on the page entitled "Aptitudes":

Draws a lot when 5 1/2 and thinks she will illustrate a book. Also likes to write letters and tries to see how many words she can write from memory. Loves to act and invites all the children in the neighborhood to come over for a show.

With my mother plying me with fairy tales to ponder and my father devising home movie scripts for me to act out, I began to write. My first written works were picture stories crayoned onto the pulpy pages of blank photo albums where one might detect the seeds of plots germinating in my overactive brain.

Jungle adventure

In one we see an exotic jungle setting with a cast of flying tigers, a nimble monkey and a would-be tightrope aerialist.

My piece *It is Cold* might be interpreted as a meteorological metaphor on the rocky road of romance. A similarly-hatted couple battles a dark and stormy night unaware of the rainbow they have left behind.

Chilly romance

A later work featured a more layered plot with hints of irony, ethnic awareness and psychological insight. A pig-tailed, dark-skinned lone Latina lass sits stiffly in a bare, barred room with her pig-tailed bank. Perhaps her plight represents the futility of great riches when one is closed behind the bars of self-imposed isolation—or that I was studying Mexico in third grade social studies.

Mexican melancholy

Budding writer in plaid, front row middle, hair down, saddle oxfords crossed

Despite these promising early illustrated narratives, my creative destiny would lie in expressing myself in words rather than pictures. As Voltaire wrote, "Writing is the painting of the voice." My desire to write was sparked when my teacher Annabelle Doss endowed me with a lifelong love of language. She read from the book *Homer Price* as we fourth graders sat cross-legged and spellbound in a circle before her. I particularly enjoyed Homer's doughnut machine escapade. Miss Doss encouraged my own writing. She let me dictate stories that she would then type up and I could illustrate.

Patins on ice

One of these stories gives a happy twist to a true-life embarrassing incident caught on film. The documentary sequence shows me fearfully clutching the barricade and then being dragged around the rink, ankles splayed, as my father attempts unsuccessfully to teach me to skate.

Miss Doss typed, and I illustrated an autobiographically wishful story based on this incident and my nascent interest in the opposite sex. Illustrated with a cinematic split screen, the story is called "Jeanie Learns to Skate." The plot conflict centers on a boyfriend who proposes a skating date to Jeanie Price (an homage to Miss Doss's *Homer,* perchance?). But she can't accept the invitation because she doesn't know how, and her mother never got around to teaching her.

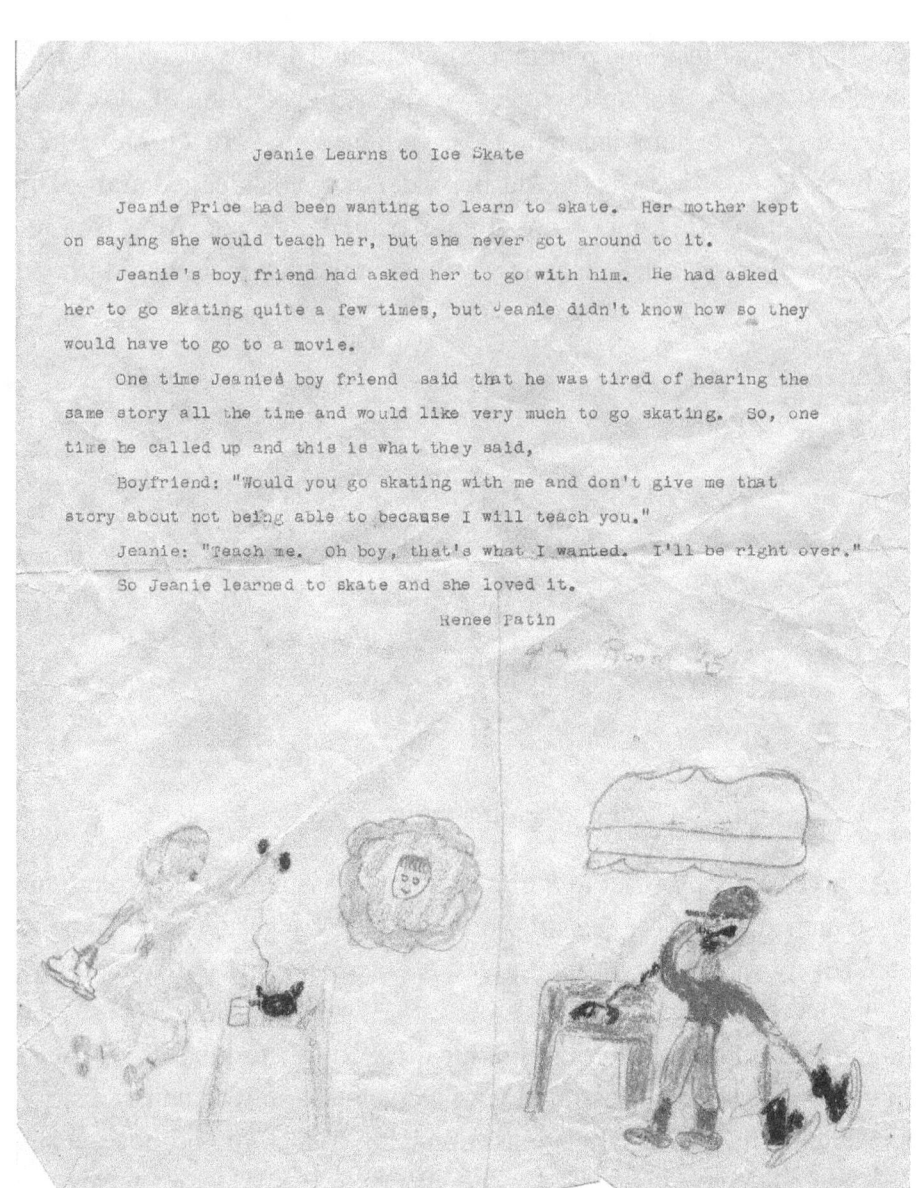

"Jeanie Learns to Ice Skate"

After repeated calls from her patient paramour, we rapidly reach the happily-ever-after denouement when her boyfriend causes her to jump for joy at his offer to teach her. Perhaps the saga of Jeanie is not likely material for a Harlequin Romance novel, but seeing my work on paper tickled my vision of becoming a real writer. I began to pour out my non-fiction thoughts in my diaries and my make-believe versions in the thickest Big Chief lined tablets my allowance allowed. I discovered that writing provided the serenity to soothe my prodigally active mind and was more age appropriate than losing myself in mud pie making or bubble blowing.

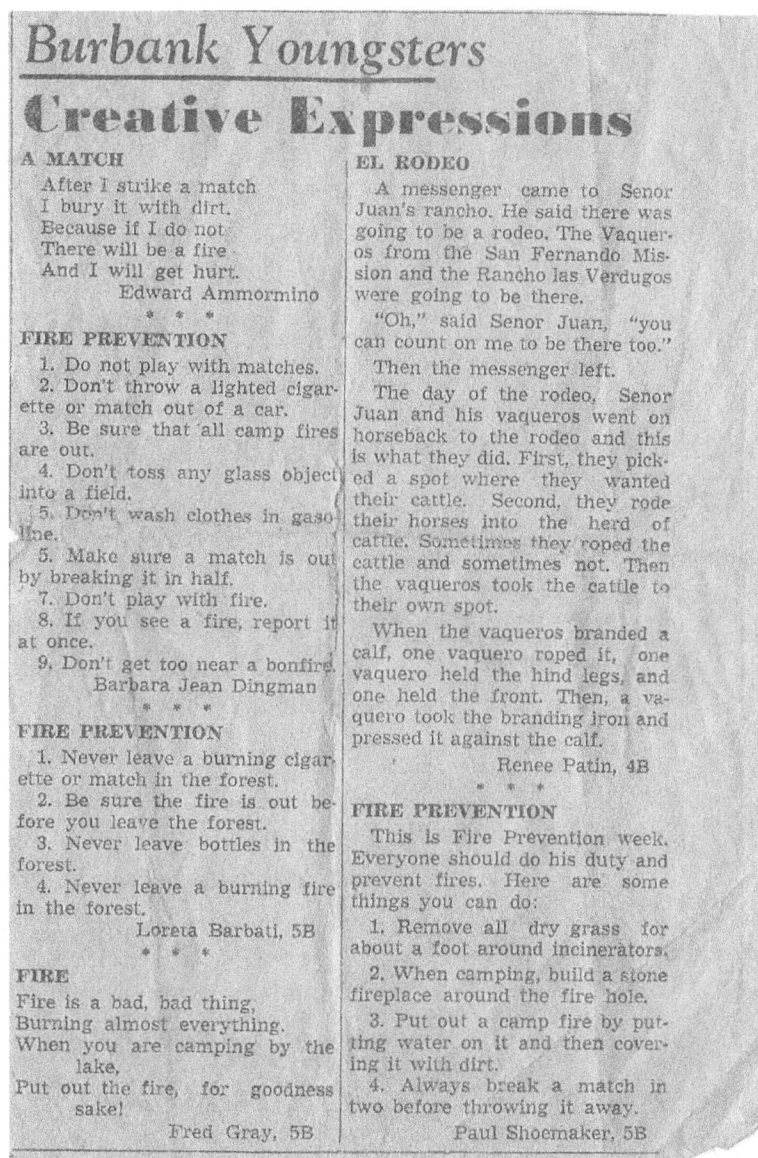

Published!

Miss Doss also provided my first pride-puffing opportunity to see my byline actually published in the *Burbank Youngsters* section of our local newspaper. Inspired by our current social studies topic, "El Rodeo" begins with a rather promising introductory sentence: "A messenger came to Sr. Juan's rancho." What follows is a description of the ranchero near the San Fernando Mission where his compadre vaqueros ride and rope without benefit of either adjectives or adverbs.

In fifth grade at age ten, I wrote a book. Though it was only a 5" x 7" spiral-bound volume, I took it very seriously and even wrote a Table of Contents in the front which I referred to as the Index. It was filled with highly creative and creatively-spelled pieces of prose such as "The Three Gaints" (sic) wherein one of the large people invited a character called "the girl" to take a nap with him. Snappy dialog included, "I want to tell you that my brother is going to eat you. Well goodbye now."

The piece de resistance in the book is what I entitled "Televtion (sic) Show" (three years before we had a TV set). The production begins with the Master of Ceremonies' rather pessimistic introduction: "Hello Girls. I'm very happy to see you all here tonight. Although you probibley (sic) won't be here at the end. I suppose I better give you station idenifaction (sic). This is TPPS–translation–Treadway Playrooom Pupit (sic) Show." After a number of acts designed with

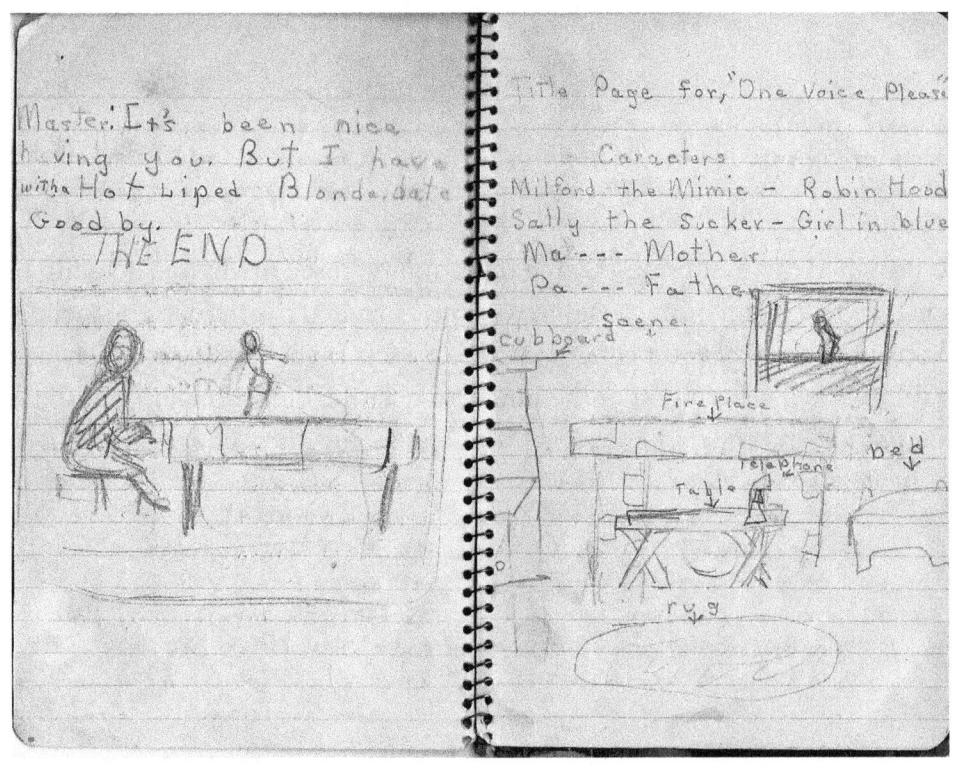

Pages from my first book

marionettes' capabilities in mind, the Master concludes with, "And now for our last number Hot Lips Holahan[1] (sic) will sing her own vershon (sic) of "Buttons and Bows." Hot Lips' first words sound as if she is channeling Mae West: "Hello baby, how's bought (sic) a date tonight, huh?" The Master then gulps and rushes off the stage shouting back, "It's been nice having you. But I have a date with a hot lipped blonde. Good by (sic)." My father was helpful in drawing out the stage setting for the "Televtion (sic) Show." But I can't recall whether the Treadway sisters let me perform the production on their puppet stage. They were funny about that.

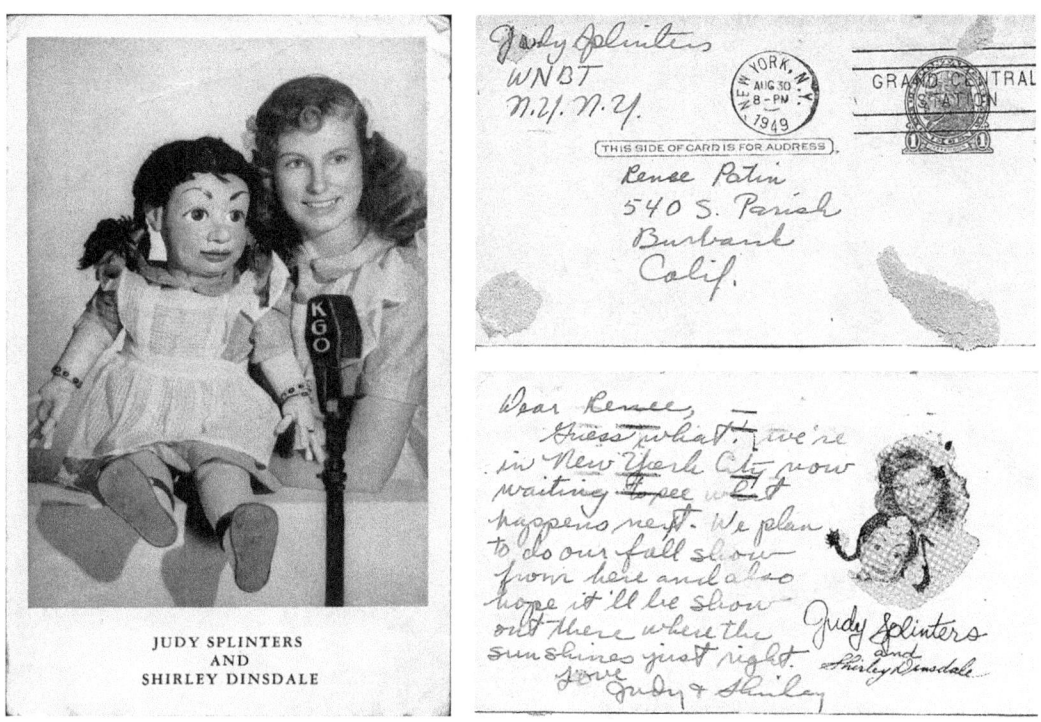

From Judy and Shirley to me!

My ten-year-old writing aspirations led me to seek even wider readership. I mailed one of my creations to the *Judy Splinters* TV show[2] where Judy, "who is unfortunately, but officially called a dummy"—or rather her ventriloquist Shirley Dinsdale—read my work on air. I have forgotten what I wrote, but not the warm rush of accomplishment as I listened to my words broadcast to the multitudes—or at least to the Los Angeles area juvenile viewers who were among the few who had television sets.

---

[1] In the interest of accuracy, I must acknowledge that this anachronism is as baffling to me as it may be to the reader. Though I wrote the piece when I was ten, Hot Lips Houlihan did not appear on the TV series M*A*S*H (based on a 1968 novel and 1970 movie) until I was in my thirties.

[2] Shirley Dinsdale had her own Western-themed weekly children's show (entitled simply *Judy Splinters*) that ran from 1949 to 1950. It originated at KNBH in Los Angeles.

I was almost as excited when Judy and Shirley actually sent me a postcard from New York City, postmarked Grand Central Station. Just think, they thought enough of me to tell me where they were working! The card still holds a little of the scrapbook page where I preserved it. This brush with fame was just one of my little boosts upward toward a writing career.

In 1949, Ms. Dinsdale won the very first Emmy Award for "Outstanding Television Personality" while she was a student at UCLA. I, however, would win no awards for my ventriloquism. Despite many practice sessions in the privacy of my room, I was unsuccessful at "throwing my voice" through my dolls. None of them had mouths that moved and mine always did.

Budding writer Ray

Eschewing ventriloquism as my means of self-expression, I continued my path in writing. My ease with pencil and paper was perhaps a proclivity passed through my Patin genes. My grandfather was a journalist and editor, and his son, my father, showed his ambitions in that arena in a self-portrait as a pipe-smoking budding writer.

Junior sleuth

My father's youthful writing was also published in a local paper, again the *Los Angeles Times* Junior Supplement. One of his ongoing creations was inspired by that master of mystery writing, Sir Arthur Conan Doyle. The strips featured the formidable Dickey Holmes, a detective based on you-know-who. My father—who was nineteen at the time—even showed a talent for poetry when Detective Dickey described his disguises:

I'm called by many "Dickey Holmes"
Never known by the ones I spy on.
So I'll tell in my little poems
'Bout the make-ups that I try on

I shadowed once a miser
Who wouldn't pay his rent.
He was clever. I was wiser.
In jail you'll find this gent!

And now I'm a "dude"
With manners just so.
Detectives are rude
But I act don cha know.

Nobody'd know me now.
I'm a rube, a homely "hick."
I learned to milk a cow,
To know every sleuthing trick.

Now in every social whirl
Trouble's bound to come,
So I have to have to be a girl
When called to smooth up some.

But I like these clothes the best,
The ones I'm often seen in.
And I'm not completely dressed
Without my T.J.C. (Times Junior Club) pin!!!

Lovely Vinnie, a lady of letters

Daddy's big sister Vinnie wrote too. Two years ahead of Ray at Poly High, she is featured in the *Poly Optimist,* the school paper her kid brother illustrated. The headline claims that "girls write well, but boys are better as editors."

My Aunt Vinnie grew into a red-haired beauty and at twenty-two married my Uncle Wally. In 1928, Richard "Dickey/Dicky" Wallace, the first of their four boys, was born. His birth put a damper on her writing aspirations, which she often lamented in front of them and others. I thought it was most admirable—the missed vocation, not the lamenting.

The Shannons' second born, Patrick Maurice, is also a writer. He has published several books and won eight literary awards. Works like his early-day memoirs—from which I have borrowed family background—often demonstrate the "chip off the old humor block" he inherited from his Uncle Ray—along with our grandfather's name.

Don't miss a single episode

Daddy's sibling nemesis was also his muse—or at least her firstborn was. Apparently, my father was so taken with his first nephew that he used his name, now spelled Dicky as opposed to Detective Dickey, as the hero in his California history adventure series. After the concluding cliff hanger of one installment he drew his heroes setting off on their next adventure and toasting Vinnie's husband Uncle Wally. Daddy presaged his future advertising acumen by touting his adventure-writing:

> *Do not miss a single episode of the amusing, interesting and thrilling adventures of Don K. Hooty and Dicky Shannon in their quest of the seven cities of Cibola.*[3]

My early output was far from amusing, interesting or thrilling, but I may have inherited a smidgen of my father's flair for humor. My first monetary compensation for an original idea came during one of my parents' cocktail parties. I was around nine or ten. Mingling waist high through the tipplers, I homed in on a cartoonist I'd never met and whose name I forget. In the big voice that always startled adults when first issued from such a small person, I proceeded to entertain my new friend with my best party repartee. Either in admiration for my gift of gab or in an effort to stifle it, he offered to give me a dollar if I would give him an idea for a cartoon.

---

[3] Mystical cities of gold in the Southwest

Delighted at the assignment, I went to my room and returned shortly to pitch my idea. Here's how it went. The scene is a dress shop window with a sign that says, "Dresses Half Off." The joke was that ALL THE DRESSES ARE CUT IT HALF! Not a knee-slapper, but it earned me my first dollar for an original creative story idea. I wish I'd framed it (the money, not the cartoon that I never did see in print). What I DID see in print fifty years later were signs in a store window reminiscent of my first stab at humor. The signs ask the shopper to take 50% off all the clothes storewide. The style of the dresses would have indeed looked as if they were cut in half to the ladies of the forties!

Dresses half off

Renée Patin, the author

About nine years later, at eighteen, the age my father was penning Dickey Holmes, I published my first paid article. "I Wonder…What Makes 'em Move?" My tediously technical explanation of the process of animation demonstrated no sign of the Patin creative writing gene. But it was published in *Telefilm Magazine* where, probably not coincidentally, my father bought advertising for Ray Patin Productions.

I don't know how much my father paid for the ad or how much I was paid for the piece. But I do know that I added yet another persona to my ever-growing cast of Renées—Writer.

As I wrote my way through my university education, I developed an erudite style that, as I have noted, seemed to please my professors. It would take many years to de-eruditify my prose to a place where even I could enjoy reading it. Now I love creating language the way my father created his cartoons. I take pleasure in doing all the wrong things that would horrify my instructors. My fun is playing with words and even inventing them. And tossing grammar rules to the wind when creating rule-breaking sentences (such as this fragment).

Miss Patin, the publisher

Of course, I wouldn't have told my students about my tendency to break the rules. For a time, I was the Creative Writing Teacher at West High School in Torrance, an LA suburb. The honor came with the responsibility of supervising the school's literary magazine. As a throwback to my school days of indigenous people school logos, we were the Warriors, and our magazine publication was called *Arrowheads.* Primarily I strived to keep up the literary standards and make sure disgruntled students didn't insert blasphemies in nefarious ways that I had heard happened in other schools.

Ah, the perils of the writer's life!

38
X is for XOXO

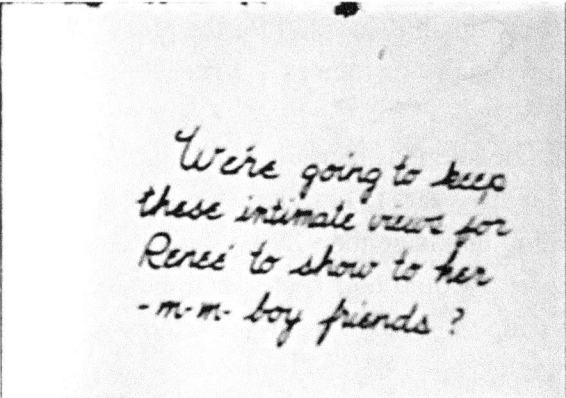 

Footage: *For Future Boyfriends*

Now, as we near the end of the story of my *Becoming* a grown-up, we reprise a refrain oft repeated in the *Beginning* chapters—the Boyfriend!

Whenever Daddy screened his movies for our guests, I cringed each time I spotted the title, "We're going to keep these intimate views to show her m-m boyfriends?" The sequence begins with a nude mini Michelin me approaching full frontally at a determined—if not alluring—crawl.

Pretty putti

At the climax of the scene I am propped up, booty cameraward, to perform a "bouncing baby" performance. The scene is framed as lovingly as a Renaissance cherub painting (which will substitute for the footage which may not be appropriate for all readers). My future suitors are treated to a provocative shimmy featuring close-ups of each jiggly, wiggly dumpling and dimple. The dance was prompted no doubt by off-camera parental rhythmic clapping. No boyfriends have been subjected to this footage.

A birthday party in the park and a visit with Michael who is just exactly her age

According to this little cinematic enactment, my father faced, at an early date, the reality that he would one day encounter his daughter's boyfriends. He even fixed me up on my first date and recorded it on film. The occasion is my first birthday. I am, thankfully, dressed in dainty dimity, wandering in my mother's flowerbed before joining my (arranged) date, Michael. The rendezvous consisted of our tug o' war over my Taylor Tot[1] and my clobbering his bald head as if it were another birthday present to examine.

Movie: *First Birthday, First Date…*   …*and First Lovers' Quarrel*

First kiss

---

[1] A now coveted "vintage" stroller/walker combo

Young Love by Ray Patin

When my father was actively playing the dating game, the artwork for his correspondence course pictured a romantic take on the art of wooing. He pictured poignant expressions of doubt and anticipation in the faces of the couple after what may have been an over the bannister proposal in an amorous antebellum setting. And then there was the one in Chapter 36 showing the devastation of the suitor's request to marry his true love. In a more realistic vein, his drawing of the young boy artist in knickerbockers admiring a young girl artist in her class uniform middy blouse and pleated skirt may reflect my father's courting of my mother.

I, as you may have noted, began my pursuit for boyfriends at a very early age. I would not be fulfilled until I was chosen the fairest of them all by a member of the opposite sex who would sweep me off my feet and provide bliss everlasting. I was determined to prove movie-star-worthy of adoration and affection. I often worshipped my crushes from afar. I sighed the names of star athletes and big men on campus before pulling the petals from "he loves me/loves me not" daisies. I covered notebooks with their names scrawled in different fonts, often combining their last name with my first. I listed them and chronicled real and imagined encounters with them in my diaries and made my presence known to them whenever or wherever I could find them.

Sweet sixteen

Finally, I began indulging in relationships with Burroughs boys whom I could call my boyfriends. Some were nice like my fellow valedictorian Mike who joined us for Christmas. And some were naughty, like the ones whose idea of a date was a drive into the hills to Stough Park, Burbank's lovers' lane, where they practiced their wooing skills.

By the time I entered the college dating pool, I was a fierce protector of my virginity. Despite his humorous threats of showing my naked baby footage to future boyfriends, my father was very serious about my amorous activities. He was my moral chastity belt. I joined the camp of the "good" girls who were saving IT, something I had hazily formed from *True Confessions* magazines. I demurred at "going too far" during what must have been extraordinarily uncomfortable end-of-the-evening goodbyes for my frustrated escorts. Time after time the first date was the last date with a boy who was unsuccessful in convincing me that the next base would be the best base.

How I longed for a phone call saying I had been chosen to rendezvous with an eligible gentleman caller—one whom I had deemed date worthy. I remember the heavy importance I put on the upstairs landing at the DG house where the black rotary phone perched atop a twisty-legged little wooden table. I could hear it ring from our room in the back of the house and—along with a houseful of suddenly silent DGs—pause with anticipation and a little prayer waiting to hear my name called as the recipient of the call.

I dated, but sparks seldom flew. Photographs taken at formal outings reveal me gazing lovingly into the eyes of perfectly fine fellows whose company I didn't long pursue. Their shining armor wasn't bright enough or their steed wasn't white enough to carry this damsel off into the Pacific sunset.

At Gerry's side in sophisticated sheath

I enjoyed a series of increasingly amorous, but virtuous, dates with a junior named Gerry—even a visit with my parents on the *Trinket*. I REALLY enjoyed getting "pinned," a sort of beyond-a-boyfriend, commitment to exclusivity. The bestower of the fraternity pin was a Kappa Sig history major/athlete. I announced our pre-engagement liaison in the darkened DG living room as a candle I had bedazzled in bronze, pink and blue was passed around a circle of my sisters. When it came to me, I was supposed to reveal my pinning by blowing out the flame whereupon I was regaled with the Delta Gamma Sweetheart Song. My shining moment dimmed a little when three other girls announced their secret as their candles circled after mine. That night we gorged on four boxes of See's candy that we, the newly pinned, had purchased for our special moment. In the month that the Kappa Sigs needed to cobble together a serenade for Gerry and me, we had ended the relationship.

Rich, the grad

Then there was Rich, the painter. Here's our story—or at least how it began.

"Hey, Patin, can you name the Seven Dwarfs?"

The question was posed by our hasher, the name we called the boys who served our dinners around the dining room table in the DG house. I was passing through the kitchen where he was helping our cook, Mrs. Kelly, wash the evening's dinnerware. Maybe he was flirting with me?

For a coed who had honed the art of detecting interest on the part of the opposite sex, the rather startling question was not posed by a prime catch. Our disheveled server had none of the buttoned-down features of the ideal collegiate. This guy had kinky dark hair that seemed almost electric in its disarray. He was stocky—what they call a fireplug. But in his case, he was best compared with a firecracker as if at any minute he might explode with energy building inside him. His pants were baggy and back-buckleless, his shirt flannel, and his heavy brown work boots were scuffed and bereft of style. This junior certainly couldn't be a Big Man on Campus or wealthy if he had to hash for his supper in the Delta Gamma house where I, in my senior superiority, was serving as president.

But I found Rich kind of attractive in a tousled way. And I knew he was intelligent because he was one of the select English majors in Huxley's seminar. So, I tried to answer his challenge of Snow White's minions. I named six of the little people (darn that forgettable Bashful), and fudged a little, "You know, my father MADE *Snow White*.

His craggy face, usually so serious with penetrating Picasso eyes under bushy brows, broke into a big mischievous grin. "Well, that explains why you never get a tan," he fired back.

His quick wit was just enough to make me think maybe this guy had something going for him other than a way with serving utensils. Besides, he was right. A bronze body was not included in my beauty résumé. The instant tanning potion I slathered on my legs always rubbed off on my skirts and was often replaced with white calamine lotion necessitated by run-ins with poison oak. I gave an appreciative come-hither laugh at his quip and continued across the yellow kitchen linoleum to climb the narrow back stairs toward the president's room.

Our clever repartee continued after more and more meals, and it became apparent that we both had little flutterings of mutual admiration. A change in venue was called for, however, after I fired him. The dismissal came about when he entered the dining room where we were all seated and made what I considered a flirtatious thumb-to-nose wave in greeting. Apparently, there were those for whom the gesture had tawdry implications. One of these was our housemother, who insisted I let him go.

Rich and Renée's rendezvous

Our relationship would have to continue outside the hallowed halls of Delta Gamma. We chose the art building on campus near where he lived in the Green Stamp-papered former fisherman's shack in Isla Vista. In the evenings, we would walk in the damp sea dusk to one of the classrooms where he, though an English major, often painted into the night for the classes that allowed him to follow his passion. I doubt that we held hands, as he was always a few steps in front of me, anxious to get ahead. But I do remember the smell of eucalyptus and jasmine and the lagoon covered with a blanket of mist. He would set to work on his latest painting, and I, ever the French major, set to imagining the easel-filled classroom transformed into Parisian garret and myself at Rich's talented elbow, the lovely muse to the starving artist. He lamented that I wasn't fat enough so he couldn't use me as a model. (Where's that Michelin Man body when you need it?) I loved the crowded workroom watching him paint, splashing his canvas and himself with nose tingly paints. The smell of oils and turpentine still give me the warm fuzzies these many years later.

Then one night whilst demonstrating our mutual affection in the front seat of my Hillman Minx, I complained that his new growth of reddish whiskers gave me a beard burn on my cheek. When I added that it didn't really bother me, he said that was because I was in love with him. And I knew he was right.

Plow & Angel

Cold Spring Tavern

Although Rich was also a Kappa Sig, he was not a participant in proms, pinnings and such shenanigans. Our circle of friends was more bohemian than fraternal, our gatherings were informal and on the (correct) edge of propriety. I worked hard to fit in but preferred our times alone. We played chess and looked at art. We indulged in drinks and music at the posh Plow & Angel at the San Ysidro Ranch in Montecito where the sleeves of Rich's required jacket lent by the maître d' hung laughingly long. On a jaunt through the San Marcos Pass in my top-down Hillman, we sojourned at the rustic, romantic Cold Spring Tavern where Rich proposed an undefined future together that he called a five-year plan.

My mission was accomplished. I would be the tail on Rich's soaring creative kite. As shall be seen, he did soar into great heights, but without benefit of me as his muse.

39
Y is for Youth Begone

When I was a child, I spoke as a child, I felt as a child, I thought as a child. Now that I have become a man, I have put away childish things.
St. Paul, 1 Corinthians 13 verse 11

Oh you kid!

The year was 1960. It was time to put away childish things and act like an adult. Legally I was. I was twenty-one. I drank alcohol. I smoked. I could vote. I was about to be a college graduate. I knew stuff.

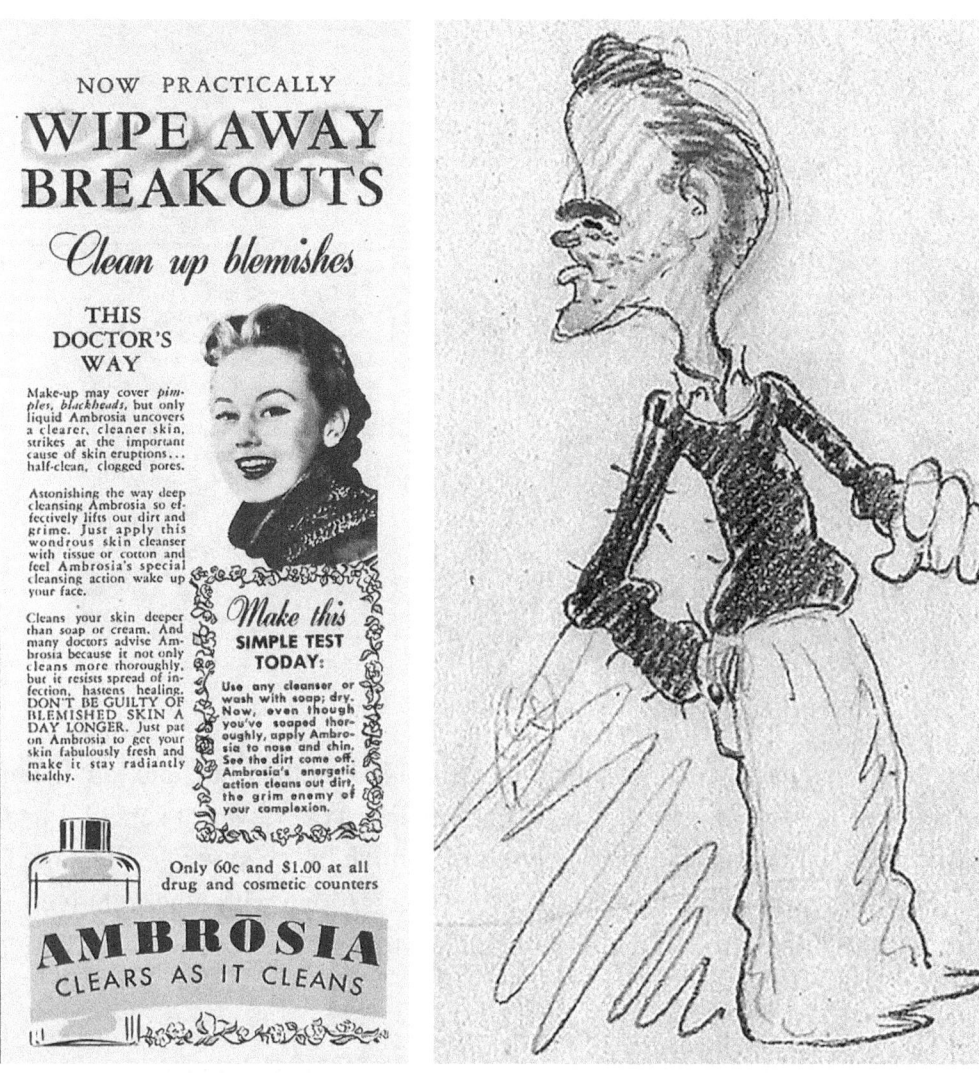

        Out damned spot!   Dapper Daddy

I thought I could wipe away the trappings of youth the same way I tried vanishing cream[1] to obliterate my freckles or skin cleanser to wipe away breakouts, those red badges of being a teenager.

I was a new persona and wanted to mold myself to fit the part. I felt like my father must have felt when he drew this spirited self-portrait at twenty-one, the same age I was when I graduated. He often caricatured his red-haired self, reflecting just the Ray he wanted to portray—not an easy feat at any age. He almost struts off the page, hand stuffed casually in the pocket of his very pleated pants. Although I didn't feel the swagger, I was set to act as though I did.

---

[1] I had misunderstood the use of the old-fashioned term "vanishing" which means that the moisturizer vanishes on the skin. The freckles stayed, and I prayed they would grow together and look like a tan.

Homesick

I began a conscious campaign to wean myself from the shadow of the Sign, and that meant the home I was raised in and the parents who raised me. During my four years away at school, I had been too busy chasing success to suffer homesickness. Certainly not like the coed whose message I spotted on a bathroom visit during one of my nostalgic campus tours. Along with other relatively erudite and philosophical comments on the wall of the stall, it read: "I really miss home and my family. I cry every night…"

After all, I had a substitute parent in the DG house. I could find her anytime at the bottom of the stairway that the pledges kept gleaming with Pledge polish—a product with no connection to sorority newbies. Sharing the entry hall with the log book where we were required to sign in and out was the suite of "Mom" Hanson, our housemother, a prim and proper middle-ager who seemed ancient to us. She was a lady of the Deep South, the sword-in-velvet-glove variety, who always dressed as if for an afternoon tea at the Biltmore or a visit from a DG alum. She would make her rounds inspecting house and residents to the sound of clicking high heels and a sort of tuneless humming that we enjoyed mimicking. This was behind her back, of course, as Mrs. Hanson was not one to suffer the silliness of sorority girls. She was there to help us become proper young women. Here's how she is remembered by my sorority sister, Doris:

> *Remember "Mom" Hanson and her drive to civilize us? Asking the rabbi to Friday night dinner and then serving him pork chops? And the lovely (and I'm not being sarcastic here) practice of enjoying coffee in the living room out of cups sitting on actual saucers. I remember Mrs. Hanson was incredulous when I answered her questions about tennis and bridge, saying I played neither. "My dear, whatever will you do?!"* (Actually, Doris did a lot like becoming the President of our National Council.)

I don't know about Doris, but as I prepared to become an adult woman, I had only a vague picture of Renée as a grown-up. I didn't have a dream of what my future as an adult would look like. I just wanted to excel at doing whatever IT was. Although I knew I was going to UCLA for graduate school to get a teaching credential, I didn't picture myself as a teacher, nor did I really believe Rich and I would spend a lifetime together.

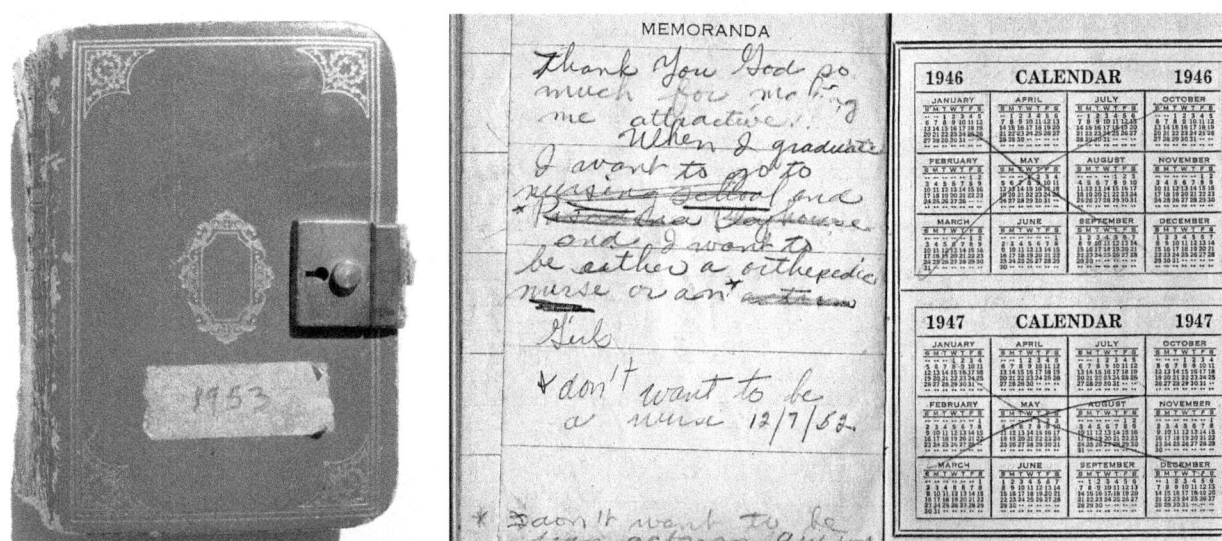

Prayers for the future

I had forgotten some of the dreams of my pre-college youth. At fourteen I was already reflecting on my postgraduate days in my red leatherette, gold embellished diary with a real lock and key that actually worked for a while. I began with a prayer of gratitude and finished with some hints to God as to what I would like my future to be.

Thank you, God, so much for making me attractive.

When I graduate, I want to go to *nursing school* *and* Pasadena Playhouse *and I want to be either* *a orthopedic nurse* *or an **actress*

*don't want to be a nurse 12/7/52

**don't want to be an actress 9/4/53

Renée Diane Patin,
Bachelor of Arts

Seven years later I was ready to undergo the rite of passage that would attest—in writing—that I, Renée Patin, was academically qualified to handle whatever came her way.

Here's what I remember from that hot June graduation day in 1960:

- I was nervous as I took my place in our class of 270[2] who lined up near the atrium of the new Music Building. I looked in vain for Mama and Daddy sitting on folding chairs out on the lawn.

- It was hot, and I was uncomfortable in a sort of liturgical black gown and mortarboard with a tassel flapping annoyingly on my right cheek. I had arranged my waist-length ponytail into a bulky bun I thought more befitting my soon-to-be alumna status.

- I didn't know what to expect or how to behave on this landmark day. I practiced and re-practiced the words to "The Star-Spangled Banner" I'd memorized for the occasion. I watched the passing faculty and sprinkling of graduate students, trying to figure out the significance of their regalia.

---

[2] The graduating class of 2019 numbered nearly 7,000!

Perfection

- I spotted my Adolescent Growth and Development professor and was surprised when she came toward me. Her purpose was to tell me I had earned an A in her class. It was the only grade I hadn't known and meant I had received all A's on my final grade report. So far I have resisted the temptation to falsely brag to those who might be impressed that I graduated from college with straight A's.

Proof

- Once I heard the first chords of "Pomp and Circumstance" I felt the tears flow, and they continued throughout the whole ceremony.

- I took my place in line and accepted my temporary ceremonial diploma with a sort of "is that all there is?" kind of feeling mingling with pride.

- Later when I received my real diploma I spotted a blue strip under the gold seal of the University of California. In tiny gold letters, it said that I had graduated "With Honors" from a school where we didn't have Magna Cum Laude or Summa Cum Laude. My diploma bears the name of the governor, Edmund G. "Pat" Brown Sr., not his son Edmund G. "Jerry" Brown Jr., who was also governor…twice.

- I found my name on the program and learned The Alliance Francaise awarded me a lovely Bronze Medal for being a French major. The ceremony is a blur. I don't remember who spoke, just moving the tassel to the left as a ritual gesture that I'd made it.

- When I spotted my parents, I cried even harder and broke the recessional ranks to hug them both and burble a thank you I knew was inadequate to what I felt. I'm pretty sure their eyes weren't dry either.

- Dinner at the restaurant in the old El Paseo was hosted by my proud father flaunting the first college graduate on either side of the family, some of the members of which were represented at the table. I joined them to imbibe legally and a lot as I had turned twenty-one the summer before—officially "of age" in California.

At seventeen and twenty-one

When I returned home to Burbank as a college graduate, I saw myself stepping triumphantly out of the shadow of the Sign. I knew I would somehow find my place in the spotlight. What I would be doing in that lofty luminescence was unclear, but I would work like hell to get there. This sophisticated new self was ready to take on the rest of the world. It would be a long time before I began to stop trying to get an A on being Renée.

40
Z is for Zip-A-Dee-Doo-Dah

When I became a man I put away childish things, including the fear of childishness and the desire to be very grown-up.

C. S. Lewis

Swing so high on a zip-a-dee-doo-dah day

Sadly, adding "Bachelor of Arts" to my bag of who I thought I was brought a degree of self-centered seriousness that I deemed essential in order to get an A as an adult. As my college days came to a close, my suddenly grown-up self put away the youthful things that filled my Potsy days and collegiate days. It would take a while before I lost the fear of being childish and remembered to let myself go to the sometimes silly, always liberating joys of zip-a-dee-doo-dah moments.

Zip-a-dee-doo-dah, zip-a-dee-ay
My, oh, my, what a wonderful day
Plenty of sunshine headin' my way
Zip-a-dee-doo-dah, zip-a-dee-ay!

Mister Bluebird's on my shoulder
It's the truth, it's "actch'll"
Ev'rything is "satisfactch'll"
Zip-a-dee-doo-dah, zip-a-dee-ay!
Wonderful feeling, wonderful day!

Yes, sir!
Zip-a-dee-doo-dah, zip-a-dee-ay
My, oh, my, what a wonderful day
Plenty of sunshine headin' my way
Zip-a-dee-doo-dah, zip-a-dee-ay!

Mister Bluebird's on my shoulder
It's the truth, it's actual
Ev'rything is satisfactual
Zip-a-dee-doo-dah, zip-a-dee-ay!
Wonderful feeling, feeling this way

Mister Bluebird's on my shoulder
It is the truth, it's "actch'll"
Ev'rything is "satisfactch'll"
Zip-a-dee-doo-dah...

Is there a song that better embodies the Disney spirit of sunshiny, bird-tweeting happiness and well-being? I was nine when I watched Uncle Remus sing the optimistic ditty in the Disney movie *Song of the South.* It won the Academy Award for Best Original Song for the 1946 movie and was on the Billboard charts again in 1963. It's used at Splash Mountain (based on *Song of the South*) at Disneyland Park and the Magic Kingdom Park in the Walt Disney World Resort and Tokyo Disneyland in Japan. Tom Hanks even sang it in the movie Splash!

When I saw that magical movie, a breakthrough in animation and live action, I loved the story it told. It helped that sad little Johnny was played by cute little Bobby Driscoll who immediately became my temporary crush. And I liked how Uncle Remus makes Johnny happy by taking him to a "laughing place," a magic storytelling place.

Potsy finds her Easter basket

My father with his cartoons and my mother with her fairy tales often led me to a laughing, storytelling place. When I look back on my journey, I see lots of days filled with "plenty of sunshine" when I was a kid. I often drew pictures of my zip-a-dee days. Many were holidays like my rendition of a be-bowed me coming upon one of the elaborate Easter baskets Mama created each year, both of us knowing they were not brought by a big bunny. In my imagination, magic was possible, like the smoke emitting idyllically from our chimney in mid spring.

Then I put youth aside and became mighty serious and driven. I left those Zip-A-Dee-Doo-Dah days behind me and spent more time in a self-imposed shadow where magic gave way to "reality."
If I could talk with newly-graduated Miss Renée Diane Patin, B.A., about what lies ahead for her, I would tell her that she will have plenty of sunshine heading her way. But there will dark and stormy times too. Academia will serve her well. She will have a life filled with lots of books and art and teaching and learning. She will never be a movie star but will have a career Potsy never could have imagined. Those nautical interludes will become a way of life. There will be many gentlemen callers and even a marriage made and unmade. She will have incredible adventures by land, sea and air. She will keep friends from the block and those all along her path, and she'll lose some, too. Many of the grown-ups who were part of her story will go on to the happily ever after.

I would tell her to learn all she can learn from artists and storytellers like Uncle Remus, Walt Disney and her parents—people who could see with wonder and sprinkle the dark days with pixie dust. I'd make her a promise that she will keep the Potsy in Renée and have plenty of zip-a-dee-doo-dah wonderful, satisfactual days...

A puppeteer...　　　　a vine Halloween costume...　　　...and a big birthday surprise

Part III Being

41
I Gotta Have Art

An art study by Ray Patin, 1929, age 23

I was at UCLA, rushing down the hall to my grad school teaching assistant job in the phonetics lab, when I stopped in my tracks. The attraction was a poster that would make my dreams come true: summer classes in art history at the Louvre Museum. THE Louvre, in PARIS! I was hooked on all things French and taking as many art history classes as I could fit in while I studied for my teaching credential. This was perfect! My pitch to my father was so enthusiastic that I actually convinced him that he needed to finance a trip to Europe to further my studies.

I flew Air Canada and tried to behave as if international flying was something I did all the time. That is until I realized I had been chatting with my seatmate while sporting a bright yellow sponge tip from my headphones stuck in my ear. I then sprayed both of us with ink from the fountain pen I whipped out to fill out my landing documents.

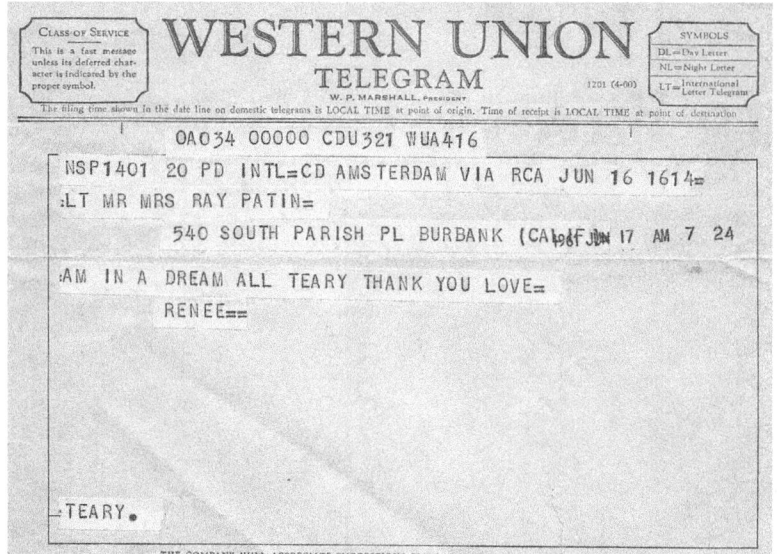

In a dream

We stopped in Reykjavik, Iceland before landing in Amsterdam for my first overnight stay in a foreign country. I was overcome by the crystal-clear air that I decided must have inspired the Dutch painters. I particularly noticed the sparkling clear windows that Vermeer would have loved, before I realized they weren't covered with screens or curtains or blinds, as they would be at home. In my first European euphoria, I sent a telegram to my parents: "AM IN A DREAM ALL TEARY THANK YOU LOVE = RENEE"

Watch where you go!

My first impression of Paris was that it was a film set like the ones that filled the Burbank back lots. It looked just too much like I had imagined it would from the movies, magazines and textbooks that made me long to travel there. It was the smells that surprised me, like the soft sweet fragrances of shops dedicated just to baked goods or to chocolate. And the sharp acrid street odors of coal dust and the corners where scofflaws ignored the little metal fences and signs that said *DEFENSE D'URINER,* warning those tempted to do so not to relieve themselves.

The signs were quite menacing, usually followed by the date the ancient law against public *plein air* pit stops went into effect. On a recent visit to France, I was interested to note that the problem of ill-advised urination locations seems not to have been solved. On a public *pissoir*, now called a *sanisette*, passersby in need were advised to make use of the facilities free of charge as opposed to being fined 450 euros for doing so on the street.

My home in Paris

I stayed in a sparse little room with a very nice Dutch roommate in a female student hostel called "Foyer International des Etudiantes." From the Boulevard St. Michel below I heard the chitchatting and swish-swishing of the street sweepers and the distinctive ominous siren wails unique to Paris ambulances. You always hear them in movies along with a shot of the Eiffel Tower to let you know the action will take place in Paris.

Echoing college days in Isla Vista, I was in the Left Bank student area called the Latin Quarter for the language of learning used there during the Middle Ages. Unfortunately, I learned that my French language learning at UCSB was a little light on conversational skills. (That's why at my teaching assistant job at UCLA, I loaded pronunciation records onto turntables in the phonetics lab instead of teaching in a classroom.) My linguistic shortcomings became apparent in Paris when I dined at the apartment of a distant Louisiana relative and got stuck on the French word for "nightmare." My elderly but elegant cousin told me the word but said I would just forget it like all Americans do, and insisted we converse in English. Though I forget why I needed to employ the word, I'll never forget *cauchemar*.

I loved wandering the streets of Paris, stopping in cafes to people watch, playing as if I were one of Hemingway's circle at Shakespeare & Company, the bookstore he frequented across from the Seine. I never tired of discovering something new and fascinating around every corner. I started learning what makes an American an American.

I was afraid of the Parisians, their suave sophistication, their ease at speaking a language I was still learning, and their disdain at my mistakes. I found myself in a contretemps in a shop near the Opéra where I had bought leather gloves to send to my Aunt Vinnie in Long Beach. The shop girl insisted I was insolent when I gave the delivery address as 3315-1/2 Corona Avenue. She insisted this was impossible. I insisted she was a *cochon*, a pig, the only name-calling word I had learned.

But I loved Paris. Each morning after brushing myself free of croissant crumbs acquired at a sidewalk cafe next to my student foyer, I walked down the Boule Miche (the boulevard's nickname for the cognoscenti). Where it joined the Seine, I turned left to walk along the quai lined with little open-faced booksellers' stalls, then across the Pont des Arts (not yet weighed down by lovers' locks now removed) to the Right Bank and the courtyard of the Louvre (not yet dominated by the looming pyramid). The classes were held in a dark, echoing room under one of the side arcades, and we were taken on tours of the art treasures of Paris and its environs. There were about fifteen students including one American movie star, Jean Seberg, who had been chosen from 18,000 hopefuls to play Joan of Arc in Otto Preminger's *Saint Joan.* I remember she wore Chanel suits and didn't mingle. I read later that she took her own life in Paris.

The Palais du Louvre and certificate of attendance at its school

 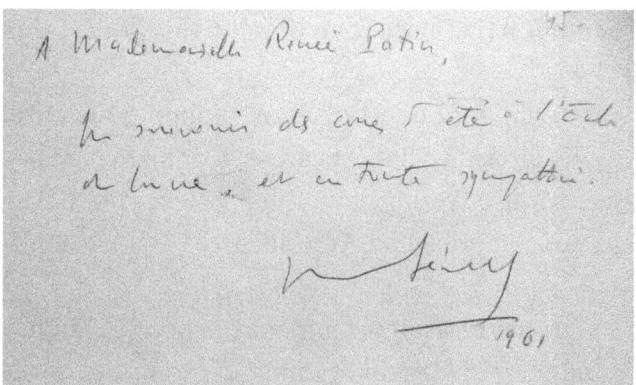

Treasures from the Louvre

I loved looking at the artwork and devoured with gusto every French word that I could understand in the same way I devoured the French pastries. I did my best to understand the text on Impressionist painters written by our teacher M. Serrulaz. I loved the lush magenta cloth binding pressed with gold on the book that came in its own sleeve, and I poured over the colored prints pasted on its pages. However, my professor's *note* (or grade) of 10.7 out of 20, bore witness to my less-than-stellar academic performance—too much time soaking in all that Paris had to offer. For me the Louvre was like Disneyland when I had a Magic Kingdom pass. I could go in and out at will, looking perhaps for only one painting like Rembrandt's *Carcass of Beef* or one sculpture like Michelangelo's *Slave.* As I went about my wanders, I was a great snob, ignoring the works I didn't care for like the huge Delacroix war pictures that bored me and Reubens' fat ladies that M. Serrulaz said resembled the Michelin Man. I looked with disdain at the tourists crowding around the *Mona Lisa* for their one and only chance to see her, grumbling about how small she was and not understanding what made her so famous. I looked over the shoulders of the painters copying the famous paintings and once, when a palette was left unattended, snuck a little dab of the turpentiney paint and breathed in a big, romantic whiff as a Proustian prompt of my painter Rich back in Santa Barbara.

Mary Jane joined me when the summer classes ended. In Paris, we marveled at the light and color of the incandescent Impressionist paintings in the Musée du Jeu de Paume galleries with names like Salle Degas, Salle Cézanne, or Salle Monet. This was the former tennis court for the Louvre Palace that displayed all the nineteenth century work deemed unworthy of the halls of the Louvre. During World War II it is where the Nazis stored their plunder of artworks. In 1986, the Impressionist paintings from the Jeu de Paume went on view at the Musée d'Orsay that had been converted from a train station.

It was from this station, the Gare d'Orsay, that Mary Jane and I ventured on an art odyssey to the great museums of Europe after I finished my courses at the Louvre. We likened our European romp to the book we'd both read called *Our Hearts Were Young and Gay* where Cornelia Otis Skinner and Emily Kimbrough roared through Europe in the twenties when they too were just out of college. We flashed our Eurail Pass, hopping from train to train and city to city chosen for the art we would find there. We marveled at the glow of the frosting-thick paint of the headgear on Rembrandt's *The Man in the Golden Helmet* in Berlin. I'm glad I believed it was Rembrandt who slathered on the thick golden oils and not, as has now been determined, some unknown artist in his circle. We pondered and wondered at Bosch's *Garden of Earthly Delights* in Madrid. We tittered at the anatomy of Michelangelo's towering *David* (without his Forest Lawn fig leaf) and stood in awe at the beauty of Botticelli's *Birth of Venus* in Florence. We would leave a museum and talk about what we saw as if we had seen different works. Mary Jane would talk about the content, and I would wax ineloquently about the technique, completely overlooking what the picture was about.

Mary Jane & Renée in Fort Worth, 2015

Over fifty years later the great paintings from the Musée d'Orsay came to the Kimball Art Museum in Fort Worth near Dallas where Mary Jane now lives. Once again, we wandered through the paintings, more slowly now, but no less enthusiastically. We posed together under a poster of a Degas that adorns a greeting card we have been passing back and forth for birthdays for twenty years. Neither of us remembers why. But we remember when our hearts were young and gay on our first Grand Tour.

The Patin/Riley artistic heritage from my parents didn't stop with my parents after all. I developed a lifelong love of looking at and learning about art and still teach classes to help others find the same joy that I have found. One artist I have followed is my old Santa Barbara boyfriend, Rich, now known as Richard Serra. Our romance ended when he was at Yale, but our paths would cross over the years. Once, several years after our romance was no more, I took a Christmas shopping trip to Florence. I was coming from an art exhibition on what happened to be Rich's birthday when I saw him crossing the street. I wished him many happy returns and he took me to meet the artist Nancy Graves, his Yale girlfriend and now wife. I'm not sure she had begun work yet on the camel sculptures for which she would be famous.

Early Serra

I had another chance meeting with the creative couple on another trip to Italy, this time to show Mama Rome for her first visit to Europe. I had left my flu-ridden parent at the hotel and gone out to the farmacia for soothing drugs. Nancy and I waited over coffees in a café while Rich rushed out for an appointment with Vincent Price, returning in exultation saying that the noted actor and art collector understood the pornographic intent of his assemblages of cages and hoses and assorted detritus. I didn't. Far be it from me in my limited imagination to predict that his other creative cages that included live animals would become newsworthy.

Several years later, I started noticing that his reputation as an artist was growing fast. With great interest (and a little pride) I began to see his work displayed in the museums I visited. I read about his massive steel sculptures and the groundbreaking case in 1987 where he sued the United States of America that removed his *Tilted Arc* from the Federal Plaza in New York. The piece was a wall-like sculpture not unlike the Vietnam Wall designed by Maya Lin who studied with Rich at Yale. It blocked the workers' path in the plaza and went to a junkyard in Brooklyn. Although he lost the case, site-specific art would never be the same.

Not a banana

I made trips to see Serra works like the dizzying steel torqued ellipses in New York. I visited *My Curves Are Not Mad* in Dallas and posed with his giant *Vortex* that locals in Fort Worth call "The Banana." And I traveled to see Serras throughout Europe. At the Louisiana Museum of Modern Art in Denmark, I examined a rusty wall-like piece. I was told the Danes didn't like it because it blocks their view of the sound.

 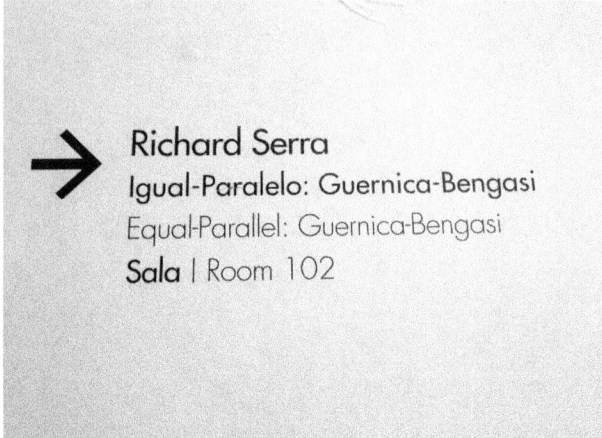

Serra or not a Serra?

In Madrid at the Museo Reina Sofia I took it upon myself to explain to ladies who were wondering out loud about the rusty structure in a museum courtyard that it was not, in fact, a Serra. His installation commemorating the Guernica (1937) and Benghazi (1986) tragedies was inside.

At the Guggenheim in Bilbao, Spain I was awestruck walking through his colossal torqued ellipse piece called *The Matter of Time*[1] that filled the 80' x 430' space, the biggest gallery in the museum.

---

[1] You can see and read all about the piece on the Guggenheim Bilbao site: https://www.guggenheim.org/artwork/21794

Some of the 2013 Venice Biennale pavilions

Russia   Portugal

The Netherlands   United States

I often plan my vacation trips around art I want to see. I've gone to several Venice Biennales when the whole town is taken over by art of all sorts from all over the world. At one exhibition, Russia gave umbrellas only to women, so they could walk through a shower of golden coins. Portugal did an installation on a boat, while The Netherlands chose an earthier display of rocks. And inside our permanent pavilion in the park, the United States displayed assemblages featuring twigs and tiny treasures. The entrance to our stately Greek-columned temple of art looked like kids gone amok with Tinkertoys.

I have a passion for looking at art wherever I can find it. Wandering in museums is transfixing and transcending. Artists show me that there is something more in this universe other than what my eye can see and my mind can understand. Now, rather than ponder the artistic attributes of the object I am contemplating, I engage with it. I sort of have a silent conversation with the artists, wondering what they are trying to communicate to me. What did they see or think or imagine as they painted the canvas or created the sculpture? It is the spark that is created when the artist and I meet through the work that makes the piece come alive.

Gallery hopping

I no longer ask, "Is it art?" But I do have a sort of ongoing game in my head where I make up silly stories about what I am seeing. For example, are those cardboard cartons on the floor art or poor housekeeping? Art. And is that a fire extinguisher or a sculpture? A fire extinguisher.

Almost 60 years after it was my first stop in Europe before attending classes at the Louvre in Paris, I revisited the Rijksmuseum in Amsterdam. As I walked through the grounds to the museum, I passed the monumental sculpture *Sight Point (for Leo Castelli)*. It was created by none other than Richard Serra.

The Night Watch

In the museum, I watched folks taking selfies in front of masterpieces like one of Rembrandt's turbaned Slavic noblemen and thought of Daddy's *Noble Snob*. My destination was one of the Dutch master's most famous works called *The Night Watch*.[2] Once I made my way through the throngs who were gathered around the huge 11'11" x 14'4" painting hanging majestically in its own room, I realized the massive work was behind a glass enclosure where a team was x-ray scanning every pigment of the painting

---

[2] That's not its real name. It was originally called *Militia Company of District II under the Command of Captain Frans Banninck Cocq,* also known as *The Shooting Company of Frans Banning Cocq and Willem van Ruytenburch.* It was called *Night Watch* after it was neglected and turned dark.

of an animated group of men all belonging to the same militia-type group. The 21st century copying would aid in later restoration. I thought of the 20th century art students at their easels copying the great works in the great museums Mary Jane and I toured after my Louvre classes.

Next door to the room where the painting is enthroned was a representation of groups of a different sort. It was a three-screen video, larger than life like *The Night Watch* and also featuring gatherings of like-minded folks like teenagers and well-dressed matrons who discussed the painting from different, often very amusing, perspectives. The biggest kick were the Japanese businessmen who, tongue in cheek, described all the ways the famous work would be commercialized in Japan.

When I left the exhibits, I exited through the gift shop, examining masterpiece-inspired merchandise, when lo and behold what to my astonished eyes should appear but an entire line of items ranging from comic books to tote bags to mugs featuring Donald Duck himself as a member of Captain Cocq's coterie and engaged in other artful activities. My father's quackeries were right there in the museum getting their due! As I selected an armful of offerings, my thoughts turned to how art has taken on a wider appeal, sometimes in what may seem irreverent ways. Perhaps it is commercialization, but it takes some of the intimidation out of enjoying art. And I did laugh at some of the ideas of the Japanese businessmen such as reproductions of *The Night Watch* with holes where the men's heads should be so that art patrons could pay to pose as members of the group who paid to pose for Rembrandt.

Tribute to Henri de Toulouse-Lautrec

The next stop on my recent art odyssey was Albi, France where I went to worship at the birthplace of and see the great collection of works by Toulouse-Lautrec. On my way through the streets of the old village, I couldn't resist the lure of the empty space formerly occupied by the cabaret singer Aristide Bruant in a sidewalk reproduction of T-L's famous poster. (No, I did not perform my Moulin Rouge act while posing.)

Ah, art. I love it all!

Honoring Henri

42
Potsy in Grown-Up Land

The teacher and the taught

I reluctantly returned from Europe to finish graduate school. I enjoyed as many art history courses as I could fit into my schedule and did all my studying in the art department library. The required education courses were far less stimulating, but I found I really enjoyed student teaching. I loved the one-on-one interaction with the kids. So, it was time to enter the real world of making a living.

My career path climbed from the halls of academia to the halls of high school and finally to Potsy's playground. It may seem like a reverse course, but zig zagging along this ever-winding path, I found my true calling.

It all started at Emerson Junior High in Westwood, California where I was hired as a teacher after getting a general secondary credential a few blocks away at UCLA. As I set all in order for my first class, I felt as if I was still playing school in my Parish Place bedroom. I was only a few years older than my older students, and I felt almost all of them were worldlier than I.

Most of the kids at Emerson Junior High were among the over-privileged. Some were daughters and sons of liberal-minded movie stars who lived in the pricey enclaves of Bel Air and the mansion-dotted canyons, but they chose not to isolate their children in private schools. There were the Bridges boys, Jeff and Beau—before his Dude days; Billy Lancaster, son of Burt; Bonnie Raitt, musical heir to her father John; Jayne Mansfield's namesake Jayne, and composer Sammy Cahn's daughter, Laurie. Star sightings were frequent fodder for faculty room gossip. Someone said they spotted the elder Mansfield walking her pet ocelot in the downstairs hall. Rumor.

I enjoyed the spotlight in front of the blackboard. Finding ways to communicate knowledge was like acting. The more I hammed it up, the more they seemed to learn. We got excited together by our animated exchanges of facts and opinions.

Although my teaching manner tended to boil exuberantly over the top, I tried to maintain a teacherly mien. I replaced my collegiate ponytail with a sophisticated bob. I forget the Beverly Hills hairdresser's name, maybe Mr. Michael, or maybe Antoine, but I remember he looked at my waist-length mane and declared that the only suitable place for hair that long was on the pillow. I wore girdles and sensible, stacked heels my students called my "orthopedic" shoes.

Maintaining my composure was not always easy in the face of a few rookie year faux pas. One time, while teaching World History, not my strongest subject, I tried to dramatize the voyage of Magellan. With great drama I asked the class, "Can you imagine how excited they were in Seville when he returned? The town folk would have thought he was dead." One of the students, who had read further in the text than I, volunteered, "He was, Miss Patin. He died in the Philippines and didn't return to Spain with the ship."

Then there was the moment I thought a boy was having an attack of some sort, only to learn he was making surf bubbles—an intricately contrived approximation of sea foam that I took for foaming at the mouth. And my ninth graders delighted in watching me turn red the time I wanted to take the pressure off when announcing some upcoming exams. I called them "testies."

I remember the class clown, John Landis, who was likable despite his continual comedic calls for attention. In not too many years he was to get attention aplenty when he directed *National Lampoon's Animal House* and directed and wrote the *Thriller* video along with Michael Jackson. Once, a cast of my dramatically-inclined English students produced an oral presentation in the form of a skit. The leading role was a very thinly-disguised impression of their teacher. They managed a hilariously accurate imitation of my foibles and idiosyncrasies strutting my pedantic self in front of the classroom. I laughed so hard that I almost re-earned the right to be called "Stinky Pee Tail." They and my other charges made up for the pastiche by choosing me as their Teacher of the Year all three years I taught there.

There were serious times too, like the November day in 1963 when our principal, Mr. Campbell, announced over the intercom that President Kennedy had died. The class and I shared the horrifying moment in stunned silence after I told them they could each deal with the shock in their own way.

After three years at Emerson, I went to Mr. Campbell and told him that I was leaving because I found another job. I would be going to Switzerland to teach in a girls' high school and finishing school. What I didn't tell him was that I had been spending the last three years building a résumé that would qualify me to work in Europe. This was my dream, even when I was suffering through the education courses at UCSB and UCLA.

I think Daddy was pleased, and maybe a little proud, when Mama took our picture at the Los Angeles Airport before TWA flew me away from the safety behind the Sign. I was pleased and proud too, posing in my imitation Chanel suit, all ready to become an international woman. But a very big part of me felt like Potsy pretending I was a grown-up going off to work.

My second school was the Institut Montesano in Gstaad, a jet set ski resort in the Swiss Alps. The school was located in seven chalets scattered on the hill behind a postcard-perfect village. Once again, I was teaching the children of the well-endowed.

Transworld traveler

Gstaad today

Gstaad yesterday where students posed on snow and lived and learned in chalets

Faculty fondue (on right, second from front)

I tried to model myself after the European women I saw around town and tame my personality to fit in with my staid staff colleagues. But I was not successful. It was hard to make friends with the faculty. I felt like a kid in the midst of the teachers who found me a little too La La—an interloper from that fabled land. My teaching methods, like playing games in the manner of *Hollywood Squares,* were frowned upon by the more traditional instructors.

However, not too long ago I received an email from one of the teenagers who sat at the tables crowded into a chalet classroom. We reestablished contact after she recognized my name on an online forum where I was inquiring about a visit to Gstaad. Her purpose in emailing about her *grandchildren's* great new tutor was not to make me feel ancient, but to comment on my teaching style. Here's what she said:

> *No one knows better than I the difference one teacher can make to one's life. My love of literature started with you and your refusal to allow boredom in your classroom. If all teachers taught like you and this tutor, there would be no bored students and the world would be a better place.*

I'm glad to know my effort to entertain my students resulted in some learning as well.

Mlle[1] Patin poses pensively

Most of the hundred girls were American, but I was the only American teacher. I felt a little lonely trying to shape myself into my new role as a cosmopolitan ex-patriot educator. Adult jet setters and local Swiss stuck to their own ilk. A photo taken at my desk shows a wistful woman whose blond hair, made darker by the photo, seemed to match her melancholy.

Rubbing elbows with the jet set
(I'm the lady in white, cigarette in hand)

I befriended a British governess whose charges played with the widow Kennedy's son when they visited town. Therefore, I had secondhand knowledge of the son of our late president when I met two handsome gentlemen in the movie house. They spoke with Boston accents, and I was quick to tell them that little John John did too. "That's funny," the older of the two attractive gentlemen replied, "I hadn't noticed. We are his bodyguards." We left the theater together and drank the night away at the Chesery.

I wandered the village, scoring only two star-sightings: Mrs. Kennedy leaving in her helicopter, and Richard Burton shopping without Elizabeth who was no doubt lounging with champagne and puppy dogs in their chalet.

---

[1] Yes, I was a Mademoiselle, a term now deemed sexist and officially banned on French forms

Creative Playthings

My career in Gstaad was cut short to a year because of difficulties with a former teacher/boyfriend at Emerson Junior High (where we pursued our dalliance passing notes carried by students between our classrooms). In my loneliness, I had obtained him a job at Montesano, and before the semester began, we indulged in a romantic tour of Europe. We broke up on a far from romantic Greek island, and I left him and the job.

Back in the US, I returned, not only to the shadow of the Sign, but to my Parish Place homestead. I took a job as a substitute teacher in both the Burbank and the Glendale school districts, teaching in the same classrooms at Burroughs and Glendale College where I had dreamed of what I would become. After my wanderings, I again had the same wonderings.

I decided that a career as an educator was not conducive for catching a husband. And catching a husband at twenty-eight was top priority. I would enter the world of business. I answered a want ad placed by CBS (Columbia Broadcasting System) for a subsidiary that required teaching as well as retail experience. With plenty of both under my belt, I headed to the Western Division headquarters of Creative Playthings near the Los Angeles Airport where I was to be interviewed by the vice president on whom I plied my charms. Even though my teaching had been in secondary school, I was hired as a consultant on early childhood teaching toys and as manager of the retail stores.

My office was a kindergarten, or at least a room set up to look like one. I gave demonstrations on how to play and teach with our hands-on innovative materials. My talks always began with the quote "I hear, and I forget; I see, and I remember; I do, and I understand." And I always included the philosophies about childhood I'd learned from Rachel Carson and Antoine de St. Exupéry.

Renée at work

I actually made it to Hollywood for an appearance on Les Crane's TV talk show where I introduced America's first "anatomically correct" doll called the "Little Brother Doll." My job took me around the country spreading the word about the wonder of childhood learning and the power of play to bring it about. Creative Playthings catalogs were filled with early learning innovations. They had a separate learning center and even did research into prenatal learning.

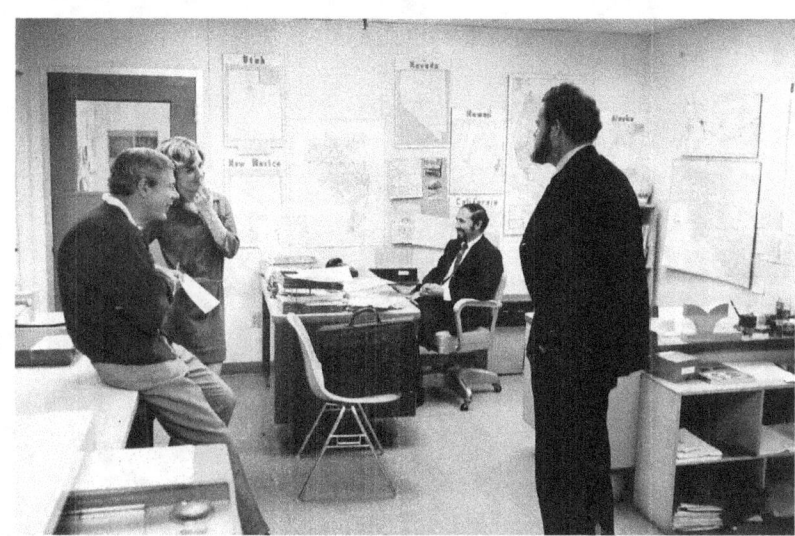

Look carefully. There are some clues to the future.

I felt like a big deal. I rented a series of apartments as my salary increased, ending in one near Sunset Boulevard in Brentwood. I pictured myself as the kind of career woman on the rise that Katherine Hepburn would have played—but I wore skirts. From time to time I visited with the big boys in suits at the home office in Princeton, New Jersey. I saw their interplay as a game I didn't really want to play. I preferred playing with the toys I was helping to sell. It was the first of four similar companies I worked for that sold toys and educational materials to schools and homes.

Come play with me

Magnifying stand　　　　　　　　　Sculpted family

Giant abacus　　　　　　　　　Wooly lamb ride-on

I was proud of playthings so beautiful and unique that they were featured in a "Good Design in Toys" museum exhibit that traveled around the country. But eventually the company veered away from education and toward toys sold in retail stores. My job was phased out, and I went to the headquarters in Princeton where my job was to put sticky notes with frowny faces on rejected new toy idea submission letters. The end came after I quit on the spot when my problematic boss at the Princeton headquarters—not the one I left behind in LA—had me fetching coffee for the big boys.

It was while employed at my third toy company when I realized I could design the very products we were buying from others. Remember the movie *Big,* where Tom Hanks plays a twelve-year-old living in a grown-up's body? He gets a job doing product development at a toy company and is a huge success because he thinks like a kid. That is my story. Potsy was inside me thinking up ideas for toys, and Renée helped make them come true. It was the career I was meant to have.

You may remember the movie my father did on my first introduction to toys. Despite my father's cinematic comments on my preferring Christmas decorations to the playthings under my first tree,

I have always loved toys. I played hard as a kid and gave my toys stress tests worthy of *Consumer Reports,* including the taste test on my ceramic bunny buddies from *Snow White and the Seven Dwarfs.* I'm sure the Three Little Pigs got their share of tough love, too. I know Pluto became my well-loved/mangled best friend. I called on my experience to create products for other tots to enjoy. I also learned a few practical tips, like the fact crockery of any sort is not ideal for infant Christmases. And I taught others, including Gretchen, what I had learned, growing a thriving Product Development department.

My first great success was Grandma's Dress-Up Trunk, based on my love of dressing up as a movie star with the kids on the block. It is still being sold over 30 years later. I had my mother, in her mid-fifties at the time, sew a collection of mix and match glamour pieces from taffetas and tulles I bought at a Burbank fabric store. I gave my boss a runway-worthy presentation using the daughters of co-workers to model all the ensembles created from the pieces. He was so excited that he rewarded Mama and me with dinner for two at the place of our choice. Another big seller was Kids' Business, a chest with drawers that contained my dream collection of all the forms, rubber stamps, signs and office supplies I had bought with my allowance as a kid.

For years, I traveled to New York, Hong Kong and Nuremburg to the toy shows. Potsy and I (and often Gretchen) walked the miles of aisles, marveling at a kid's dream of an enchanted land of toys. We traveled to the factories in Asia that brought my imagination to reality. It was a creativity I had never imagined I had inside me.

Two companies, two offices

When I retired from my last educational materials business in 2003, I was vice president of research and development for a company in Monterey, California. I had spent 20 years playing in four different companies on two coasts. The third company sued the fourth when I began developing products for them, and the fourth bought the second. Sound like a game? I never stopped thinking of corporate twists and turns as a somewhat silly game and my job as child's play.

43
Marriage Afloat and on the Rocks

Wavy paramour and performer

When my knight in shining armor finally appeared to carry me off into the sunset, it was not astride a snow-white steed. It was aboard a resplendent white yacht. But let's begin at the "once upon a time" part of our story. It all started with my interview with the vice president of Creative Playthings, John Thomas Farrington. Yes. He was the one. You actually saw him first in Chapter 42. He was the imposing figure standing in profile before his sales staff. The article shown in Chapter 42 with my picture begins, "L.A. MEANS LOTS OF ACCOLADES—Kudos to Mr. Farrington's Western Division Headquarters." It goes on to talk of my speaking engagements around California—often accompanied by Mr. Farrington.

Like most knights, "Jack" was a handsome fellow. He told me he'd been likened to Van Heflin, that matinee idol of the forties and fifties. And, like Van and the knights of yore, he was a military man.

Military man

Renée's rendition of a bomber flown by the bomber pilot she married

When I was drawing crayon pictures of bomber planes, Jack was a B-17 "Flying Fortress" bomber pilot, flying out of a base in Italy that British troops had captured. He was shot down and survived a year as a prisoner in a German stalag. When he hired me, I was twenty-eight, and he was forty-four.

I remember the moment I knew I was falling in love with my boss. It was after work at the Proud Bird Restaurant. We were watching the planes land at LAX and sipping cocktails garnished with faux-feathered birds and gay umbrellas. When Mr. Farrington couldn't hear what I was saying, he grabbed the captain's chair I was sitting in and pulled it closer to himself. Maybe it was the show of strength from a war hero, or the aphrodisiac of his executive power, or that the sixteen-year age difference made him seem more like a man than the fellows of my own age I had dated. It could even have been his Van Heflin looks, but I knew I was falling. And so it came about that Mr. Farrington and Miss Patin became Jack and Renée.

Jack and Renée

Admiration

My mother, who along with my father, still called my boyfriend Mr. Farrington, even sketched us as a couple. One might say she was drawing a caricature of my La La Land coiffure. But Mama was not a satirist. My curly locks were a hairdresser's attempt to make me look like the businesswoman I was becoming.

Come see my toys

Not only did Jack and I share a love for the business of toys, but we enjoyed playing together. There was a lot of fantasy involved in our romance. We were like kids pretending when we set up exhibit displays at early childhood education conventions. Even at home, Jack loved to create elaborate block creations around the Christmas tree.

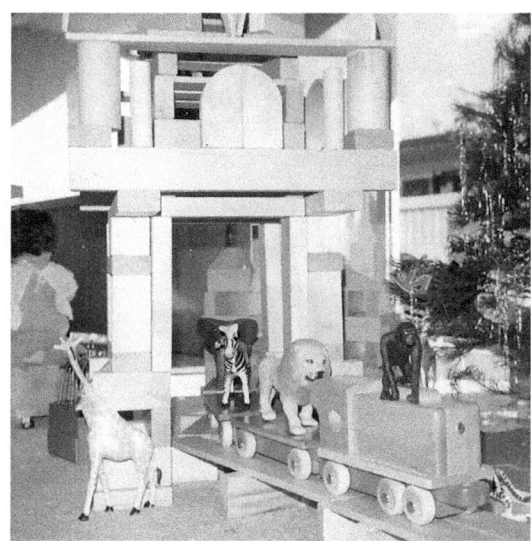 

Christmas surprise

It was on one of these Christmas mornings that Jack hid a baroque black pearl engagement ring in a music box that was the last of the shower of gifts he placed around one of his Christmas creations. I shared the grand present opening with the Little Brother doll discretely riding atop the Wooly Lamb.

But not all was copacetic in toy land. The Princeton powers that be took exception to their West Coast head honcho, Jack, consorting with a consultant, me. And they did not like that I had abruptly quit and returned to California to be near him. So, Jack was fired, and we were jobless. Not long after we left Creative Playthings, we were married in Las Vegas. And not long after that, Jack had an idea. We would build a boat and spend our days cruising wherever the winds took us. It would take about a year, he told me, and then we would "slip the surly bonds"[1] of land and make the water our home. Boat? Travel? Count me in!

---

[1] Jack often quoted the John Magee poem *High Flight,* beloved by airmen that begins,
  Oh! I have slipped the surly bonds of Earth
  And danced the skies on laughter-silvered wings.

Advent of an ark

We began construction on our dream boat in a Marina del Rey boatyard. On the back of a picture he took of our very first day of construction, our friend Art Herman wrote: "From these blocks and string..." In the distance, Jack and I are kneeling at the end of a formation of cinder blocks that outlines our future yacht's broad beam (14 feet). The sticks and string in the middle run the 50 feet down her length. It would be five years before the dream became a floating reality.

Jack began work full-time on the boat, first in the boatyard, and then, when the hull was finished, in the backyard of a little house we rented in Redondo Beach, thirteen miles away from Marina del Rey where the boat was begun. Along with the backyard came the ability to have a dog, so we went to the local animal shelter, and Jack fell in love. The object of his affections was a magnificent German shepherd/Norwegian elkhound sitting in a car next to ours in the parking lot while its owner was inside the shelter arranging to give him up. We named our new constant companion Schatz (a German term of endearment). Among his many talents was climbing the six-foot ladder to get up onto the deck of the boat while we worked on her completion.

I went back to teaching. Each year I returned, I had to tell my students that no, we hadn't gone around the world yet. We put everything in our bank account and in our possession and in us into the creation of our floating home. By launch time, we had nothing but her. She sat in our backyard, her glistening hull an object of wonder to both her creators and the passers-by in the wide alley she overlooked.

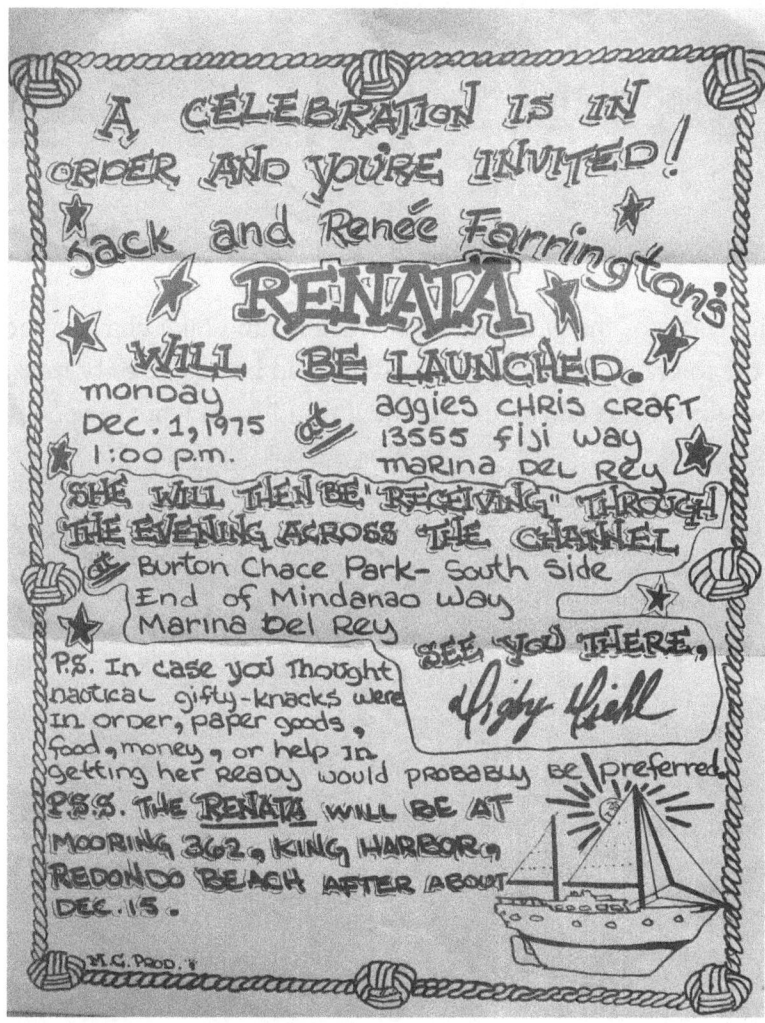

Invitation to launch

As we readied *Renata* for her debut launching, our dear friend Digby, the book editor at the *Los Angeles Times,* readied the party at the dock. The studio musician father of one of my students rehearsed his musicians with a song composed for the occasion. It is sung to the tune of "Granada," and heralds *Renata,* my name in Spanish.

> *Renata, Renata, you just gotta gotta float.*
> *Remember you're a ship, not a boat…*

Reluctant *Renata*

Champagne was at the ready for the gathered well-wishers, and fake champagne was ready in its breakaway bottle for me to crack on *Renata's* lovely curved bow. The only missing element from the party was *Renata.* A week of rains had saturated the ground from where the 32-ton beauty would not budge from our backyard.

On her way!

Two weeks later we loaded the reluctant craft onto a lowboy truck and followed her the ten miles back to Marina del Rey. She turned heads along the way, especially as she barely made her way under freeway overpasses.

She floats!

At the launch ramp we were met by a small group of friends. *Renata* was gingerly placed in a sling, and with life-jacketed Jack on deck, slowly lowered into the water. I watched with held breath and said a prayer as she descended into the murky waters and stopped, right at her sunflower yellow waterline. The straps were undone, and she floated free, Jack optimistically and proudly standing on her deck. My breath and tears exploded at once, and Jack's eyes were damp too.

For another six months we lived aboard, tied to a buoy. Jack continued to work non-stop to step the masts and rig our new home. He shared my father's love of working on the boat. In *The Wind in the Willows,* the Water Rat said:

> *Simply messing...about in boats–or with boats... In or out of 'em it doesn't matter. Nothing seems to matter, that's the charm of it. Whether you get away, or whether you don't; whether you arrive at your destination or whether you reach somewhere else, or whether you never get anywhere at all, you're always busy, and you never do anything in particular; and when you've done it there's always something else to do, and you can do it if you like, but you'd much better not."*

I however, had the attitude of Mr. Toad. I was in it for the adventure and the messing about was going on far too long for this impatient wanderlust-filled future circumnavigator.

Shakedown and at anchor with Renée in dinghy (Jack and Schatz on board)

But before we headed south, we needed to have a shakedown cruise to be sure we and *Renata* were seaworthy. We survived a blustery cruise north thanks to a friend who gave Jack lessons in sailing on the way. Actually, Jack had never *sailed* before. His boats had been power cruisers, a passion he shared with his father-in-law, Ray.

Our shakedown was six weeks in Santa Barbara, an ironic sojourn for the coed who had led a life of learning and leisure in the same town. If I had envisioned a marriage when I was a student, this was not how I imagined Renée playing the role of happy housewife. Whenever I wanted to come ashore to perform my wifely errands, Jack would dinghy me to Stearns Wharf where I climbed the rusty gap-toothed ladder onto splintery wood planks, hoisting my wire shopping cart behind me on a rope.

Renata at anchor in Santa Barbara

Errands completed, cart filled, and a jug of screw top wine on top, I would catch the bus back to the pier, blow my whistle for Jack to bring the dinghy, drop him the rope to haul up canvas bags to load my purchases, inch them down to him, and gingerly back myself down the ladder to dinghy back to the *Renata*. Before I could go below to enjoy the wine, I had to remove each can from the paper bag, remove the label and mark the can lest cockroaches feast on the glue they love so much.

The Harbor on Stearns Wharf 1959

Ahh, the price of paradise! If the Harbor Restaurant diners—like the Patin family in the fifties—only knew the stories playing out on those yachts at anchor they admired from their sea-view tables.

Domesticity afloat in our salon/living room, galley/kitchen, cabin/bedroom

Renata was roomy—for a boat. Her salon was comfy and filled with light. I boasted of a 3-section sink with Mexican-tiled backsplash, two stoves—electric and kerosene—and a small and tight-enough space to wedge myself in when cooking in rough seas. Our cabin had large, louvered teak lockers and next to my bunk, a roll-top desk my father made as a copy of the child's desk my grandfather made for my mother.

Finally, her shakedown complete, *Renata* was deemed mature enough—and her captain willing enough—to embark on our trip south through the Panama Canal and across to Europe.

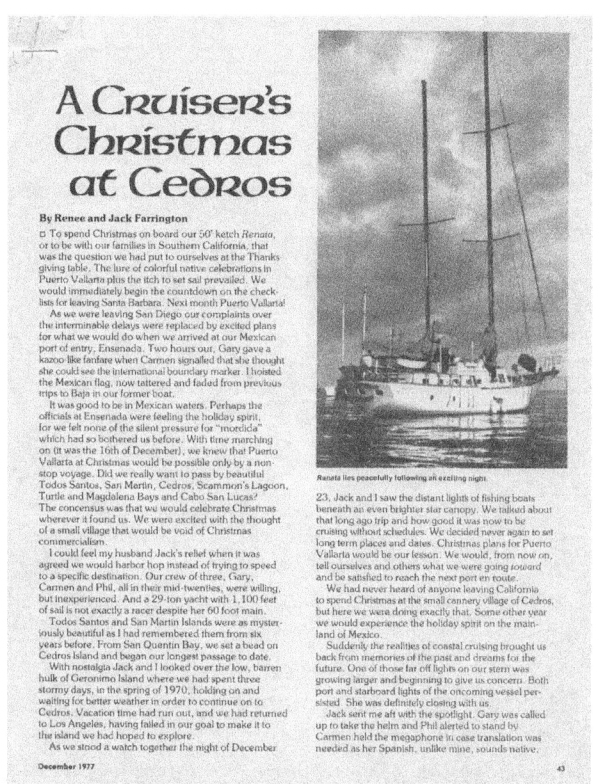

Sea story in print

Proud author with a true Christmas story and Maxine's illustration for it

Our first encounter with danger on the other side of the border came on tiny Cedros Island. A storm came up while we were at anchor, and the cove we had chosen became unsafe. A Mexican seaman rowed toward us in the heavy wind, boarded and led us to safety. He disappeared before we could thank him. He was probably on his way to Christmas Eve festivities on shore. A few months later, tied up in a dock in Puerto Vallarta, I wrote my first boating magazine article. It was about that incident. Mama illustrated the article showing the Good Samaritan and the Christmas tree attached to our bowsprit. Digby visited us and brought a copy of the magazine with the story of our Christmas at Cedros. I proudly displayed it on the balcony of his nearby hotel room, showing the page with Mama's illustration of the church she imagined our rescuer attended that Christmas Eve.

JO JO JO!—a Mexican holiday on the beach

The following Christmas in Puerto Vallarta we "yachties" gathered in the coconut palms for the arrival of Santa Claus with a dinghy filled with goodies for the live-aboard kids from our floating neighborhood.

Tulum and Puerto Vallarta, Mexico: this isn't Newport anymore

We gunkholed in hidden coves and docked in the harbors of the west coast of Mexico and Central America. In various ports, we picked up new amateur crewmembers because the two of us couldn't handle the big, beautiful, but unwieldy yacht on our own.

PANAMANIAN PASSAGE
story and photo by Reneé and Jack Farrington

Locks and lakes

We continued to write articles for yachting magazines chronicling our experiences. The last of these was "Panamanian Passage." We had a Panamanian pilot come on board to help navigate the giant locks and postcard perfect lakes. The extraordinary beauty of the daylong trip and the pride of having built a yacht that qualified for the passage were among the greatest highlights of our cruising days.

From the Canal we headed north. When we came upon land, we hoped we had discovered America and hailed a sport fisherman to ask our position. No doubt wondering how such a weathered, salty vessel and crew could be completely lost, he answered that we were in the Marquesas. This would put us back in the Pacific. We agreed my navigation wasn't that bad and were reassured when our guide informed us we were in the Marquesas Keys, 20 miles from Key West, Florida. Determined not to hit that or any other key, we set a bead for Miami where our crew left us. We picked up new crew to head north into the Intracoastal Waterway, that lovely connection of inside passages that would take us through rivers and creeks and bays with none of the fear-inducing threats of ocean passages. Immediately upon entering the inland route at Fort Pierce, we went aground—twice—only to be humiliatingly hauled off each time by the U.S. Coast Guard.

Seafarers

I loved the nomadic life at sea with a man I loved. I was proud of him and of *Renata* each time we sailed into a new harbor. It seemed a luxury to have lovely sea-view accommodations wherever we were. Ours was a constantly changing front yard whether it be a grassy marsh, a fishing village, a yacht club marina or a palm-circled cove. I loved the tiny tug of the anchor line announcing we were safely anchored in a new port—and the cocktails that toasted our arrival. I loved the soft lapping of the oars of a dugout canoe as residents from thatched huts approached the new yacht in town, offering coconuts and fruit or fresh caught seafood to trade for *Playboy* magazines or other bounty. I loved exploring a new port with a surprise around each corner and hopefully food other than live, leashed iguanas and mystery veggies. I loved sharing adventures with Jack and Schatz. I loved living simply, deliberately without the masks acquired in my life in the shadow of the Sign.

Life afloat

The Owl and the Pussy-cat went to sea
In a beautiful pea-green boat,
They took some honey, and plenty of money,
Wrapped up in a five-pound note.

The Farringtons at home

But, unlike the species-crossed couple of Edward Lear's poem, our life afloat was not perpetual paradise. We did not have plenty of money from living off Jack's Air Force pension and my writing. We enjoyed commiserating with fellow "yachties" who agreed that "a boat is a hole in the water into which you pour money" and "the most expensive way to go last class."

The "Dangers" and Delights of Mexican Cruising

by Renee and Jack Farrington

March 1, 1978; Santa Cruz, Mexico. "Keep calm, everybody. Act natural. That gunboat launched a small boat, and it looks like it's coming this way!"

April 6, 1978; Puerto Madero, Mexico. The captain and first mate of the 50-ft. ketch Renata *are escorted by two armed guards into the base headquarters of the Mexican Navy!*

These two encounters with the Mexican Navy actually befell *Renata* and her crew during 14 months of cruising in Mexico. The reports, however, are similar to many passed on to others planning cruises to Mexico. Only half the story is told, and that half is usually exaggerated.

The truth is: we were boarded once, for about 10 minutes. A very polite officer was brought alongside while we were at anchor. We invited him aboard and offered him a tour. He was complimentary and interested in the fact that we had built the boat ourselves. He checked its documentation, thanked us profusely, and left.

At Puerto Madero, three female members of the crew anxiously approached the beautiful new naval installation. We needed water, we told the armed sentry. He led us through a series of officers, each one bearing more scrambled eggs on the bill of his hat. Finally, I was taken to the office of the base commander, Capitan Jose Rivera Arreola, who arranged for us to acquire as much water as we needed from their purification system.

The next morning my husband, Jack, and I tied our Avon to the Armada pier. An officer greeted us and saw us into the waiting jeep—complete with chauffeur and two (armed) escorts.

Later, 75 gallons of water having been transported in jerry jugs to the *Renata*, Jack and I said our thanks and headed for the dinghy. Coming the other way on the road were about 50 troops being mustered

to roll call. As they passed us they executed a perfect hat salute at the command of their leader, the sentry who had first greeted us. What a send-off from our last port in Mexico!

From Ensenada to the border of Guatemala we found the Mexican Navy a true source of aid. One invaluable service we discovered was the willingness to share weather radiograms. Glancing back over the reports we kept, I ran across one headed by the following advisory (it's easy to see how a minor error in word choice and a few exaggerations could lead to rumors about the Mexicans trying to get innocent yachtsmen within range of their lethal cannons):

"February 17, 1978; Puerto Madero, Mexico. Advisory: Mexican Navy will effect cannon shot practice on Feb. 20 and 25 . . . Please take care to sail on (sic) these areas at date and time above."

While on the topic of clearances and supply runs, what about "mordida" for port officials? We were never asked for, nor gave money to port captains, immigration, or customs officers in the 10 ports we cleared. The procedures are simple and often loosely followed. We used Larry Baldwin's "Crew Lists For Spanish Speaking Countries" and followed the directions inside. They lasted through Mexico.

However, two encounters with port officials stand out.

Jack and I were ashore in the tiny, colorful village of Puerto Magdalena, unaware that it is a port of entry. We were therefore surprised that a house we had hoped to be a restaurant was the home of the port captain. After our visit, we had to return immediately to *Renata*. This was not due to any irregularity in our papers. It was just too hard to carry the 15 live lobsters the port captain's wife had presented us on leaving.

After repeated visits to a closed office, it became clear that the immigration officer

The pleasures and pains of the boating life

Advice to the seaborne

Jack agonized over the constant responsibility of captaining a 32-ton vessel with no insurance, the constant danger of bridges that would not open for us in time as we were being pushed by the current, uncharted rocks, banditos and breakdowns of boat or body. It seemed whatever could go wrong did. We often stayed weeks or even months in a port fixing one thing or another or waiting for just the right time to pull up our anchor. Many of our magazine articles centered on repairs, a topic about which we were becoming experts. We offered advice on navigating both the waters and harbors.

Our stories were both cautionary and amusing. We recounted our tales of going through the rigmarole entering each port and warned about paying "mordida"—the bite/bribe—to port officials in order to get permission to stay at anchor. Our many adventures and misadventures became content for our chronicles.

The other side of paradise

New port, new home

We had been almost "two years before the mast"[2] when we pulled into the Downtown Marina in Beaufort, South Carolina. On the old sailing ships, the sailors bunked in the area in the very cramped narrow bow in front of (before) the foreword mast. The captain and officers slept in more comfortable quarters in the broad stern (back). Flaunting tradition, Jack and I bunked in the forward (front) cabin with the mainmast (the longer one) in the middle of our cabin, fire extinguisher attached, as you can see in the photo. Beaufort, South Carolina, forty miles from Savannah and sixty miles from Charleston, is pronounced "Bee-ew-fort." Beaufort, North Carolina is pronounced "Bow-fort"—like the Beaufort

---

[2] Richard Henry Dana's voyage as described in his 1841 book *Two Years Before the Mast* was the reverse of ours. He set off from Boston and arrived (without benefit of a canal) in Mexico's Alta California where he describes his adventures in the Port of Los Angeles, Santa Barbara, Monterey and San Francisco.

wind speed scale. If you've seen the movies *The Great Santini*[3] or *Forrest Gump,* you've seen the charm of Beaufort's antebellum mansions and the net-draped shrimpers.

We were entranced, and that night, as we celebrated our wedding anniversary at a dinner under the low ceiling of the wavy-floored old John Cross Tavern, we decided to spend a couple of days, then continue north. We ended up spending five years.

Here's why we stayed. The owner of an educational products company came knocking on the side of the boat when he heard from our friend, the co-founder of Creative Playthings, that Jack could offer some help with operations. So, Jack went back to went to work, and I later joined him working on product selection and setting up a toy store on Bay Street, the main street, not far from the John Cross Tavern.

Our plantation home

At first, we lived on board, at the Downtown Marina on the river, then bought a remodeled caretakers' cottage on a plantation on the sea island of St. Helena. Our entrance was a dirt road through an *allée* (alley) under an archway of moss-dripping oaks that reminded me of Louisiana. The island is known for its golden marshes, the Gullah culture of the African-Americans and for the Penn Center that educated the freed slaves when the area fell to the Union early in the war.

We learned that we needed an education in the subtleties of our new southern society. Although our arrival aboard a yacht helped us fit into many levels of the stratified hierarchy, we were something of an oddity having sailed from Southern California. One member of the "town's finest" commented on our La La Land origin, "You don't even have to leave the LA Airport to see all the weirdos." When we told our new friends that we had enjoyed the Memorial Day parade to the cemetery, we were told it was traditionally a celebration for the black population who originated the holiday to commemorate the end of the Civil War and emancipation of the slaves. When we invited black supporters of a politician friend for a campaign fund-raising river cruise aboard *Renata,* Jack was called "Captain Bwana."

We were proud when *Renata* survived a small hurricane as we watched from an inn on land. She only tore up the marina dock a little. But when a company came to town to shoot *The Big Chill,* and we were asked to sail her in a background shot, Jack refused—despite my cajoling and their offer of a tidy sum. I think he was afraid of not doing it well.

---

[3] Pat Conroy grew up in Beaufort and wrote about his father, whose nickname was "The Great Santini." He made the town and the Lowcountry co-stars in his many books.

Maxine's Christmas card created for the Farringtons of Beaufort

I was fascinated by life in the "Lowcountry." It was like living in a foreign country at another period of time. Our new double income made that living a lot easier. Mama came to stay and created our Christmas card with Santa on a shrimper, a Christmas tree in the rigging and an angel blessing Beaufort. It was nice to visit friends for drinks and bridge in one of our his and hers company cars rather than by dinghy. We entertained with ping pong on our broad porch and croquet between oaks and azaleas. Our social circle included retired military "snowbirds" who came for the climate and for the nearby Parris Island Marine Corps Recruit Depot where we shopped and dined. From Charleston Air Force Base, we flew military standby to Europe where we visited Weiner Neustadt, the town near Vienna where Jack was shot down and captured as a POW. It is a lovely town, but we knew that these thirty plus years later, the men of Jack's age could have been his captors.

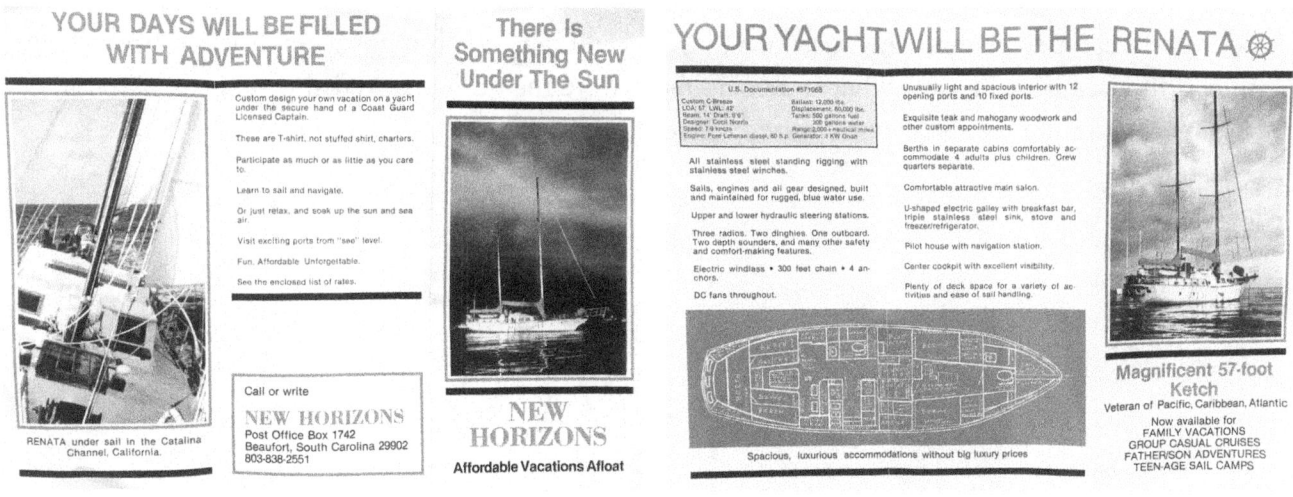

Charter brochure: *Renata* goes to work

I wrote articles for the chamber of commerce and even tried out for the Little Theater role of the addled Abby in *Arsenic and Old Lace*. (The director who auditioned me gave herself the role.) I got involved a little with some charities and learned that when we prepared for luncheons, the ladies of higher standing arranged flowers, and vegetable cutting for crudités went to those of lesser rank. I did both. Jack and our crewman got their pilot's licenses, so we could charter *Renata* to Beaufortonians. We took guests to Hilton Head Island and hosted parties aboard.

Shrimp boats draped with nets

But our party came to an end when our jobs did. We sold our little red house and moved back aboard *Renata* at the Beaufort Marina, where our neighbors were the net-bedecked shrimp boats. We turned our sights back to the sea. New ports were calling.

Under the Brooklyn Bridge

We hired new crew, and headed north, staying in the safety of the Intracoastal, sailing in and out of quiet bays and villages and even Manhattan where we ogled the skyline from sea level. Our most northern port on the East Coast was Newport, Rhode Island, where we watched the United States lose the America's Cup for the first time in its history. We loved exploring Martha's Vineyard and Block Island and the Chesapeake.

But our romance at sea was not as romantic as the tale of *The Owl and The Pussy-cat:*

> *And hand in hand, on the edge of the sand,*
> *They danced by the light of the moon,*
> *The moon,*
> *The moon,*
> *They danced by the light of the moon*

It became increasingly clear to both of us that there would be no more walking hand in hand on the edge of the sand or dancing by the light of the moon for Jack and Renée. Instead of setting our intended course for Europe, we sailed slowly back down South with no particular plan. Although we now had enough money to insure the boat and live more comfortably, Jack did not enjoy the cruising. We had various crews and sometimes hired professional captains to continue our trek south. We stopped again in Beaufort where Jack would have liked to remain. He told me he just wanted to stay in port as a "beach bum." Jack was sixty-one and tired. I was forty-five and not ready to stop playing. I returned to the West Coast and my third educational toy company. Jack stayed on *Renata* on the East Coast. It was 1983. Our "ever afters," happily or not, would be lived separately.

Safe haven

In 2004 Jack died and was buried with full honors at Arlington National Cemetery in Washington, D.C. I, too, honor Jack. He was a man who could imagine the impossible and achieve it. He arrived at a place on his journey that I am only beginning to glimpse—a place when being is enough. I learned a lot from my seafaring knight. Like our life afloat, I have encountered both hazardous rocks and untradeable wonders. Thanks to Jack and *Renata,* I am learning not to fight the wind, but adjust my sails.

44
Adventures Far from the Sign

Heir mail

My chronic case of wanderlust might be blamed on a letter from my father. The missive is dated July 1961 and sent to my address in Paris. He was answering my letter to let him know that Nicole, the sorority sister who had accompanied me to Paris, had to return to the States and couldn't travel with me after my classes. I would be on my own.

The salutation "Hi Honey" is written on an "Air Letter," a tissue-thin sky-blue form that folds into its own envelope, pre-stamped with ten cent overseas postage. After a few tidbits of local news, my father, who was writing the letter on board the *Trinket,* interrupted his narrative:

This is going to be a very disconnected letter—I see there is not other stationery on board so I'm going to have to switch to a paper towel. I hope it works. Paper Mates are supposed to...

Then at the top of a bumpy paper towel, he drew a trial squiggle and continued:

...work over butter so they should work on—By Golly! They do!!

With that transition out of the way, he finished his long letter on said sheaf of towels:

I want to be sure and let you know that we want you to relax and enjoy your European trip. You'll make every moment count. I know you will, but I don't want you to do it with any feeling of guilt or obligation. You are not building up a debt that we ever expect to have you repay in a monetary sense. You have earned every bit of it by being just what you are—someone we're very proud of. We know that even though she has to leave, you'll take good care of yourself and come back to us with a bubbling barrelful of knowledge and experiences.

My father always found it easier to express himself on paper—whether stationery, animation paper or towels. As I read the letter while sitting on my bed in my little student foyer room, I was struck to tears by his faith in me, his encouragement and praise. Daddy's nudge toward plunging myself into that European exploration left me with self-confidence and a lifelong spirit of adventure. He followed the letter by lending the money to Mary Jane to join me.

Ballooning over Turkey and Kenya

Ever after I have been gallivanting and gathering a "bubbling barrelful"[1] of experiences—and perhaps a trickle of knowledge. I have often shared my globe-hopping with Gretchen. We've explored on and off the beaten track ever since.

In the spirit of my father, I have documented my ramblings on film. Like his, my documentation is often photographed through a slightly whimsical lens. Although I have shelves of snapshots and slide-holding carousels, and thousands of digital pictures of postcard views and must-see monuments, I've chosen to share scenes according to themes that capture that special something that makes me want to keep on wandering and wondering.

---

[1] Looks as if even my alliteration addiction was inherited.

Here's looking at you, kid in Casablanca, Morocco

ACTING ON THE WORLD'S STAGE

Travel allows us to become peripatetic pretenders. This was the case when we traveled to Rick's Cafe in Casablanca, Morocco. Our "first class" trip from Fez by train was long and arduous just so we could dine and pose in the lovely music-filled real restaurant. Before leaving we bought souvenirs at this reproduction of a place that never existed until it was created on a Warner Bros. set in my hometown, Burbank.

Acting like Chinese royalty in Beijing, China

In the Forbidden City, we learned how uncomfortable it must have been for the non-forbidden to live there.

Camel hopping in Cappadocia

In Cappadocia, Turkey, sporting a change of headgear, we learned the same thing about camel riding. The setting amidst suggestively-shaped rock formations added an exotic touch, but the camel wrangler's rambling cell phone conversation did not.

Messing about in the Masai Mara, Kenya

I'LL HAVE WHAT SHE'S HAVING

When we were on a photo safari in Kenya, we were treated to a culinary lesson. A Masai elder demonstrated the recipe for their only meal, a concoction of cow's blood and milk. As his explanation became more animated, Gretchen fainted, sliding down the side of a dung-plastered hut. She revived, however, and was able to laugh and pose with the calabash in which the delicacy is served.

No-snake noodle shop in Tainan, Taiwan

Although I have not added the Masai concoction to my list of favored foods, I've always been an ecumenical eater. That comes from my father who fed me chocolate-covered ants and pigs' knuckles and other exotic fare that appalled my mother. I have a when-in-Rome attitude at foreign dining establishments. Taiwan presented a couple of challenges, but I managed to swallow the plasticky fish eyeball pushed on me as a delicacy and was game for the snake soup I was offered by my Taiwanese friend, Michael. Having heard of Snake Alley in Taipei where the delicacy was served, I asked him what kind of snake it was, whereupon he looked confused. He replied it was the kind of snake you have between meals. I then realized I would not have a tale to tell about devouring serpents. It was a problem with pronunciation. I would be having a "snack," not a "snake."

In Puebla, Mexico I decided to photograph rather than indulge in the contents of two buckets of snacks I spotted side-by-side on the sidewalk, both garnished with limes. One pail contained deceased crickets and the other was filled with confusingly similar nuts. I chose neither.

Vegetarian or not—they're better with lime

More to my delight is the variety of ice cream confections I indulge in throughout Europe. I always heed the call of stands where, arrayed under glass, tubs of colorful flavors await my choice for inclusion on a multi-tiered cone. The award winner for the most creative cone artistry was the masterpiece called "Pinocchio" offered near Dubrovnik, Croatia.

Pinocchio sundae near Dubrovnik, Croatia

Essaouira, Morocco—I kid you not

ANIMALIA

I get rather excited when I can have a significant interaction with native fauna. I had anticipated one such moment from research I had done before our trip to Morocco. We were approaching Essaouira on a day trip from Marrakesh when I spied a tree filled with goats. I had read how they climb trees to eat the precious argan nut kernels that are gathered after the goats have digested and eliminated them. The end products of this process are ground into the oils that make hair and skin glisten. Camera ready, I hopped out of the car to photograph this fascinating phenomenon. My enthusiasm was considerably dimmed when I learned the poor guys had been tethered in the tree in hopes of tourists like me.

Monkey business

Animal watching on safari in Kenya was one of the most extraordinary experiences of my travels. Sometimes semi-domesticated creatures were also memorable. For example, the monkeys who would scamper in what sounded like all-night revelries around our cabins. Their day job was to pester the guests at our lodge, watching and waiting in anticipation to snatch a morsel dropped by a careless diner. There was even an employee whose business it was to swish the monkeys off the terrace of our lodge.

Close encounter from on high

My post-safari hotel was the posh Giraffe Manor in a suburb of Nairobi, near the home of Karen Blixen, the Danish baroness, who, under the pen name Isak Dinesen, wrote *Out of Africa*. Here I had visitors who were quite a bit larger than the monkeys. The roaming tall guys joined us through the window for a snack at breakfast and could peek into the second-floor rooms.

Celebrating

KID BUSINESS

In Tokyo and Kyoto, I watched Japanese boys and girls celebrate rites of passage at prescribed ages. At temples I mingled with proud parents and grandparents accompanied by excited children, all dressed in their best. The boys or girls entered and exited dutifully leaving their shoes and putting them back on the porch. Post passage ritual, they posed for photos with their celebration toys, rang the temple bells and chased each other around the courtyard.

Mexican balloonery in Puebla and Oaxaca

Filled with the same delight as a child who wants every balloon she sees, I never pass up a balloon photo op. No country can beat Mexico for the wonders of its balloonery.

Toys for sale: Mexico and Turkey

Always interested in the toy business, I photographed two women in different parts of the world as they sold their toy temptations. One whistled her birdie tweeter while she worked in the plaza of a church near Oaxaca, and the other demonstrated her bubble-blowing toy in Istanbul between the Blue Mosque and the Hagia Sophia.

The little prince returns   Mustachioed mini Juan Diego

In a village in the Dordogne, France, I managed to find a tourist-free back street where I came upon an earthly reincarnation of my little prince, sword in hand.

This mustachioed Mexican child in Oaxaca is one of many dressed as the humble Juan Diego who was visited by the Virgin of Guadalupe, the Patroness of the Americas.

Celebration

These boys in Istanbul are in full, furry sultan-worthy regalia and swords, but not for play. Their regalia is part of the celebration for their circumcisions at nine years of age.

Child protection

VITAL SIGNS OF LIFE

I know that if my father had given himself time to travel instead of encouraging me to, he would have documented his trips with the same humor he brought to his art and home movies. I, too, find myself looking at scenes with a cartoony gleam in my eye. For example, I like to collect and photograph signs. They add a pinch of whimsical spice to a foreign trip.

Sometimes it helps to know the language when the signs don't make it clear what you are supposed to do or not do. In the Danish countryside, the sign seems to warn children about the dangers of emitting certain bodily gasses, but actually it reminds drivers to slow down for the little darlings.

Protection from children

Then there is the cute illustration of what looks like locals helping a tourist at Chillon Castle near Lake Geneva. On closer examination, you see it is one of the many pickpocket warnings posted in the area.

Bra burning?

Even the ones that don't have language can be confusing. Look at the sign on our Bosporus tour boat posted, apparently, because members of the crew prefer female passengers to go without bikini tops.

Rethink your wardrobe

Was that also the message on the sign in a church in Dubrovnik?

Pause that refreshes

Sometimes it doesn't help to know the language, like in the unfortunate choice of the Japanese soda name brand.

Old mother goose-stuffer

Finally, in Sarlat, France, there was the poster in a shop window showing a sweet little white-haired grandmother. It's only when you read that the product for sale is made from the fatted liver of geese that you realize that granny is pictured stuffing the goose's gullet through a funnel.

> *The real voyage of discovery consists not in seeking new landscapes but in having new eyes.*
>
> Marcel Proust

NEW EYES

Now that I have crossed many destinations off my bucket list, I enjoy returning to locations where I have already seen all the mandatory landmarks and can just relax into the rhythm of the place. I love revisiting places and remembering how I experienced them through the mindset I had then and seeing them now through new eyes.

Roses for Edith

Revisiting old Paris stomping grounds

In 2015, I took a selfie in front of my old student residence under my former room. Then I wandered all over the massive Père Lachaise Cemetery to find the grave of Edith Piaf. After many twists and turns passing the resting places of the famous and the forgotten, I finally found her rose-strewn memorial. I gave thanks for her song, and I contemplated her sad life that was so far from rose-colored.

Bovine moments in Switzerland and Southern California

I took Gretchen to see Gstaad and dipped into more reminiscing. I saw the locale where I had been a lonely and yearning schoolteacher in a whole different way. As we walked down the main street, I realized what a fairy tale setting I'd chosen for my teaching abroad experience. We watched a family lead their herd from alpine grazing grounds through the old main street now lined with chic shops in renovated chalets. The moment was transcendent not just for the beauty of the animals with their enormous flower headdresses and the soft clanging of their giant antique bells. I felt we were witnessing a family tradition performed with pride and love. I couldn't help but remember thirty years before when Gretchen and I made products at a company where Halloween was a big occasion. We chose to celebrate the cow western-style.

With Judy and jack-o'-lanterns

On another Halloween in another country my old DG roommate Judy and I met in Copenhagen. Rather than the iconic harbor as the focal point for our photo, we chose jack-o'-lanterns and celebrated the time in our lives when we could seek fun rather than campus fame.

Old friends in old Santa Barbara:
Gretchen, Renée and Mary Jane

I had the chance to choose any guests and any venue for my seventy-fifth birthday celebration. My pick was Santa Barbara where I posed with Gretchen and Mary Jane at the same fountain where Mama posed with me three quarters of a century before.

Now all my travel experiences flash and float in my memory like looking through a teleidoscope. Have you ever looked through one? It's like a kaleidoscope, but instead of looking at tiny pieces of colored glass, you look out at the world around you through magic designs. That's what travel has been to me. It has allowed me to view today's passing parade through fabulous, everchanging designs composed of all my yesterdays—near and far from the Sign.

45
The Cast of Characters

If the movies of my first years had continued throughout my lifetime, the credits for the cast of characters streaming at the end would go on for hours. Since it would be a mighty long movie, I'd need to speed it up, and the major players would make rapid entrances and exits, often playing different roles depending on what was going on in my self-written script. I have chosen a handful of these leading players to take the spotlight before I reveal the final plot twists in the story of the Patins of Parish Place.

Spotlight on success

MARY JANE

In 1955, the John Burroughs *Akela* reflected nearby Hollywood with a movie theme throughout. The teachers were called "producers," class officers were "directors," and the big folks on campus were the "leads." Mary Jane was listed among the latter as one of the graduating seniors. I was a junior, but she deigned to sign my yearbook, the pages of which look as if they provided nourishment to all creatures great and small who inhabited the attic at my house next door to hers.

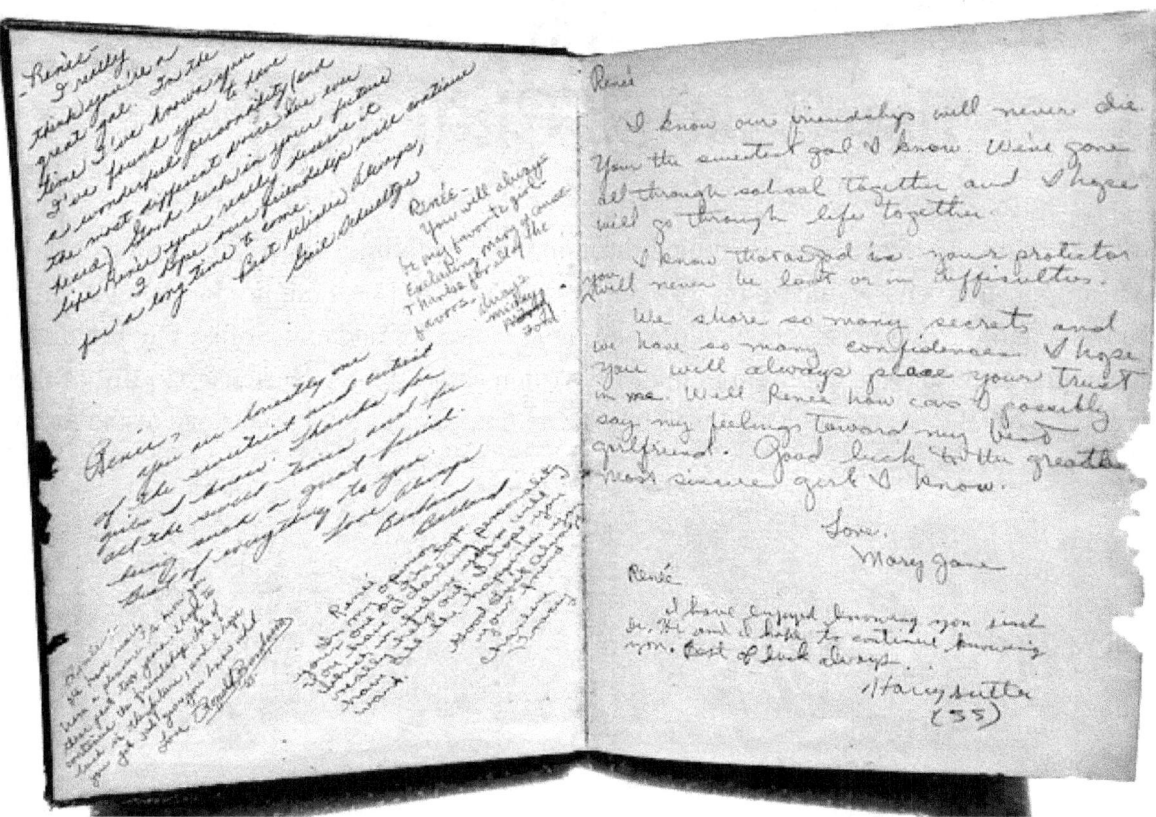

Burroughs BFFs

Here's what she said:

Renée

I know our friendship will never die. Your (sic) *the sweetest gal I know. We've gone all through school together and I hope we'll go through life together.*

I know that as God is your protector, you will never be lost or in difficulties.

We share so many secrets and we have so many confidences. I hope you will always place your trust in me. Well Renée how can I possibly say my feelings toward my best girlfriend. Good luck to the greatest most sincere girl I know.

Love,
Mary Jane

The bride-to-be

Mary Jane's words written so many years ago proved prophetic. At ten months my senior, Mary Jane always got to play the juicy roles before I had a chance. And I was as jealous as hell. Take, for example, this headline I've saved from where it blared out sixty years ago in the *Burbank Leader:* "Burbank Actor to Wed Miss Mary Jane Bennett."

The article announces her upcoming nuptials with John Wilder who had changed his name from Johnny McGovern, the stage name he'd used as a child actor. You may remember when he made his appearance in "Sex Lessons and How I Learned Them." His very presence in her life prompted the boyfriend envy I'd harbored toward Mary Jane since junior high. Once again, my best friend beat me in a race, this one to the grail of holy matrimony.

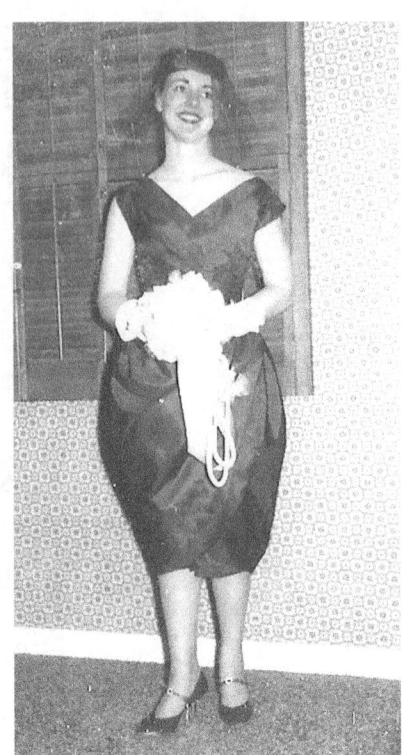

Bride and maid

As a twenty-year-old maid of honor to Mary Jane's twenty-one-year-old bride, I dutifully adorned myself in a red satin balloon-skirted dress and matching pointy satin shoes. Witch shoes, I called them. They carried me successfully down the aisle where I was conscious of the presence of Johnny's friend Chuck Connors, the 6'6" actor who was currently starring as *The Rifleman.* Behind my smiles and unseemly harlot-red veil, I harbored visions of eternal bridesmaid-hood; a modern Miss Havisham[1] stuck in the Burbank shadows.

Johnny and Mary Jane were better suited as sweethearts than as marriage partners. It only lasted four years (thus allowing her to join me in Paris after classes at the Louvre). In a role less prestigious than that of maid of honor, I was the designated server of Johnny's divorce papers. Mary Jane returned to Europe to teach in Rome when I taught in Switzerland. She put her entrepreneurial expertise from our Parish Place enterprises to good use. Her childhood work experience was supplemented by a UCLA Bachelor of Science degree and an MBA from USC. As if those initials were not enough, she carved out a career at IBM. She was one of the first systems representatives who helped end users to understand the tech-speak of instructions written by the inventors of the new business machines.

As an attractive businesswoman, Mary Jane actively played the field and was married twice before I went to the Las Vegas "altar" for the first and only time.

---

[1] For those not versed in Dickensian literature, she is the creepy crone in *Great Expectations* who was jilted at the altar. She spends the rest of her very long life in seclusion, her wedding dress rotting on her spurned, wasted body.

Mr. and Mrs. Ralph Williams

Her second husband was the colorful car dealer Ralph Williams. He was well-known around Southern California mostly for his ubiquitous TV commercials flogging his Fords. I remember how Johnny Carson would don a bald wig and imitate him and even had Ralph as a surprise guest on *The Tonight Show.* I was proud to know Ralph, though I must admit to feeling a little self-conscious when he would unexpectedly pop up on my TV when I passed by in my all-together. Of course, the green-eyed monster of jealousy attacked me when Mary Jane became once again romantically connected to a male of the celebrity persuasion.

Unfortunately, I did not improve my standing with MJ and her famous new husband when I visited, navigating the winding mansion-hiding Beverly Hills roads to their new enclave there. When I parked my poorly-maintained, old Renault in their porte cochere, I hailed my arrival in our old familiar way—I yodeled at the top of my lungs. Her Chinese butler greeted me inscrutably and announced that "Minnie Cotton" had arrived—his version of Renée Patin.

Postscript: Hi, Friends, Ralph Williams Here— and Still in Trouble for Sales Tactics

Godzilla would be zapping people with his breath, drop-kicking skyscrapers all over Tokyo and generally making a nuisance of himself on the late-night movie, when, all of a sudden, a line of shiny used cars would appear on the television screen.

And a nasal monotone voice would say, "Hi friends, Ralph Williams here, owner of Ralph Williams Ford."

And then a balding man with a perpetual smile would come into view and proceed to rattle off a series of bargains in a remarkable display of speed-talking. That was Ralph Williams' style during his heyday in the 1960s.

Some local TV car salesmen, like Chick Lambert with his dog Storm, had gimmicks. Some, like Frank ("No-Sunday-selling") Taylor and Les ("Get off your couch and come on down to Hermosa Beach") Bacon had slogans.

But Williams' route to renown was through his idea of saturation advertising on the late movie (drama and, especially, horror films; never musicals).

His fame also derived in part from the fact that Southern California and used-car dealers have been synonomous since the early 1940s when Earl (Madman) Muntz of Glendale started drawing attention with billboard messages like: I WANT TO GIVE 'EM AWAY BUT MY WIFE WON'T LET ME. SHE'S CRAZY.

In the mid-1960s, Johnny Carson and other comics took to mimicking the ubiquitous Williams; Carson even had him as a surprise guest on one skit. And by 1969, the Associated Press was calling Williams the best known auto-dealer in the United States.

But the 1970s brought trouble for Williams. The Federal Trade Commission charged him with violating the Truth in Lending Act in 1970 and, two years later, the state of California and Los Angeles County jointly sued him for false advertising.

Both matters were settled through consent decrees in which Williams admitted no guilt but promised not to violate advertising standards in the future. Williams also paid $10,000 to settle the state-county suit.

Williams' 1971 divorce and property settlement cost him more than $450,000. (he later sued his attorney for malpractice and lost).

And then, in 1976, the Washington state Supreme Court upheld contempt-of-court and consumer protection findings against Williams in connection with a dealership he owned in Seattle. The state put Williams' tab at more than $800,000 including court fines and costs.

But only about $20,000 was paid, officials say. Williams, meanwhile, shed his dealerships and moved to Dallas, Tex.

Recently, the Texas state Supreme Court ruled that Texas can collect the money Williams owes on behalf of Washington. Williams' attorneys have filed a motion for a new hearing, but they may have reached the end of the legal road.

In the meantime, Thomas Boeder, of the Washington state attorney general's office says: "He (Williams) is being fined $100 a day and there is a warrant out for his arrest here (Washington)."

Williams' attorneys refused comment on the case and Williams could not be reached.

Williams, who now works for a Dallas firm that extends auto warranties for a fee, no longer makes television commercials. And his reruns never play on the late-night movie.

—Steve Harvey

Trouble

Ralph was often in the news for better or worse. And as time went by, and he indulged in some shady trading practices, the articles recounted more of the worse. I saved an article about his career that is as tattered and torn as his career became. The piece in the *Los Angeles Times* by the writer (not the entertainer) Steve Harvey began:

Godzilla would be zapping people with his breath, drop-kicking skyscrapers all over Tokyo and generally making a nuisance of himself on the late-night movie, when all of a sudden a line of shiny new cars would appear on the television screen.

And a nasal monotone voice would say, "Hi friends. Ralph Williams here, owner of Ralph Williams Ford."

And then a balding man with a perpetual smile would come into view and proceed to rattle off a series of bargains in a remarkable display of speed-talking. That was Ralph Williams' style during the 1960s.

... by 1969 the Associated Press was calling Williams the best-known auto-dealer in the United States. But the 1970s brought trouble for Williams.

The article concludes with details of less than legal dealership dealings in two states. The Williams family, now including toddler Jennifer, who is my goddaughter, moved to Dallas.

Lifestyle of the rich and infamous

Gretchen and I visited the Williams family at their mansion on Turtle Creek while we were on business in Dallas. They sent their limo and chauffeur to pick us up at the airport. On the license plate holder was the message, "My other car is a Testarossa." It was true. Ralph did own said Ferrari sports car, and I rode with him after he awkwardly folded his very large self into its very small sleekness. He hunched over the wheel and drove around the neighborhood, acknowledging the gawkers who gave the car a thumbs-up.

The limo and the Ferrari and other vehicles were housed at their mansion nestled in a tony Dallas neighborhood. That is until Ralph's businesses again fizzled and so did the marriage. Ralph left MJ with some big money woes, but she pulled herself up by the ankle straps and started a second career as a successful realtor at age fifty-seven and took care of the debts, bought a house, dusted herself off and started all over again. She still lives there and enjoys her family, including Jennifer's boy and girl teen twins. Mary Jane prefers the tranquility of a far-from-headline-making life.

Jennifer's daughter Mary Kate, now a teenager, in front of the Burbank homestead

We are still best friends, and we still see the world through very differently-colored glasses, but our arguments are without the whiskey bottles or irons we used as weapons during our childhood play. We love each other very much. Gretchen and I joined her for a celebration of her 80th at the other Mansion on Turtle Creek in Dallas. Each time we celebrate she comments on how she misses the oilcloth bibs embellished with our names. But we manage to be silly without them.

Potsy and Janie celebrate

Playing with a tortilla and speaking at my retirement party

LORNA

Lorna and I are still friends too, still in California, but far from the Burbank block where we played so hard as kids. Though my junior by a year, I always found what Lorna had enviable. There were, for example, the golden-bronze tan she sported when she worked on Balboa Island and the office she held at Burroughs and the bay window apartment she rented when she was a teacher in San Francisco.

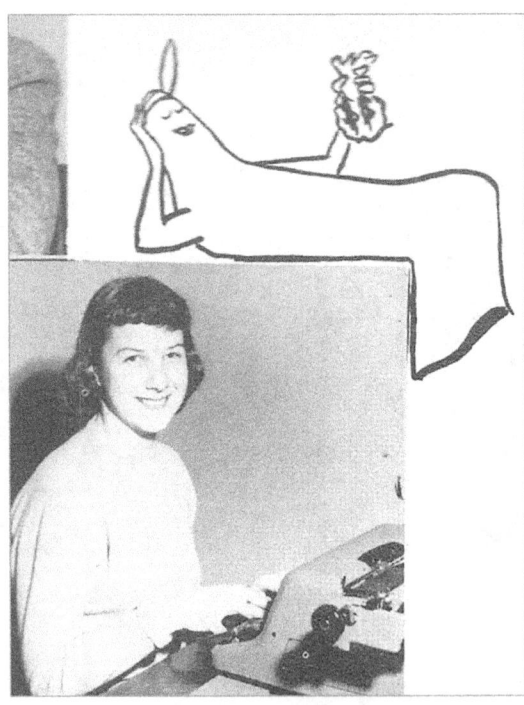

Lorna, Associated Student Body Secretary,
under a wampum-holding Indian

When we returned to Parish Place as grown-ups to visit my mother, we posed with Mae West who was removed for the occasion from her niche in the bathroom. Now Lorna visits me near Monterey with her husband Lyle who listens patiently as we reminisce about how hard we played at pretending. We talk of stories we created with our *Little Women* dolls and dressing up to become movie stars. Lyle tries to look as if understands as we describe our marble orphanage laid out on her rug. We get most animated describing our dual dollhouse sessions where we spent the whole time as interior decorators—never adding pretend people to enjoy our creations.

Grown-up Renée and Lorna and Mae

Welcome to the house of Snow White

Meet Dopey and the Evil Queen

I don't think Lorna was at all surprised the first time she visited my home and discovered an ornate Victorian dollhouse taking up most of my den that was lined with shelves of toys, art books and travel guides. The miniature mansion was my first gift to myself after I retired at sixty-five. It was electric—a feature I had always coveted in Lorna's house. It was furnished with the finest pieces. And it was inhabited. The residents of my fantasy folly were, like Lorna and me, all from Burbank. But unlike us, they were all characters from the imagination of Walt Disney and company.[2] The doyenne of the fancy spread was Snow White, and the Dwarfs could be found throughout the upstairs and downstairs rooms. Dopey, my favorite, occupied the boudoir with its four-poster bed. The Evil Queen had her mirror in the attic—near a Singer sewing machine just like Mama's. I know both Lorna and I would have liked to play in that house, but after all, there are times when grown-ups must be grown-ups. The next time she visited, the room was converted to a writer's nook, and the Disneyana was confined to the bookshelves.

Reunion

JOANIE

Joanie and I didn't play together after our Parish Place childhood. But I saw her and her husband on my 80th birthday in Seattle where she lives and works as a writer and travels the world. I was still wearing my "All the Best Things Were Made in 1938" button Gretchen gave me and the one from the zoo that allowed me a free birthday ride on the carousel. But it wasn't an elephant in the room with us at our reunion brunch discussion. It was the Black Widow Club initiation disaster that Joanie recounted in embarrassing detail. She showed me the long scar on her arm and said she always covered it with long sleeves throughout school. I felt the same prickles of shame that I had on entering her hospital room those many years ago. But she never mentioned the Indian burns for her grammatical trespasses. And there was far more laughter than remorse as we reminisced over those polliwog pond days with the old kids on the block.

---

[2] Along with the miniature residents of my dollhouse, the title of this chapter may also have been inspired by The Walt Disney Company whose theme park and store employees are called "cast members."

Judy and Finn at home   Welcome to Denmark!

JUDY

I was so in awe of Judy's accomplishments at Santa Barbara that I didn't really appreciate just how special she was. Now, after all these years, I know all she already had gone through when I met her at nineteen. Much of what I know I learned reading her book *Life Line*.

Her parents met while making movies in Hollywood. They moved to Hawaii where Judy was born. Right before WW II broke out, her father went to the Philippines to establish a newspaper, with plans for the family to follow. The family's flight to the Philippines was scheduled for December 10, and the attack on Pearl Harbor was December 7. If the attack had happened later, they would have been in the Philippines and ended up prisoners of the Japanese. Judy's mother fell ill while her father was presumed dead in the Philippines. She died on the plane carrying Judy and her brother home to the Mainland. Ironically, her father had survived the Bataan Death March and returned home only be killed in a car crash when Judy was a teen. So, Judy was an orphan when she and I became lifelong friends in Santa Barbara.

After graduation Judy chose not to climb either an academic or a career ladder of success. Instead she became a nanny for a French family and traveled to Africa. Back home in San Francisco she met a great Dane named Finn and moved to Denmark, the country that has often topped the World Happiness Report. Her book *To Denmark, With Love* describes how she learned the ways of the Danish philosophy of *hygge* (pucker your lips and pronounce it something between hoo-gah and hue-gah). I have often enjoyed the serenity of sharing her home and hearth-centered life so far from the turmoil of her upbringing.

Judy's husband Finn has now gone to Valhalla to join the pantheon of great Vikings. I miss my old drinking buddy. We shared a certain sensibility, becoming lifelong friends when I gave him a remote-controlled whoopee cushion. Judy and I have continued a close friendship, now unhindered by my jealousy[3] of her days as big woman on campus. She still has a great sense of fun and adventure mixed with a very keen sense of the humor in human foibles and frivolities.

---

[3] Perhaps by now you are detecting a bit of a "second best" syndrome. Let's blame it on the shadow.

Gerry performs and prepares for the Ugly Man contest he deservedly did not win

GERRY/MICHAEL

While on a very long layover in Munich during a flight from Istanbul to Dubrovnik, Gretchen and I went into the city to look at the art in Pinakothek der Moderne. On our way out, I spotted a fellow standing staring up at the museum. I decided it was either a lost homeless person or Gerry, my old boyfriend who was a history professor and went by the name Michael.

Gerry (with a name tag with an alternatively-spelled first name) at our 50th reunion

It was, in fact, said suitor from the past, who was deciding whether to go modern or look at the more classic pieces in the nearby Alte Pinakothek. I whispered this to Gretchen who, eager to encourage an end to my single status, pushed me toward the surprised wanderer. Always nervous in boy-girl situations even in my seventies, I chatted with Gerry briefly, all the while backing away, saying we had a taxi to catch. Gretchen reminded me we had plenty of time and weren't in a hurry. Her thinly-disguised matchmaking was to no avail though I still enjoy occasional encounters with the old beau who gave me a briefly-held fraternity pin, a belated serenade and memories of young romance.

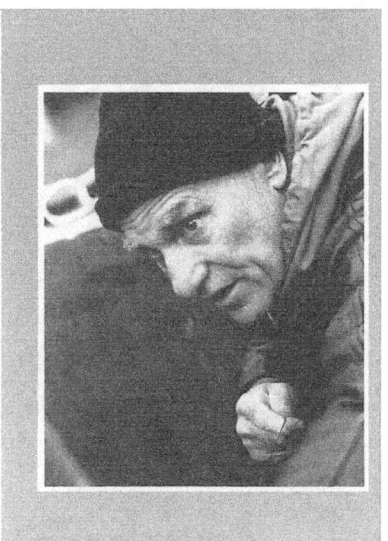

UCSB Distinguished Alumnus and I

RICH

In 1994, Richard Serra was honored with the UCSB Alumni Association Distinguished Alumni Award. I sat next to him at the head table and enjoyed catching up after thirty years. We'd both traveled long paths from that first meeting in the DG house kitchen. For a memento of times gone by, I traded programs with him after he sketched a rendering of an upcoming project on his.

I last saw Rich in 2011 when he had a one-man show of his drawings at the Museum of Modern Art in San Francisco. With echoes of our Distinguished Alumni meeting, I was so nervous about appearing at my most fetching best that I bought a new head-to-toe ensemble. This included my first and last pair of Spanx, the full armor kind that take forever to adjust at the most crucial of times.

Rich making it big in print and in his sculptures

Dashingly dressed, I entered the lobby of SFMOMA. This is before the installation of his massive walk-through torqued ellipse piece *Sequence*—shown on the cover of his book. I joined the line of patrons waiting to have Richard Serra sign the catalog for the show. When I finally got to the man himself (whom I had earlier spotted with his tall, elegant art historian wife), he was intent on eating cookies. Finally, when it was my turn, he nodded graciously and continued munching. Hardly a Spanx-worthy reunion. But I still follow his meteoric career. It has been as much fun as a whirlwind romp in a Hollywood rise-to-riches-and-fame movie.

46
Ray Redux

A kid with dreams

My father's message to me arrived, as if from on high, forty years after his death, when I was in the midst of writing this book. Like so many of his messages, this was a cartoon. But I doubt that it was intended to be seen, and it wasn't funny.

While I was writing his story, I found a tattered and torn sheet of 12" x 15" animation paper tucked away in one of the many boxes of papers and photos my father saved. It was a self-portrait à la *MAD* Magazine's Alfred E. Neuman. Remember him? He was the freckle-faced, jug-eared, red-headed cover boy and mascot for *MAD*. He was always spouting, "What...Me Worry?" This is the expression my father used to title a cartoon revealing the barrage of worries he was suffering. It hit me like a thunderbolt that the Patin patriarch I had so worshipped and feared was threatened by all the slings and arrows we are all heir to.[1]

---

[1] With apologies to Shakespeare. And to those of you who thought you'd never need to remember Hamlet's soliloquy "To be or not to be," perhaps now you see the wisdom of your high school English teacher who made you memorize it. However, she may have an objection to the sentence-ending preposition.

The dream becomes a nightmare

The artist, who thirty years before drew a cartoon of an exuberant kid with a dream of working for Disney, now caricatured himself as a frazzled, crazy-eyed old man sprouting only a few tufts of his signature red hair. Labels point to his deteriorating appearance: "no hair," "bum eyesight," "shave rash," "shaky hand," "potbelly," "worn pants" and "moth holes" (this on his tie using the hole in the animation paper). A frenzy of demons attacks him like wasps. He knows he drinks too much and fears the consequences: "skid row," "Camarillo" (mental hospital) or "Alcoholics Anonymous." His animators threaten to strike, deadlines loom, agencies make too many demands. Financial and familial woes buzz and swarm frenetically around him.

I was completely oblivious to what was going on in my father's head as his fifties came to an end. I was busy finding my own way to as yet undefined great heights and fighting any obstacles that stood in my way. In my intensity to climb as high as possible on the ladder of success, I was completely unaware that the man I had put on a pedestal was toppling.

But rather than plummeting downward, my father took arms against his sea of troubles.[2] The transformation began when he disbanded Ray Patin Productions in 1967. He moved his favorite possessions and pieces of fading green furniture to the overflowing room that we called "the goody room." This was a storage room built in the area where we had raised chickens and tended our Victory Garden during the war. It was intended as Mama's art studio, but she preferred the light-

---

[2] Yup. More from Hamlet.

Dry dock

filled lanai. He set about enjoying himself. Weekends on the *Trinket* helped restore serenity, but she became too demanding as boats tend to do and was sold to someone better able to meet her constant upkeep.

I was teaching in Gstaad when he gave up the studio. He also quit smoking and drinking at the same time—cold turkey, no rehab. He was sixty. In the den at 540 South Parish the *Trinket's* cocktail flag now hung upside down. Many years later, at the same age, I followed his example. I didn't have a happy hour flag to turn upside down as we had no need of such announcements of our heavy drinking on board the *Renata.* But I did have help that brought me the serenity I don't think Daddy found from the disease he and I both inherited from our fathers.

He became a new man, a renaissance man. With the luxury to stop and think and act, he got involved in the world around him. In 1970, he wrote to Jack Smith, the much-loved columnist of the *Los Angeles Times.* My father's cause was the deplorable condition of the merry-go-round in Griffith Park, the one he and Mama had often watched Potsy ride with a rapture I've continued to this day, especially on my birthdays. It was fenced in, and the gallant wooden steeds had lost their tails and were splattered with paint. All due to kids, my father was told. Jack not only put the plight in print, but he quoted from my father's dramatic letter:

When you have the time, Jack, drop over there and see those little horses, if you are as sensitive as I am, you'll shed a tear. These charming little chargers are suffering the indignities of working day after day in a dismal cage, leading a splotchy, humiliating, tailless existence.

Writing that he would not want to be considered less sensitive than anyone from Burbank, Mr. Smith went to Griffith Park to check out the degradation. His conclusion was that the cause was not trivial, that people who foul their merry-go-round will foul their world.

New beginnings with Brother Buzz

Buzzy business

He was able to put his talents to work for real animals, too. He created films for the Latham Foundation that promotes humane issues, especially between humans and animals. The artist Ray returned. The animation station was active again as he sought and found satisfying freelance work.

He animated Brother Buzz cartoons. I even got to do some voice-overs for him. I remember my line as Brother Buzz's girlfriend when I used my back-of the-throat silly screech to shout, "Did you get his license plate, Brother Buzz?" Then there was my role as the mother of a deer family when I exaggerated my contralto tones with, "Come into the forest, my dears/deers."

He continued his work with the Academy of Motion Picture Arts and Sciences helping to judge the Short Subjects that were potentially Oscar-worthy. Sometimes Mama and I went with him to watch a round of potential nominees. Once we went to a screening after Daddy died and were taken aback to see his picture fill the screen during a memorial tribute.

He talked to me about a script he was writing. It's a story about how man brags about his inventions when it is nature who should get the credit. He used Peter Pan as an example, saying man bragging about what he did not create is like Peter Pan bragging about finding his shadow, when it was really Wendy's doing. Peter Pan? Shadow? Now as I look at that script from long ago, I wonder whether my father ever noticed that his daughter was becoming a mirror of himself.

I remember at Creative Playthings the time I was promoted to National Educational Consultant and would receive $13,000 a year. My father pasted up a fake telegram to my boss, "Mr. Farrington," with a picture of a little girl reaching on tippy toes to open a door. It said to raise all the doorknobs, so I wouldn't get too big for my britches in my new position.

A creative dream

Then Jack and I had a vision of how the educational companies of CBS could be combined into one great learning center. We asked my father to design it. His rendering for our dream that never became reality showed a magnificent galaxy with displays for the different subsidiaries like Creative Playthings and Holt, Rinehart and Winston publishing.

Tales of times shared by two aging animators

Daddy filled folders with all the research he did for various projects and with letters that showed he finally had time to give free reign to his galloping intellect. He wrote me in South Carolina about one of my first articles on boating. He said it was great but wondered if it was commercial enough for a boating magazine. (It wasn't.) He signed the letter of literary advice, "Love and smooches." He wrote to family in Louisiana and animators, like Chuck Jones, the Oscar-winning creator of many Warner Bros. characters. He spent time with another Jones, his best friend Volus, who was the star of so many early Patin features like *Flying Feathers,* a documentary on archery.

Loewy poses with his design

He transferred his love of the *Trinket* to another beloved form of transportation, his 1953 Studebaker Starliner that had become a classic. He coddled his sleek treasure because it was the creation of Raymond Loewy, the "father of industrial design," who was on the cover of *Time* in 1949. It added to Mr. Loewy's caché that he is also the fellow who modernized Daddy's beloved Lucky Strike package from green to white.

Renata's trail boards by Ray Patin

My father loved sharing his nautical knowledge with Jack as we built the boat. Daddy carved and painted beautiful teak trail boards with her name and home port (Princeton because we had our mail sent to Jack's sister there). To thank him, we had a friend take a picture of us with the boards while the boat was being finished in the backyard. Since the stern (the rear end) was 15 feet off the ground, we propped the boards behind us on deck before we attached them. You may have noticed them on *Renata's* lovely stern as she traveled under the bridge for her launch. Sadly, my father was too sick with pancreatic cancer to ever see his creations on the finished boat.

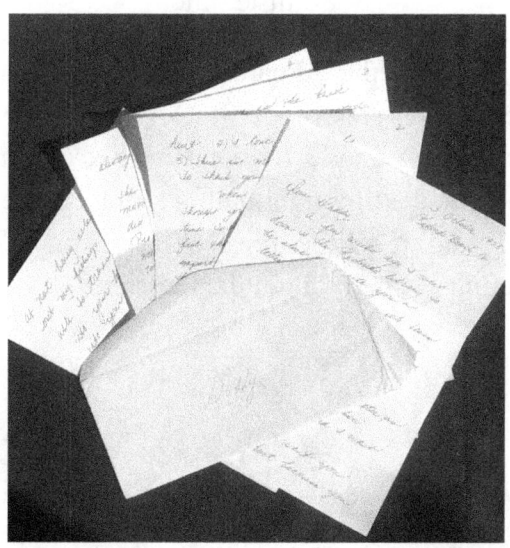

Dear Daddy

Another discovery I found among the treasures my father held dear was the letter I wrote to him when we knew he didn't have long to live. Along with thanks for the way he raised me and the many gifts he gave me, I wrote:

Thank you for being a great man. Great is vague and kinda corny, but so are words like moral, vibrantly curious, strong and so many you'd just shrug off. It's true though that I'm proud of you and in awe of what you've accomplished as a body of work as well as the kind of Ray Patin you've created.

I wrote the letter at the big salon table aboard *Renata* in King Harbor in Redondo Beach where we were mooring while we rigged her. I had a long-term substitute teaching assignment, and Jack would dinghy me in each day and drive me to work.

One day I was teaching Creative Writing when the principal entered the room and said, "It's your father." I got a ride to the harbor, and from the water's edge yelled out to Jack. "It's my father." I drove to Burbank and was able to say goodbye before he died in St. Joseph's Hospital where his mother died, across the street from The Walt Disney Studios.

So little time

My father's final message was also something I came upon by accident after he died. It was in my childhood bedroom that had become his sick room. Stuck back in a corner of the bookshelf that had held my toys and books, I found a lovely geode. In its cavern-like center, Daddy had placed a miniature clock left over from my dollhouse and a tiny light bulb. I still have the display but gone is the label he had attached to the tableau. It said, "So little time." When he knew his light would soon go dark, he once again expressed his feelings visually. I got the message.

At rest in the middle of La La Land's hustle-bustle

Celebrating a legacy of love, art and marvelous memories

My father's ashes were scattered in a rose garden in what was then called Westwood Memorial Park, a little cemetery near UCLA. It is now called Pierce Brothers Westwood Village Memorial Park and Mortuary and is a lovely oasis of tranquility hidden among the high rises of Wilshire Boulevard. His earthly remains lie near those of A-listers who starred in his Hollywood story: Marilyn Monroe, the model for his treasured playing cards, Natalie Wood, my school days' idol who drowned off his beloved Catalina, and many more. I got the feeling that's why he chose this little pantheon of glitterati from the right side of the Sign.

Although he felt there was so little time, he had fulfilled the dreams of that redhead from the bayou. I'm so grateful to have that kid as part of me.

Ray Maurice Patin 1906–1976

47
I Remember Mama

The movie *I Remember Mama* and Mama's painting of Daddy's family in the same era

In the fifties, my mother and I were big fans of the television show called *Mama*. We had watched the 1948 movie *I Remember Mama* it was based on, all about a family of immigrants from Norway. I think my mother loved the stories about the early years of the twentieth century when she was a child because the Hansen household was so loving and stable and so different from the Rileys of Culver City or from the Patins of Parish Place. Once she painted a picture from a photograph of Daddy, his mother and sister that was taken in an era that continued to fascinate her and appear in her art.

Just like ours

We would cuddle together on the couch pushed up close to the tiny 10" screen of our RCA TV that didn't look a lot different from the radio it replaced. The weekly black and white show always began with a Maxwell House Commercial about how the luscious-looking liquid was "Good to the last drop." We could almost smell the coffee brewing as we settled in to see the close-up of the percolating pot followed by a shot of an old-fashioned photo album like the one Daddy put together. Then came the daughter Katrin's opening words:

This old album makes me remember so many things in the past... I remember my family as we were then. My big brother Nels, my little sister Dagmar, and of course, Papa. But most of all when I look back to those days so long ago, most of all, I remember Mama.

Victorians à la Maxine

Mama loved the Victorians like the Hansen house that still line Steiner Street in San Francisco where the show took place. I think it was because they have a storybook quality, as if all those gingerbready turrets and towers and nooks and crannies hid wondrous secrets and surprises. She made meticulous line drawings of these "painted ladies," as the houses are called in San Francisco. She embellished them with her own architectural flourishes. And, like much of the art she would later paint, she placed a flying angel above them. She made our Christmas card with an angel-winged Santa Claus flying over curlicue mansions. She printed them on oatmeal paper with names like "Grandma's House" and "Old Timer."

Victoriana in Sacramento and Los Angeles (Mama in the middle)

She made a serigraph drawing of the Governor's Mansion in Sacramento that Governor Reagan had left empty. In Los Angeles, she joined a troupe of painting ladies who immortalized the fast disappearing Victorians on Bunker Hill and on Carroll Avenue in Angelino Heights.

Maxine paints a barn

One of Maxine's barns

Maxine's mindscape

Mama's first paintings were acrylics in what could be called a folk art, or Grandma Moses style, like the picture she painted of her family. She signed them at first "Max," then "Maxine." She took snapshots that she would paint later, never passing a barn or weathered building that might be the subject for her art. She painted everything she saw from objects in the house to what she saw in books and magazines. And she created mindscapes from her very active imagination.

Maxine shows Maxines a few years apart

She began to sign her paintings "Maxine Patin." She showed her work and won prizes for it. She had the thrill of seeing her work appreciated and even purchased. I watched my mother communicate through color what she found difficult in words. I saw her love of paint and shared her passion.

Wheels for Maxine

When I went to college, she did too, taking as many adult-education painting classes as she could find. She became more independent when she finally learned to drive. Daddy bought her a 1953 Chevrolet Bel Air. The man on the used car lot said the hard top was previously owned by the actress Angela Lansbury.[1] If, in fact this was true, the esteemed actress must have had very exclusive taste to match her supreme status as a movie star, because the vehicle came equipped with detachable chrome Cadillac-ish tailfins. I found a picture of the now classic car at an exhibit in a golden oldies car show, but sadly, sans fins. I'm happy that we believed and perpetuated the myth provided by the salesman. For our starstruck family it was far more fun than the truth that I received from Dame Lansbury's representatives. She never owned said Bel Air and certainly never one with chrome fins!

---

[1] British born, perpetually performing, stage, movie and TV actress famous as *Auntie Mame* and Jessica Fletcher in TV's *Murder, She Wrote*.

Mama drove all around the county in search of paintable settings; the older and more ramshackle the better. Her repertoire of the last of LA's barns and tumbledown buildings and Victorian mansions grew. And she grew in confidence and competence, not only as a painter, but also as a woman.

In the goody room, Daddy built shelves that rapidly filled with her work side by side with all that he stored there for posterity. My father may have been proud of my mother, but there was a little envy there too. Perhaps the envy was that she got so much joy out of something he did for a living, never for fun.

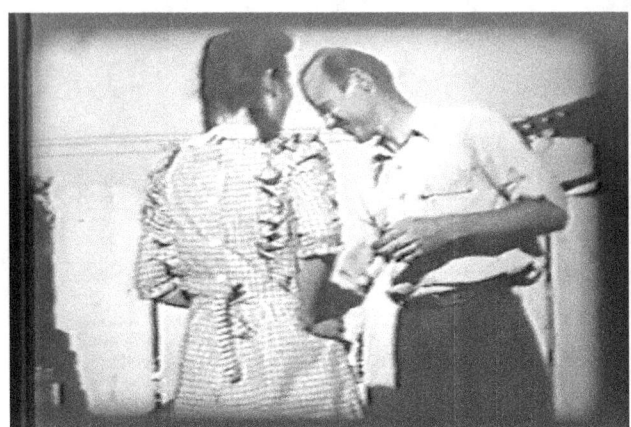 

Romcom movie forties style: *A Little Backyard Romance*

Throughout their 43-year marriage my father continued to express his semi-romantic feelings with humor. One outlet for his expressions was to create humorous scenarios staged for his movies. In a film taken at a party in our Parish Place backyard, we see the Riley kids all grown up. Gerry has brought home her Air Force fiancé who plays ping-pong with Jack. Nonnie chatters and laughs for the camera followed by some odd mouth motions that are perhaps suggested by my "director" father to indicate that my mother's food was delicious. In the movie, my mother and I are in matching braids and mother/daughter ruffled pinafores.[2] She is shown cooking then serving at the barbeque my father built from plans in *Sunset* magazine. The grown-ups and I parade by the brick masterwork to fill our plates, hamming our delight at Mama's offerings. Daddy, however, comes out from behind the camera in the final scene and refuses the food with a wrinkled nose. In the end, he takes a kiss from his wife instead.

His cartoons demonstrate how he viewed Maxine, and how he imagined she saw him. Gradually the scenes change from his gaga adoration of the docile young teenager who needed training in wifely duties to an appreciation that she was a talented woman with her own mind. And at times her mind found his mind a bit annoying.

---

[2] Potsy makes a pouty appearance at the party in her matching braids and pinafore in Chapter 7.

Artistic envy?

In one he showed himself holding up a *Peanuts*[3] cartoon where Charlie Brown is trying unsuccessfully to explain to his little sister Sally how to make Valentines.

Daddy, whose image is surrounded by laughter, announces, "Hey look Honey, this is me trying to teach you to draw!!!"—which, in fact, he did not do. Her reaction is, "You are the ink blob in the beautiful portrait of my life!!!"

Santa Maxie does a yuletide jig

---

[3] Unfortunately, due to legal restrictions, we are unable to show the contents of the cartoon.

Ikkus in her birthday suit

Mama was cursed by having a December 29 birthday, so it was often melded into Christmas. When she was about to turn fifty-five, her devoted-though-less-than-sentimental husband combined the two holidays showing his forever young wife performing a burlesque in two acts, casting off her Santa costume, and posing semi-demurely in her birthday suit.

With a love that's true

In another slightly suggestive cartoon my grizzly-bearded father, in his last year of life, drew his "Ikkus" looking angrily confused when he offered her a double entendre Valentine gift of nuts.

This Valentine's Day
with a love that's true,
I'm giving my heart
and nuts* to you.
*$1.25 LB, shelled

But I know they loved each other and found each other amusing. Usually.

When Daddy died, my mother, sixty-two, showed her great strength just as she had after breast cancer surgery fifteen years before. Little Maxie was no longer the easily teasable child bride, living in her successful husband's shadow. She threw herself into her art and traveled in search of new sites to translate into paint. She took courses at home and at Cambridge in England. She grew more independent, partly since she had to. Jack and I sailed off soon after she became a widow. She visited us at various ports in Mexico and on the East Coast.

San Blas in Mexico and the white villages in Spain

Her watercolors from the village of San Blas, Mexico illustrated my article on cruising there. A reader who admired them in *Sea* magazine contacted her and bought the originals. I took photographs to send her when I traveled, and she turned them into paintings like the *White Villages in Spain*.

Sea Island sanctuary

After we stopped in Beaufort, she visited us and painted there too. Once while she was painting a church nestled in the moss-dripping trees, a school bus disgorged a clutch of kids who clustered around her to see what she found so interesting in their neighborhood. Their faces lit up with pride and joy when they learned she chose their house of worship as worthy of art.

Art in Beaufort

She painted new meaning into common sites around Beaufort in the same way she had illuminated her Culver City home. She found it fascinating. So did the film companies who shot *The Big Chill, Forces of Nature, G.I. Jane, The Prince of Tides* and *Midnight in the Garden of Good and Evil* on location in the picturesque area. She had her own show at a Beaufort waterfront art festival. I'm not sure whether she or I was most proud of the reaction of the folks who admired her work.

As we grew older together, Mama and I grew closer. We became best friends and shared our observations and feelings. Now that she was not restricted by our mother and daughter roles, she taught me life lessons that she learned through experience. I began to know us both in a deeper way.

This world is but a canvas to our imagination.
Henry David Thoreau

Mama kept painting through her eighties. Her last series featured a panoply of medieval settings with queens and kings in all their finery. She was giving free rein to the fairy tales that had paraded through her imagination since childhood.

Then, the painting stopped. When Mama was ninety, she grew tired. The house became too much, and she left the shadow of the Sign to come to live near me in Monterey County. Our roles changed again. I took on the mothering role she had performed so well for me.

She moved into assisted living across from the fields that form Salinas' "salad bowl for the world." The painting materials didn't come with her. Instead she returned to fantasy and began to create an episodic fairy tale in her head. It was her girlhood way of coping with difficult situations, in this case her dislocation from her house of sixty years. Mama's fantasy saga was an elaborate one. Each day I returned to visit her in her new home, she had added a bit more to her story. I wrote down what she recounted to me. Here are just a few excerpts from what I call her *Bunny Tales:*

I first saw them from my window out in the lettuce fields under the fluffy clouds. In the lead was an Easter Rabbit, hopping proudly, clutching her umbrella over her head. Behind her followed a line of little ducks and yellow chicks. Pulling up the rear, as you might expect, was a determined snail with a multi-colored raincoat.

The next day all the Easter animals climbed onto the back of a huge turkey. They worried about the dark when the gobbler flew them into the thick fog. "No problem," said the turkey, "Just switch on the lights behind my ears."

(Which answers the question of whether turkeys, like Mrs. Wurtle, have ears.)

She even brought Mary Jane and me into her imaginative story:

Renée wanted to voyage to the bottom of the sea, but Mary Jane was afraid to. However, a turtle took them both and they traveled through magnificent jewel studded coral and seaweed to the bottom. Here they met the beautiful mermaid with long golden hair and iridescent tail. (From the Submarine Ride?)

Here it was that Renée was crowned Queen of the Fairies. The gnomes made Renée a jewel-encrusted wand. She was promised that if she waved it, she could have whatever she wished for.

What wonderful fantasies, worthy of a Disney movie!

Front page feature

My mother, the queen

On November 2, 2009, there was a front-page article in the *Monterey County Herald* called "Painting Opens Way to Fantasy." It shows Mama dressed in a shimmery blue queen's gown. This surprise sartorial selection came about because on the day she was interviewed it was Halloween, and she had asked her caretaker if she could borrow her costume. In the article she is shown wearing it next to the painting she did of the Riley family. She described the setting and the family and Mrs. Wurtle for the interviewer. Prompted by his questions, she talked of her father's violence and her husband's kindness. She talked of her life as the wife of a Disney animator, and how important art had been in her life. She told about the upcoming one-woman show at her Assisted Living home: "It's wonderful that people like my art so much that they would display it in their home. It's very flattering."

The article then quotes me: That humility, Renée Farrington says, is typical of her mom. "She doesn't know how to put on airs." And Farrington says the show has injected new life into her mother. "She has rallied for this show. She's like a new person. I haven't seen my mother sparkle like this in 20 years."

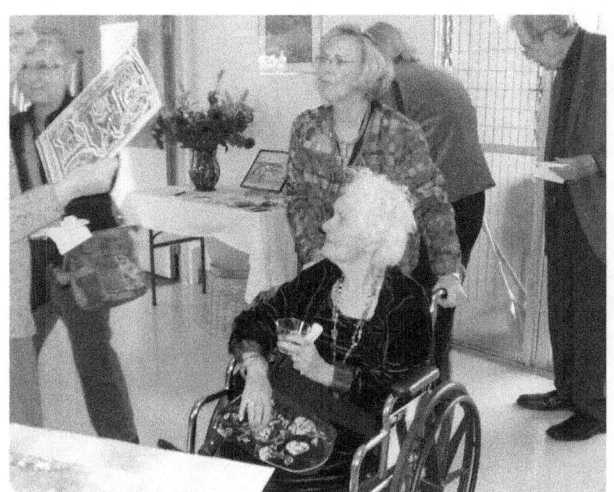 

Renée brings in the artist who signs her paintings

My mother's final show was a triumph. Mary Jane came from Dallas, and people Mama knew and didn't know came from all over. When I wheeled her into the hall filled with all her work that my friends and I had hung on the walls and displayed on easels, she was overwhelmed to see that she had done so much over the years. There was a lot despite all that she had sold and given away, so I priced it to sell. When I returned her to her room, she was tired, but exhilarated. I congratulated her on the success of selling so many paintings. "Oh, you know," she said, "I priced them very low."

It was at the show when I realized the importance of my mother's art in her life. My mother was her art. Since she was a little girl it was her way of understanding an often-confusing world and her way of expressing what she saw and felt.

Maxine Riley Patin
December 29, 1914 ~ January 18, 2010

SALINAS, CA – Maxine, 95, died peacefully at Skyline Care Center where she had great, joyful care.

She was born in Los Angeles, a tiny preemie, and placed in a shoebox that substituted for a not-yet invented incubator. She was the eldest of six children living through the Depression in Culver City.

Maxine graduated from Venice High in 1931 and married Ray Patin the following year at 17. For over 60 years she created a beautiful home in Burbank where they moved for Ray's job as a Disney animator. Ray, who later pioneered animated television commercials through Ray Patin Productions, died in 1976. In 2001 Maxine moved to Salinas to be near her daughter.

Maxine's creative imagination and art brought her joy throughout her life. She traveled throughout America and Europe and shared her observations in drawings and paintings that today hang in private collections throughout the world. Two months before her death, Maxine enjoyed a triumphant art show in her honor at Skyline.

Maxine had a beauty, intelligence, talent and nobility she was completely unaware of – and that was part of her greatness.

She is survived by her daughter, Renée Farrington of Salinas, who feels privileged to have had such a great mother/friend for as long as she did; as well as by her sister, Geraldine Linn of Santa Rosa; brother, Jack Riley (Barbara) of Lompoc; her brother Dick Riley's widow, Therese, of Oceanside; plus many nieces and nephews. She knew that her family and friends from Dallas to Denmark and throughout California loved and admired her.

Maxine was a 50-year breast cancer survivor. Contributions may be sent to Susan G. Komen for the Cure 1-877-465-6636 or ww5.komen.org. A private celebration of her life is pending.

Remembering Mama

Two months later, Mama died. She had been telling me she wanted to. She was tired. Being 95 was too difficult. She refused treatment for a bad cold and went peacefully. Now it was time to rest.

Celebrating Mama with Mary Jane and Gretchen

Family and friends gathered on Fisherman's Wharf in Monterey where I had chartered a sport fishing boat. Some stayed on shore and others, including Aunt Gerry at eighty, climbed aboard for my mother's final boat trip. Mary Jane and Gretchen passed out roses to drop in the sea to celebrate her long, full life. Mary Jane and I hugged the same way we did when we scattered her mother's ashes.

The land celebration was in a restaurant owned by a friend, the son of one of the early Sicilian fishermen on the wharf. When it was time for me to say a few words, for once they did not come easily. Art helped. I held up the little painting of her family and tried hard to describe the Maxine we all knew. I pointed out the angels she painted over her chldhood home. Her no-longer baby brother Jack shouted, "Now she is one!"

I don't need to remember Mama because she is always with me, like an angel on my shoulder.

As a matter of fact, my mother visited just the other day. It was her connection to my father that brought her to me. I was in one of my OLLI[4] classes for people of, as the French say, a certain age. The course was on the "Screwball Comedies of the Thirties" that Mama loved, and—as if seated in one of her beloved, Hollywood movie palaces—we were treated to a cartoon. It was *The Autograph Hound*, the 1939 production starring Donald Duck and a cast of caricatured movie stars. Mama would have seen it, maybe at the Hyperion studio where Daddy was one of the animators who created it. Our teacher introduced me as our resident Disney expert.

After class, a fellow student approached me to say—as is often the case when my Disney connection is brought up—that she had something to show me that was connected to a studio animator. It was a very long shot as there have quite a few Disney employees since 1937. But I told her to bring it in. The next week she approached me with a large tote bag and began to take out an object. I could see it was a small painting.

---

[4] Osher Lifelong Learning Institute, "An adventure in intellectual, cultural and social exploration for adults age 50 and better" where I learn and teach.

The visit

Then I saw a photo of my mother on the back. It was from the announcement of her last show. Then I saw the lovely watercolor of Mexico my mother painted. Tears tugged. My comment was, "She's here. That's immortality."

Mama not only made beauty, but she had a beauty, intelligence and nobility of which she was completely unaware—and that was part of her greatness. There was a touch of innocent, make-believe magic about her. If I could wish upon her star, it would be to have more of her in me. But I'm working on it, and maybe with more of these visits I'll get there.

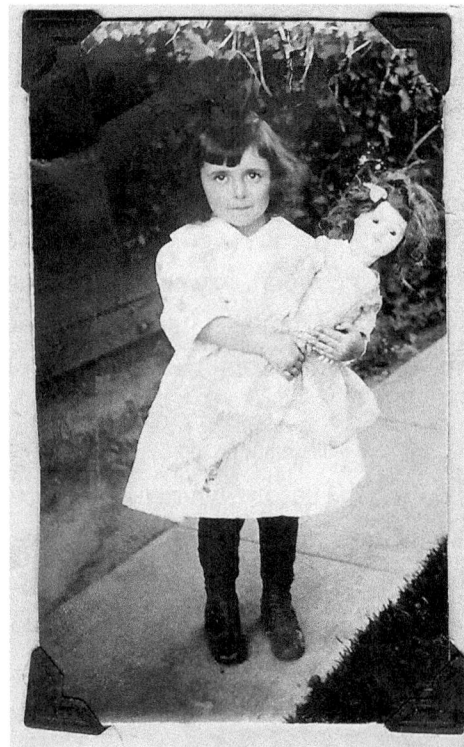

Maxine Jane Riley Patin 1914–2010

48
Lessons from Beyond the Shadow

We shall not cease from exploration, and the end of all our exploring will be to arrive where we started and know the place for the first time.

T. S. Eliot

Eliot was right. I learned this lesson in Burbank. That's right, back in the shadow of the Sign. The occasion was the 2017 meeting of the Hyperion Historical Alliance, a professional organization that seeks to advance member-initiated projects related to Disney history. I was joined by Gretchen who came in from Sedona, Arizona.

I learned about the organization when I was researching my father's work on the Disney Gallery of Old Masters and found the story of its inception on a site run by Didier Ghez, the founder of the Alliance. He invited me to their annual meeting to share the movies my father made at Disney's Hyperion studio and of the strike at the "new" Burbank studio.

Restaurant to the stars

The first night of the annual get-together was at the Smoke House Restaurant where I had celebrated my high school graduation. Since then, George Clooney in his *ER* television days, named his production company Smoke House Pictures after the landmark eatery where we were meeting. Across the street from the restaurant is Warner Bros.

We were meeting at the watering hole for stars who acted on that lot and for Toluca Lake residents like Bing Crosby and Bob Hope. We were not far from what I grew up perceiving as the "wrong" side of the Hollywood Sign. In reality, the Sign looks out on Hollywood, but it is a reminder that the action in this film/TV capital of the world takes place all over Los Angeles County, including Burbank. The Sign is a symbol of that action, kind of like Broadway is to New York.

Gretchen and I found the private room where some members were excitedly chatting in small groups. We found seats at a long table near a rustic stone fireplace. My seat partner, Vanessa, was an art historian of visual culture. Like Didier and many of the Hyperion members she has published and lectured about the world of Disney. The longer we chatted, the more I learned we had a lot in common: a love of art and a delight in all that's whimsical and child-pleasing like circuses. We discovered we were both Francophiles who love Paris, and when I mentioned Creative Playthings, she lit up saying with tongue in cheek that those toys she played with are the reason she's so smart.

Where animation magic happens

It was a rare and wonderful exchange with someone who looked at the world with the clear wonder of a child. She's helped me understand that the way I look at the world is a legacy from a father who was an animator. "They can make the impossible happen—like people walking through walls or surviving a piano falling on their heads." And as I listened to her, I thought it's the way a child thinks—the way Walt thought. I felt as if my father was not on high looking down on us, but inside me looking out and feeling honored. So much I had taken for granted seemed extraordinary for the first time.

When it was my turn to address the gathering, I described Daddy's 1931 cartoon dream of working for Walt Disney. I told of his perpetual picture-making with an 8 mm camera. Then I introduced the movies he made at the Hyperion studio. I was thrilled and proud as the group hung on every frame, laughing at the drawing contests between the animators, pointing out folks they recognized as they gamboled at Walt's Field Day celebration when *Snow White and the Seven Dwarfs* was finished.

On the second night, I was excited to finally enter the "new" Roy E. Disney Animation Building on Riverside Drive that I had driven by so many times. We drove through a gate topped with Mickey ears. The complex is set in the "wilds" where we kids menaced polliwogs and let our imaginations loose in the pond. As the sun was just going down, we could see the Don Lee tower sharing the mountaintop with the Hollywood Sign hidden on the other side. The entrance to the building was under the iconic, stars-and-moon-adorned magical hat Mickey wore as the Sorcerer's Apprentice in *Fantasia*.

Me at the Mouse factory

The auditorium was filled when I was introduced and given a mic to narrate my father's film. I explained that we Patins lived close by in the neighborhood, and that my father worked across the street from where we were gathered. It was where the animators went on strike over seventy-five years ago. As the film rolled, I pointed out Mama and her best friend Susan Jones as they filled the screen marching, chatting, holding pickets and pretending they were Ink & Paint girls, not wives of animators. I got a laugh when I showed Potsy topless in the rocking boat at the nursery. As the camera panned along a row of whimsical protest posters, I remarked that this is what happens when creative people go on strike. I said I had spoken with Walt's granddaughter at the meeting and hoped she wouldn't be offended by the images of "Grandpa."

As Gretchen and I left the studio sharing our impressions of the wonderful two-day whirlwind, I was struck with much more than nostalgia for the olden times. I was filled with new understandings. One thing I learned was that Thomas Wolfe was wrong. You *can* go home again, and on this return trip to the shadow, what I learned was that nothing in my now long life has been by chance. My love of art, success in the toy business, love of the sea and adventure, and especially my childlike wonder. Everything is connected.

I look back on those old movies of my wonder years and see Potsy plunging into each new experience with great gusto, eyes darting in anticipation for what's next. And I see my mother and father playing alongside me, enjoying the ride as much as I was.

As I traveled far away from the Potsy days, I began to tell myself stories like the ones recounted by the absurd adults the little prince met: we are second best because we live on the wrong side of the Sign; Daddy may work for a film studio, but the films are only animated, not the real thing like Hollywood movies; sure my father is an artist, but not a real one—he just draws cartoons; Mama's a painter, but not famous; maybe I'm successful, but not as successful as…you name him or her. My self-image of second best was my own self-created shadow. The quest to be best prevented me from seeing life through the rose-colored glasses I sang about in "La Vie en Rose." I needed to clean my lenses so that I could look through the glass brightly.

It took digging through years of stored memories to teach me how wrong I had been. My father was one of a rarified group of artists who can make magic with the stroke of a pencil. Walt Disney wasn't just Daddy's boss and the man he went on strike against. He was a visionary with the spirit of a wide-eyed boy. He was a sorcerer whose animators were his apprentices. He went out on a limb to make *Snow White and the Seven Dwarfs* and *Fantasia* and in so doing, legitimized animation as an art form. He brought to life the fairy tales that my mother so loved. I learned from Mama's fairy tales and from Disney's movies that there would be dark times in the frightening forest. But there will be light on the other side of the shadow.

It took many years for me to regain all I lost when I thought I had to put away childish things. But now the sense of wonder and whimsy and even an occasional fairy and cricket have returned. Potsy as well as Daddy and Mama are alive and kicking inside this kid.

Ice cream at one and seventy-one in Burbank and Dubrovnik

I was a very lucky to have been chosen as the daughter of Maxine and Ray who prophetically named me Renée, "reborn." In the winding plot of life's play, I have been reborn into several different roles. Today I live with a great hunger and enthusiasm for whatever I can experience wherever I can find it. It's the same zeal that led me to my overly enthusiastic first feeding. I have been hungry ever since to gobble up all I can from little treats like ice cream as well as grown-up enterprises like jobs and my next adventure.

Merrily going around at four and four score, a birthday tradition

On the morning of my eightieth birthday, Gretchen and I went to the Seattle Zoo so I could carry out a birthday tradition, a ride on the merry-go-round. I felt the same exhilaration on my speeding white steed as Potsy felt in Griffith Park at four. And I didn't even need to be strapped in!

Celebrating at five and eighty

The ride was the culmination of a four-day celebration hosted in Seattle by Gretchen and her fiancé Mike. They arranged an extravaganza filled with all my favorite things: boating, seaplaning, exploring, playing, fine dining and companionship.

For my birthday party Gretchen decorated me with a sparkly tiara, button and banner announcing my standing as an octogenarian, followed by a shower of gifts and cards opened amid lavish decorations. My cake arrived with an icing photo of me in my Minnie ears. The memories of our times together, the carousel, the décor, the gifts and the outpouring of love—all topped with the cake were overwhelming. I broke out in a flood of tears. I looked just a little bit more overwhelmed than oilcloth-bibbed Potsy at five.

A kid with a shadow

Many of my most favorite folks have the magic to see through the eyes of a child. James Barrie said that genius is the power to be a boy again. He's the one who wrote about that boy called Peter Pan who didn't want to grow up and played with his own shadow.

Starting the journey together

"Mouseketeers" Cisco and Renée

There just may be a hint of Walt still animating the way I look at life. I no longer play with my first friend, Pluto, although several plush Disney playmates grace my house. For fourteen years, until losing him recently, I played with Cisco, a real live dog that I loved as much as my first cuddly friend. He was just as patient as Pluto, even wearing his own Mickey Mouse hat. In 2015, I wore my Minnie Mouse creation to the Rose Parade when it celebrated the 60th anniversary of Disneyland. It seems like yesterday I visited The Happiest Place on Earth when it was brand new.

My exploring has not ceased, but it has slowed down. I have learned that I don't have to fly at full speed to encounter serendipity. It will find me. In playing with the word I was delighted to learn that if you take the "dip" out of *serendipity* and take a deep breath, you have *serenity.* And in my serenity, I no longer identify with the dragonfly I long ago chose as my symbol. I used to see myself as a creature who came off as a strong, attractive dragon. But underneath I was as fearful and skittish as a fly.

Like the dragonfly, I flitter fluttered over the surface, never stopping long enough to settle and dive deep. Today I am enjoying coming off as just who I am. Although I am still driven like Potsy who rushed headlong between adventures, I take more breaks to slow down, go deep and reflect on all the wonders I have seen and have yet to see.

The best part of traveling back to childhood is to know myself for the first time. And here's the biggest lesson of all. *There was never a shadow from the Sign.* The bright lights I thought shone only on the "right" side of the Sign have been inside me all the time. Yes, T.S. Eliot got it right. And so did Walt Whitman, that eloquent celebrator of life. He said, "Keep your face always toward the sunshine—and shadows will fall behind you."

So that's the story of me and my shadow. Now, go out and play in the sun!

Potsy/Renée at play 1941 and 2018

What Renée Didn't Say

Renée and Gretchen in faraway places

I don't know anyone who loves life like Renée. She epitomizes the phrase *joie de vivre*—an exultation of spirit.

Do you know anyone who spent five years building a yacht then living on it for five more years, with no permanent address?

Do you know any 80-year-old women who travel to a foreign country by themselves when things aren't so incredibly safe there?

That's our Renée—in the center of a far-away town, blonde, standing out like a bright star with "tourist" practically written on her back, camera in hand taking pictures of the locals, chatting it up with the shopkeepers in their native tongue, oblivious to any possible danger—clearly that child-like wonder overtaking potential fear.

I've known Renée for thirty-five years and not only did she generously take me under her wing and teach me everything I know about bringing a product to market, she became a confidante, fellow traveler and another mother to a very lucky me. (Somehow "second" mother doesn't seem right—no offense to my own mother.)

When we worked together in the toy industry in China or Nuremberg, there are hilarious images of Renée with her bad hip squatting low over an Eastern style toilet (aka, hole in floor with no porcelain fixture) and getting stuck in the down position, unable to stand up without some assistance. Or as guest of honor at a dinner in Taiwan graciously nibbling the eyeballs of a large fish on a garnished silver platter to show gratitude to the host for selecting this amazing delicacy. Or walking twelve miles a day up and down rows of toys, searching for new ideas, showing me how to do it even though she was exhausted and tired of pulling a rolling briefcase.

These are some of her favorite things:
Renée loves, loves, loves to play games <u>and</u> win; take daily naps; read and take classes on many topics that most of us would say "no thanks" like how to appreciate the most difficult books ever written; sing "La Vie en Rose" as well as any French cabaret singer; plan itineraries to exotic locales; celebrate birthdays with silly hats; wrap over-the-top presents; and totally over-prepare for guests to the point of getting a sweaty upper lip.

She's a teacher, toy maker, traveler and tale-teller. Even today, she teaches multiple classes on art and writing in her community. Whimsy is her middle name (no, it's actually Diane), and she's got a great big feverish case of wanderlust. She's also a dedicated journal keeper. I've not gotten into journaling but after you read her story, you'll see what amazing details a journal helps you recall. I could never figure out why someone who spent a great part of the working day writing would like to spend more time at home writing about the day spent writing…but now I see one of the big advantages. She can recall in an instant exactly what she was doing and feeling on that date 365 days ago—and what her friends were doing.

Over a decade ago, while having lunch in Washington DC, I suggested Renée write down some of the amazing stories of her life and voilà, she's done it!

Gretchen Van Tassel
Sedona, Arizona

Thank You Notes

The book before the book

Once upon a morning many years ago I shared a little Shutterfly photo book with my Writers' Circle. I told them I might want to turn it into something. And when my fellow writers showed an interest, a book was born. I had no conception of what I was going to create. I won't say it was a monster, but definitely, like me, an unruly imp that didn't want to grow up and needed lots of taming. So, my list is long of those to thank for their help in bringing my picture storybook to a happily ever after.

To Gretchen Van Tassel who finally convinced me I had a story to tell and had it in me to write a book. She lit the spark that got me started, and she fanned the flame when I didn't think I could. Thanks for the countless hours spent getting permissions for the outside photos I so blithely included in my text. Thank you for editing that text with great skill, even noting that the title of my first Shutterfly book is graced with a typo that no one else had seen. Most of all, thank you for your patience as a partner and guide through every step of the way from idea to reality. Without you there would be no book.

To Brenda Aronowitz, my writing partner, reader and writer extraordinaire. You discovered insights in my book even before I did. Thanks, too, for animating the writing as well as the writer.

Thanks to the other members of my writing team–Leslie Dunn and Carol Kaplan–for all your expertise and friendship. And appreciation goes out to all the members of Michele Crompton's stimulating OLLI classes at CSUMB for their help and encouragement. Big thanks to my writing teachers Elin Kelsey and Roxan McDonald for your encouragement and help. Thanks to Dr. Renée

Curry for nourishing my passion for words well-written and teaching me I am not too old to learn all manner of fascinating wonders. Sadly, Mary Jane Williams passed away before the book that she so looked forward to reading was published. I owe her my thanks for all the memory boosters from more than eighty years of best friendship and for not letting our childhood rivalries stand in the way of telling me that my grown-up writing was pretty good. To her daughter, Jennifer Ferguson, I give my thanks for her contributions to the book that preserves cherished memories of her mother whose story is so much a part of mine.

Thanks go to Lorna Fleming, Joan Sells and Doris Flint for contributing their memories of our younger days to mine and making them better.

Thank you, Judith Falck-Madsen, my UCSB Judy, for your encouragement and patience in helping me tell your story and ours. Thanks to Mary Jane Salcido for all the time devoted to enriching my knowledge of UCSB, Delta Gamma and Santa Barbara.

To my cousins Pat, Jeff and Brian Shannon and uncle Jack Riley and aunt Geraldine Riley Linn, thank you for the written and oral stories of our shared families. And to the members of those families no longer with us, I thank you for the wonderful collection of lessons and stories you left me.

To Didier Ghez, Founder and President of the Hyperion Historical Alliance, thanks go to you and the HHA members who generously shared their knowledge of all things Disney and helped me add Walt's story to mine. Thanks, too, go to Margaret Adamic and Maxine Raley, the Image Permissions Team at Disney Enterprises, Inc. We gave them an overwhelming amount of material to review. Thank you for your care and consideration of my book and the permissions to enrich it with fantastic images. Thanks to Rebecca Cline, Director of the Walt Disney Company Archives, for the tour revisiting the Studio where my father would go to work.

To Ben Ohmart and his BearManor Media for his patience. Thank you for bringing *In the Shadow of the Sign* out of the shadows.

To Lucas Seastrom and Jenna Benton for all the hours spent on organizing the photos and to Lorne C. Dokie of Razorwire Design for his patience and excellent partnership in providing the layout, photo work and awesome art.

Thank you, Carla and Eric Burgett, for sending me the treasures that my parents had stored in what is now your attic.

Thanks for the memoirists I can only hope to model: Norah Ephron, Jeannette Walls, Mary Karr, Tina Fey, Jessi Klein, David Sedaris and so many others who write the truth with wisdom and whimsy.

And finally, though there are many more I'm leaving off, I want to thank all the people– from celebrities and their estates to artists and corporations and publications–who granted us permissions for photographs, quotations and lyrics. They are listed in the long credits section to follow.

Credit Where It's Due

PHOTOGRAPHS

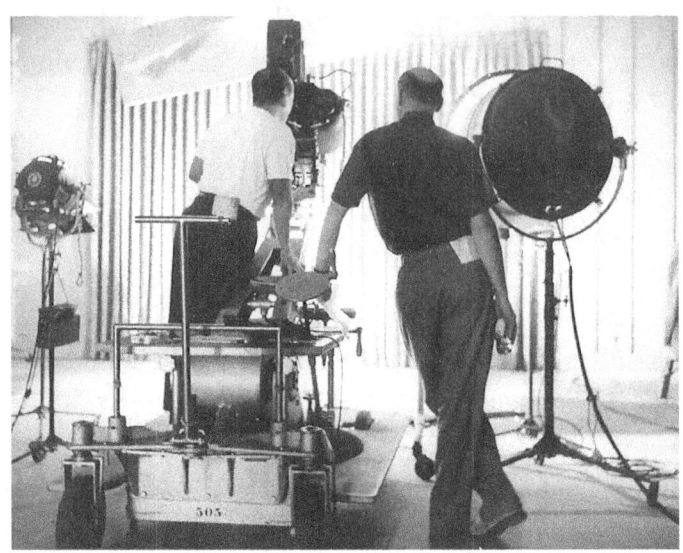

Front Cover
Front cover illustration by Lorne C. Dokie, razorwiredesign.com and **HOLLYWOOD**™ & Design © 2017 Hollywood Chamber of Commerce. The Hollywood Sign and Hollywood Walk of Fame™ are trademarks and intellectual property of Hollywood Chamber of Commerce. All Rights Reserved.

Before Beginning
Hollywoodland sign photo courtesy of Bison Archives/Marc Wanamaker/ HollywoodHistoricPhotos.com and **HOLLYWOOD**™ & Design © 2017 Hollywood Chamber of Commerce. The Hollywood Sign and Hollywood Walk of Fame™ are trademarks and intellectual property of Hollywood Chamber of Commerce. All Rights Reserved.

Chapter 1
Sir Winston Leonard Spencer Churchill photo 1874-1965, Contributor: Ian Dagnall Computing/Alamy Stock Photo

Hyperion studio photo © Disney

Chapter 2
Vivien Leigh
Fawcett Publications (https://commons.wikimedia.org/wiki/File:Vivien_Leigh_Scarlet.jpg), "Vivien Leigh Scarlett", marked as public domain, more details on Wikimedia Commons: https://commons.wikimedia.org/wiki/Template:PD-US

"Popeye" cartoon by Elzie Crisler Segar © Distributed by King Features Syndicate, Inc. World Rights Reserved

Chapter 3
George Young by unknown author (https://commons.wikimedia.org/wiki/File:Canadian_swimmer_George_Young.jpg), "Canadian swimmer George Young", marked as public domain, more details on Wikimedia Commons: https://commons.wikimedia.org/wiki/Template:PD-Canada

The Junior Times cover illustration by Ray Patin © 1925, 1979 Los Angeles Times, used with permission.

"Hey Red! Cartoon" by Ray Patin; Mickey Mouse © Disney

"Won't You Draw Us a Mickey Mouse?" cartoon by Ray Patin; Krazy Kat © Distributed by King Features Syndicate, Inc. World Rights Reserved

Disclaimer: All reasonable efforts have been made to contact the copyright/trademark holders. Anyone who believes their intellectual property has been infringed should contact the author.

Chapter 4

Mintz letterhead letter by Ray Patin; Krazy Kat © Distributed by King Features Syndicate, Inc. World Rights Reserved. Scrappy courtesy of Columbia Pictures/Screen Gems.

Plum Nerts cartoon by Ray Patin; Krazy Kat © Distributed by King Features Syndicate, Inc. World Rights Reserved

Rumble seat photo by Stephen Foskett (Wikipedia User: sfoskett) (https://commons.wikimedia.org/wiki/File:1931_Ford_Model_A_roadster_rumble_seat.JPG), "1931 Ford Model A roadster rumble seat", https://creativecommons.org/licenses/by-sa/3.0/legalcode

Cartoon-covered letter by Ray Patin; Krazy Kat © Distributed by King Features Syndicate, Inc. World Rights Reserved

Baby Betty Boop by Ray Patin; Betty Boop © Distributed by King Features Syndicate, Inc. World Rights Reserved

Hollywoodland photo courtesy of Bison Archives/Marc Wanamaker/HollywoodHistoricPhotos.com and **HOLLYWOOD**™ & Design © 2017 Hollywood Chamber of Commerce. The Hollywood Sign and Hollywood Walk of Fame™ are trademarks and intellectual property of Hollywood Chamber of Commerce. All Rights Reserved.

Mulholland Dam and Hollywood Hills postcard courtesy of the California History Room, California State Library, Sacramento, California and used with permission of Christopher Frasher/Frashers Fotos, Pomona

Lake Hollywood reservoir
Clinton Steeds from Los Angeles, USA (https://commons.wikimedia.org/wiki/File:Lake_Hollywood_Reservoir_by_clinton_steeds.jpg), "Lake Hollywood Reservoir by Clinton Steeds", https://creativecommons.org/licenses/by-sa/2.0/legalcode

Ray's letter to Ub Iwerks used by permission of the estate of Ub Iwerks

Art of animation cartoon by Ray Patin; Krazy Kat © Distributed by King Features Syndicate, Inc. World Rights Reserved

Walt's Field Day photo © Disney

Chapter 5

Walt Disney, Shirley Temple and special Oscar photo © Disney. Shirley Temple's image used with permission of Shirley's World, LP. The Oscar statuette is a registered trademark and copyrighted property of the Academy of Motion Picture Arts and Sciences.

Original Animation building photo © Disney

Walt Disney Studios signpost photo © Disney

Ray drawing Donald Duck still photo © Disney

Grizzly Flats railroad photo used with permission of Ward Kimball estate

Mr. and Mrs. Ward Kimball at train photo used with permission of Ward Kimball estate

Renée on caboose photo used with permission of Ward Kimball estate

Dear Walt title card photo © Disney

Ray Patin on strike, photo by Kosti Ruohomaa, courtesy of the Neelo Lofman Estate

Chapter 6

Citrus Fruit Label courtesy of Gavilan Citrus Association, Marquita Brand, Collection of citrus labels (MS 038), box 1, image 017. Special Collections & University Archives, University of California, Riverside

Welcome to Los Angeles postcard
Tichnor Brothers, Publisher (https://commons.wikimedia.org/wiki/File:Greetings_from_Los_Angeles,_California_(63828).jpg), "Greetings from Los Angeles, California (63828)", marked as public domain, more details on Wikimedia Commons: https://commons.wikimedia.org/wiki/Template:PD-US

Platform house historic district photo courtesy of Los Angeles Office of Historic Resources, Department of City Planning, Historic Resources Group, www.preservation.lacity.org

Tail O' the Pup
Alan Taylor (https://commons.wikimedia.org/wiki/File:Tail-o-thePup.jpg),"Tail-o-the Pup", https://creativecommons.org/licenses/by/2.0/legalcode, used with permission of the 1933 Group

Randy's Donuts photo used with permission of Randy's Donuts
This work is from the Carol M. Highsmith Archive Collection at the Library of Congress,
Prints & Photographs Division, LC-HS503-532 Carol M. Highsmith creator QS:P170,Q5044454
(https://commons.wikimedia.org/wiki/File:Randy's_Donuts_LA_California_LC-HS503-532.jpg), "Randy's Donuts LA California LC-HS503-532", marked as public domain, more details on Wikimedia Commons:
https://commons.wikimedia.org/wiki/Template:Library of Congress-no known copyright restrictions

Hollywood Sign by Gnaphron (https://www.flickr.com/photos/gnaphron/8485148958/in/photostream/), Hollywood Sign, https://creativecommons.org/licenses/by-sa/2.0/ and **HOLLYWOOD**™ & Design © 2017 Hollywood Chamber of Commerce. The Hollywood Sign and Hollywood Walk of Fame™ are trademarks and intellectual property of Hollywood Chamber of Commerce. All Rights Reserved.

Southern California map by Lorne C. Dokie, razorwiredesign.com and **HOLLYWOOD**™ & Design © 2017 Hollywood Chamber of Commerce. The Hollywood Sign and Hollywood Walk of Fame™ are trademarks and intellectual property of Hollywood Chamber of Commerce. All Rights Reserved.

Home of Bing Crosby postcard
The Tichnor Brothers Collection, Boston Public Library, https://ark.digitalcommonwealth.org/ark:/50959/2n49tg14d
"Home of Bing Crosby, Toluca Lake, near Hollywood, California", no known copyright restrictions or restrictions on use

Bob Hope's Toluca estate photo, https://virtualglobetrotting.com/map/bob-hopes-house-former/view/google/, tlp333, map data © 2018 Google Imagery Google Maps/Google Earth

Forest Lawn Hollywood Hills photo used with permission of Forest Lawn Memorial-Parks & Mortuaries

Gene Autry grave marker photo courtesy of Gene Autry Entertainment and used with permission of Forest Lawn Memorial-Parks & Mortuaries

Gene Autry publicity photo circa 1951 courtesy of Gene Autry Entertainment

Bette Davis tomb
Floatjon (https://commons.wikimedia.org/wiki/File:Bette_Davis_Tomb.JPG), „Bette Davis Tomb",
https://creativecommons.org/licenses/by-sa/3.0/legalcode
and used with permission of CMG Worldwide and Forest Lawn Memorial-Parks & Mortuaries

Bette Davis trailer screenshot
https://web.archive.org/web/20080321033709/http://www.sabucat.com/?pg=copyright and
http://www.creativeclearance.com/guidelines.html#D2
(https://commons.wikimedia.org/wiki/File:Bette_Davis_in_All_About_Eve_trailer.jpg), "Bette Davis in All About Eve trailer", marked as public domain, more details on Wikimedia Commons:
https://commons.wikimedia.org/wiki/Template:PD-US and used with permission of CMG Worldwide

TV transmitter on Mt. Lee photo
HOLLYWOOD™ & Design © 2017 Hollywood Chamber of Commerce. The Hollywood Sign and Hollywood Walk of Fame™ are trademarks and intellectual property of Hollywood Chamber of Commerce. All Rights Reserved.

Behind the Hollywood Sign by Oliver Dodd, Behind the Hollywood Sign,
https://www.flickr.com/photos/oliverdodd/8964602905, licensed by
https://creativecommons.org/licenses/by/2.0/ and **HOLLYWOOD**™ & Design © 2017 Hollywood Chamber of Commerce.
The Hollywood Sign and Hollywood Walk of Fame™ are trademarks and intellectual property of Hollywood Chamber of Commerce. All Rights Reserved.

Hollywood at night lights and palms photo Moviestore Collection Ltd/Alamy Stock Photo

Sunset Ranch photo used with permission © Sunset Ranch and **HOLLYWOOD** ™ & Design © 2017 Hollywood Chamber of Commerce. The Hollywood Sign and Hollywood Walk of Fame™ are trademarks and intellectual property of Hollywood Chamber of Commerce. All Rights Reserved.

Mickey ears fence topper photo © Disney

The Walt Disney Studios water tower photo © Disney

The Walt Disney Company Alameda entrance photo © Disney

Seven Dwarfs holding up Team Disney building photo © Disney

Johnny's Burbank map used with permission of Carson Entertainment Group

The Wonder Years house photo used by permission of Iamnotastalker.com

Bob's Big Boy with Mary Kate photo courtesy of Jennifer Ferguson. The word marks BOB'S, BOB'S BIG BOY and BIG BOY along with the associated logos and statues are registered trademarks or trademarks owned by Big Boy Restaurant Group, LLC and are used herein with permission.

Warner Bros. water tower by traveljunction, water tower on Warner Brothers movie studio lot, Burbank, CA, https://www.flickr.com/photos/128012202@N05/15606339691 licensed under https://creativecommons.org/licenses/by-sa/2.0/

Warner Bros. Studio
Rebell18190 (https://commons.wikimedia.org/wiki/File:WarnerStudio.jpg), "WarnerStudio", https://creativecommons.org/licenses/by-sa/3.0/legalcode

Crossroads of the World at The Walt Disney World Resort photo © Disney

Crossroads of the World photo MixPix/Alamy Stock Photo used with permission of Crossroads Properties.

Griffith Observatory photo, Los Angeles
The Jon B. Lovelace Collection of California Photographs in Carol M. Highsmith's America Project, Library of Congress, Prints and Photographs Division. No known restrictions on publication.

Star map seller photo Visions of America, LLC/Alamy Stock Photo

James Dean statue by Prayitno, James Dean,
https://www.flickr.com/photos/prayitnophotography/5054435505/in/photostream/
is licensed under https://creativecommons.org/licenses/by/2.0/ and CMG Worldwide and
HOLLYWOOD ™ & Design © 2017 Hollywood Chamber of Commerce. The Hollywood Sign and Hollywood Walk of Fame™ are trademarks and intellectual property of Hollywood Chamber of Commerce. All Rights Reserved.

Walt Disney's Star on Hollywood Walk of Fame
Witchblue (https://commons.wikimedia.org/wiki/File:Walt_Disney_Walk_of_fame.jpg),
"Walt Disney Walk of Fame", marked as public domain, more details on Wikimedia Commons:
https://commons.wikimedia.org/wiki/Template:PD-user and
HOLLYWOOD ™ & Design © 2017 Hollywood Chamber of Commerce. The Hollywood Sign and Hollywood Walk of Fame ™ are trademarks and intellectual property of Hollywood Chamber of Commerce. All Rights Reserved.

Grauman's Chinese Theatre photo used with permission of TCL Chinese Theaters
This work is from the Carol M. Highsmith Archive Collection at the Library of Congress, Prints & Photographs Division, LC-HS503-489. The original uploader was Moondigger at English Wikipedia.
(https://commons.wikimedia.org/wiki/File:Grauman's_Chinese_Theatre_Highsmith_medium.jpg),
"Grauman's Chinese Theatre Highsmith", marked as public domain, more details on Wikimedia Commons:
https://commons.wikimedia.org/wiki/Template:PD-retouched-user

Jimmy Stewart's hand and footprints photo, Grauman's Chinese Theatre, Los Angeles used with permission of TCL Chinese Theaters. Photograph from Carol M. Highsmith's America, Library of Congress, Prints and Photographs Division. No known restrictions on publication.

Jim Henson Studios photo MixPix/Alamy Stock Photo. Image provided courtesy of The Jim Henson Company.

Capitol Records building by Eva, Capitol Records, https://www.flickr.com/photos/easternblot/2781958360 licensed under https://creativecommons.org/licenses/by-nd/2.0/

Chapter 7
Renée portrait smiling by Jose Reyes of Hollywood

Renée portrait frowning by Jose Reyes of Hollywood

Hollywood United Methodist Church photo used with permission of Hollywood UMC and **HOLLYWOOD**™ & Design © 2017 Hollywood Chamber of Commerce. The Hollywood Sign and Hollywood Walk of Fame™ are trademarks and intellectual property of Hollywood Chamber of Commerce. All Rights Reserved.

Renée with hat by Jose Reyes of Hollywood

Renée with purse by Jose Reyes of Hollywood

Renée side view by Jose Reyes of Hollywood

Renée disgruntled by Jose Reyes of Hollywood

Chapter 8
1940s classroom photo reprinted with permission from the February 2014 issue of *Illinois State* magazine.

Portrait of Louise de Keroualle, Duchess of Portsmouth by Peter Lely, digital image courtesy of the Getty Museum's Open Content Program. Appeared on one of the *Forever Amber* book covers.

Valentine sundae by Mark Gstohl, Valentines Day Cards, https://www.flickr.com/photos/howieluvzus/2854946002/in/photostream/ licensed under https://creativecommons.org/licenses/by/2.0/

Valentine tennis players by Joe Haupt, Vintage Valentine Day Card – You're Hard to Beat Valentine, Made in USA, Circa 1963 https://www.flickr.com/photos/51764518@N02/15019110501 licensed under https://creativecommons.org/licenses/by/2.0/

Natalie Wood with braids photo used with permission of Natasha Gregson Wagner
20th Century Fox (https://commons.wikimedia.org/wiki/File:Natalie_Wood_1947_photo.jpg), "Natalie Wood 1947 photo", marked as public domain, more details on Wikimedia Commons: https://commons.wikimedia.org/wiki/Template:PD-US

Renée with braids by Jose Reyes of Hollywood

Red Goose Shoes sign by Steve Snodgrass, Juvenile Shoe Store, https://www.flickr.com/photos/stevensnodgrass/8712923536 licensed by https://creativecommons.org/licenses/by/2.0/

Fluoroscope
The Pedescope Company (manufacturer) (https://commons.wikimedia.org/wiki/File:Podoscope_par_The_Pedoscope_Compagny_01.jpg) https://creativecommons.org/licenses/by-sa/4.0/legalcode

Pinocchio photo © 1940 Disney

Chapter 9
Service on the Home Front poster
Work Projects Administration Poster Collection (https://commons.wikimedia.org/wiki/File:Service_on_the_home_front_LCCN98518713.jpg), "Service on the home front LCCN98518713", marked as public domain, more details on Wikimedia Commons: https://commons.wikimedia.org/wiki/Template:PD-US

Milk or bread model truck by Alden Jewell, 1941 Brooks E-Z Route Milk Truck and Baker's Model Van, https://www.flickr.com/photos/autohistorian/28993939606 licensed by https://creativecommons.org/licenses/by/2.0/

Helms Bakery truck with mom, daughter 1936, Security Pacific National Bank Collection,
Los Angeles Public Library; used with permission of Wally Marks, WALTER N. MARKS, INC. Helms Hall of Fame

Good Humor Truck
GRUBBXDN (https://commons.wikimedia.org/wiki/File:Good_Humor_Vendor_1966.jpg),
https://creativecommons.org/licenses/by-sa/4.0/legalcode and used with permission of Good Humor/Unilever

Cudahy's Delrich margarine ad 1948 by Newell Convers Wyeth, Internet Archive Book Images,
Ladies' Home Journal, https://www.flickr.com/photos/internetarchivebookimages/14786167483/ No known copyright restrictions

How to shop with war ration book two
Office of Price Administration, Online Archive of California
(https://commons.wikimedia.org/wiki/File:"How_to_Shop_With_Ration_Book_Two"_-_OAC_-_bk0007t0n59.jpg),
"How to Shop With Ration Book Two" - OAC - bk0007t0n59", marked as public domain, more details on Wikimedia Commons:
https://commons.wikimedia.org/wiki/Template:PD-US

Your victory garden poster by The U.S. National Archives, Your Victory Garden Counts More Than Ever!", created by Office for Emergency Management. Office of War Information. Domestic Operations Branch. Bureau of Special Services from World War II posters,
https://www.flickr.com/photos/usnationalarchives/4546092598/in/photostream/, no known copyright restrictions

Plant a victory garden poster by Boston Public Library, Plant a victory garden. Our food is fighting, U.S. Government Printing Office,
United States Office of War Information
https://www.flickr.com/photos/boston_public_library/2351906637, is licensed by
https://creativecommons.org/licenses/by/2.0/

Can All You Can poster from National Archives Catalog, Can all you can. It's a real war job!,
created by Office for Emergency Management, Office of War Information from World War II posters,
https://catalog.archives.gov/id/513566, no known use restrictions

We Can Do It!
J. Howard Miller (1918–2004), artist employed by Westinghouse, poster used by the War Production Coordinating Committee,
National Museum of American History, Smithsonian Institution
(https://commons.wikimedia.org/wiki/File:We_Can_Do_It!.jpg),
"We Can Do It!", marked as public domain, more details on Wikimedia Commons:
https://commons.wikimedia.org/wiki/Template:PD-US

Women wearing snoods, Unknown author
(https://commons.wikimedia.org/wiki/File:Women_workers_in_snoods_1942.gif),
"Women workers in snoods 1942", Franklin D. Roosevelt Library & Museum, Library ID: 65716(8),
marked as public domain, more details on Wikimedia Commons:
https://commons.wikimedia.org/wiki/Template:PD-because

Women aircraft workers, Library of Congress Prints and Photographs Division Washington, D.C., Women man America's machines in a West Coast airplane factory, where the swing shift of drill press operators is composed almost entirely of women.
http://www.loc.gov/pictures/resource/fsa.8b02895/

Leg Silque Liquid Stockings, Shade P244 Suntan by Langlois, Inc., Gift of Sidney Glaser, Division of Medicine & Science,
National Museum of American History, Smithsonian Institution
http://americanhistory.si.edu/collections/search/object/nmah_765873

War ration book front
Bill Faulk (https://commons.wikimedia.org/wiki/File:WWII_USA_Ration_Book_3_Front.jpg), "WWII USA Ration Book 3 Front",
marked as public domain, more details on Wikimedia Commons: https://commons.wikimedia.org/wiki/Template:PD-US

Is YOUR trip necessary? poster
Unknown author or not provided
(https://commons.wikimedia.org/wiki/File:"Is_Your_Trip_Necessary%5E_Millions_of_Troops_are_on_the_Move"_-_NARA_-_515012.jpg), "Is Your Trip Necessary? Millions of Troops are on the Move" - NARA - 515012", marked as public domain, more details on Wikimedia Commons: https://commons.wikimedia.org/wiki/Template:PD-US

Children in front of war bonds poster
John Vachon creator QS:P170,Q3182639
(https://commons.wikimedia.org/wiki/File:Homefront_posters.jpg),
"Homefront posters", marked as public domain, more details on Wikimedia Commons:
https://commons.wikimedia.org/wiki/Template:PD-US

Adolf Hitler
Bundesarchiv, Bild 146-1990-048-29A / CC-BY-SA 3.0
(https://commons.wikimedia.org/wiki/File:Adolf_Hitler_Berghof-1936.jpg),
"Adolf Hitler Berghof-1936",
https://creativecommons.org/licenses/by-sa/3.0/de/legalcode

Benito Mussolini
Martianmister and Vps (https://commons.wikimedia.org/wiki/File:Benito_Mussolini_colored.jpg), "Benito Mussolini colored",
marked as public domain, more details on Wikimedia Commons: https://commons.wikimedia.org/wiki/Template:PD-Italy

Tojo Hideki
Unknown author (https://commons.wikimedia.org/wiki/File:Prime_Minister_Tojo_Hideki_photograph.jpg),
"Prime Minister Tojo Hideki photograph", marked as public domain, more details on Wikimedia Commons:
https://commons.wikimedia.org/wiki/Template:PD-Japan

Our carelessness their secret weapon–prevent forest fires poster
Uncredited artist working for U.S. Department of Agriculture
(https://commons.wikimedia.org/wiki/File:PropagandaHitlerTojo.jpg),
"PropagandaHitlerTojo", marked as public domain, more details on Wikimedia Commons:
https://commons.wikimedia.org/wiki/Template:PD-US

They're watching us…plenty! poster
Unknown author or not provided
(https://commons.wikimedia.org/wiki/File:They're_watching_us...Plenty^_-_NARA_-_534523.jpg), "They're watching us...Plenty! - NARA - 534523", marked as public domain, more details on Wikimedia Commons:
https://commons.wikimedia.org/wiki/Template:PD-US

Jappy so-o-o happy poster
Unknown author or not provided (https://commons.wikimedia.org/wiki/File:"Jappy_So-o-o_Happy_When_This_Happen_to_You"_-_NARA_-_514676.jpg),
"Jappy So-o-o Happy When This Happen to You" - NARA - 514676", marked as public domain, more details on Wikimedia Commons:
https://commons.wikimedia.org/wiki/Template:PD-US

Winston Churchill by OliBac, Sir Winston Leonard Spencer Churchill
https://www.flickr.com/photos/olibac/4790225095 licensed by https://creativecommons.org/licenses/by/2.0/

Kilroy was here by Jinx!, Kilroy was here, a WWII staple of graffiti,
https://www.flickr.com/photos/span112/3477696360
licensed by https://creativecommons.org/licenses/by-sa/2.0/

Truck with Kilroy was here by Lee Cannon, World War II Display at 2011 Wings & Wheels,
https://www.flickr.com/photos/leecannon/6221786597
licensed by https://creativecommons.org/licenses/by-sa/2.0/

Swastika
Ant Allan (https://commons.wikimedia.org/wiki/File:Swastika_flag_(Nazi_Germany).ant.png), "Swastika flag (Nazi Germany).ant",
marked as public domain, more details on Wikimedia Commons: https://commons.wikimedia.org/wiki/Template:PD-Coa-Germany

Lockheed P-38 Lightning
USAF Museum Photo Archive
(https://commons.wikimedia.org/wiki/File:Lockheed_P-38_Lightning_USAF.JPG),
"Lockheed P-38 Lightning USAF", marked as public domain, more details on Wikimedia Commons:
https://commons.wikimedia.org/wiki/Template:PD-US
Used with permission of LM Aero, owner of Lockheed intellectual property.

Lockheed P-38 conveyor lines
U.S. Air Force Airman or employee
(https://commons.wikimedia.org/wiki/File:Mechanized_P-38_conveyor_lines.jpg),
"Mechanized P-38 conveyor lines", marked as public domain, more details on Wikimedia Commons:
https://commons.wikimedia.org/wiki/Template:PD-US
Used with permission of LM Aero, owner of Lockheed intellectual property.

Lockheed planes under camouflage, courtesy of Wes Clark/Mike McDaniel, Burbank Historical Society and used with permission of LM Aero, owner of Lockheed intellectual property.

Lockheed cars under camouflage, courtesy of Wes Clark/Mike McDaniel, Burbank Historical Society and used with permission of LM Aero, owner of Lockheed intellectual property.

Lockheed passengers under camouflage, courtesy of Wes Clark/Mike McDaniel, Burbank Historical Society and used with permission of LM Aero, owner of Lockheed intellectual property.

Franklin D. Roosevelt fireside chat
Unknown author (https://commons.wikimedia.org/wiki/File:FDR-January-11-1944.jpg),
"FDR-January-11-1944", marked as public domain, more details on Wikimedia Commons:
https://commons.wikimedia.org/wiki/Template:PD-US

Woman in gas mask, State Library Victoria Collections from the Argus collection of wartime photographs,
https://www.flickr.com/photos/statelibraryofvictoria_collections/5551751234
licensed by https://creativecommons.org/licenses/by/2.0/

WW II civil defense helmet
Curiosandrelics (https://commons.wikimedia.org/wiki/File:CD_Helmet.jpg),
"CD Helmet", https://creativecommons.org/licenses/by-sa/3.0/legalcode

Service Ribbin' Screen Cartoonists Guild pamphlet cartoon by Carmichael 1944 used with permission of The Animation Guild.

"Abide by the laws" cartoon by Ray Patin, Screen Cartoonists Guild pamphlet used with permission of The Animation Guild.

Soldiers and girl cartoon by Ray Patin, Screen Cartoonists Guild pamphlet used with permission of The Animation Guild.

Service flags display at Kettering Hall at the National Museum of the U.S. Air Force, USAF photo,
https://www.nationalmuseum.af.mil/Visit/Museum-Exhibits/Fact-Sheets/Display/Article/196842/service-flags-and-pins/

Resident of Rodger Young Village Housing Project, Louis Clyde Stoumen, Housing Authority of the City of Los Angeles Photo Collection, Los Angeles Public Library

Family outside Quonset hut at Rodger Young Village 1940s, Stoumen, Louis C., Southern California Library for Social Studies & Research, Housing Authority of the City of Los Angeles Photograph Collection; Lou Stoumen Archive used with permission of The Edmund L and Nancy K Dubois Library, Museum of Photographic Arts

Chapter 10
"Rosemary" Madame Alexander doll; Madame Alexander is a trademark of Madame Alexander Doll Company, used with permission

Renée with Madame Alexander doll; Madame Alexander is a trademark of Madame Alexander Doll Company, used with permission

Renée and Joanie courtesy of Joan Sells

Pollywog pond photo courtesy of Joan Sells

Madame Alexander "Jo" doll and clothes; Madame Alexander is a trademark of Madame Alexander Doll Company, used with permission

Renée in skirt and sweater by Jose Reyes of Hollywood

Renée, Joanie and Lorna photo courtesy of Joan Sells

Chapter 11

The Little Prince book cover
Cover and illustrations THE LITTLE PRINCE by Antoine de Saint-Exupery. Copyright © 1943 by Houghton Mifflin Harcourt Publishing Company, renewed 1971 by Consuelo de Saint-Exupery, English translation copyright © 2000 by Richard Howard. Reprinted by permission of Houghton Mifflin Harcourt Publishing Company. All rights reserved.

The Little Prince interior pages
Cover and illustrations THE LITTLE PRINCE by Antoine de Saint-Exupery. Copyright © 1943 by Houghton Mifflin Harcourt Publishing Company, renewed 1971 by Consuelo de Saint-Exupery, English translation copyright © 2000 by Richard Howard. Reprinted by permission of Houghton Mifflin Harcourt Publishing Company. All rights reserved.

Brown "hat" illustration from *The Little Prince*
Cover and illustrations THE LITTLE PRINCE by Antoine de Saint-Exupery. Copyright © 1943 by Houghton Mifflin Harcourt Publishing Company, renewed 1971 by Consuelo de Saint-Exupery, English translation copyright © 2000 by Richard Howard. Reprinted by permission of Houghton Mifflin Harcourt Publishing Company. All rights reserved.

Boa constrictor illustration from *The Little Prince*
Cover and illustrations THE LITTLE PRINCE by Antoine de Saint-Exupery. Copyright © 1943 by Houghton Mifflin Harcourt Publishing Company, renewed 1971 by Consuelo de Saint-Exupery, English translation copyright © 2000 by Richard Howard. Reprinted by permission of Houghton Mifflin Harcourt Publishing Company. All rights reserved.

Antoine de St. Exupery on 50 franc note
Monnaie de Paris (banknote), Banque de France (photograph)
(https://commons.wikimedia.org/wiki/File:50_francs_banknote_A.jpg),
"50 francs banknote A", marked as public domain, more details on Wikimedia Commons:
https://commons.wikimedia.org/wiki/Template:PD-JORF

Nana's grave used with permission of Find a Grave.com member #48534895 and Inglewood Park Cemetery

Los Angeles Orphan Asylum 1890, William H. Fletcher Collection, Courtesy of the California History Room, California State Library, Sacramento, California.

The Hollywood Hotel
Unknown author (https://commons.wikimedia.org/wiki/File:Hollywood-hotel-1905.jpg),
"Hollywood-hotel-1905", marked as public domain, more details on Wikimedia Commons:
https://commons.wikimedia.org/wiki/Template:PD-US

Chapter 12

Mae West in 1953
Los Angeles Times (https://commons.wikimedia.org/wiki/File:Mae_West_in_1953.jpg),
"Mae West in 1953", marked as public domain, more details on Wikimedia Commons:
https://commons.wikimedia.org/wiki/Template:PD-US

Kotex mother-daughter ad courtesy Kimberly-Clark Corporation

Are you in the know? Kotex ad courtesy Harry Finley, Museum of Menstruation & Women's Health and Kimberly-Clark Corporation

Tampax chained to calendar ad used by permission of Procter & Gamble

True Confessions reprinted with permission from True Renditions, LLC

Tangee Lipstick ad courtesy of Cynthia Petrovic, www.tangoland.com. Tangee is a registered trademark of Fairbanks Group, LLC; used with permission.

Ponds Cold Cream ad used with permission of Pond's/Unilever

Johnny McGovern as child actor, courtesy of John Wilder

John Wilder as teen, courtesy of John Wilder

Chapter 13
Renée before braces by Jose Reyes of Hollywood

We're Going Steady used with permission of Image Cascade Publishing, LLC

45 RPM record player by Joe Haupt
Vintage RCA Automatic Phonograph, Model 45-EY-2, 3 Vacuum Tubes, Made In USA, Circa 1950 – 1952,
https://www.flickr.com/photos/51764518@N02/38016540112
licensed by https://creativecommons.org/licenses/by-sa/2.0/

The Four Aces
TGC-Topps Gum Cards-photo from Decca Records
(https://commons.wikimedia.org/wiki/File:The_Four_Aces_1957.JPG),
"The Four Aces 1957", marked as public domain, more details on Wikimedia Commons:
https://commons.wikimedia.org/wiki/Template:PD-US

Betty Cornell Teen Popularity Guide ad used with permission of the estate of Betty Cornell

Lux Radio Theater
Macfadden Publications (https://commons.wikimedia.org/wiki/File:Lux_Radio_Theatre_1948.jpg), "Lux Radio Theatre 1948",
marked as public domain, more details on Wikimedia Commons:
https://commons.wikimedia.org/wiki/Template:PD-US

Seventeen Magazine October 1956 cover used with permission of *Seventeen*, Hearst Magazine
Media, Inc. Cover photo of model Ann Klem by photographer Tom Palumbo, used with permission of the estates of Ann Klem and Tom Palumbo.

Chapter 14
John Burroughs High School 1955, Burbank rehabilitates Burroughs High, Valley Times Photo Collection, Los Angeles Public Library

Mary Frances Reynolds Girl Scout photo courtesy of Hollywood Motion Picture Experience/Todd Fisher

Mary Frances Reynolds Miss Burbank 1948 photo courtesy of HMPE/Todd Fisher

Debbie Frannie Reynolds comes to microphone 1948 photo courtesy of Wes Clark/Mike McDaniel, Burbank Historical Society; used with permission of HMPE/Todd Fisher

Debbie Reynolds and her 1955 T Bird, 1955 photo. © 1978 Joe Shere/mptvimages.com; used with permission of HMPE/Todd Fisher. The word marks BOB'S, BOB'S BIG BOY and BIG BOY along with the associated logos and statues are registered trademarks or trademarks owned by Big Boy Restaurant Group, LLC and are used herein with permission.

Elizabeth I of England
Unknown author, Formerly attributed to George Gower QS:P170,Q4233718,P?,Q2126008
(https://commons.wikimedia.org/wiki/File:Elizabeth_I_(Armada_Portrait).jpg),
"Elizabeth I (Armada Portrait)", marked as public domain, more details on Wikimedia Commons:
https://commons.wikimedia.org/wiki/Template:PD-old

Chapter 15
Mr. Belvedere Goes to College movie poster
MR. BELVEDERE GOES TO COLLEGE AF Archive/Alamy Stock Photo © Twentieth Century Fox. All rights reserved.
Shirley Temple's image used with permission of Shirley's World, LP.

Aldous Huxley photo courtesy of UCSB La Cumbre yearbook; used with permission of Huxley estate.

Student with book on head photo courtesy of UCSB La Cumbre yearbook

Chapter 16
Buff guys with surfboards photo courtesy of UCSB La Cumbre yearbook

Chapter 17

UCSB campus as it looked in 1944
1960 U.S. military/National Archives and Records Administration (https://commons.wikimedia.org/wiki/File:Overhead_MCAS_Santa_Barbara_in_April_of_1944.jpg), "Overhead MCAS Santa Barbara in April of 1944", marked as public domain

UCSB campus now photo by Tony Mastres/UCSB, used with permission.

Santa Rosa Hall 1957 photo courtesy of UCSB La Cumbre yearbook

Dorm life 1 photo courtesy of UCSB La Cumbre yearbook

Dorm life 2 photo courtesy of UCSB La Cumbre yearbook

Dorm life 3 photo courtesy of UCSB La Cumbre yearbook

Scenic campus dwelling photo courtesy of UCSB La Cumbre yearbook

Golden Gaucho reunion logo from UCSB Alumni Association Awards Ceremony brochure cover courtesy of UC Santa Barbara 1994 Alumni Association

El Colegio Road 1959 photo courtesy of UCSB La Cumbre yearbook

Fifties collegiates on campus photo courtesy of UCSB La Cumbre yearbook

Student union 1 photo courtesy of John Dickson, santabarbara.com

Student union 2 photo courtesy of UCSB La Cumbre yearbook

Chapter 18

Kappa Alpha Theta house photo courtesy of UCSB La Cumbre yearbook, used with permission of Kappa Alpha Theta Fraternity

Pi Beta Phi house photo courtesy of UCSB La Cumbre yearbook, used with permission of Pi Beta Phi Fraternity for Women

Delta Gamma pledge pin photo by Mary Jane Salcido, used with permission of Delta Gamma Fraternity

Delta Gamma anchor pin photo by Mary Jane Salcido, used with permission of Delta Gamma Fraternity

Renée as Delta Gamma president photo courtesy of UCSB La Cumbre yearbook

Joe's Café on State Street photo courtesy of Bill Heller Photography, www.billheller.com and used by permission of Joe's Cafe

Chapter 19

Renée at photo studio by Jose Reyes of Hollywood

Delta Gamma Hawaiian party photo courtesy of UCSB La Cumbre yearbook

Renée as the queen in *Carmen* photo courtesy of UCSB La Cumbre yearbook

Moulin Rouge ensemble cast photo courtesy of UCSB La Cumbre yearbook

Moulin Rouge lithograph 1891 (La Goulue)
Toulouse-Lautrec, Henri de (1864 - 1901) – Artist (French) Details of artist on Google Art Project (https://commons.wikimedia.org/wiki/File:Toulouse-Lautrec,_Henri_de_-_Moulin_Rouge-La_Goulue_-_Google_Art_Project.jpg), "Toulouse-Lautrec, Henri de - Moulin Rouge-La Goulue - Google Art Project", marked as public domain, more details on Wikimedia Commons: https://commons.wikimedia.org/wiki/Template:PD-1923

Renée and DGs in Barbary Coast show 1957/58 photo courtesy of UCSB La Cumbre yearbook

Newspaper clipping "Crowds Brave Fog for *Barbary Coast*" reprinted with permission of *Santa Barbara News-Press*

Henri de Toulouse-Lautrec
Paul Sescau40002 (https://commons.wikimedia.org/wiki/File:Photolautrec.jpg),
"Photolautrec", marked as public domain, more details on Wikimedia Commons:
https://commons.wikimedia.org/wiki/Template:PD-old

Chapter 20
La Cumbre 1957 front and back yearbook cover photos used with permission of UCSB La Cumbre yearbook

Back collar button photo courtesy of GANT, used with permission
http://www.gant.com/shirtguide/the-anatomy-of-the-gant-shirt

Female co-ed wearing stripes photo courtesy of UCSB La Cumbre yearbook

Male co-ed wearing stripes photo courtesy of UCSB La Cumbre yearbook

Renée wearing stripes photo courtesy of UCSB La Cumbre yearbook

Female cheerleaders in plaid photo courtesy of UCSB La Cumbre yearbook

Male cheerleaders in plaid photo courtesy of UCSB La Cumbre yearbook

Students on VW in plaid photo courtesy of UCSB La Cumbre yearbook

Students with surfboard in plaid photo courtesy of UCSB La Cumbre yearbook

Freshman in plaid photo courtesy of UCSB La Cumbre yearbook

Saddle shoes
Paul A Hernandez (https://commons.wikimedia.org/wiki/File:Saddle_shoes_-_02.jpg),
"Saddle shoes - 02", https://creativecommons.org/licenses/by/2.0/legalcode

White House of Santa Barbara ad photo courtesy of UCSB La Cumbre yearbook

Duffle coat (also known as toggle coat)
The original uploader was Daniel Case at English Wikipedia.
(https://commons.wikimedia.org/wiki/File:Duffle_coat.jpg), "Duffle coat",
https://creativecommons.org/licenses/by/2.0/legalcode

Newsboy cap
Sylvain1972 at English Wikipedia
(https://commons.wikimedia.org/wiki/File:Eight_panel.JPG),
"Eight panel", marked as public domain, more details on Wikimedia Commons:
https://commons.wikimedia.org/wiki/Template:PD-user

The Merry Widow by iClassical Com, The Merry Widow Unchained Melodie Classical,
https://www.flickr.com/photos/130720149@N05/17630311820 licensed by
https://creativecommons.org/licenses/by/2.0/

Corset shop
Eugène Atget creator QS:P170,Q322030
(https://commons.wikimedia.org/wiki/File:Eugène_Atget,_Boulevard_de_Strasbourg,_Corsets,_Paris,_1912.jpg),
"Eugène Atget, Boulevard de Strasbourg, Corsets, Paris, 1912",
https://creativecommons.org/publicdomain/zero/1.0/legalcode

Chapter 21
The Three Caballeros poster © Disney

Walt Disney dressed as gaucho with Donald Duck photo © Disney

Gaucho 1868
Courret Hermanos Fotogs., Lima, Peru.
(https://commons.wikimedia.org/wiki/File:Gaucho1868b.jpg),
"Gaucho1868b", marked as public domain, more details on Wikimedia Commons:
https://commons.wikimedia.org/wiki/Template:PD-1923

Gaucho in wheatfield 1940
Toni Frissell creator QS:P170,Q260658 derivative work: Arad
(https://commons.wikimedia.org/wiki/File:Gauchowheat_edit2.jpg),
"Gauchowheat edit2", marked as public domain, more details on Wikimedia Commons:
https://commons.wikimedia.org/wiki/Template:Library of Congress-no known copyright restrictions

Gaucho fashion photo used with permission of R.Voong.

Douglas Fairbanks as *The Gaucho* poster
United Artists (https://commons.wikimedia.org/wiki/File:The-gaucho-1927.jpg),
"The-gaucho-1927", marked as public domain, more details on Wikimedia Commons:
https://commons.wikimedia.org/wiki/Template:PD-US

The Mark of Zorro movie poster 1920
Unknown author (https://commons.wikimedia.org/wiki/File:FairbanksMarkofZorro.jpg),
"FairbanksMarkofZorro", marked as public domain, more details on Wikimedia Commons:
https://commons.wikimedia.org/wiki/Template:PD-US

Olé, UCSB gaucho mascot, used with permission of University of California, Santa Barbara Intercollegiate Athletics Department

Gaucho burger snack stand photo courtesy of UCSB La Cumbre yearbook

Gaucho float photo courtesy of UCSB La Cumbre yearbook

UCSB *Gaucho* statue by sculptor Teresa Farga de Corominas, used with permission of UCSB Alumni Affairs

Chapter 22
Security First National Bank ad featuring Milford Muddle by Ray Patin Productions, courtesy of the Bank of America Historical Collection

Boat loan storyboard for Detroit Bank and Trust by Ray Patin Productions reprinted with permission from Comerica Bank

Crossroads of the World advertisement and photo used with permission of Crossroads Properties

Patin Productions ad by Ray Patin Productions, Libby's Brand™ used with permission of Libby's Brand Holding, JELL-O brand used with permission of Kraft Heinz Foods Company, and Kellogg's Sugar Pops © Kellogg Company used with permission

Patin Productions ad by Ray Patin Productions, used by permission of the 3-M Company; Libby's Brand™ used with permission of Libby's Brand Holding; Post Consumer Brands, LLC; Hudepohl Beer, courtesy of Gregory Hardman, Christian Moerlein Brewing Co. Cincinnati, Ohio; Sealy used with permission of TempurSealy; JELL-O brand and Heinz Baby Food brand used with permission of Kraft Heinz Foods Company; Kellogg's Sugar Pops © Kellogg Company used with permission

Blacky Carbon and Dirty Sludge illustrations by Ray Patin Productions. The Grime Gang characters are used with permission of Bardahl Manufacturing Corporation, Seattle, WA

Chapter 23
Renée and Mary Jane at Disneyland photo © Disney PhotoPass

Mermaids at Disneyland's Submarine Voyage attraction photo © Disney

Animation Academy interior at The Walt Disney World Resort photo © Disney

Tomorrowland Art Corner interior © Disney

Renée with train engineer used with permission of Ward Kimball estate

Ward Kimball engine at Disneyland used with permission of Ward Kimball estate

Chapter 24
Joe's Café interior photo courtesy of Dawn Sherry, Sherry & Associates, Architects Inc. and used with permission of Joe's Café

Hand holding joint by Torben Hansen, marijuana joint, https://www.flickr.com/photos/torbenh/2298921212 licensed by https://creativecommons.org/licenses/by/2.0/

DGs and Delts photo courtesy of UCSB La Cumbre yearbook and used with permission of Delta Tau Delta Fraternity

Kappa Sig's joints photo courtesy of UCSB La Cumbre yearbook

Delta Tau Delta "function" and house photo courtesy of UCSB La Cumbre yearbook and Delta Tau Delta Fraternity

Steps to Delt house used by permission of Delta Tau Delta Fraternity

Renée on Waiting Bench used by permission of Delta Tau Delta Fraternity

Chapter 25
College bookstore photo courtesy of UCSB La Cumbre yearbook

Santa Barbara office supply store Dennett & Denmun photo courtesy of UCSB La Cumbre yearbook

Registration photo courtesy of UCSB La Cumbre yearbook

Professor with Blue Book courtesy of UCSB La Cumbre yearbook

Chapter 26
Cinderella and the Prince dancing photo © 1950 Disney

Slow dance photo courtesy of UCSB La Cumbre yearbook

Slow dancing couples photo courtesy of UCSB La Cumbre yearbook

Renée dancing photo courtesy of the Glendale College 1957 *La Reata* yearbook

UCSB dancers photo courtesy of UCSB La Cumbre yearbook

Informal dancing photo courtesy of UCSB La Cumbre yearbook

Coral Casino Beach & Cabana Club by Chronicle/Alamy Stock Photo, used with permission of Four Seasons Resort/The Biltmore Santa Barbara

Large group of students dancing photo courtesy of UCSB La Cumbre yearbook

Chapter 27
"The Skeleton Dance" A Disney Silly Symphony poster © Disney

Fantasia DVD © Disney

Mushrooms from *Fantasia* dancing photo © 1940 Disney

Peter and the Wolf courtesy of Peter Pan Records and Inspired Studios Inc.
Photo by Ted Van Pelt, Peter and the Wolf 45 rpm,
https://www.flickr.com/photos/bantam10/5317270927 is licensed by
https://creativecommons.org/licenses/by/2.0/,

Scheherazade painting
Ferdinand Keller creator QS:P170,Q565569
(https://commons.wikimedia.org/wiki/File:Ferdinand_Keller_-_Scheherazade_und_Sultan_Schariar_(1880).jpg),
"Ferdinand Keller - Scheherazade und Sultan Schariar (1880)", marked as public domain, more details on Wikimedia Commons:
https://commons.wikimedia.org/wiki/Template:PD-1923

Spike Jones and His City Slickers photo courtesy of the estate of Spike Jones, used with permission.

Antique pump organ
Tim Drury from Cambridge, Cambridgeshire
(https://commons.wikimedia.org/wiki/File:Pump_organ.jpg),
"Pump organ", https://creativecommons.org/licenses/by-sa/3.0/legalcode

Old organ, close up of organ stops @yb_woodstock
(https://commons.wikimedia.org/wiki/File:Old_organ,_Marumo_Ryokan_(inn),_Matsumoto,_2009-09-19.jpg),
"Old organ, Marumo Ryokan (inn), Matsumoto, 2009-09-19",
https://creativecommons.org/licenses/by-sa/2.0/legalcode

Spring Sing photo courtesy of UCSB La Cumbre yearbook

Chapter 28
Studious Ray at work still photo © Disney

Animated Ray at projector still photo © Disney

Fellow animator with clip on nose still photo © Disney

Title card for *Sea Scouts* © Disney

Pencil test for *Sea Scouts* © Disney

Steamboat Willie © 1928 Disney

Newport Harbor postcard by Orange County Archives, Balboa Motel postcard, circa 1950,
https://www.flickr.com/photos/ocarchives/4725189371 is licensed by
https://creativecommons.org/licenses/by/2.0/

Wild Goose yacht photo courtesy of Hornblower Cruises & Events

Balboa Island Ferry postcard by George Watson

El Viejo y el Mar (Old Man & the Sea) sculpture, La Paz, Mexico. Photo courtesy of Renée Patin Farrington of sculpture *El Viejo y el Mar* by Guillermo Gomez Macias donated by Tenaja Holdings and the International Community Foundation.

Chapter 29
The Dyspeptic movie advertisement
Unknown author (https://commons.wikimedia.org/wiki/File:American_Film_Company_4.jpg),
"American Film Company 4", marked as public domain, more details on Wikimedia Commons:
https://commons.wikimedia.org/wiki/Template:PD-US

Flying A Film Studio in Santa Barbara, CA, circa 1915, Micky Moore Collection, Pepperdine University Special Collections and University Archives

Flying A Studio today photo used by permission of Becker Henson Niksto Architects

Flying A sign photo used by permission of Becker Henson Niksto Architects

Montecito Inn then, photo courtesy of Montecito Inn http://www.montecitoinn.com

Montecito Inn today, photo courtesy of Montecito Inn http://www.montecitoinn.com

California Riviera/Santa Barbara coastline
John Wiley User:Jw4nvc - Santa Barbara, California (https://commons.wikimedia.org/wiki/File:Aerial-SantaBarbaraCA10-28-08.jpg),
"Aerial-SantaBarbaraCA10-28-08",
https://creativecommons.org/licenses/by/3.0/legalcode

Cabrillo Blvd today
Niranjan Arminius (https://commons.wikimedia.org/wiki/File:SB_EastBeachPark_20140909.jpg),
https://creativecommons.org/licenses/by-sa/4.0/legalcode

Delta Gamma house 1950s photo courtesy of UCSB La Cumbre yearbook, used with permission of Delta Gamma Fraternity

Delta Gamma house site today photo used with permission of Delta Gamma Fraternity

Delta Gamma house 2015 photo used with permission of Delta Gamma Fraternity

Renée in front of Delta Gamma house 2015 photo used with permission of Delta Gamma Fraternity Welcome to Isla Vista sign photo by Mary Jane Salcido

Isla Vista Temporary Closures sign photo by Mary Jane Salcido

Chapter 30
Brown "hat" illustration from *The Little Prince*
Cover and illustrations THE LITTLE PRINCE by Antoine de Saint-Exupery. Copyright © 1943 by Houghton Mifflin Harcourt Publishing Company, renewed 1971 by Consuelo de Saint-Exupery, English translation copyright © 2000 by Richard Howard. Reprinted by permission of Houghton Mifflin Harcourt Publishing Company. All rights reserved.

The Blue Boy
Thomas Gainsborough creator QS:P170,Q192720
(https://commons.wikimedia.org/wiki/File:The_Blue_Boy.jpg),
"The Blue Boy", marked as public domain, more details on Wikimedia Commons:
https://commons.wikimedia.org/wiki/Template:PD-1923

The Blue Duck by Ray Patin © Disney
Thanks to the Collection of Dennis Books, Seattle, WA comicartfans.com

Man in Oriental Costume ("The Noble Slav")
Rembrandt creator QS:P170,Q5598
(https://commons.wikimedia.org/wiki/File:Man_in_Oriental_Costume_("The_Noble_Slav")_MET_DP146479.jpg),
"Man in Oriental Costume ("The Noble Slav") MET DP146479",
https://creativecommons.org/publicdomain/zero/1.0/legalcode

The Noble Snob by Ray Patin © Disney
Thanks to the Collection of Dennis Books, Seattle, WA comicartfans.com

Dancers Bending Down
Edgar Degas creator QS:P170,Q46373
(https://commons.wikimedia.org/wiki/File:Edgar_Germain_Hilaire_Degas_062.jpg),
"Edgar Germain Hilaire Degas 062", marked as public domain, more details on Wikimedia Commons:
https://commons.wikimedia.org/wiki/Template:PD-Art-YorckProject

Two Dancing Ducks by Ray Patin © Disney
Thanks to the Collection of Dennis Books, Seattle, WA comicartfans.com

Robert Benchley at the Gallery photo from *The Reluctant Dragon* © Disney, used with permission of the Robert Benchley and Ward Kimball estates.

Chapter 31
Evil Queen from *Snow White* © Disney

Drawing the Evil Queen from *Snow White* © Disney

Jack Bailey, host of *Queen for a Day*
ABC Television (https://commons.wikimedia.org/wiki/File:Queen_for_a_Day.JPG),
"Queen for a Day", marked as public domain, more details on Wikimedia Commons:
https://commons.wikimedia.org/wiki/Template:PD-US

College yearbook royalty photo courtesy of UCSB La Cumbre yearbook

Homecoming queen and court photos courtesy of UCSB La Cumbre yearbook

Elaine Nobel as Homecoming Queen photo courtesy of UCSB La Cumbre yearbook

Anita Barton as Homecoming Queen photo courtesy of UCSB La Cumbre yearbook

Coeds walking and saluting photo courtesy of UCSB La Cumbre yearbook

Military sweethearts photo courtesy of UCSB La Cumbre yearbook

"Glendale College Girl of the Week" Vol. 26 No. 12 January 14, 1957 article, *El Vaquero*,
Glendale Junior College, used with permission of *El Vaquero* Newspaper, GCC's official student publication.

Stan Freberg at piano photo by Ray Patin Productions, used with permission of Hunter Freberg

Chapter 32
1958 La Cumbre inside front cover "Somebody opened the gates to the zoo," courtesy of
UCSB La Cumbre yearbook and illustrator Dick Phipps (aka Richard Phipps)

Saul Steinberg, *View of the World from 9th Avenue*, 1976 cover drawing for The New Yorker, March 29, 1976
© The Saul Steinberg Foundation / Artists Rights Society (ARS), New York
*Reproduction, including downloading of Steinberg works, is prohibited by copyright laws and
international conventions without the express written permission of Artists Rights Society (ARS), New York.*

Delta Gamma 1957 yearbook spread photo courtesy of UCSB La Cumbre yearbook

Sigma Phi Epsilon yearbook spread photo courtesy of UCSB La Cumbre yearbook

Residence halls photo courtesy of UCSB La Cumbre yearbook

Girls' residence halls photo courtesy of UCSB La Cumbre yearbook

Boys' residence halls photo courtesy of UCSB La Cumbre yearbook

Rally Committee photo courtesy of UCSB La Cumbre yearbook

Spurs photo courtesy of UCSB La Cumbre yearbook

La Cumbre yearbooks 1957-1960 photo used with permission of UCSB La Cumbre yearbook

The Club Club photo courtesy of UCSB La Cumbre yearbook

Rho Rho Rho photo courtesy of UCSB La Cumbre yearbook

The Goleta Sophists photo courtesy of UCSB La Cumbre yearbook

Chapter 33
Fraternity page photo courtesy of UCSB La Cumbre yearbook

Delta Gamma beer stein 1962 photo courtesy Mary Jane Salcido

Chapter 34
UCSB faculty desk photo courtesy of UCSB La Cumbre yearbook

Faculty yearbook cartoon courtesy of UCSB La Cumbre yearbook and illustrator Dick Phipps (aka Richard Phipps)

English Department faculty photo courtesy of UCSB La Cumbre yearbook

Art Department faculty photo courtesy of UCSB La Cumbre yearbook

Polyglot professors photo courtesy of UCSB La Cumbre yearbook

Jean Paul Sartre
https://www.flickr.com/people/69061470@N05 (https://commons.wikimedia.org/wiki/File:
Sartre_1967_crop.jpg), "Sartre 1967 crop", https://creativecommons.org/licenses/by/3.0/legalcode

Sig Ep's Odyssey float photo courtesy of UCSB La Cumbre yearbook
Industrial Arts Rousseau float photo courtesy of UCSB La Cumbre yearbook

Kappa Sig's Hemingway float photo courtesy of UCSB La Cumbre yearbook

Collage of Educators 1960 photo courtesy of UCSB La Cumbre yearbook

Chapter 35
JELL-O storyboard by Ray Patin Productions; JELL-O brand used with permission of Kraft Heinz Foods Company

The Musso & Frank Grill photo by Musso & Frank Grill; used with permission

Chapter 36
Jiminy Cricket photo © 1940 Disney

Children's storybooks used with permission of Penguin Random House

Tenggren's Story Book inside front cover used with permission of Penguin Random House

Chapter 37
Shirley Dinsdale with Judy Splinters postcards used with permission of Shirley Dinsdale estate

Chapter 38
Cherubs on clouds
Wenceslaus Hollar creator QS:P170,Q448555
(https://commons.wikimedia.org/wiki/File: Wenceslas_Hollar_-_Three_cherubs_and_two_boys_on_clouds_(State_2)_2.jpg#file),
"Wenceslas Hollar - Three cherubs and two boys on clouds (State 2) 2", marked as public domain, more details on Wikimedia Commons: https://commons.wikimedia.org/wiki/Template:PD-1923

Richard Serra yearbook photo courtesy of UCSB La Cumbre yearbook

UCSB lagoon and Arts Building photos used with permission of UCSB

Plow & Angel Restaurant photo courtesy of San Ysidro Ranch

Cold Spring Tavern photo used with permission of Cold Spring Tavern

Chapter 41
Defense d'uriner
The original uploader was YPS at German Wikipedia. (https://commons.wikimedia.org/wiki/File:Defense_d'uriner.jpg), „Defense d'uriner", https://creativecommons.org/licenses/by-sa/3.0/legalcode

Louvre Museum photo courtesy of © RMN-Grand Palais / Art Resource, NY, used with permission of Musee du Louvre

Art installation at Pavilion of Russia at the Biennale Arte 2013 (the 55th International Art Exhibition of La Biennale di Venezia), used with permission

Art installation at Pavilion of Portugal at the Biennale Arte 2013 (the 55th International Art Exhibition of La Biennale di Venezia), used with permission

Art installation at Pavilion of The Netherlands at the Biennale Arte 2013 (the 55th International Art Exhibition of La Biennale di Venezia), used with permission

Art installation at Pavilion of United States of America at the Biennale Arte 2013 (the 55th International Art Exhibition of La Biennale di Venezia), used with permission

Art installation at Central Pavilion at the Biennale Arte 2013 (the 55th International Art Exhibition of La Biennale di Venezia), used with permission

Art installation at Central Pavilion at the Biennale Arte 2013 (the 55th International Art Exhibition of La Biennale di Venezia), used with permission

The Night Watch
Rembrandt artist QS:P170,Q5598 (https://commons.wikimedia.org/wiki/File:The_Nightwatch_by_Rembrandt_-_Rijksmuseum.jpg),

"The Nightwatch by Rembrandt - Rijksmuseum", marked as public domain, more details on Wikimedia Commons: https://commons.wikimedia.org/wiki/Template:PD-old

Chapter 42
Creative Playthings button used with permission of Creative Playthings, Ltd., www.creativeplaythings.com

Creative Playthings store photo by Joseph Schumacher, Jr. used with permission of Creative Playthings, Ltd., www.creativeplaythings.com

Creative Playthings Renée office photo used with permission of Creative Playthings, Ltd., www.creativeplaythings.com

Renée "accolades" article used with permission of Creative Playthings, Ltd., www.creativeplaythings.com

Creative Playthings executive meeting 1970-71 photo used with permission of Creative Playthings, Ltd., www.creativeplaythings.com

Child looking through magnifier photo by Joseph Schumacher, Jr. used with permission of Creative Playthings, Ltd., www.creativeplaythings.com

Child with wooden figures photo by Joseph Schumacher, Jr. used with permission of Creative Playthings, Ltd., www.creativeplaythings.com

Child with abacus photo by Joseph Schumacher, Jr. used with permission of Creative Playthings, Ltd., www.creativeplaythings.com

Sheep ride-on photo by Joseph Schumacher, Jr. used with permission of Creative Playthings, Ltd., www.creativeplaythings.com

Chapter 43
Jack Farrington photo used with permission of Creative Playthings, Ltd., www.creativeplaythings.com

Van Heflin
Clarence Bull (https://commons.wikimedia.org/wiki/File:Van_Heflin_-_1941.jpg),
"Van Heflin - 1941", marked as public domain, more details on Wikimedia Commons:
https://commons.wikimedia.org/wiki/Template:PD-US and permission of estate of Van Heflin

Creative Playthings trade show booth photo used with permission of Creative Playthings, Ltd., www.creativeplaythings.com

Tableaux of wooden blocks and animals photo used with permission of Creative Playthings, Ltd., www.creativeplaythings.com

Renée with Little Brother doll and other toys used with permission of Creative Playthings, Ltd., www.creativeplaythings.com

Harbor Restaurant, end of the wharf Santa Barbara, photo courtesy of UCSB La Cumbre yearbook

"Panamanian Passage" article courtesy of Duncan McIntosh Co./Sea Magazine

Children in rowboat used with permission of CanalBlog

"Dangers and Delights of Mexican Cruising" article courtesy of Duncan McIntosh Co./Sea Magazine

"Outwitting Murphy" article reprinted courtesy of Duncan McIntosh Co./Sea Magazine

"Fair Haven: Beaufort" article courtesy of Beaufort Regional Chamber of Commerce

Brooklyn Bridge photo used with permission of NYC Department of Transportation

Jack Farrington grave photo by Melyssa Webb, courtesy of Billiongraves.com

Chapter 45
"Burbank Actor to Marry Miss Mary Jane Bennett" by *Los Angeles Times Staff,* Copyright © 1925, 1979 *Los Angeles Times*; used with permission.

"Postscript: Hi, Friends, Ralph Williams Here – and Still in Trouble for Sales Tactics" by Steve Harvey, Copyright © 1925, 1979 *Los Angeles Times*; used with permission.
Mary Kate in front of Burbank house photo courtesy of Jennifer Williams

Renée and Joanie photo courtesy of Carl Sells

Gerry performing photo courtesy of UCSB La Cumbre yearbook, used with permission of Gerry Mullin

Gerry competing in 1958 Ugly Man Contest photo courtesy of UCSB La Cumbre yearbook, used with permission of Gerry Mullin

Gerry today photo used with permission of Gerry Mullin

Richard Serra Distinguished Alumni Award program photo used with permission of UCSB Alumni Association and permission of Richard Serra

Richard Serra drawing on program used with permission of UCSB Alumni Association and permission of Richard Serra

Rich and Renée photo by UCSB Alumni staff and used with permission of Richard Serra

Chapter 46
Wonderful World of Brother Buzz photo used with permission of The Latham Foundation

Brother Buzz cartoons photo used with permission of The Latham Foundation

Creative Playthings rendering by Ray Patin photo used with permission of Creative Playthings, Ltd., www.creativeplaythings.com

Loewy and Studebaker photo from the collection of the Studebaker National Museum, South Bend, Indiana. Used with permission of the estate of Raymond Loewy.

Chapter 47
I Remember Mama movie photo Moviestore Collection Ltd / Alamy Stock Photo

RCA TV with 10" screen photo courtesy of Phil's Old Radios (https://antiqueradio.org/index.html)

1951 Chevrolet Deluxe Bel Air Hardtop Coupe front
Mr.choppers (https://commons.wikimedia.org/wiki/File:1951_Chevrolet_Deluxe_Bel_Air_Hardtop_Coupé.jpg),
"1951 Chevrolet Deluxe Bel Air Hardtop Coupé",
https://creativecommons.org/licenses/by-sa/3.0/legalcode

1951 Chevrolet Deluxe Bel Air HT Coupe back
Mr.choppers (https://commons.wikimedia.org/wiki/File:1951_Chevrolet_Deluxe_Bel_Air_HT_Coupé.jpg),
"1951 Chevrolet Deluxe Bel Air HT Coupé",
https://creativecommons.org/licenses/by-sa/3.0/legalcode

"Painting Opens Way to Fantasy" article by Dennis Taylor, *Herald Staff Writer* and Vern Fisher, photographer, used with permission of *The Monterey County Herald* www.montereyherald.com

Maxine and Renée at art show photo courtesy of Ashley Tedesco

Maxine Riley Patin obituary used with permission of *The Monterey County Herald* www.montereyherald.com

Maxine Patin portrait courtesy of Ashley Tedesco

Chapter 48
Hollywood Sign by Mark Fugarino/Creative Commons and **HOLLYWOOD**™ & Design © 2017 Hollywood Chamber of Commerce. The Hollywood Sign and Hollywood Walk of Fame™ are trademarks and intellectual property of Hollywood Chamber of Commerce. All Rights Reserved.

Smoke House Restaurant with George Clooney © Smoke House, used with permission of Stan Rosenfield & Associates

Roy E. Disney Animation Building photo © Disney

Peter Pan and Shadow photo © 1953 Disney
Walt and Mickey Partners statue at Walt Disney World Resort photo © Disney

Back Cover
Southern California map by Lorne C. Dokie, razorwiredesign.com and **HOLLYWOOD**™ & Design © 2017 Hollywood Chamber of Commerce. The Hollywood Sign and Hollywood Walk of Fame™ are trademarks and intellectual property of Hollywood Chamber of Commerce. All Rights Reserved.

Hollywood Sign by Mark Fugarino/Creative Commons and **HOLLYWOOD**™ & Design © 2017 Hollywood Chamber of Commerce. The Hollywood Sign and Hollywood Walk of Fame™ are trademarks and intellectual property of Hollywood Chamber of Commerce. All Rights Reserved.

QUOTATIONS

Epigraph
T.S. Eliot quote excerpt from "Little Gidding" by T.S. Eliot from FOUR QUARTETS. Copyright © 1943 by T.S. Eliot. Copyright renewed 1971 by Esme Valerie Eliot. Reprinted by permission of Houghton Mifflin Harcourt Publishing Company. All rights reserved.

Chapter 6
Saul Bellow quote from "*Seize the Day*," copyright © 1956, renewed © 1984 by Saul Bellow; from SEIZE THE DAY by Saul Bellow. Used by permission of Viking Books, an imprint of Penguin Publishing Group, a division of Penguin Random House LLC. All rights reserved.

Michael Eisner quote © Disney

Chapter 10
Rachel Carson quote from THE SENSE OF WONDER by RACHEL CARSON. Copyright © 1956 by Rachel L. Carson. Reprinted by permission of HarperCollins Publishers.

Chapter 11
Excerpt from THE LITTLE PRINCE by Antoine de Saint-Exupery. Copyright © 1943 by Houghton Mifflin Harcourt Publishing Company, renewed 1971 by Consuelo de Saint-Exupery, English translation copyright © 2000 by Richard Howard. Reprinted by permission of Houghton Mifflin Harcourt Publishing Company. All rights reserved.

Chapter 23
Walt Disney quote © Disney

Chapter 39
1 Cor. 13:11, *World English Bible*. Rainbow Missions, Web. 2000.

Chapter 40
CS Lewis quote from OF OTHER WORLDS by CS Lewis © copyright CS Lewis Pte Ltd 1966.

Chapter 48
T.S. Eliot quote excerpt from "Little Gidding" by T.S. Eliot from FOUR QUARTETS. Copyright © 1943 by T.S. Eliot. Copyright renewed 1971 by Esme Valerie Eliot. Reprinted by permission of Houghton Mifflin Harcourt Publishing Company. All rights reserved.

LYRICS

Chapter 3
"26 Miles (Santa Catalina)"
Words and Music by Glen Larson and Bruce Belland
© 1957 (Renewed 1985) BEECHWOOD MUSIC CORP.
All Rights Reserved International Copyright Secured Used by Permission
Reprinted by Permission of Hal Leonard LLC

Chapter 17
"UCSB at G" lyrics courtesy of UCSB Alumni Association archives

Chapter 27
"Mairzy Doats"
Words and Music by Milton Drake, Al Hoffman and Jerry Livingston
Copyright © 1943 Sony/ATV Music Publishing LLC, Hallmark Music Company and Al Hoffman Songs, Inc.
Copyright Renewed
All Rights on behalf of Sony/ATV Music Publishing LLC Administered by Sony/ATV Music Publishing LLC, 424 Church Street, Suite 1200, Nashville, TN 37219
All Rights on behalf of Hallmark Music Company Controlled and Administered by Spirit Two Music, Inc.
International Copyright Secured All Rights Reserved
Reprinted by Permission of Hal Leonard LLC

Chapter 33
"Smoke! Smoke! Smoke! (That Cigarette)"
Words and Music by MERLE TRAVIS and TEX WILLIAMS
© 1947 (Renewed) UNICHAPPELL MUSIC INC., ELVIS PRESLEY MUSIC, INC. and MERLE'S GIRLS MUSIC
All Rights on behalf of itself and ELVIS PRESLEY MUSIC, INC. Administered by UNICHAPPELL MUSIC, INC.
All Rights for of MERLE'S GIRLS MUSIC Administered by WARNER-TAMERLANE PUBLISHING CORP.
All Rights Reserved
Used By Permission of ALFRED MUSIC

Chapter 40
"Zip-A-Dee-Doo-Dah"
From SONG OF THE SOUTH
Music by Allie Wrubel
Words by Ray Gilbert
© 1945 Walt Disney Music Company
Copyright Renewed
All Rights Reserved. Used by Permission.
Reprinted by Permission of Hal Leonard LLC

THE END

www.ingramcontent.com/pod-product-compliance
Lightning Source LLC
Chambersburg PA
CBHW060503300426
44112CB00017B/2528